The Invention of the English Landscape

The Invention of the English Landscape

c. 1700–1939

Peter Borsay with Rosemary Sweet

BLOOMSBURY ACADEMIC
LONDON • NEW YORK • OXFORD • NEW DELHI • SYDNEY

BLOOMSBURY ACADEMIC
Bloomsbury Publishing Plc
50 Bedford Square, London, WC1B 3DP, UK
1385 Broadway, New York, NY 10018, USA
29 Earlsfort Terrace, Dublin 2, Ireland

BLOOMSBURY, BLOOMSBURY ACADEMIC and the Diana logo are
trademarks of Bloomsbury Publishing Plc

First published in Great Britain 2023
This paperback edition published 2025

Copyright © Rosemary Sweet, 2023

Rosemary Sweet has asserted her right under the Copyright,
Designs and Patents Act, 1988, to be identified as Author of this work.

For legal purposes the Acknowledgements on p. xii constitute
an extension of this copyright page.

Cover image © *The Cotswolds Poster* by Chater
(Photo by Swim Ink 2, LLC/CORBIS/Corbis via Getty Images)

All rights reserved. No part of this publication may be reproduced or transmitted
in any form or by any means, electronic or mechanical, including photocopying,
recording, or any information storage or retrieval system, without prior
permission in writing from the publishers.

Bloomsbury Publishing Plc does not have any control over, or responsibility for,
any third-party websites referred to or in this book. All internet addresses given
in this book were correct at the time of going to press. The author and publisher
regret any inconvenience caused if addresses have changed or sites have ceased
to exist, but can accept no responsibility for any such changes.

A catalogue record for this book is available from the British Library.

A catalog record for this book is available from the Library of Congress.

ISBN: HB: 978-1-3500-3167-8
       PB: 978-1-3502-6976-7
       ePDF: 978-1-3500-3165-4
       eBook: 978-1-3500-3166-1

Typeset by Integra Software Services Pvt. Ltd.

To find out more about our authors and books visit www.bloomsbury.com
and sign up for our newsletters.

In memory of Peter Borsay
9 January 1950–13 November 2020

Contents

List of illustrations	ix
Foreword	xi
Acknowledgements	xii

1 Introduction — 1

2 Revealing the early modern landscape — 9
    Exploration and tourism — 9
    The discovery of the natural landscape — 15
    Exploring the human landscape — 21

3 Ideas and representations — 27
    The Reformation — 28
    The Enlightenment — 33
    Romanticism — 35
    Representations — 38

4 Reconfiguring the landscape — 49
    Ideas — 49
    Cultural media — 54
    Production and performance — 78
    Reception — 83

5 New geographies and topographies — 87
    Imagined spaces — 87
    Town: Grey space — 89
    Country: Green space — 95
    Water: Blue space — 106
    Frameworks of spaces — 110

6 Timescapes — 117
    Landscapes of memory and myth; stories and landscape — 118
    Deep history: Geology and natural history — 119
    Pre-history — 122
    Recent pasts and competing pasts — 129

	Old towns and villages	138
	Landscape as modernism; the modernist seaside and countryside	148
7	Economic and social change	155
	Industrialization	155
	Urbanization	164
	Leisure	174
8	The transport revolution and the journey	179
	The transport revolution and recreational travel	181
	Walking	194
	Experiencing the journey	203
9	Identities	211
	Landscape, identities and nation	212
	The British paradox	221
	Race and empire	224
	Religion, class and gender	231
10	Conclusion: The Second World War and beyond	245
	The Second World War	247
	Modernity and the post-war decades	252
	Towards the millennium and beyond	255

Select bibliography	260
Index	272

Illustrations

2.1	Charles Grignion after Nathan Drake, 'A Noble Terras Walk', York (1756). © The Trustees of the British Museum	14
2.2	The Valley of the Rocks, near Linton, Devonshire, from John Britton and E. W. Brayley, *Devonshire Illustrated in a Series of Views* (London: Fisher, 1829). Reproduced by kind permission of the David Wilson Library, University of Leicester	17
3.1	Tintern Abbey from the River Wye from William Gilpin, *Observations on the River Wye, and Several Parts of South Wales &c.: Relative Chiefly to Picturesque Beauty*, 3rd edn (London: R. Blamire, 1792). Reproduced by kind permission of the David Wilson Library, University of Leicester	36
3.2	Francis Nicholson, 'The Waterfall or Cascade falling into the Paddock Pond opposite Garden Lake', from 'Rural Scenery at Stourhead in the County of Wilts, the Seat of Sir Richard Hoare, Bt.' © The Trustees of the British Museum	47
4.1	Helen Allingham, 'At the Cottage Gate' (1900). © Getty Images	68
4.2	John Wheely Gough Gutch, 'View of Tenby from the Croft' (1857). © Getty Images	71
4.3	Whitlingham Vale from Postwick, *c.* 1883 from *The Scenery of the Broads and Rivers of Norfolk and Suffolk* (Norwich: Jarrold & Sons, 1883). © Getty Images	72
4.4	'Over-photographed' Clovelly: Clovelly, Harbour and Red Lion Hotel 1930. © The Francis Frith Collection	72
4.5	Ernest William Haslehurst, 'Anne Hathaway's Cottage', from Walter Jerrold, *Shakespeare-land* (London: Blackie, 1910). Reproduced by kind permission of the David Wilson Library, University of Leicester	74
4.6	Strip map from John Ogilby, *Britannia* (London: John Ogilby, 1675). © British Library Creative Commons	76
5.1	Frederick Henry Henshaw, 'A Forest Glade, Arden' (1844–5), photo by Birmingham Museums Trust	100
5.2	Paul Nash, 'The Wood on the Hill' (Wittenham Clumps) (1912). © Ashmolean Museum	105

6.1	'A view of the landslip from Great Bindon, looking westward to the Sidmouth hills and estuary of the Exe', from W. D. Conybeare and William Buckland, *Ten Plates Comprising a Plan, Sections, and Views, Representing the Changes Produced on the Coast of East Devon, between Axmouth and Lyme Regis* (London: John Murray, 1840). Reproduced by kind permission of the Geological Society of London	122
6.2	Members of the Woolhope Naturalists' Field Club viewing Arthur's Stone from *Transactions of the Woolhope Naturalists' Field Club 1881–82* (1882). Reproduced by kind permission of the David Wilson Library, University of Leicester	125
6.3	Mr Alfred Watkins addressing a meeting at the Woodcraft Folk Camp at the Queen Stone, Huntsham, 9 August 1933. Herefordshire County Library Service www.herefordshirehistory.org.uk	128
6.4	Lamb House from A. G. Bradley, *An Old Gate of England. Rye, Romney Marsh, and the Western Cinque Ports* (London: Robert Scott, 1918). Reproduced by kind permission of the David Wilson Library, University of Leicester	142
6.5	South Shore Blackpool, contemporary postcard, *c.* 1933	151
6.6	'Mousehole, Penzance' (1932), poster design for Shell by Alexander Stuart-Hill. © Shell Heritage Art Collection	152
7.1	Philip James de Loutherbourg, 'Coalbrookdale by Night' (1801). © The Science Museum Group	157
7.2	Gustave Doré, 'Dudley Street in the Seven Dials' (1872). © Getty Images	168
8.1	'Whitsun in the Country' (1935), poster design by Herry Perry for London Transport. © TFL from the London Transport Museum Collection	185
8.2	Bronze statue of Edward Elgar with his Sunbeam bicycle, Hereford Cathedral Close. © Getty Images	189
8.3	'Faringdon Folly' (1936), poster design for Shell by Lord Berners. © Shell Heritage Art Collection	192
8.4	'View from the Ivy Rock, Malvern', *c.* 1830–40. © The Trustees of the British Museum	199
9.1	Thomas Gainsborough, 'Mr and Mrs Andrews' (*c.* 1750). © Getty Images	214
9.2	David Lucas after John Constable, 'Summer Evening', from *English Landscape: Various Subjects of Landscape, Characteristic of Scenery from Pictures Painted by John Constable RA* (1829–31). The Metropolitan Museum of Art, New York, Harris Brisbane Dick Fund, 1940, www.metmuseum.org	216
10.1	Frank Newbould, 'Your Britain – Fight for It Now' (1942). © The Imperial War Museum	249

Foreword

Peter Borsay died in November 2020 leaving a draft manuscript for *The Invention of the English Landscape* largely complete. It was, however, some way from being ready for publication and, at the request of his family, I have had the privilege of bringing it to completion. The manuscript was too long, the footnotes existed in note form only, and there was still much that Peter had wished to do in terms of tightening the argument and working in more discussion of secondary literature. As editor, I have done my best accurately to complete the footnotes and to reduce the text to an acceptable length for the publishers: much detail and some nuance have necessarily been lost but I trust that Peter would consider that the core arguments remain unchanged. I have introduced some additional references to secondary literature, but mindful of the need to abbreviate rather than lengthen the text, these interventions have been limited. Instead, I have preferred to prioritize Peter's text over the introduction of extended historiographical discussion or lengthy footnotes. Peter left no instructions concerning illustrations; the choice therefore has been mine and I have endeavoured to reflect what I hope Peter's wishes would have been.

The one element that Peter left unfinished was the introduction. Where the text was incomplete, he had provided notes for each section. I have attempted to convert these into coherent prose and have tried to avoid projecting my own interpretation of what I believe Peter's intentions to have been. The result is briefer and more schematic than Peter would have intended but the argument is his, not mine.

In the interests of length, and in discussion with Bloomsbury, it was agreed that one chapter would be omitted from the book. This chapter examines the interactions between property ownership, power and the state that have historically shaped the conditions of recreational access to the countryside with a particular focus upon the activities of the Malvern Hills Conservators and the Oxford Preservation Trust. The intention is to submit this material to a historical journal as a standalone article at a later date.

Undoubtedly this is not the book that Peter would have published, but I hope that it is a reasonable approximation to what he intended it to be and that readers will be able to recognize the characteristic hallmarks of Peter's scholarship. Fittingly for a final work it draws together many strands of Peter's earlier work, including his groundbreaking interpretation of the urban landscape in the *English Urban Renaissance*, his study of Bath's complex relationship with its history and the heritage industry, his long-standing interest in the evolution of spas and resorts and his work on leisure and consumption. It is also clearly inspired by Peter's personal love of walking, music and literature.

Rosemary Sweet

Acknowledgements

Peter died before he was able to draft any acknowledgements. However, this book draws deeply on a long career of research on urban history, the histories of leisure and consumption, and the emergence of the heritage movement and I know that he would have wished to thank Lampeter University, where he spent much of his career, Aberystwyth University, which he joined in 2007, and the National Library of Wales where much of the research for this book was conducted. Upon retirement, Peter moved to Oxford, and his research and writing also clearly benefited from access to the Bodleian. Peter's modesty would also have demanded that he acknowledge the insights, support and suggestions of friends and colleagues, both at Lampeter and Aberystwyth, within the UK and further afield. Peter collaborated with many colleagues through *Urban History*, the Pre-Modern Towns Group, the European Association of Urban Historians and other academic networks. These colleagues will have to remain nameless but their influence may often be detected in the footnotes. Although Anne, his wife, died in 2014 their shared interests, particularly in the history of health, are much in evidence. Finally, his daughters, Sarah and Clare, with whose help this book is finally being published, would have most certainly been named. Anyone who knew Peter also knew how proud he was of both his daughters and how much their conversation, company and support meant to him, particularly after Anne's death.

In completing Peter's manuscript, I too have incurred some obligations. First, I must thank Abigail Lane and Megan Harris at Bloomsbury who provided prompt and efficient support at all stages of the book's production. I would also like to thank the Trustees of the Marc Fitch Fund who generously provided financial support to cover the cost of illustrations and the Centre for Regional and Local History, University of Leicester, for funding towards the cost of preparing the index. I am grateful to the David Wilson Library, University of Leicester, which supplied copies of and to Ian Swirles for undertaking the scans. The following institutions and organizations also gave permission to reproduce images from their collections: the Ashmolean Museum, Birmingham Museums Trust, the British Museum, the Geological Society of London, Herefordshire Council, the Imperial War Museum, the Science Museum Group, London Transport Museum and the Shell Heritage Art Collection the Francis Frith Collection and Getty Images. Paul Readman and Katy Layton Jones generously read and commented on a draft. I am grateful to Samantha Clark for compiling the index promptly and professionally. Finally, I must thank my head of school, Krista Cowman, for supporting me in undertaking a project that may not contribute to my university's REF return but will make a much bigger contribution to our understanding of the English landscape and its meanings.

1

Introduction

This book is about the invention of the English landscape between about 1700 and 1939. The emphasis here is upon the three words 'landscape', 'English' and 'invention'. By landscape is meant both the built and natural environment. The term 'English' is used to denote not only a specific geographic space but also the mythic space embodied in the idea of England. The word 'invention' is chosen because this is not primarily a study of how the 'real' landscape of England developed in this period – as we will see many others have already undertaken this task – but of how an idealized vision of the landscape, which became closely associated with the idea of England, was created – or invented – in the years after 1700. Central to this process was the emergence of the landscape as a recreational good, and so this is a history of the landscape in which leisure (rather than work) plays a central role.

The starting point for this book is another volume that has a similar name but a very different objective, and which has become a classic, W. G. Hoskins's *The Making of the English Landscape*. Published in 1955 it has been described by John Beckett as 'the first serious attempt to study the landscape in a systematic way in order to assess how it has changed and altered through time, and to relate the findings to what it tells us about past communities'.[1] Its influence has been huge, not only among historians, archaeologists and geographers but also – and more importantly – a recreational public eager to learn more about the landscape they visit and in which their local communities are embedded. Hoskins was keen to demonstrate that the landscape was a record of the past in its own right, arguing that 'the English landscape ... to those who know how to read it aright, is the richest historical record we possess. There are discoveries to be made in it for which no written documents exist, or have ever existed'.[2] This was a reaction against historians' exclusive reliance on written records, especially those of the central state, an approach that had emerged with the professionalization of the discipline in the late-nineteenth century. Hoskins saw landscape as an empirical record of the past, in John Wylie's words, 'an objective, external, material assembly of facts and things which is realised through direct encounter and observation'.[3] Historians,

---

[1] John Beckett, *Writing Local History* (Manchester: Manchester University Press, 2007), 111.
[2] W. G. Hoskins, *Midland England: A Survey of the Country between the Chilterns and the Trent* (London: Batsford, 1949), v; idem, *The Making of the English Landscape* (London: Hodder & Stoughton, 1970), 14.
[3] John Wylie, *Landscape* (London: Routledge, 2007), 33.

and in particular local historians, were encouraged to take to the fields and streets to rediscover, through intelligent reading of the surviving landscape, the *reality* of economic and social life in the past. Hoskins claimed that 'no book exists to describe the manner in which the various landscapes of this country came to assume the shape and appearance they now have', but he was well aware that a large literature already existed on how to read the landscape in the form of the popular guidebook and travelogue that had proliferated in the inter-war years. However, he dismissed the romanticized and emotive vision of the country conveyed in such literature as 'sentimental and formless slush'.[4] An economic historian by background, he sought to introduce a new empiricism and realism into the way that the landscape was observed, reflecting the developing influence of the social sciences on academic study. At the same time he was also eager to engage with a lay public that was seeking a form of history that had a strong recreational content to it: 'a new kind of history which it is hoped will appeal to all those who like to travel intelligently, to get away from the guide-book show pieces now and then, and to unearth the reason behind what they are looking at'.[5] This bridge between the academic and popular was something that Hoskins sought to build, not only in his publications but also in the two television series of six programmes that he presented in 1976 and 1978.[6]

The Making of the English Landscape has spawned a wide range of publications from academic to popular. Hoskins himself edited and contributed to series of county histories of the landscape published by Hodder and Stoughton, and in 2006 English Heritage published a multi-volume series of regionally based volumes on the *English Landscape*. Two general surveys, aimed at the general market, have been published in the last decade by an archaeologist and a geographer with a high television profile; both possess the same title that exactly – except for the significant change of one word – mirrors Hoskins's original title: Francis Pryor's *The Making of the British Landscape* (2010) and Nicholas Crane's *The Making of the British Landscape* (2016).[7] Both acknowledge the inspirational influence of Hoskins's book, and both produce broadly chronological surveys of the evolution of the nation's landscape from the Ice Age to the present day. Both give much more space to the pre-Saxon period than Hoskins, and the story that they tell is enriched by the great volume of research produced since the 1950s. But the approach, using material evidence supported by documentation, to recover a real process of change is the same. The replacement of the word 'English' by 'British' has more to it than simply a wish to be geographically embracing. Much as Hoskins saw his mission to introduce a new historical robustness into looking at the landscape, it is clear that his views were heavily coloured by social and political

---

[4] Hoskins, *English Landscape*, 13.
[5] Ibid., 15.
[6] For Hoskins's life, see Joan Thirsk, 'Hoskins, William George (1908–1992), Historian of the English Landscape', *Oxford Dictionary of National Biography*, 23 Sep. 2004 https://www.oxforddnb.com/view/10.1093/ref:odnb/9780198614128.001.0001/odnb-9780198614128-e-38631, accessed 15 Jun. 2022.
[7] Francis Pryor, *The Making of the British Landscape: How We Have Transformed the Land, from Prehistory to Today* (London: Allen Lane, 2010); Nicholas Crane, *The Making of the British Landscape: From the Ice Age to the Present* (London: Weidenfeld & Nicolson, 2016).

attitudes. His was decidedly a study of the *English* landscape – in fact predominantly of the south and Midlands. Despite their hugely connected histories and landscapes, there is no attempt to accommodate Wales, Scotland or Ireland into his narrative. In all probability this reflected the pre-war trend to associate landscape and national identity.

Hoskins's treatment of the Tudor and early Stuart era, and the yeoman and peasantry of that period, as England's golden age, also resonates with late Victorian and early-twentieth-century trends in historiography. Hoskins possessed an aversion to modernity, so much so that he claimed, 'Since that time [the late-nineteenth century], and especially since 1914, every single change in the English landscape has either uglified it or destroyed its meaning, or both.'[8] This has prompted Francis Pryor to argue that Hoskins's views were 'reactionary in the extreme'. Hoskins's detestation of the modern world and his harking back to a non-existent rural idyll should locate him in the Romantic tradition of landscape appreciation, as exemplified by Wordsworth.[9] This might – though Pryor does not suggest this – point to another way of reading landscape and of reading Hoskins himself – landscape not as a piece of objective reality, an historical source which if interpreted correctly may reveal more about the true past lived by our ancestors, but as something invented in the mind of the writer, poet and artist, imbued with all their prejudices and values, and those of the society that they service. Hoskins's *Making of the English Landscape* was an attempt, in the context of the times, to introduce a new social-scientific reality into landscape studies. But it may be the poetic quality of his writing that represents its enduring legacy. It is not something that he would have acknowledged, but it does suggest that a survey of the invention of the English landscape is overdue to parallel that of the making. It is easy now to spot where Hoskins's prejudices affected his judgement. But, as David Matless has pointed out, we need to get beyond the process of simply 'outing' these prejudices to understand the role of imagination, imagery and myth in influencing the way that we interact with and use landscape.[10]

Such an approach is possible because of the wealth of research across a series of disciplines that has been undertaken as a result of the 'cultural turn' in the later twentieth century. In many respects geographers have led the way, with major contributions, particularly on the relationship between landscape and national identity, by figures such as Stephen Daniels, David Lowenthal, David Matless and Denis Cosgrove. Historians have tended to be somewhat slower to acknowledge the invented character of landscape, more inclined – to the extent that they do engage with the subject – to view, in the manner of Hoskins, the physical traces of the past as another empirical historical source. However, Simon Schama in his influential *Landscape and Memory* has pointed to another way of reading the past in the landscape, in which the emphasis is upon how we mould the material world to reflect our beliefs, aspirations and myths.[11] More recently Alexandra Walsham has demonstrated the importance of

---

[8] Hoskins, *English Landscape*, 298.
[9] Pryor, *Making of the British Landscape*, 14.
[10] David Matless, 'One Man's England: W. G. Hoskins and the English Culture of Landscape', *Rural History* 40:2 (1993): 203–4.
[11] Simon Schama, *Landscape and Memory* (London: Fontana Press, 1996).

religious beliefs in shaping early modern perceptions of landscape, and Paul Readman powerfully demonstrated how in the nineteenth century the landscape was, in a quite new way, invested with meanings that played a key part in 'the shaping of English identity'.[12] One of Readman's case studies is of the Lake District, and this has been the focus of attention of a collection of essays edited by the historian John Walton and the archaeologist Jason Wood under the title of *The Making of a Cultural Landscape: The English Lake District as Tourist Destination, 1750-2010* (2013).

The notion of a cultural landscape is central to this book, as is the role of leisure in determining the extent and character of the cultural overlay. In the contributions to the volume, however, it is not so much the association of the Lake District with a purported English identity or even the role of the past in shaping perceptions of the area that predominate; more significant would seem to be the Lakes as a repository of unsullied Nature. History and Nature are not of course unconnected. The further we go back in the past the more closely we approach the wilderness and the state of nature, a world unaffected by human intervention. Nonetheless, it is important to recognize that where landscapes are invested with meaning, it is as much about their green credentials as their historic ones. However, what constitutes a green or natural landscape – indeed what constitutes Nature – is profoundly problematic. So much of contemporary discourse and debate revolves around connecting with Nature,[13] or appealing to Nature to legitimize or stigmatize a particular course of action. Yet frequently little attempt is made to define what Nature is; it is often simply treated as an objective category, and assumptions are made to that effect. But approaching it as part of culture, and a historically and geographically defined culture, leads to a very different and richer perspective. In this context it turns out to be a highly fluid and malleable concept, capable of quite radical changes in meaning across relatively short periods of time. This book will argue that from the seventeenth century in Britain, there was a growing interest in 'Nature' and the natural world. This was accompanied, and to a degree facilitated, by a shift in the meaning of 'nature', away from one located predominantly in the human body and mind (their characteristics and urges) and in a concept of a natural order defined by God, to one that while retaining the human elements increasingly, and paradoxically, looked to the natural non-human environment – of which landscape was to prove a key part – and life forms for its meaning.[14] Driving this change was a series of linked economic, social and intellectual 'revolutions' – the Scientific Revolution and the rise of natural philosophy, the Industrial Revolution, and accelerating urbanization – which will be explored in detail in later chapters.

---

[12] Alexandra Walsham, *The Reformation of the Landscape: Religion, Identity and Memory in Early Modern Britain and Ireland* (Oxford: Oxford University Press, 2012); Paul Readman, *Storied Ground: Landscape and the Shaping of English National Identity* (Cambridge: Cambridge University Press, 2018).

[13] Tristan Gooley, *How to Connect with Nature* (London: Macmillan, 2014).

[14] K. V. Thomas, *Man and the Natural World* (London: Penguin, 1984). For the historic meanings and development of the term 'nature', and compounds of it, see the Oxford English Dictionary, https://www.oed.com/view/Entry/125353?rskey=LHS8s6&result=1#eid. For a discussion of the idea of Nature see Noel Castree, *Making Sense of Nature: Representations, Politics and Democracy* (Abingdon: Routledge, 2014).

These historiographical developments have been paralleled by trends in economic, social and cultural history that have fed into the idea of 'invention' of a concept that was imagined, disseminated and consumed. The wider hinterland of the invention of the English landscape includes the changes consequent upon the processes of commercialization that accelerated rapidly from the early-eighteenth century, driving increasing consumption and a service economy.[15] One form of consumption that is of particular relevance to this book was that of health and leisure: during the eighteenth century both health and leisure were increasingly commodified, with the growth of recreational travel and the rise of a medical marketplace, processes that were – as manifested in the phenomenon of the spa town – clearly symbiotic.[16] The English landscape was the backdrop against which travel in the pursuit of health and recreation was pursued by those who could afford it, and in the process the landscape itself was discovered, represented or invented. Questions of who had access to this landscape, however, became ever more pressing in the nineteenth century against the context of rapid urban population growth. Landscape was increasingly reimagined as a recreational good, a source of both physical and moral well-being for urban workers as well as the landed elite. Meanwhile, specific landscapes were revealed, modelled and commodified (through the proliferating genres of guidebooks, fictional works, paintings and photographs) as recreational green spaces in order to quench the thirst of the urban dwellers for contact with nature. From Dartmoor to the Lakes, from the West Country and Wessex to the Cotswolds and Broads, imagined countrysides and wildernesses were being created, tied umbilically for their lifeblood to the cities by the revolutions in personal mobility and transport provided by steamer, rail, cycle, charabanc and automobile. In this sense, the rural landscape as a whole was being transformed into urban green space.[17]

Today, popular interest in the countryside as a site of leisure and recreation is arguably greater than ever before. Heritage organizations such as the National Trust have seen a steady increase in membership (at the time of writing it is 5.7 million) while English Heritage claims to attract over 10 million visitors to its sites each year.[18] Leisure pursuits such as walking and bicycling that emerged in the nineteenth century are attracting a growing and increasingly diverse constituency. With the growth of population, access to the countryside – Right to Roam – is becoming increasingly contentious as organizations such as the Open Spaces Society campaign to preserve and restore public footpaths and to maintain public access to commons.[19] The impact of Covid-related travel restrictions during 2020–21 in particular prompted a boom in domestic tourism as holiday makers were forced to 'staycation'. At the same time many commuters took advantage of working from home to pursue a less-pressurized

---

[15] See, e.g., Neil McKendrick, John Brewer and J. H. Plumb (eds.), *The Birth of a Consumer Society: The Commercialization of Eighteenth-Century England* (London: Hutchinson, 1983); John Brewer and Roy Porter (eds.), *Consumption and the World of Goods* (London: Routledge, 1993).
[16] Phyllis Hembry, *The English Spa, 1560–1815: A Social History* (London: Athlone, 1990).
[17] Peter Borsay, 'Nature, the Past and the English Town: A Counter-cultural History', *Urban History* 44:1 (2017): 27–43.
[18] https://www.english-heritage.org.uk/about-us/, accessed 29 Jul. 2022.
[19] https://www.oss.org.uk/about-us/, accessed 29 Jul. 2022.

lifestyle in the country with estate agents seeing a dramatic increase in buyers seeking to purchase rural properties. Within towns and cities, the impact of Covid has inspired a new appreciation of the value of gardens and parks as public amenities and as sites of mental and physical recreation. Recognition of the value of green space, both in the countryside and within towns and cities, is also being fuelled by increasing concern over climate change and debates over land management and rewilding. Catastrophic weather events and 'climate breakdown' that are occurring with ever greater frequency have focused attention on the vulnerability of 'Nature' and the ecosystem that sustains it.

The invention of the English landscape, it is argued here, was in large part a response to the social and cultural changes consequent upon urbanization. Urban historians, however, have traditionally focused upon man-made or 'grey space' and the modern and have paid relatively little attention to nature or what might be termed 'green' and 'blue space' (the countryside and the sea). Yet to understand the relationship between town and 'nature', we have to look not just at the countryside but inside the town: at the domestic garden, the public walks and promenades, the parks and pleasure gardens, the civic buildings and cathedrals. But the most significant intersection between town and country was probably on the urban edge and beyond: in the suburbs and deep suburbia, the maritime margins and the imaginary territories being created, especially from the late-nineteenth century.[20] As a result, this book focuses upon both the built and the visible material landscape but inevitably strays into geology, flora and fauna, and people as well.

The focus of this book is very roughly contained within a triangle, which has London, Lyme Regis and Ludlow as its three corners (or, to put it in the language of the railways, which did so much to open up the countryside, within a triangle of GWR lines connecting London, Shrewsbury and Taunton). But it will also consider landscapes elsewhere in England: the Broads and Poppyland to the east; Dartmoor further west, and the Sussex Downs to the south. Many areas of England, however, have not been covered: the Peak District and the Lake District, first popularized by the domestic tourists of the eighteenth century, for example, can only receive passing mention. And a rather different narrative might have been written from the perspective of the north of England, where the border with Scotland, the richness of the Roman military heritage and the industrial economy have generated landscapes which are not only distinctive in appearance but represent histories that challenge some of the London-centric narratives of the south.

This book is about the 'invention', 'discovery' and 'representation' of the landscape: it asks how knowledge about the landscape and its meaning was created and disseminated. In many senses this was a literary phenomenon, created through the writing and consumption of the printed word, but it was also one in which visual and even musical representations played a key role. The sources are, therefore, predominantly the printed texts that a wider reading public consumed and through which their own experiences were shaped and imagined ideals of the landscape were formed. Thus, this study is in part a commentary on England's rich heritage of antiquarian and topographical writing, from the heavyweight tomes of Camden's *Britannia* and the county histories of

[20] Ibid., 42–3.

the eighteenth century to the specialist publications of the proliferating local historical and antiquarian societies of the nineteenth century. But the information that they contain was also abridged, repackaged, revised and recycled in publications aimed at a more general readership, finding its way into a broad array of guidebooks, which have equally proved essential in charting the changing perceptions and representations of the natural and built environment. From the late-nineteenth century, prompted by the expansion of recreational travel a new form of topographical writing emerged that wore its learning more lightly and was aimed at a more general reader. The publications of travel writers-cum-journalists such as H. V. Morton or S. P. B. Mais played a central role in introducing townspeople to the countryside and investing it with significance and meaning and the chapters that follow draw heavily on this oeuvre.[21] Although this book does not pretend to offer a survey of the 'literary' representation of landscape, novels and poems have been hugely influential in endowing specific sites or landscapes with meaning or significance. And alongside the written text, visual representations have been equally powerful in shaping perceptions of landscape and in reflecting or enabling new modes of viewing. The visual image – from the topographical prints of the eighteenth century, the landscape paintings and photography of the nineteenth century, and the railway posters, postcards and map art of the twentieth – play a crucial role in the analysis that follows.

The next chapter that follows establishes the early modern contexts to the 'invention' of the English landscape when domestic travel for leisure and recreation first became established, accompanied by an expansion in print culture which allowed travellers to record what they had seen and for readers to follow them vicariously. The study of antiquities, natural history and geology flourished in the eighteenth century in an era of pre-disciplinary scholarship when authors could move seamlessly from botany to Roman antiquities or to rock formations as the landscape, and its human past, was opened up to new forms of investigation. Such investigations were informed by wider cultural trends that are examined in Chapter 3, which explores the intellectual and cultural changes associated with the Reformation, the Enlightenment and Romanticism and their consequences for attitudes towards and representations of the natural and man-made environment. The intellectual and aesthetic changes described in Chapter 3 continued to reverberate through the nineteenth and early twentieth centuries and were joined by new movements such as democracy, socialism and nationalism. Against this backdrop, as Chapter 4 shows, the forms of representation and reproduction that had emerged in the eighteenth century expanded hugely, becoming mass commodities, consumed by a rapidly growing urban population for whom the countryside had become a recreational landscape.

With the environment now seen as a recreational good, Chapter 5 examines the texts that were produced in response to public demand for representations of

---

[21] Bernard Smith, 'Mais, Stuart Petre Brodie (1885–1975), Writer and Radio Broadcaster', *Oxford Dictionary of National Biography*, 23 Sep. 2004 https://www.oxforddnb.com/view/10.1093/ref:odnb/9780198614128.001.0001/odnb-9780198614128-e-46344, accessed 29 Jul. 2022. and C. R. Perry, 'Morton, Henry Canova Vollam (1892–1979), Travel Writer and Journalist', *Oxford Dictionary of National Biography*, 23 Sep. 2004 https://www.oxforddnb.com/view/10.1093/ref:odnb/9780198614128.001.0001/odnb-9780198614128-e-46343, accessed 29 Jul. 2022.

the landscape and the way that these collectively redefined it, creating a variegated recreational map of blue, green and grey space. Some places and spaces were sites of intensive interest and commentary – tourist hotspots, but equally telling, other places were invisible, unnoticed and unmarked. Chapter 6 explores the relationship between landscape, memory and myth in terms of deep history, pre-history and 'recent' history, focusing on the way that landscapes were invested with historical meaning in the century following the accession of Queen Victoria. Whereas previous chapters chiefly discuss the rural landscape and the reconfiguration of its meaning in response to urbanization, in this chapter towns, and specifically the historic urban environment, come into focus. Historic towns and villages, redolent of 'olden time', became a desirable tourist attraction in their own right. Finally, the chapter considers future timescapes, exploring those parts of the urban and rural landscape that attracted the tourist gaze precisely because they were associated with ideas of modernity. The forces of economic and social change that precipitated the 'discovery' of the natural landscape are the focus of Chapter 7. The fact that the 'natural' world became a source of solace reflects fundamental changes in attitudes towards the landscape, which was no longer simply an enduring physical reality but also a mutable mental concept that could undergo radical change. Chapter 8 explores the impact of the 'transport revolution' on landscape tourism as railways, bicycles and motor cars facilitated access for tourists. However, despite these innovations, or indeed thanks to the improved access they offered, walking continued to be the preferred mode of exploring the landscape for a growing community of ramblers and hikers. Finally, the chapter explores how different modes of transport – from trains to pedestrianism – affected how the landscape itself was experienced.

The focus of Chapter 9 is upon the relationship between the landscape and identities. By the early-twentieth century the landscape had become a central element in the construction of an English national identity, but this was not a straightforward process and has to be seen in the context of England's place within Britain and the wider empire. Moreover, the way in which the landscape was engaged with was also inflected by the religious, class and gender identities of the consumers. Finally, the concluding chapter looks forward to how the 'invention' of the English landscape continued to unfold in the years following the Second World War until the beginning of the new millennium.

2

Revealing the early modern landscape

In the 1920s, the journalist and travel writer H. V. Morton embarked on his 'search' for England, admitting that 'I was humiliated … to realize how little I knew about England. I was shamed to think that I had wandered so far and so often over the world neglecting those lovely things near at home'.[1] Less than a decade later, another journalist, S. P. B. Mais, was declaring to his readers that '[m]y aim is quite simple. It is to set out with you on a voyage partly of discovery, partly of re-discovery'. Perhaps the most extraordinary aspect of this whole exercise of discovery was the need to do it. Since the mid-Victorian period, tens of thousands of natives and foreigners had been intensively engaged in visiting, exploring, protecting, describing and portraying what they conceived of as the landscape of England. Their peregrinations and investigations, and the attempts to represent these, will be the subject of much of the following chapters. But, for centuries before, smaller numbers of people had also been engaged in a similar epic voyage of discovery that laid the foundations for what was to come. In many respects the raw material – the knowledge base and intellectual framework – for the transformation ahead was established in the early modern and early Victorian eras. This chapter examines the search for England and its landscape before the emergence of this as a mass experience in the later nineteenth century.

Exploration and tourism

The global voyages of discovery undertaken by expansionist and neo-imperialist societies in Western Europe from the fifteenth century, during the so-called Age of Adventure, were motivated primarily by economic, political and religious motives.[2] However, they also initiated a number of important shifts in attitude that were to spread beyond the tiny numbers who undertook the expeditions, not least through the spread of printing after 1450. The notion of exploration per se was elevated into

---

[1] H. V. Morton, *In Search of England* (London: Methuen, 1927), 2; S. P. B. Mais, *Round about England* (London: Richards, 1935), 179.
[2] See Merry Wiesner-Hanks, *Early Modern Europe, 1450–1789* (Cambridge: Cambridge University Press, 2006), chapters 1, 7, 13.

a cultural ideal, there developed a greater sense of spatial awareness and – through contact with other natural worlds and cultures – deeper consciousness of and curiosity about landscape forms. Many expeditions had mixed scientific and politico-economic motives, such as Captain Cooke's three epic voyages of 1768–80 (the first two to the Pacific and Australia sponsored by the Royal Society) when he sailed under secret instructions from the crown aimed at establishing British control over newly discovered territory and reporting on natural resources located there.[3] However, the fact that political factors were so influential in promoting overseas expeditions – John Cabot had the backing of Henry VII as he undertook the first English voyage to North America in 1497[4] – also helped fuse ideas of discovery, place and identity into a potent amalgam in a way that was of critical significance for the future. The act of exploration became a form of national and local patriotism. This soon became the case for not only those who opened up new territories beyond their native countries but also those who drilled deep into their homelands. Paradoxically – and this will become a recurrent theme – as external exploration expanded so it appears, at times at least, to have stimulated an eagerness to investigate internal spaces. The earliest ventures into local cartography, topography and history were underpinned by a wish to explore and celebrate place identities such as those of the parish, town and county, alongside that of England and Britain. By the nineteenth century this process may have been enhanced by the way European overseas exploration was increasingly turning away from the investigation of coastlines, much of which had already been mapped, to that of interiors, such as those Africa and Asia.[5] Penetrating the Congo had its counterpart for the domestic explorer in searching deepest Herefordshire.

The great voyages of discovery of the early modern era often involved heavy investment and high levels of personal and economic risk, justified ultimately by the serious returns – such as commercial benefits – that they promised. Such attitudes to journeying grew naturally out of the long association between work and travel embodied in the practice of trade. The notion that travel could be undertaken for pleasure, and that exploration could be a form of recreation, was another matter. The closest parallel to this was probably the experience of the medieval pilgrimage, which propelled devotees into lengthy journeys not only across their own countries, such as to Canterbury in England, but also into transnational travel, such as to Santiago de Compostela in northern Spain and Jerusalem in the Holy Land. Such journeys, whatever their religious purpose, would have provided opportunities for sightseeing and pleasure. It was the development of the Grand Tour, however, originating in England in the sixteenth and seventeenth centuries, and reaching maturity in the eighteenth century, that turned travel from something intended to service other ends, such as commercial or religious ones, into an end in itself, a form of recreation that

---

[3] Wiesner-Hanks, *Early Modern Europe*, 444–6; David N. Livingstone, *The Geographical Tradition: Episodes in the History of a Contested Enterprise* (Oxford: Blackwell, 1992), 129.
[4] Wiesner-Hanks, *Early Modern Europe*, 227.
[5] Ibid., 447.

today – using a modern term – we would call tourism.⁶ The European Grand Tour was initially the pastime of a tiny number of people – one of the principal *rites de passage* for young members of the elite – but by the early-nineteenth century its appeal was spreading. In 1819 William and Sampson Sandys could proclaim,

> Never probably was the passion for tourizing [*sic*] so prevalent as it is now; in time past one who had travelled to the end of Europe or who had entered the borders of Asia was looked upon as a superior being and the marvellous relation of a Mandeville received with implicit credit. At present … the tour of Europe formerly the *ultimatum* of travellers has now become the summer excursion of a mere party of pleasures; 'Every body now makes the grand tour' as a lady said who had been to Ostend via a Margate Steam Packet, accompanying her remarks with two, or three, very expressive rotations of her finger on the table.⁷

Pleasures of all sorts were undoubtedly an important feature of it, but recreation was also defined in serious educational terms. Encountering foreign landscapes was an important element of this. Initially the principal destinations were the great centres of urban culture, Paris and in Italy Rome, Venice, Florence, Naples and Turin (later the options expanded to include central European cities such as Dresden and Vienna), where antique, Renaissance and modern classical styles in art and architecture could be absorbed.⁸ But the extensive journeys involved inevitably carried the grand tourists across a wide variety of non-urban terrains. If traversing these was treated at first as a necessary and often considerable inconvenience, by the mid-eighteenth century, if not before, the seas, mountain ranges, lakes and rivers that had previously been seen as potential obstructions to travel were viewed increasingly in a positive light and became a significant, even essential, part of the 'tourist' experience.⁹

The *Oxford English Dictionary* gives the first use of the word 'tourist' as dating from 1780 and significantly drawn not from a work about the Grand Tour but one entitled *Ode to the Genius of the Lakes in the North of England*. By this period the domestic tour, around England and various parts of Britain, was firmly established on the tourist map.¹⁰ Its origins lie in the journeys, beginning on the cusp of the medieval and early

---

⁶ Richard Ansell, *Complete Gentlemen Educational Travel and Family Strategy, 1650–1750* (Oxford: British Academy 2022); Jeremy Black, *The British Abroad: The Grand Tour in the Eighteenth Century* (Stroud: Alan Sutton, 1985); Edward Chaney, *The Evolution of the Grand Tour: Anglo-Italian Cultural Relations since the Renaissance* (Abingdon: Routledge, 2006); John Towner, 'The Grand Tour: A Key Stage in the History of Tourism', *Annals of Tourism Research* 12 (1985): 297–333.
⁷ National Library of Wales, Cwrtmawr 393C 'Walk through South Wales in October 1819', f. III.
⁸ Rosemary Sweet, *Cities and the Grand Tour: The British in Italy c. 1690–1820* (Cambridge: Cambridge University Press, 2012).
⁹ Paul Bernard, *Rush to the Alps: The Evolution of Vacationing in Switzerland* (Boulder: Columbia University Press, 1987); G. De Beer, *Early Travellers in the Alps* (London: Sidgwick & Jackson, 1966); Robert Macfarlane, *Mountains of the Mind: A History of a Fascination* (London: Granta Books, 2003); Jim Ring, *How the English Made the Alps* (London: Faber & Faber, 2011).
¹⁰ Esther Moir, *The Discovery of Britain. The English Tourists, 1540–1840* (London: Routledge & Kegan Paul, 1964); Ian Ousby, *The Englishman's England* (Cambridge: Cambridge University Press, 1990).

modern period, undertaken to furnish genealogical, antiquarian and topographic details for intended chorographies. William of Worcester compiled notes during a series of trips through Norfolk and the south-west in 1477–80, and John Leland spent almost a decade collecting material for his unpublished *Itinerary*, in 1546 reporting to Henry VIII, who had commissioned the project,

> I have so travelled in your dominions both by the sea coasts and the middle parts, sparing neither labour nor costs, by the space of these six years past, that there is almost neither cape, nor bay, haven, creek, or pier, river or confluence of rivers, breacks, washes, lakes, meres, fenny waters, mountains, valleys, moors, hearths, forests, woods, cities, burgs, castles, principal manor places, monasteries, and colleges, but I have seen them, and noted in so doing a whole world of things very memorable.[11]

The notion of a journey was embodied in the title of the first of the county histories, William Lambarde's *A Perambulation of Kent* (1576). Journeying and discovery (whether local or further afield) underpinned the work of many of the early natural historians and 'scientists', such as Edward Lhwyd, who explored Wales, Cornwall, Devon, Brittany, Ireland, the Isle of Man, the Lake District and Scotland.[12] It would, of course, be misleading to describe the travels undertaken on these occasions as simply recreational; these were journeys of discovery, driven by curiosity and structured around the historic and contemporary landscape and unconnected with trade or business. Later commercial publications like Daniel Defoe's *Tour thro' the Whole Island of Great Britain*, published in three volumes between 1724 and 1726, were written around the model of a journey. Defoe stated that his guide was based on a series of recently undertaken trips or 'circuits', though this contained a heavy dose of fabrication.[13] Much of the detail was garnered during spying missions on which he had been engaged decades earlier for the Tory politician and courtier, Robert Harley, or information that he had accumulated from other sources, including rival publications.[14] That he felt the need to construct this elaborate ruse reflected not only a contemporary thirst for up-to-date information but also the fact that it was increasingly common for well-off men and women to tour their native shores for recreational purposes, and that they would want a guide that reflected the actual format of their pastime.

Hundreds of manuscript diaries survive of tours undertaken in Britain. One catalogue, based on a trawl of the forty-nine county record offices, lists 608 diaries

---

[11] Beckett, *Writing Local History*, 8–10.
[12] John Cramsie, *British Travellers and the Encounter with Britain, 1450–1700* (Woodbridge: Boydell Press, 2015), 168–73, 357–94.
[13] Daniel Defoe, *A Tour thro' the Whole Island of Great Britain*, 3 vols. (London: G. Strahan, 1724–6), vol. 1, 1–2.
[14] J. H. Andrews, 'Defoe and the Sources for His Tour', *Geographical Journal* 126 (1960): 268–77; Pat Rogers, 'Defoe's Tour and the Historiography of Early Modern Britain', *Journal for Eighteenth-Century Studies* 2:3 (2019): 365–79; Peter Borsay, 'Urban Development in the Age of Defoe', in *Britain in the First Age of Party, 1680–1750. Essays Presented to Geoffrey Holmes*, ed. Clyve Jones (London: Hambledon, 1987), 195–219.

(representing 'probably well over 700' separate journeys), two-thirds of which were compiled between 1750 and 1850. Favoured destinations were Scotland, Wales and the north and south-west of England. Those areas less well represented, the south and east of England, appear to have been where most of the compliers came from, reflecting where the core of tourist demand lay, and the thirst for exploration of an unknown Britain that underpinned this demand. A number of the diaries (forty-six) were also illustrated, indicative of the fact that visiting and recording landscape features was an important part of the touring experience.[15] It should also be said that during the eighteenth and nineteenth centuries a sort of grand tour in reverse existed with a sizeable number of wealthy foreigners visiting Britain to view what they perceived of as its enlightened and progressive economic and political systems.[16]

Though the journeys undertaken by overseas and domestic tourists had an educational function, it is clear that more often than not pedagogy merged seamlessly into pleasure. Many of the expeditions involved a visit to one of the country's burgeoning watering places such as Tunbridge Wells and Bath. The first wave of spa development took place in the late Tudor and early Stuart period, but their numbers begin to proliferate from the late-seventeenth century, and during the eighteenth century they were joined by the seaside resort to create an extensive network of urban settlements geared to providing health and leisure services. Merging the journey and holiday into a single package, they underpinned the development of the domestic tourist industry.[17] The first seaside resorts, established in the early to mid-eighteenth century, were concentrated in the south-east of England, servicing the London market, but by the later-eighteenth and early-nineteenth century they were spreading out along much of the British coastline, including East Anglia, north and south Devon, south and mid-Wales, Lancashire and Yorkshire, and the Scottish coasts closest to Edinburgh and Glasgow. This widened the opportunities for exploration, particularly since a number of these locations – such as Ilfracombe in north Devon and Tenby and Aberystwyth in Wales – were sited in places remote from large centres of population surrounded by spectacular natural landscapes.[18]

In the early-nineteenth century William Sanford, a wealthy but sick landed gentleman from Somerset, was advised by his doctors to seek a health cure at the seaside. He chose not one of the already fashionable large resorts but the tiny village of Lynton – just beginning to emerge as a resort – suspended between Exmoor and the rugged coast of north Devon. No doubt much of its appeal derived from its wild and romantic setting, reinforced not only by its isolation and inaccessibility but the way that the dramatic scenery mimicked the Alpine element that was

---

[15] Robin Gard (ed.), *The Observant Traveller: Diaries of Travel in England, Wales and Scotland in the County Record Offices of England and Wales* (London: H.M.S.O., 1989), ix–xi.
[16] See, e.g., Norman Scarfe (ed. and transl.), *Innocent Espionage: The La Rochefoucauld Brothers' Tour of England in 1785* (Woodbridge: Boydell Press, 1995).
[17] Hembry, *The English Spa*; Peter Borsay and John Walton (eds.), *Resorts and Ports: European Seaside Towns since 1700* (Bristol: Channel View, 2011); Allan Brodie and Gary Winter, *England's Seaside Resorts* (Swindon: English Heritage, 2007).
[18] Peter Borsay, 'From Port to Resort: Tenby and Narratives of Transition, 1760–1914', in *Resorts and Ports*, ed. Borsay and Walton, 86–112.

Figure 2.1 Charles Grignion after Nathan Drake, 'A Noble Terras Walk', York (1756). © The Trustees of the British Museum.

increasingly one of the key features of the European Tour. Sanford purchased land and built a large house on a magnificent cliff-top site and later, in 1817, funded the construction of a communal walk cut vertiginously into the sea cliff, which led from the village to the extraordinary Valley of the Rocks.[19] It was an extreme version of an amenity that had become a growing feature for any town with social pretensions since the early-seventeenth century, a public promenade. Though some of these were locked within the urban core, the clear majority were sited on the periphery, occasionally following the course of a river, and often with fine views of the countryside. The tree-lined New Walk constructed in the 1730s and 1740s at York ran along the bank of the River Ouse and decanted those who strolled along it into the surrounding meadows (see Figure 2.1), while the Park Walk at the hilltop town of Shaftesbury, laid out in 1753, enjoyed breathtaking views of Blackmore Vale.[20] The promenades and cliff-top walks that were basic features of seaside resorts emphasized not only the growing fascination with the natural landscape but also the role of walking in satisfying this.

---

[19] John Travis, *An Illustrated History of Lynton and Lynmouth* (Derby: Breedon Books, 1995), 18–19, 23, 46–7, 163; Peter Keene and Brian Pearce, *Valley of Rocks, Lynton* (Oxford: Thematic Trails, 1993).

[20] Peter Borsay, *The English Urban Renaissance: Culture and Society in the Provincial Town, 1660–1770* (Oxford: Oxford University Press, 1989), 162–72, 350–4.

The discovery of the natural landscape

The early modern period in Britain had seen the rise of two phenomena that were both practices and ideals: exploration and recreational travel. They fused together in what might be called tourism, which in itself was part of a wider consumer 'revolution' gathering pace in the seventeenth and eighteenth centuries.[21] Travel and exploration became part of an increasingly commercialized leisure economy. However, what exactly was being consumed by these early, predominantly well-off 'tourists'? Various factors might be singled out – health, food and drink, sex, good company, adventure – but one common element that fills the accounts of those engaged in travel for pleasure, particularly towards the end of the early modern period, is – in the broadest sense – the landscape. Discovering the material world, consuming through visual interaction its elements, became a growing passion for the elite. In this process of exploration and consumption, crudely speaking two types of landscape were involved: the natural and human.

In his path-breaking study, *Man and the Natural World* (1983), Keith Thomas demonstrates – perhaps to the surprise of a generation who might claim to have forged a new agenda of animal rights, biodiversity and eco-ethics – how far modern concerns with nature can be traced back to the early modern era.[22] Between 1500 and 1800 there was a major re-evaluation of man's relationship with the nature; Thomas has written, 'It was these centuries which generated both an intense interest in the natural world and those doubts and anxieties about man's relationship to it which we have inherited in magnified form.'[23] Thomas's study is primarily concerned with animals and plants. Both of these contribute in some fashion to appearance and form of the landscape, the latter more than the former.

But for the building blocks of the landscape we must turn to rocks, which as we will see in the work of early scientists become intimately associated with historic forms of flora and fauna. Like Thomas, Roy Porter looks to the early modern era for the emergence of changing perspectives on the formation of the earth's crust. Contrary to the picture cultivated by early-nineteenth-century geologists, 'from whom most historians have taken their cue', Porter proposed that a transformation in attitudes towards the Earth and its investigation took place in the period between the mid-seventeenth and early-nineteenth centuries.[24] Up until the 1660s there had been little attempt to probe the Earth's structure or its crust. This changed with the application of empirical methods of investigation, the emergence of early institutional structures to support scientific enquiry, and a growing commitment to take to the field and travel. As data upon rocks and their location amassed, geological strata 'very gradually … became an increasingly significant focus of enquiry'.[25] But in 1700 any attempt at

---

[21] McKendrick, Brewer and Plumb (eds.), *Birth of a Consumer Society*.
[22] Thomas, *Man and the Natural World*.
[23] Ibid., 15.
[24] Roy Porter, *The Making of Geology: Earth Science in Britain, 1660–1815* (Cambridge: Cambridge University Press, 1977), 3.
[25] Ibid., 58.

theorizing remained constrained by the continuing biblically centred belief in a Creator, a moment (as opposed to a long process) of creation and the deluge.

The later-eighteenth and early-nineteenth centuries saw developments that pointed the way towards the establishment of a systematic geology, with an emphasis upon the regular ordering of the strata, and the use of fossils to identify this; on the great antiquity of the earth; and on changes in its crust being the product of ongoing and naturally determined processes of rock formation and erosion.[26] James Hutton's *Theory of the Earth* (1795) promulgated the idea of uniformitarianism – a conviction that the changes in the earth's geology were slow and even, as opposed to the 'catastrophism' implied in the notion of the deluge.[27] His work, and that of William (Strata) Smith, underpinned foundational texts such as Charles Lyell's *Principles of Geology* (1830) and the research of major figures of Victorian geology such as Roderick Murchison and Adam Sedgwick.

A key factor in facilitating change was the blossoming of societies, many with published transactions, based upon a shared interest in science (rather than narrow social ties), not only at the centre, such as the influential Geological Society of London (f. 1807), but also in the provinces – such as the Literary and Philosophical Society of Newcastle-upon-Tyne (f. 1793) and the Royal Geological Society of Cornwall (f. 1814) – these being regions with a strong interest in mining.[28] In the nineteenth century, as we shall see, county and regional field societies and naturalists' clubs proliferated from the middle of the nineteenth century, building upon the model of the scientific societies pioneered in the eighteenth century. Members of these clubs were rarely engaged in raw acts of discovery, either in terms of their organizations or their field of investigation. They tended to add to knowledge by extending its bank of data rather than reconceptualizing it. Where they often were pioneers was in exploring their neighbouring environs and the local application of new ideas. It was this localizing impulse that was central to their impact.

If the emergence of geology provided one tool for viewing the landscape in new ways, the same might also be argued of the allied discipline of geography, which received its institutional crystallization with the foundation of the Royal Geographical Society in 1830 with the geologist Sir Roderick Murchison becoming 'its chief architect during the mid-Victorian era'.[29] How much this contributed to new ways of looking at the English landscape is a matter of question. The Society's resources and energies – those that remained after dining and socializing – seem primarily to have been directed overseas with prestigious foreign expeditions, but, through contrast and comparison, the reports of these ventures sensitized those at home to their native landscape. The rise of geography was also closely tied up with cartography, whose development during the early modern period – as we shall see – provided a major resource for conceptualizing and rethinking the landscape.

---

[26] J. Yolton, P. Rogers, R. Porter and B. M. Stafford (eds.), *The Blackwell Companion to the Enlightenment* (Oxford: Blackwell, 1991), 189–90.
[27] Livingstone, *The Geographical Tradition*, 119–20.
[28] Porter, *Geology*, chapter 6.
[29] Livingstone, *The Geographical Tradition*, 159.

Figure 2.2 The Valley of the Rocks, near Linton, Devonshire, from John Britton and E. W. Brayley, *Devonshire Illustrated in a Series of Views* (London: Fisher, 1829). Reproduced by kind permission of the David Wilson Library, University of Leicester.

The new geology, long in its gestation, had potentially momentous implications for how the English landscape was viewed. However, early accounts of two sites of spectacular geological formations, which later attracted a great deal of scientific attention, suggest that their impact was not immediate. When in 1789 the Revd John Swete 'sallied forth, in quest of the "Valley of Stones" [the Valley of the Rocks, Lynton]', he was bowled over by the scene, but he could do little more than find architectural analogies for the rock forms: (see Figure 2.2) 'Soon the tops of the succeeding hills became more and more wild and craggy – taking the shapes of disparting towers, gigantic obelisks and a thousand other fantastic forms.'[30] The Revd J. Bartlett's *Description of Malvern* (1796) seemed to promise some recognition of the emerging research into stratigraphy with his opening remarks that '[t]he *strata* in these elevated tracts are arranged in a perpendicular direction, which is the distinctive mark, or characteristic, of a mountain, always attended to by those who have treated scientifically of this branch of knowledge.'[31] But this comment is simply delivered in the context of whether to call the Malverns hills or mountains. His later account went little beyond describing the superficial appearance and practical use of individual rocks ('rugged and brittle'

---

[30] Peter Hunt (ed.), *Devon's Age of Elegance: Described by the Diaries of the Reverend John Swete, Lady Paterson, and Miss Mary Cornish* (Exeter: Devon Books, 1984), 26.
[31] J. Barrett, *A Description of Malvern and Its Environs* (Worcester: T. Holl, 1796), 13–14; Porter, *Geology*, 122, 176–83.

and 'unfit for carving'), without any speculation as to their relationship to each other or the processes which brought them into being.[32]

Geological knowledge was to prove persistently difficult for the lay observer to absorb. This was partly because of its highly scientific nature, but of equal if not more importance was that it related to an essentially hidden landscape concealed beneath the surface of the earth. On occasions it is revealed in coastal cliff formations, but inland the most revealing sites are quarries, not the most attractive of locations for the tourist. Flora and fauna were another matter. These were a part of the natural world that was regularly in people's sights, and, as living organisms, they were something with which it was possible to empathize. Their strict definition as landscape, particularly in the case of animals, might be questioned, but they were inextricably bound up with the way the landscape was viewed and perceived. The notion of an expanding knowledge of the natural world in the early modern period, and therefore of the landscape, needs treating with care. Humans had long had a relationship with and often intimate knowledge of the plant and animal world – necessarily so to carry out many aspects of their lives, from agriculture to medicine. What emerged in the early modern period was a new type of knowledge in which the natural world began to be perceived as a phenomenon in its own right rather than just an adjunct of human need. The invention of the microscope in the late-sixteenth century led, from the seventeenth century, to the discovery of natural processes and organisms too small for human sight, as well as allowing the detailed investigation of observable creatures.[33] New ways of classifying plants and animals were introduced from the seventeenth century, based on their intrinsic structures and characteristics, rather than anthropomorphic criteria. From the 1760s the Linnaean system – founded on the work of the Swedish scientist Carolus Linnaeus (1707–78), and classifying flora according to sexual characteristics and using Lain terminology – was accepted in educated circles. These 'new modes of classification', though still retaining human analogies, 'represented an important attempt to escape from the old man-centred viewpoint',[34] and to understand nature in its own terms.

These developments in classification built on an immense curiosity in the workings of nature, and a powerful sense that a new world was being discovered quite as strange, unexplored and exciting as that overseas; though in this case it existed literally in one's own village and back garden. By the latter half of the eighteenth century scores of amateur observers, many of them clergymen, were interrogating nature and communicating their findings to each other.[35] One of these was of course Gilbert White (1720–93) the curate of Selborne in Hampshire.[36] His minute observations of natural phenomena were recorded in correspondence, journals and eventually – drawing on these manuscript records – his celebrated publication, *The Natural History and Antiquities of*

---

[32] Barrett, *Description*, 16–17.
[33] Thomas, *Man and Natural World*, 87–8, 167–8.
[34] Ibid., 66.
[35] Ibid.; Jan Golinski, *British Weather and the Climate of Enlightenment* (Chicago: Chicago University Press, 2007); Vladimir Jankovic, *Reading the Skies. A Cultural History of English Weather, 1650–1820* (Manchester: Manchester University Press, 2000), chapter 5.
[36] Richard Mabey, *Gilbert White: A Biography of the Naturalist and Author of the Natural History of Selborne* (London: Pimlico, 1999).

Selborne (1789). It was the existence of a manuscript culture of letter writing and diary keeping, and of a print culture that nurtured and fed on this, that gave structure and meaning to White's observations. Many of his letters were written to Thomas Pennant, the naturalist and travel writer, who was planning a new edition of his *British Zoology* (1761–6) and seeking additional data. White's latter journal (it had been preceded by an earlier journal the 'Garden Kalendar'), kept for twenty-five years, was compiled using Daines Barrington's (another of White's correspondents) *Naturalist's Journal* (1767). This was a printed diary (reinforcing the notion that a significant number of other amateur naturalists were keeping such a record) providing eleven different blank headings for the daily collection of information on natural phenomena.[37] Fragment by fragment, detail by detail – White soon spread beyond the narrow confines of the printed format – he revealed the workings of natural world that polite human sight in the past had largely failed to register or at least record. As he grew older White appears to have become more and more attached to Selborne and the surrounding district, and less and less willing to travel.[38] His failure to obtain a full-time post at Oxford in 1758 probably marked the end of any serious attempt to leave Selborne. In some respects his work represented the very opposite of the expansive tourist impulse that underpinned the discovery of the landscape. Yet White demonstrated that a commitment to place and locality was as much a part of that journey of discovery as a sense of *wanderlust*. Without his close attachment to Selborne, it is unlikely that he would have committed the energies necessary to reveal the workings of its unique natural micro-environment.

The entries in his journals demonstrate both the range and focus of his vision: 26 September 1781, 'Our building-sand from Wolmer-forest seems pure from dirt; but examined thro' a microscope proves not to be sharp, & angular, but smooth as from collision'; 28 March 1790,

> A neighbour complained to me that her house was over-run with a kind of *black-beetle*, or, as she expressed herself, with a kind of *black-bob*, which swarmed in her kitchen when they get up in a morning before day-break. Soon after this account, I observed an unusual insect in one of my dark chimney closets; & find since that in the night they swarm also in my kitchen. On examination I soon ascertained the Species to be the *Blatta orientalis* of Linnaeus, & the *Blatta molendinaria* of Mouffet. The male is winged, the female is not; but shows somewhat like the rudiments of wings, as if in the pupa state. These insects belonged originally to the warmer parts of America, & were conveyed from thence by shipping to the East Indies; and by means of commerce begin to prevail in the more N. parts of Europe, as Russia, Sweden, &c. How long they have abounded in England, I cannot say.[39]

Here is a mixture of the homely and scientific; a locating of natural phenomena in a domestic and village topography; and a minuteness of vision; and the value of

---

[37] Walter Johnson (ed.), *Journals of Gilbert White* (Newton Abbot: David & Charles, 1970), xxxvii–xliv; Gilbert White, *The Natural History of Selborne*, ed. P. Foster (Oxford: Oxford University Press, 1993), x–xviii.
[38] Mabey, *Gilbert White*, 78, 170.
[39] Johnson (ed.), *Journals of Gilbert White*, 194, 355.

local investigation, coupled with an awareness of the wider scientific world and the international dimension of natural history. White was not the first to adopt a local perspective. Richard Carew's *Survey of Cornwall* (1603) contained an avifaunal list as did Robert Plot's *Natural History of Oxfordshire* (1677), but White's concentration on the village and particularity of his vision brought the exploration of the local context to a new level. At heart White was also an observer rather than a classifier, unlike several of his contemporaries such as Pennant.[40] It was an approach that underpinned much of the studies of amateur naturalists in the nineteenth century.

White's early letters to Pennant, forming the opening section of the *Natural History*, sketch in the landscape of Selborne and its environs.

> The soils of this district are almost as various and diversified as the views and aspects. The high part to the south-west consists of a vast hill of chalk, rising three hundred feet above the village; and is divided into a sheep down, the high wood, and a long hanging wood called The Hangar. ... The down, or sheep-walk, is a pleasing park-like spot ... jutting out on the verge of the hill-country, where it begins to break down into the plains, and commanding a very engaging view, being an assemblage of hill, dale, wood-lands, heath, and water. The prospect is bounded to the south-east and east by the vast range of mountains called the Sussex Downs ... Should I omit to describe with some exactness the forest of Wolmer, of which three fifths perhaps lie in this parish, my account of Selborne would be very imperfect, as it is a district abounding with many curious productions, both animal and vegetable.[41]

Is this merely context for the detailed accounts of flora and fauna which occupy most of the book or does it demonstrate a sensitivity to and pleasure in landscape forms – 'hill, dale, wood-lands, heath, and water' – as such? Though Defoe's *Tour*, published seventy years earlier, also contains accounts of natural landscapes, such as heath, moorland and mountains, his approach was very different. Bagshot Heath in Surrey is condemned as 'quite steril, given up to barrenness, horrid and frightful to look on', the so-called wonders of the Peak District in Derbyshire dismissed as 'wonderless wonders', and the fells of the Lake District condemned as not only 'high and formidable ... but they had a kind of an unhospitable terror in them. Here were ... no lead mines and veins of rich oar [*sic*], as in the Peak; no coal pits as in the hills about Halifax'. The best that can be claimed for such wild areas is that, as Defoe writes of Bagshot, they act 'as a foil to the beauty of the rest of England'.[42] In fact, Defoe shows little interest in natural landscape forms as such, with the focus on towns, and with features like rivers praised essentially as arteries of communication. Natural landscape was something to be avoided rather than explored.[43]

---

[40] Peter Bircham, *A History of Ornithology* (London: Collins, 2007), 76–81, 100–11; White, *Selborne*, ed. Foster, xx.
[41] White, *Selborne*, ed. Foster, 11–12, 20.
[42] Defoe, *Tour*, vol. 1, 83–4; vol. 3, 168, 223.
[43] Borsay, 'Urban Development in the Age of Defoe', 195–217.

White's approach to the landscape was clearly a world away from that of Defoe. In particular his attachment to the Hangar located to the rear of his house suggests that the steep wooded incline came to have a special meaning for him. Gilbert and his brother John cut two paths into the Hangar, the Zig-zag (John's idea) and the Bostall, the former more open and 'alpine', the latter 'a secluded tunnel into the heart of the woods', allowing White to explore regularly its inner secrets.[44] It is likely that it was the Hangar's accommodation of living phenomena – trees and birds – that appealed most to White rather than its formal qualities. However, it was the discovery of the aesthetic qualities of landscape with the concept of the picturesque that celebrated the wilder types of nature – hills, lakes, rivers and coastlines – more perhaps than their natural history where the greatest development occurred in the eighteenth century.

Exploring the human landscape

Consciousness of landscape forms, and variations in these, was already well developed by the end of the eighteenth century. Samuel Rudder's *New History of Gloucestershire* (1779), for example, divides the county into three distinct environmentally based regions, the 'Coteswold', the 'Vale' and the Forest of Dean. All of these regions are defined by natural features – hills, wood and river – yet Rudder's account emphasizes not so much this element as the human use of the landscape. 'Under the denomination of the Coteswold', he writes

> I now include all that high country on the south-east side of the … range of hills that runs through the county. It is a noble champaign country, the residence of many of the nobility and gentry, and abounds in verdant plains, downs, cornfields, parks, woods and little vallies … Within the last forty years, prodigious improvements have been made here, by a course of husbandry, first introduced into these parts by the late Mr. Richard Bishop … who brought the grass-seeds, turnips and clover into use, and taught the coteswold farmers how to become an opulent people.[45]

This account is not so much a celebration of the natural landscape as of the human use, improvement and mastery of this. It is reflective of a particular type of landscape discourse popular at the end of the eighteenth century, the county and regional surveys of agriculture undertaken by figures like William Marshall.[46] Though this type of discourse was different, even antithetical to the romantic discovery and celebration of untamed nature, it does highlight that another way of looking at landscape was to focus on the human impact. Many of the travel guides and journals, particularly

---

[44] Mabey, *Gilbert White*, 24, 69, 179–81.
[45] Samuel Rudder, *A New History of Gloucestershire* (Cirencester: Samuel Rudder, 1779), 21.
[46] G. E. Mingay, 'Marshall, William (bap. 1745, d. 1818), Agricultural Writer and Land Agent', *Oxford Dictionary of National Biography*, 23 Sep. 2004 https://www.oxforddnb.com/view/10.1093/ref:odnb/9780198614128.001.0001/odnb-9780198614128-e-18155, accessed 11 Feb. 2022.

the early ones such as those of Defoe and Celia Fiennes, were far more concerned with this aspect of the landscape than raw nature.[47] So descriptions of not only agricultural practices and scenes but also industry, towns and more generally the built environment were commonplace. When the La Rochefoucauld brothers, members of the French aristocracy, toured parts of England in 1785, they visited the Peak District, obtained 'great pleasure' in venturing into a 'a famous cave commonly called the Devil's Arse' and noted that 'Matlock's situation is very picturesque' but tellingly observed that 'the part of Derbyshire that isn't mountainous is extremely agreeable'.[48] It was towns, industry and improved landscapes that grabbed much of their attention. One of the locations that they visited was Coalbrookdale in Shropshire, at this time perhaps the most advanced centre of iron making in Britain, and they recorded in remarkable detail the industrial processes located there. Situated in a deep gorge cut by the River Severn, the site also had considerable picturesque potential, as did many rural industrial locations which involved mining and metal working. Some observers saw a close parallel between the dramatic natural scenery of such places, often situated in steep valleys or on mountain slopes, and the seemingly demonic visions of human activity that filled them, with smoke and fire belching out of the furnaces. Paul Sandby Munn's painting of Bedlam furnace, *Ironbridge* (1803), and P. J. de Loutherbourg's *Coalbrookdale by Night* – paralleled by some of the remarkable paintings of early ironworks in Wales such as that by Thomas Horner of the *Rolling Mills at Merthyr Tydfil* (*c*. 1817) – illustrate this powerful conjunction of natural and human landscapes in an aesthetic of the sublime.[49] Such conjunctions would appear less and less obvious during the nineteenth century, as industry moved increasingly into the town and as the urban and the rural and the natural and the manufactured were seen as increasingly opposing, rather than mutually reinforcing categories of landscape.

Exploring the human landscape was a powerful element in eighteenth-century tourism. It was one which readily embraced the modish and the modern, whether it was industrial plant, improved farms, urban squares and crescents, or country houses and gardens. The La Rochefoucauld brothers sought out all these types of locations, but they also visited older structures, such as Salisbury Cathedral – 'one of the most beautiful churches I have seen in my life' – Glastonbury Abbey and Tor, Warwick and Windsor Castles, and Avebury and Stonehenge.[50] Defoe emphasized the modernity of his *Tour* – 'matters of antiquity are not my enquiry', 'the situation of things is given not as they have been but as they are'[51] – but the investigation of historic buildings and structures was a concern, and in some cases a passion of many tourists. Today professionalized disciplines address the recording, interpretation and conservation of historic landscape forms, most notably archaeology and architectural history. The later nineteenth century was a crucial period in the emergence of these disciplines; long

---

[47] Christopher Morris (ed.), *The Journeys of Celia Fiennes* (London: The Cresset Press, 1947).
[48] Scarfe (ed.), *Innocent Espionage*, 48–9, 58.
[49] Catherine Clark, *English Heritage Book of Ironbridge Gorge* (London: Batsford, 1993), 122; Peter Lord, *The Visual Culture of Wales: Industrial Society* (Cardiff: University of Wales Press, 2003), 31–3.
[50] Scarfe (ed.), *Innocent Espionage*, 121–2, 147, 160, 180–6.
[51] Defoe, *Tour*, vol. 1, vi, 104.

before that date, however, their foundations were being laid through the assiduous endeavours of local antiquaries. Often perceived as obsessive, old-fashioned and retrogressive – the problem rather than the solution to understanding the past – in practice the discovery of the English landscape built heavily upon the antiquarian tradition, which remained a powerful influence on local studies and tourism throughout the Victorian and post-Victorian eras.

It is a tradition that dates back to the medieval period, but emerges in its 'modern' form in the sixteenth century in Britain, in response to the twin influences of the Reformation and the Renaissance:[52] the one threatened and damaged the fabric and records of the most influential cultural institution in the country, the church; the other introduced a new awareness of the classical past and injected high kudos into its study; both initiated the process of transforming the architectural language of the country. The effects were very long term, but the immediate impact could be seen in John Leland's *Itinerary* – notes compiled as the dissolution of the monasteries unfolded – and William Camden's hugely influential *Britannia* (1586), with its 'reconstruction' of Roman Britain, and the formation of the Society of Antiquaries of London (1585, but banned in 1604). In the seventeenth century the Scientific Revolution, and particularly Baconian empiricism, intensified the urge, in elite circles, to collect, record and publish, often on a collaborative basis – as in the case of William Dugdale's monumental *Antiquities of Warwickshire* (1656), compiled over a quarter of a century with the help of the county gentry and record keepers in London.[53] How much all this activity changed perceptions of the built environment is a moot point. Only a small circle of intellectuals and cultured gentlemen were involved, many primarily concerned with genealogy and heraldry; much of their attention focused on documents, monumental inscriptions, and small artefacts like coins. Serious archaeological field study only began to emerge in the later seventeenth century with the investigations of figures like John Aubrey at Stonehenge and Avebury; and where larger built forms were examined and recorded, such as monastic ruins, there was no framework of architectural history in which to locate and make sense of them.[54]

How far the long eighteenth century broke free of these limitations and progressed the agenda is also a matter of debate. In the history of archaeology this is often seen as a fallow era as, it is claimed, empirical field work gave way to romantic speculation. The decline of serious investigation is seen to be exemplified in the career of William Stukeley, who after undertaking important 'objective fieldwork' at sites like Stonehenge and Avebury (1718–24) in later life turned to Druidical fantasy.[55] From this perspective, it is only with the emergence of a sense of 'deep' as opposed to biblical time; the rise of

---

[52] David Hey (ed.), *The Oxford Companion to Family and Local History*, 2nd edn (Oxford: Oxford University Press, 2008), 59–66.
[53] Graham Parry, 'The Antiquities of Warwickshire', in *William Dugdale, Historian. His Life, His Writings and His County*, ed. C. Dyer and C. Richardson (Woodbridge: Boydell Press, 2009), 15–22.
[54] Graham Parry, 'Mists of Time' and 'Earliest Antiquaries', in *Making History* (London: Royal Academy, 2007), 17–19, 37–9; idem, *The Trophies of Time: English Antiquarians of the Seventeenth Century* (Oxford: Oxford University Press, 1995).
[55] Stuart Piggott, *William Stukeley: An Eighteenth-Century Antiquary* (London: Thames & Hudson, 1985), 152–3; idem, *Ancient Britons and the Antiquarian Imagination: Ideas from the Renaissance to the Regency* (London: Thames & Hudson, 1989).

the evolutionist 'New Prehistory' after 1850; and the excavations of Lieutenant-General Pitt-Rivers in the later nineteenth century (particularly on Cranborne Chase in the 1880s)[56] that we see the injection of a scientific approach – especially the introduction of the vertical stratigraphic section – and the 'birth of modern archaeology'.[57] The apparent regression of the eighteenth century owed much to the rise of the picturesque and romantic movements which subverted the progress that had been made after the Restoration in the rational study of the material past.

However, caution should be exercised in accepting this teleological view of archaeology's emergence and the negative image of the eighteenth century that it portrays. Nineteenth-century antiquaries and archaeologists self-consciously distanced themselves from what they saw as the irrational, speculative and fanciful work of their predecessors and used the language of science and reason to describe activities that often differed little, in essence, from those of their eighteenth-century forebears. Interest in and the critical evaluation of the material past strengthened and broadened, stimulated by the continuing growth of antiquarianism. The emergence of clubs and societies – most notably the second foundation of the Society of Antiquaries in 1707 – devoted in whole or part to investigating the remains of the past, provided an organizational framework to structure and sustain study. This was reinforced by the rapid growth of domestic tourism and by a proliferation in publications illustrating and describing archaeological features and old buildings. The outcome was that the knowledge base of surviving landscape features of ancient and Roman Britain expanded considerably. 'By the early-nineteenth century', it has been observed, 'the amount of detail recovered concerning Roman Britain dwarfed the information which had been available in 1695 for Gibson's first revision of *Britannia*'.[58]

In 1700 scarcely any physical remains had been discovered of Bath's Roman past. Over the next century a series of chance discoveries, a product in particular of the redevelopment of the old city, notably the rebuilding of the Pump Rooms in 1790, ensured that there was strong material evidence to demonstrate the importance of the spa in Roman times. This was made available not only in publications like John Collinson's *History and Antiquities of the County of Somerset* (1791), Richard Warner's *History of Bath* (1801), and Samuel Lysons's *Reliquiae Britannico-Romanae* (1813) – the last of these including a reconstruction of the Temple of Minerva – but also in a small museum opened in the 1790s, by the city corporation close to the baths, 'where the antiquary and virtuoso may contemplate a collection of Roman remains, more numerous and curious than any other place in the kingdom has hitherto produced'.[59] Bath's significance as a tourist centre made it something of an engine for spreading the message about the Romano-British landscape. To the south of the spa knowledge of an earlier phase in

---

[56] M. W. Thompson, *General Pitt-Rivers: Evolution and Archaeology in the Nineteenth Century* (Bradford-on-Avon: Moonraker Press, 1977), 116–17; Piggott, *Ancient Britons*, 158.
[57] Chris Evans, 'The Birth of Modern Archaeology', in *Making History*, 185–99.
[58] Rosemary Sweet, *Antiquaries: The Discovery of the Past in Eighteenth-Century Britain* (London: Hambledon and London, 2004), 185.
[59] Peter Borsay, *The Image of Georgian Bath, 1700–2000. Towns, Heritage and History* (Oxford: Oxford University Press, 2000), 56–7; *The Improved Bath Guide* (Bath: Wood & Co., 1812), 6; Barry Cunliffe, *Roman Bath Discovered* (London: Routledge and Kegan Paul, 1971), 16–19, 39–47.

the landscape's development (though how much earlier was not entirely appreciated at the time) was also being added to. At Stourhead lay the Wiltshire residence of Sir Richard Colt Hoare (1758–1838), whose estates, house and library were the hub of an antiquarian network and enterprise. Working with an assistant William Cunnington (1754–1810) Colt Hoare's team dug over 400 barrows in the first decade of the nineteenth century, the results of which were included in the two volumes of his *History of Ancient Wiltshire* (1812–19). Barrow digging was a pastime that went back some way – the Revd Bryan Faussett (1720–76) had explored over 700 Anglo-Saxon tumuli in Kent and elsewhere – and though by modern standards investigative techniques were crude and the interpretative frameworks adopted ill-informed and highly speculative, a great deal of basic information about the historic landscape was being amassed.[60]

All this *quantitative* change might have meant relatively little if it had not been accompanied by a *qualitative* change in the way people thought about and acted in relation to the historic built environment. A key development was the emergence of an appreciation for and understanding of medieval gothic architecture. Despite the presence of ancient and Romano-British remains, it was the Middle Ages that marked the effective starting point of a national architectural history. Moreover, in 1700 a good deal of the fabric of this period still survived. William Dugdale's *Monasticon Anglicanum* (1655–73) had led the way, but it was largely devoted to documentary material rather than the architectural fabric, about which he, like most of his fellow antiquaries, remained largely silent.[61] Dugdale was portrayed by some as a cryptocatholic because of his passion for the pre-Reformation monastic world,[62] and it was the popish associations of gothic architecture that long inhibited any serious attempt to analyse it or incorporate it within the national architectural heritage. Slowly but surely this began to change during the course of the eighteenth century, a turning point being the failure of the second Jacobite rebellion of 1745. From this point onwards there was no credible likelihood of returning mainland Britain to the Roman Catholic Church and gothic architecture could now be visited, studied and celebrated publically, and even deployed in new building projects, without those doing so being stigmatized as religiously heterodox or unpatriotic. The medieval period as a whole was associated in the polite mind of the eighteenth century with backwardness and barbarity, and the rediscovery of classical culture and architecture in the post-medieval era seen as part of shift towards a more civilized society. So the 'gothic revival', evident from about the mid-eighteenth century, took some time to dislodge deep-seated attitudes. However, in the long term it was fundamental in restructuring the way the historic fabric of the country was valued and perceived.[63] Recognition of the gothic was critical to a

---

[60] B. M. Marsden and Bernard Nurse, 'Opening the Tomb', in *Making History*, 95–6; Kenneth Woodbridge, *Landscape and Antiquity. Aspects of English Culture at Stourhead 1718–1838* (Oxford: Clarendon Press, 1970), 187–234; David Wright, *Bryan Faussett: Antiquary Extraordinary* (Oxford: Archaeopress, 2015).

[61] Parry, *Trophies of Time*, 240–1.

[62] Ibid., 228.

[63] Christopher Brooks, *The Gothic Revival* (London: Phaidon, 1999), 83–104; Kenneth Clark, *The Gothic Revival: An Essay in the History of Taste* (London: Penguin, 1962); Rosemary Sweet, 'Antiquarianism and Ruins', in *Writing Britain's Ruins 1700-1850*, ed. Dale Townshend, Michael Carter and Peter Lindfield (London: British Library, 2017), 43–75; Sweet, *Antiquaries*, 238–76.

comprehensive, clearer and more nuanced sense of periodization in the development of the built environment. With this came the rise of architectural history. By 1800 battle raged in publications over the appropriate way to label the 'gothic' style and the origin of the pointed arch.[64] The intellectual tools were being provided by which those who chose could debate, decode and enjoy the medieval fabric, most of whom came from the social elite. There are, however, signs of a wider constituency emerging and even of the development, stimulated by the cheaper publications, of a type of popular antiquarianism – reflected in growing range of accessible printed materials, the emergence in the early-nineteenth century of the cult of the 'olden time' (a sub-gothic period before Renaissance classicism subverted the native English style), and the early signs of the 'mass' visiting of old country houses.[65] This was accompanied by the first serious stirrings of a preservation movement and underpinning this was the revolutionary idea of a national heritage of which the landscape was a critical part.[66] Antiquarianism at the start of Queen Victoria's reign was still very much alive and well, even if some of the national societies that promoted it were in the doldrums.[67] In the long run its role in transforming attitudes to the human landscape was to be immense. This was partly due to its role as midwife to professionalized disciplines like archaeology and architectural history (something they have proved less than keen to acknowledge), but perhaps even more important was the mass of basic data that it accumulated and the spirit of discovery that it passed on to the local field societies that were to proliferate in the mid-nineteenth century.

---

[64] David Watkin, *The Rise of Architectural History* (London: Architectural Press, 1980), 49–69.
[65] Sweet, *Antiquaries*, 277–307; Peter Mandler, *The Fall and Rise of the Stately Home* (New Haven and London: Yale University Press, 1999), 21–106; Adrian Tinniswood, *The Polite Tourist: Four Centuries of Country House Visiting* (London: National Trust, 1998), 113–35.
[66] Sweet, *Antiquaries*, 309–43.
[67] Ibid., 108–12.

3

Ideas and representations

During the early modern period a combination of a spirit of exploration and the rise of tourism had generated a growing cultural interest in the landscape of Britain, both natural and human. The landscape was becoming an object of cultural consumption in which new attitudes to the natural world and the past played a vital part. These changes were underpinned by fundamental economic and social processes – such as commercialization, industrialization, urbanization – gathering pace between the sixteenth and early-nineteenth centuries, but impacting far more deeply in the century after 1840. Their role will be examined later in the book. What this chapter seeks to unpick are the intellectual processes that turned the landscape into an object of consumption in the early modern period and that were to prove so influential in framing the Victorian and Edwardian mind. In revealing the intellectual framework that underpinned change, a twin track approach is adopted, of ideas and representations. The two are, of course, inextricably intertwined, but for practical reasons, and to emphasize the part played by representation in changing attitudes to the landscape, each will be examined separately.

It is important to understand that though it is possible to talk of the 'discovery' and 'consumption' of the British landscape in the early modern period, it is an argument that needs to be carefully qualified. Local populations had always known and continued to 'know' their landscape and interact with it. Most obviously this occurred in the conduct of their everyday and working lives, where knowledge of domestic space, topography, pathways, roads and rivers, soil types, vegetation, animals, building materials, methods of construction, and such like were essential to making a living and conducting ordinary life. It is also clear that there were broader cultural perceptions of landscape, including its sacred meaning. Natural features and elements of the built environment would be sites of religious, ritual and recreational activity. Fields and hills; streams, rivers and springs; trees, copses and forests; footpaths and track ways; market squares and churchyards; churches and archaeological monuments – could all be invested and resonate with layers of meaning and memory that had accumulated and constantly changed over time.[1] The belief systems that shaped these strata were a mixture of conventional religion and what we might today characterize as 'magic',

---

[1] Thomas, *Religion and the Decline of Magic*, 54–5, 80–1; Walsham, *Reformation of the Landscape*; Nicola Whyte, *Inhabiting the Landscape: Place, Custom and Memory, 1500–1800* (Oxford: Windgather Press, 2009), chapter 5.

'folklore' or 'popular culture'. This is not the point to debate the appropriateness of these highly problematic terms. What is critical is the recognition that the landscape was not unknown, and therefore strictly speaking not an object of discovery, but re-discovery; and that perception of the landscape was closely conditioned by systems of ideas and beliefs embodied in mind and memory. As Simon Schama has written, 'before it can ever be a repose for the senses, landscape is the work of the mind. Its scenery is built up as much from strata of memory as from layers of rock'.[2] If a process of discovery or re-discovery was underway, it was because landscape was being looked at through a new religious, intellectual and aesthetic frame; because types of people (the leisured, the professional and the tourist) were growing in number and wealth and observing landscapes in which they did not work and/or they were unfamiliar with; and because tools (representations) influencing how people looked at and communicated the new cultural framework were proliferating.

During the early modern period three 'movements' in particular were forcing cultural change; the Reformation, the Enlightenment and Romanticism. The three may be seen as distinct chronological and intellectual entities, the one following on from the other in a form of reactive displacement. Though it would be wrong to dismiss the dialectical element in their relationship, in truth all three were part of an entangled process of change, which fits no neat sequential programme, and involved a constant interplay of reaction and accommodation. It was this cultural amalgam that the Victorians inherited. Throughout the nineteenth century, the aftershocks of the Reformation, the Enlightenment and Romanticism were still being felt, and their interplay – though now under rapidly changing economic, social and political circumstances – determined the way the English landscape was seen.

The Reformation

The Reformation was to have a profound impact on the way landscape looked and the manner in which it was perceived. The most physically arresting signs of this were the changes imposed on the religious built environment. Structures and spaces were remodelled and reinterpreted to meet the dictates of a Protestant theology which was reshaping the relationship between the material and spiritual worlds. Monastic complexes, some among the most physically and symbolically impressive man-made structures of the medieval period, were abandoned and left to ruinate or recycled (literally when building stone was robbed) for less-elevated secular purposes. When Defoe visited Lincoln in the early-eighteenth century he found the town 'ragged, decay'd, and still decaying ... it is so full of the ruins of monasteries and religious houses, that in short, the very barns, stables, out-houses, and, as they shew'd me, some of the very hog-styes, were built church-fashion; that is to say, with stone walls and arch'd windows and doors'.[3] The interior decoration and furnishings of churches, chapels and shrines were destroyed or damaged with the loss or mutilation of wall paintings, statuary,

---

[2] Schama, *Landscape and Memory*, 6–7.
[3] Defoe, *Tour*, vol. 2, 137.

funerary monuments, rood screens and stained glass. Churches and chapels whose fabric once resonated with mystery, whose spaces and stones were inhabited by the real presence of Christ and the Saints, were transformed into functional structures, at best symbolic of a religious presence, in which unmediated contact could be made with God. The process was not a simple linear one; there were, for example, surges of iconoclasm during the reign of Edward VI and the Civil War period, punctuated by phases when there was some attempt to reverse the flow of destruction as during the Laudian reforms of the 1630s.[4] It is also now clear that the theological changes had an impact beyond the ecclesiastical fabric to include prehistoric monuments such as megaliths and barrows, and natural phenomena like hills, unusual rock formations, springs, trees and shrubs. Under the medieval catholic system, and as a consequence of the early Christianization of Britain which had often involved the appropriation of sacred pagan sites, these had been imbued with religious meaning. Springs and wells, for example, were associated with saints and miracles and became sites of mass pilgrimage and healing. Protestantism rejected the notion of intermediary agents, intercession and the localization of space implied in designating particular places as more sacred than others.

On the face of it, the damage to the religious fabric and the changes to the way the natural world was read amounted to a wholesale de-sacralization of the landscape. However, as Alexandra Walsham has argued persuasively, this was not the case. Catholic beliefs continued to be held and vigorously prosecuted by a minority – albeit a tiny one by the seventeenth century in England – of the population, who not only defended traditional sacred sites but created new ones to reflect their recent persecution. A belief in the immanence of the holy may also have continued to be held by a larger number of people, who, though not recusants, were slow to shed this aspect of Catholicism. Within Anglicanism there was a constant reaction among the more conservative elements against the excesses of protestant zealotry and the stripping of the church of its material holiness and heritage. The rise of antiquarianism, and the pioneering work of figures like William Dugdale, author of *Monasticon Anglicanum* (1655–73), to recover the medieval ecclesiastical heritage, owed something to this.[5] Moreover, Protestantism – in spite of its penchant for iconoclasm, and whatever its rejection of the localization of the sacred – developed a new system of practices and traditions which focused religious experience on points in the material world. White walls, plain glass, and elevated pulpits can resonate with as much meaning as colourful murals, emotive statuary and elaborate altars; holy minimalism can be as powerful as holy maximalism. Domestic space became invested with a new religious meaning in a process which Christopher Hill has called the 'spiritualization of the household'.[6] Puritans and later nonconformists and Methodists took their message

---

[4] Walsham, *Reformation of the Landscape*, chapter 2; Walsham, 'Sacred Topography: Religious Change and the Landscape in Early Modern Britain and Ireland', *Journal of Religious History* 36:1 (2012): 31–51; see also Eamon Duffy, *The Stripping of the Altars: Traditional Religion in England, c. 1400–1580* (New Haven and London: Yale University Press, 1992).

[5] Parry, *Trophies of Time*, 217–48.

[6] Christopher Hill, *Society and Puritanism in Pre-Revolutionary England* (Manchester: Panther Books, 1969), 429–66.

out of formal religious buildings into the open air, meeting to worship and spread their message in small groups and on occasions en masse, sometimes in towns in market squares, at other times in the countryside in forest clearings, fields, by tree stumps and on hillsides. In part this reflected their inability to access spaces controlled by the established church or the need to maintain secrecy in a regime of religious persecution. It may also reflect the wish to demonstrate that God can be worshiped anywhere and the implied de-localization of space. But it may also be that the sites chosen already possessed a significance, locations in the landscape, perhaps displaying some distinctive natural or other feature, which were understood to be communal gathering points. Moreover, through repeated usage and the consequent layering of memory they would come to acquire for those involved a religious significance. In addition, by a process of negative association, monastic buildings for many Protestants became symbols of the corruption of the late medieval Catholic Church and sites of protestant martyrdom new points of pilgrimage. But probably most important of all was the notion that the natural world was a grand showcase of God's all-embracing power and purpose, reflecting and expressing events in biblical history (especially the creation and the deluge), battles with the forces of darkness, divine judgements on the moral errors of mankind (through, for example, evidence of natural disasters), and his extraordinary skill and benevolence in making the world the way it is. To put it in a nutshell, there was no de-sacralization as such, simply the generation of a new type of religious landscape, though in a way that entangled the old and the new.

To take the case of holy wells or springs. These were hugely popular sites of miraculous healing, many probably appropriated by the Catholic Church during the early medieval process of Christianization. It would seem likely that the tradition of sacred healing waters continued, particularly among popular society, throughout the early modern period. Yet springs, and water more generally, also became the basis of the British resort system in the form of the spa and later seaside resort. It is unlikely that the emergence of the commercialized spa in the early modern period owed nothing to the notion of the sacred or magical powers of spring water and there is evidence that some of the practices of spa visitors seeking a cure resembled those of pilgrims to holy wells.[7] However, in protestant England it was no longer acceptable to conceive of the waters as possessing an intrinsic sacred force. The powers of the waters were now taken to derive directly from their chemical constituents which could be empirically profiled, and a considerable amount of space in specialist treatises and general spa guides went to demonstrating and advertising this.[8] But the sacred character of the

---

[7] Walsham, *Reformation of the Landscape*, chapter. 6; see also eadem, 'Sacred Spas, Healing Springs and Religion in Post-Reformation Britain', in *The Impact of the European Reformation: Princes, Clergy and People*, ed. Bridget Heal and O. P. Grell (Aldershot: Ashgate, 2008), 209–30 and eadem, 'Reforming the Waters: Holy Wells and Healing Springs in Protestant England', in *Life and Thought in the Northern Church, c.1100–c.1700*, ed. D. Wood (Woodbridge: Boydell for the Ecclesiastical History Society, 1999), 227–55.

[8] N. G. Coley, 'Physicians, Chemists and the Analysis of Mineral Waters: "The Most Difficult Part of Chemistry"', in *The Medical History of Waters and Spas*, ed. Roy Porter (London: Wellcome Institute for the History of Medicine, 1990), 56–66; Christopher Hamlin, 'Chemistry, Medicine, and the Legitimization of English Spas, 1740–1840', ibid., 67–81.

waters could continue to be asserted in that their physical content reflected God's divine and benevolent purpose in creating chemical elements contained in the waters that could ease human ailments.

In this way the waters – and they might stand for the landscape as a whole – retained their sacred quality by a redefinition of what constituted the sacred. But there was no mistaking the point that something had changed. In the catholic version of the holy well the waters and the statues of saints who presided over them contained a 'real' divine presence; in the protestant version that presence was at best symbolic, and whatever power the waters possessed derived from material elements that at least in theory were open to empirical experiment. This of course reflected the change in attitude to religious belief and material culture that lay at the heart of the Reformation and was epitomized in the denial of a real presence in the wine and bread during the mass, and the transformation of the act of communion from a real to a symbolic ritual. What we see here is not so much a process of de-sacralization – the evidence seems incontrovertible that this did not take place – as of disenchantment.

Without taking the argument to its extremes, there seems a good deal of evidence that our pre-Reformation ancestors conceived of a two-dimensional world of a visible material exterior and an invisible spiritual interior. The concealed but powerful realm of spirits (sacred and pagan) was all around, infiltrating objects such as statues, hills, and of course living forms like trees, animals and human beings. The notion of possession may have reached its more dramatic forms during the confessions and accusations that attended witchcraft trials of the sixteenth and seventeenth centuries, but it was an idea that underpinned generally the way that the material and natural world was viewed.[9] Landscapes could be and often were 'possessed'. A rich and constantly evolving tradition of stories existed within all local societies of how 'archaeological' monuments (such as stone circles, earthworks and barrows) and natural features (like hills, rivers and trees) were the products of or possessed by spirit forces.[10] These forces could be beneficent, as in the case of the spirits that inhabited a healing well or spring. But they could also be seen as evil, as in the petrification of animals and humans, and the 'diabolization' of remoter landscapes like Dartmoor in Devon and the Blackdown Hills in Somerset, possibly in the later medieval period.[11] Drawing on this tradition each community would have a mental map of sites of special spiritual significance. The first half of John Wood's *Description of Bath* (1742–3), with its extraordinary description of the hills surrounding the spa in terms of a pagan mythology and archaeology, which has largely been ignored by historians, becomes understandable when seen in terms of a mental map drawing on local beliefs underpinned by magical forces.[12]

---

[9] J. A. Sharpe, *Instruments of Darkness: Witchcraft in England, 1550–1750* (London: Hamish Hamilton, 1996), chapter 8.

[10] Adam Fox, *Oral and Literate Culture in England 1500–1700* (Oxford: Oxford University Press, 2000), 213–58.

[11] Lucy Franklin, 'Imagined Landscapes: Archaeology, Perception and Folklore in the Study of Medieval Devon', in *Medieval Devon and Cornwall: Shaping an Ancient Countryside*, ed. Sam Turner (Macclesfield: Windgather Press, 2006), 144–61.

[12] Borsay, *Image of Georgian Bath*, 52.

Disenchantment of the non-sacred world, therefore, logically followed the disenchantment of the churches. However, it must be remembered that Protestants did not deny the existence of a spirit realm (war with the Devil and his minions was a constant duty, and human possession by these evil forces a persistent threat), and magical and witchcraft beliefs remained a central feature of post-Reformation culture. The most serious witch hunt in English history, that which consumed parts of East Anglia in 1645-7, was driven by puritan paranoia.[13] Nonetheless, protestant critiques of holy wells – though not of spas – and deep distrust of May Day celebrations and their overt engagement with the natural environment suggest a powerful hostility to imbuing natural forms with an active spiritual presence. In 1725 the Anglican clergyman Henry Bourne commented that

> in the dark ages of *Popery*, it was a custom if any *well* had an awful situation, and was seated in some lonely melancholy vale; if its water was clear and limpid, and beautifully margined with tender grass; or if it was looked upon, as having a medicinal quality; to give it to some *Saint*, and honour it with his name. … To these kind of wells, the common people are accustomed to go, on a summer's evening … Now this custom seems to be the remains of the superstitious practice of the Papists, of paying adoration to wells and fountains.

He also argued of May Day celebrations that

> forasmuch as many country people are of opinion, that the observation of this ceremony is a good omen, and a procurer of the success of the fruits of the earth, which is entirely a piece of superstition; and because also much wickedness and debauchery are committed that night, to the scandal of whole families, and the dishonour of religion, there is all the reason in the world for laying it aside.[14]

This de-romancing of the natural environment represented a new way of looking at landscape. But, despite its apparent negativity, it did not constitute a rejection of nature. Quite the opposite. As long as rocks and trees were seen as vessels for spirits, there was little incentive to investigate their material forms. Their meaning derived from forces that by definition were invisible and beyond investigation. However, strained of its mystery, leached of its powers of empathy, the natural environment now became an object to investigate and celebrate in its own right, an open book the unravelling of whose structures and operations was as much a journey of exploration as any overseas adventure.[15] At the same time, placed in the context of protestant theology, such an

---

[13] Malcolm Gaskill, *Witchfinders: A Seventeenth-Century English Tragedy* (London: John Murray, 2005).

[14] Henry Bourne, *Antiquitates Vulgares: Or, the Antiquities of the Common People* (Newcastle: J. White, 1725), 62-3, 256-7; D. R. Woolf, 'The "Common Voice": History, Folklore and Oral Tradition in Early Modern England', *Past and Present* 120 (1988): 26-52.

[15] S. A. E. Mendyk, *Speculum Britanniae. Regional Study, Science and Antiquarianism in Britain to 1700* (Toronto: University of Toronto Press, 1989).

enterprise was also an act of religious revelation in that the more the material wonders of nature were unravelled, the more the complex workings of nature's machine were demonstrated, the greater the glory that devolved upon the architect that lay behind it. In Britain, then, scientific and religious investigations were generally able to go hand in hand.

The Enlightenment

The Scientific Revolution and Enlightenment of the seventeenth and eighteenth centuries had the potential to change radically the way that people viewed and interacted with the man-made and natural landscape. Roy Porter has argued that 'the key Enlightenment concept was Nature', and as the previous chapter demonstrated the discovery of the natural landscape was one of the most important cultural pursuits and developments of the early modern period.[16] The term 'science' is a later invention; contemporaries used the phrase 'natural philosophy' to describe the surge of interest in the structures of the natural world and the way it operated. Central to the new approach was a belief, pioneered by Francis Bacon, in the importance of observation and experimentation. Descriptions of the world were no longer acceptable just because they made logical sense; they had to be rooted in a transparent empiricism. One particular branch of natural philosophy was to gain the upper hand, mechanical philosophy. Developed in particular by Isaac Newton in the later seventeenth century, it sought to identify material and mechanical forces in nature – most famously in Newton's case, gravity – that accounted for the way that the world functioned. To what extent the replacement of live magical forces in nature by mechanical material ones was a product of the Reformation or the rise of natural philosophy, or an interaction of the two, may be debated. What is clear is that the natural landscape was now an open book whose contents – in all their miraculous complexity, for it must be remembered that God was responsible for the marvellous mechanics of nature – were waiting to be discovered, described and celebrated.

In England the Enlightenment absorbed and popularized, through lectures and demonstrations, the basic features – if not the complex experimentation and reasoning – of the new science. It turned the observation and recording of nature, and in some cases its collection, into a fashionable pastime. Knowledge, and knowledge of nature, became a currency to trade in by those who wished to demonstrate their modernity and intellectual superiority. It was also a valuable way of distinguishing themselves from the common people, who did not possess this new type of knowledge, and many of whom continued to view nature in essentially magical terms – as a currency knowledge of nature was something that was transferrable. From the outset natural philosophers had placed emphasis upon communicating their findings and creating structures – such as correspondence, printed transactions and the meeting of clubs like

---

[16] Roy Porter, *Enlightenment: Britain and the Creation of the Modern World* (London: Penguin, 2001), 295.

the Royal Society – in which discoveries could be transferred and shared.[17] This chimed closely with the Enlightenment emphasis upon sociability. An understanding of nature thus became a form of sociable knowledge that could be used to facilitate harmonious human interaction, which in itself was seen to be a civilizing and liberating activity. In this way, the natural world became part of the public sphere, something which manifested itself in the locally based natural history clubs and societies that emerged in the early years of Victoria's reign.[18] If knowledge of nature and sociability were two of the key drivers of the Enlightenment, then the notion of improvement was probably the most important of all.[19] It was not an idea confined to the Enlightenment. Its origins probably lie in protestant theology and economics in the seventeenth century, and its language was to suffuse the public and private rhetoric of the nineteenth century, but the Enlightenment gave the notion a new integrity and force. The study of the natural world was of itself an improving activity because it encouraged sociability and understanding of God's creation. But a knowledge of nature also implied – perhaps suggested a duty to engage in – something more active. As the complex workings of nature were revealed, were those entrusted with this information simply to stand in awe of what they saw, or were they to use this information to transform nature itself? It was a question that became increasingly urgent as the level of information and the capacity to use it to effect change grew. In the context of improvement the answer was decidedly in favour of intervention. The natural world might reveal God's marvellous creation, but it was not – like mankind itself – perfect. Aspects of it had its flaws, such as the vast spaces of wild unproductive moorland occupying much of Britain, and it was becoming increasingly difficult to write all these off as God's punishment for human sinfulness. The challenge facing humankind, therefore, was to use knowledge of nature to improve it. So, for example, understanding of the chemical content and effects of limestone could be used to improve the fertility of soils and rescue some of the marginal wastelands. Geological knowledge could be deployed to locate and mine minerals and thereby turn unproductive upland areas into productive assets. Take the case of Dartmoor. Early modern commentators almost universally portray it as literally a blot on the landscape: in Leland's words, 'a wilde Morish and forest Ground', and for Camden 'squallida Montana Dertmore'. Moreover, on its fringes, it accommodated an extraordinary 'tribe' of people called the Gubbins, who seemed to mirror in human form the natural landscape. In 1662 Thomas Fuller observed, 'I have read of an England beyond Wales; but the Gubbings-Land is a Scythia within England, and they pure Heathens therein', an account reinforced by Thomas Cox who in 1700 called them a 'barbarous sort of People, rude and lawless'. More generally, Andrew

---

[17] Elizabeth Yale, *Sociable Knowledge. Natural History and the Nation in Early Modern Britain* (Philadelphia: University of Pennsylvania Press, 2016).
[18] Philippa Levine, *The Amateur and the Professional: Antiquarians, Historians and Archaeologists in Victorian England, 1838–1886* (Cambridge: Cambridge University Press, 1986), 40–69.
[19] Paul Slack, *The Invention of Improvement. Information and Material Progress in Seventeenth-Century England* (Oxford: Oxford University Press, 2015); Peter Borsay 'The Culture of Improvement', in *The Eighteenth Century, 1688–1815*, ed. Paul Langford (Oxford: Oxford University Press, 2002), 183–212; David Spadafora, *The Idea of Progress in Eighteenth-Century Britain* (New Haven and London: Yale University Press, 1990).

Brice described those living on Exmoor, Dartmoor and 'some other of the wilder parts' as 'born Clowns, their Carriage being very rustic and ungainly, and their Speech so coarse, corrupt, and uncouth, as to be scarcely intelligible to strangers', in his *Grand Gazetteer* of 1759.[20] By 1800, however, projects were underway to 'improve nature' by bringing the moor's wasteland into cultivation and by harnessing its mineral resources through mining. In Enlightenment thinking there was a duty to do this; not only did it maximize the knowledge and resources that God had provided in nature, but it also helped to civilize the landscape and people it housed. The improvement of Dartmoor was but a trial for the grander mission the British Empire was to face in civilizing the landscape and peoples of great tracts of the globe.

Romanticism

Placing Nature at the centre of the Enlightenment project, and yet claiming a duty to improve it, if not contradictory, was at the very least problematic, as was the idea of using knowledge of Nature to alter it. If Nature was not to be its own guide, who or what was to be the arbiter of where and how it needed improving? If it was to be man, did that not diminish the primacy of Nature and set the two on a collision course? Could, indeed, knowledge of nature be used not to improve but exploit and damage it? The inherent tensions in Enlightenment thinking generated countervailing flows of thought, which ultimately elevated Nature to a new level of significance. Once Nature had been let out of the bag, it could not be easily put back in again. The notion that Nature should lead can be traced back to the interface between nature and man represented by landscape gardening. In early-eighteenth-century Britain we find the first signs of a revolution in garden design as geometric structures began to give way to more free-flowing forms which it was felt better reflected the patterns of Nature. The changes are often summed up in Alexander Pope's call in 1731,

> To build, to plant, whatever you intend,
> To rear the Column, or the Arch to bend,
> To swell the Terras, or to sink the Grot;
> In all, let *Nature*, never be forgot.
> Consult the *Genius* of the *Place* in all,
> That tells the Waters or to rise, or fall.[21]

Landscape gardening is a subject that we will return to later in this chapter. For the moment the key points to note are the importance given to Nature and the natural landscape as a guide in preparing a garden, but also that this guidance should be one of consultation rather than direction. Raw nature could not necessarily be trusted; all

---

[20] Patricia Milton, *The Discovery of Dartmoor: A Wild and Wondrous Region* (Chichester: Phillimore, 2006), 19–28.

[21] Alexander Pope, *Epistles to Several Persons: Epistle IV to Richard Boyle, Earl of Burlington* (London: L. Gilliver, 1731).

ultimately had to be mediated through the human mind and hand. It always comes as something of a surprise to read William Gilpin in a work that defined and publicized the picturesque movement, *Observations on the River Wye* (1782), asserting,

> Nature ... is seldom so correct in composition, as to produce an harmonious whole. Either the foreground or the background is disproportioned; or some awkward line runs across the piece; or a tree is ill-placed; or a bank is formal; or something or other is not exactly what it should be. ... therefore, the painter who adheres strictly to the *composition* of nature, will rarely make a good picture.

This would seem to leave space for human improvement. However, he also adds, 'Nature is always great in design ... the immensity of nature is beyond human comprehension', suggesting that the problem may not be so much the existence of an inherent order in nature, as man's limited capacity to perceive it.[22]

The picturesque, which Gilpin did so much to define, gathered pace in the latter half of the eighteenth century, influenced by and influencing the broad surge of interest in nature. Aesthetically it sat somewhere between the order and stability of the 'beautiful' and the terror and flux of the 'sublime'. It also reflects the midpoint between the Enlightenment and Romanticism.

Gilpin himself showed much more interest in the natural than the built landscape – his account of Tintern Abbey (see Figure 3.1) was minimal, and more concerned with

Figure 3.1 Tintern Abbey from the River Wye from William Gilpin, *Observations on the River Wye, and Several Parts of South Wales &c.: Relative Chiefly to Picturesque Beauty*, 3rd edn (London: R. Blamire, 1792). Reproduced by kind permission of the David Wilson Library, University of Leicester.

[22] William Gilpin, *Observations on the River Wye* (London: R. Blamire, 1782), 31–2.

nature's encroachment on it, what he called 'the ornaments of time'.²³ With Romanticism, however, any ambivalence is decided firmly in favour of the primacy of nature. There is no longer felt any necessity to intervene and improve. When Wordsworth visited the Wye gorge (for a second time) in 1798 he left little doubt that he saw in the natural environment a form that not only needed no improvement but contained a force, 'a motion and a spirit', that flowed through all matter, man included:

> I have felt
> A presence that disturbs me with the joy
> Of elevated thoughts; a sense sublime
> Of something far more deeply interfused,
> Whose dwelling is the light of setting suns,
> And the round ocean and the living air,
> And the blue sky, and in the mind of man,
> A motion and a spirit, that impels
> All thinking things, all objects of all thought,
> And rolls through all things. Therefore I am still
> A lover of the meadows and the woods,
> And mountains.²⁴

Wordsworth does not define what he means by 'a motion and a spirit'. The expectation among readers would of course be God. In this context the vagueness of the term 'something' is surprising and unsettling. Though the lines are 'written a few miles above TINTERN ABBEY', there is no explicit reference to any religious subject, only to 'Nature'. It is difficult to avoid the conclusion, particularly given the rich descriptions of natural forms contained in the poem, that Nature is the 'something' referred to. Any threat that the rise of natural philosophy posed to the notion of a divine purpose and presence in the world had been counteracted by the rise of natural theology, which, by positing the notion of God as the divine architect, turned the exploration of nature into a form of religious revelation. By suggesting that Nature was a force in its own right, Wordsworth was implicitly challenging this. Nature was becoming an autonomous entity and perhaps a sacred force in its own right. It is a notion that also surfaces in another of his early works, the *Prelude* (1805). Here Wordsworth describes a formative experience in his youth, as he commandeered a shepherd's boat and rowed out into a lake surrounded by mountains.

> I dipp'd my oars into the silent Lake,
> And, as I rose upon the stroke, my Boat
> Went heaving through the water, like a Swan;
> When from behind that craggy Steep, till then
> The bound of the horizon, a huge Cliff,

---

²³ Ibid., 42.
²⁴ William Wordsworth and Samuel Taylor Coleridge, *Lyrical Ballads*, ed. Michael Mason (London: Longman, 1992), 212.

> As if with voluntary power instinct,
> Uprear'd its head. I struck, and struck again,
> And, growing still in stature, the huge Cliff
> Rose up between me and the stars, and still,
> With measur'd motion, like a living thing,
> Strode after me.[25]

In almost, if not quite, treating the mountain as a 'living thing', possessing a 'voluntary power instinct', Wordsworth appears to be suggesting that the natural landscape resonates with a force of its own. It is difficult to avoid the occult tone of the description of the cliff and the re-enchantment of the landscape implied by this. It is not of course the same sort of magic that existed in the landscape before the Reformation. There is something melodramatic and forced about the young man's reaction in the boat. But it should rather be seen as a reaction, shared by many in the Romantic movement, to the mechanistic view of nature developed by natural philosophy and the Enlightenment.

Representations

This chapter has argued that the way that the landscape was perceived and consumed was in a constant state of flux in the early modern period, as the Reformation, the Enlightenment and Romanticism altered the cultural frame through which the natural world was seen. To some extent what was underway was a series of reactions and counter reactions, with Romanticism turning the wheel full circle by suggesting a re-enchantment of the landscape. But this simplifies a much messier and entangled process, in which on the eve of Victorian Britain the Reformation, the Enlightenment and Romanticism were still all actively present forces. That this was possible, and that the cultural frame was able to shift in the way it did, owes a great deal to the process and mechanisms of representation. It was these that mediated between ideas and their practical impact on the way that people thought and behaved. What made representation such an important agent of change in the early modern period was the way in which images of landscape were being generated on an increasing scale. This was particularly the case for the sort of landscape being explored in this book, the recreational or tourist landscape. In 1770 Thomas Whately wrote,

> That a subject is recommended at least to our notice, and probably to our favour, if it has been distinguished by the pencil of an eminent painter, is indisputable; we are delighted to see those objects in the reality, which we are used to admire in the representation; and we improve upon their intrinsic merit, by recollecting their effects in the picture.[26]

---

[25] Stephen Gill, *The Prelude* (Cambridge: Cambridge University Press, 1991), 12.
[26] Thomas Whately, *Observations on Modern Gardening, Illustrated by Descriptions* (London: Thomas Payne, 1770), 146.

This was written in a treatise on gardening, but its recognition of the powerful influence of representation in determining what is looked at, and the way in which it is perceived, could apply equally to the natural landscape. It is hard to imagine any form of tourism based on visiting special landscape features, which is not accompanied by a parallel and prior process which identifies and valorises those features. Even in cases where the tourist visits sites which have not been the subject of prior accounts – where the visit is to an 'undiscovered' spot – the lens through which those locations will be viewed will be representations of other sites or of ideal landscapes; as Whately acknowledges, 'we improve their intrinsic merit, by recollecting their effects in the picture'.[27]

Representations of landscape in the early modern period took a variety of forms, primarily verbal, written (and printed) and visual. Contemporaries must have frequently exchanged views about landscape. Tourists rarely travelled alone. In August 1798 Sir Richard Colt Hoare 'sallied forth … on an excursion to the mountains' in South Wales: 'Our party consisting of about twenty dined under the canopy of the skies. Our cloth was spread out on a large flat rock. A rapid rill running at its foot cooled our wines and afforded us a delicious beverage. The scene was Alpine and gay.'[28] It is hard to imagine that on occasions like this the conversation did not revolve, at least in part, around interpreting the sight spread out, like the meal, before the company. Landscape discourse would be part of the sociability of the occasion. Though it is impossible to recover these oral encounters other than through written accounts – and Colt Hoare does not recount these in his diary – we should not underestimate the power of conversation. In Jane Austen's *Northanger Abbey* (1818), Catherine Morland's declaration, during a walk to Beechen Cliff outside Bath, that 'she would give anything in the world to be able to draw' elicited from Henry Tilney: 'a lecture on the picturesque … in which his instructions were so clear that she soon began to see beauty in every thing admired by him … He talked of fore-grounds, distances and second distances – side-screens, and perspectives – lights and shades'.[29] Tilney would probably have gathered his ideas on the picturesque from didactic publications such as Gilpin's *Observation on the River Wye*, so that conversation on landscape would have been constantly fertilized by reading prose and poetry. Indeed, in some respects the point of conversation among polite society was not so much to convey information per se, as – given the high value placed upon literacy and the membership of book clubs – to demonstrate the membership of a virtual community of readers of high status and fashionable texts.

Of these fashionable texts, James Thomson's extended 'nature-descriptive poem',[30] *The Seasons* (1730), was one of the most influential literary products of the eighteenth century (there were more than 300 separate editions between 1750 and 1850)[31] and

[27] Ibid., 150.
[28] M. W. Thompson (ed.), *The Journeys of Sir Richard Colt Hoare: Through Wales and England, 1793–1810* (Gloucester: Alan Sutton, 1983), 97.
[29] Jane Austen, *Northanger Abbey*, ed. R. W. Chapman, 3rd edn ([1817] Oxford: Oxford University Press, 1969), 111.
[30] James Thomson, *The Seasons*, ed. James Sambrook (Oxford: Clarendon Press, 1981), x.
[31] John Chalker, *The English Georgic: A Study in the Development of a Form* (London: Routledge and Kegan Paul, 1969), 90.

contains many generalized descriptions of natural landscapes, along with more specific allusions, such as that to Lord Cobham's garden, the 'fair majestic paradise of Stowe'.[32] Thomson, like his contemporaries, drew heavily on Virgil's poetry (in this case the *Georgics*) in his description of the English countryside. Early in his life Alexander Pope published four pastorals (1709), one for each season, based on the *Eclogues*, and his *Windsor Forest* (1713) likewise owes much to the *Georgics*. Thus the impact of poetical texts on perceptions of landscapes was a complicated and multi-layered one, in which images inter-acted with each other. During the long eighteenth century, and in particular the so-called Augustan age in England – loosely 1680–1730 – it was the norm among the *cognoscenti* to view the English landscape though the lens of classical culture.[33] Underpinning this was the high kudos attributed to the classics and the desire to create a vision of the English landscape that conformed to that of Greece and Rome. In its turn this was in part a political statement, a search for stability, order and authority, but also a social one in that only those of sufficient taste and knowledge would be able to perceive the allusions to antiquity and publically in conversation, and privately in self-reflection, celebrate their learning and civility.

Antique Mediterranean representations of nature remained important in shaping contemporary English ones, at least among the elite, but during the later eighteenth century there was some movement away from what was seen as over-dependence on foreign models towards ones originating in a native context.[34] In part this reflected a nascent patriotism and can also be seen in the emergence of the gothic revival, drawing as it did on the English medieval architectural heritage rather than the classical inheritance of ancient Greece and Rome. In part, however, it was due to the shift in the cultural frame from Enlightenment to Romanticism, as it was felt that nature itself, and particularly British nature, should determine the form of the representation rather than vice versa. This was something that Wordsworth and his fellow Romantic poets would have agreed upon – that their work was not just inspired by but in some sense was the materialization of the natural forms and forces that they observed. However, there is no reason to believe that the representations that they created were any less influential – or for that matter any less culturally constructed – than their predecessors. Wordsworth 'replaced Gilpin as the representative voice of the Wye',[35] not because his image was more 'authentic' but because it met the requirements of the Romantic ideal better.

Alongside poetical images of landscape ran – literally in many cases, since both could be mixed in the same output – prose ones to be found in diaries, letters, guides, histories, treatises, novels, magazines and newspapers. Several of these forms were touched upon in the first chapter. Rising levels of literacy and consumer expenditure,

---

[32] Thomson, *Seasons*, 117.
[33] Philip Ayres, *Classical Culture and the Idea of Rome in Eighteenth-Century England* (Cambridge: Cambridge University Press, 1977), 75–84.
[34] Malcolm Andrews, *The Search for the Picturesque: Landscape Aesthetics and Tourism in Britain, 1760–1800* (Aldershot: Scolar Press, 1989), 3–23; Rosemary Sweet, 'Domestic Tourism in Great Britain', https://www.bl.uk/picturing-places/articles/domestic-tourism-in-great-britain, accessed 15 Jun. 2021.
[35] Stephen Hebron, *The Romantics and the British Landscape* (London: British Library, 2006), 19.

allied to the development of the printing press and the relaxation of censorship in England after 1695, allowed the volume and range of written and printed text, and with it of representations of landscape, to expand, especially during the eighteenth century. Several of these formats – such as diaries and correspondence – were of a type which would appear intended largely for personal consumption. Though this may have limited their dissemination, it emphasizes the expectation that those engaged in travel would reflect upon and internalize their experiences, engage in the process themselves of externalizing these experiences through constructing literary images, and transmit these – in the form of letters – to family and friends. The activity of letter writing shows that in practice the line between manuscript and printed, personal and collective, private and public spheres was a thin one.[36] What reinforced this was that in composing their personal images of landscape writers would be acutely aware of the models provided by printed texts; indeed, in some respects the success of a diary or letter description would be measured by the extent to which it conformed to a canonical published account such as Virgil, Thomson, Gilpin or Wordsworth. Moreover, the fact that there was a growing market for tourist publications, and that a number of diaries and collections of correspondence appeared in print, suggests that many of those engaged in producing personal accounts had one eye trained on the possibility of publication. William Gilpin undertook his famous tour of the Wye Valley and South Wales as early as 1770 and circulated manuscripts of it and other tours to friends who encouraged him to publish, though it took a decade to do so.[37] Gilbert White's *Selborne* began life as a series of private letters to a number of different correspondents.[38] The fact that the epistolary format was retained when it was decided to publish suggests that this intimate style – the blurring of the private and public worlds – held an appeal to readers, implying their membership of an exclusive community of scientific correspondents.

The text in the diaries kept by those undertaking a tour was sometimes accompanied by a visual record of the landscapes visited. Of the 608 diaries of British tours identified by Gard forty-six are illustrated, some with printed engravings but most with drawings by the travellers themselves.[39] Visualizing the landscape, and the creation of visual representations, became a central part of the way nature and the built environment were experienced and consumed. This was reflected in the provision of artistic services in fashionable towns. *The New Bath Guide* of 1809 lists some nineteen 'artists' practising in the spa, *The Improved Bath Guide; Or Picture of Bath and Its Environs* of 1812, thirty five.[40] Many of the artists listed were of course professional portrait painters. But a significant number were identified as teachers,

---

[36] John Brewer, 'This, That and the Other', in *Shifting the Boundaries: Transformation of the Languages of Public and Private in the Eighteenth Century*, ed. Dario Castiglione and Lesley Sharpe (Exeter: Exeter University Press, 1995), 10–17.
[37] William Gilpin, *Observations on the River Wye*, introduction by R. Humphreys (London: Pallas Athene, 2005), 9, 13.
[38] White, *Selborne*, ed. Foster, xv–xvi, xxi.
[39] Gard, *Observant Traveller*, x.
[40] *The New Bath Guide; or Useful Pocket Companion* (Bath: J. Savage, 1809), 78; *The Improved Bath Guide; Or Picture of Bath and Its Environs* (Bath: Wood, 1812), 129.

drawing masters and mistresses (fifteen in *The Improved Bath Guide*) and several were specifically designated landscape painters and/or teachers (seven in *The Improved Bath Guide*). There was clearly a market not only for professionally constructed images of landscape but also for acquiring the skills to make one's own.

Such a market did not always exist. Landscape painting appears to have been introduced into England by Dutch painters in the late seventeenth century. For much of the eighteenth century it was regarded as inferior to history painting, portraiture and genre painting, and continued to be heavily influenced by foreign artists.[41] These included not only the Dutch but also French seventeenth-century landscape painters, in particular Nicolas Poussin (1594–1665) and Claude Lorrain (1600–82), and Italian artists like Gaspard Dughet (1615–75), Salvator Rosa (1615–73) and Antonio Canaletto (1697–1768). The last of these, who had serviced the grand tourist market with paintings of Venice, lived in England at points during the middle years of the eighteenth century, working for the aristocracy and producing some luminous paintings of London redolent of his native city.[42] British artists servicing the domestic market were required to conform to the norms and models set by these artists. Samuel Scott's (?1702–72) paintings of London, if not imitations, were clearly influenced by Canaletto,[43] Thomas Gainsborough's (1727–88) and Michael Angelo Rooker's landscapes (1743–1801) by Dutch painters,[44] and Richard Wilson (1714–82), who came to specialize in landscape painting and was affected by the wilder scenery of his native Wales, nonetheless presented a classical view of the countryside moulded firmly by the vision of painters like Claude.[45] Thus the visual lens through which the English expected, and were expected to view their natural and man-made landscape, was a foreign one, that of either the Netherlands, coloured heavily by the character of the Dutch countryside and cities, or the idealized and classical perspective of the French and Italians.[46] Rosa's bolder works anticipated the emergence of the sublime and became very popular in the eighteenth century, but it was perhaps only with the generation of John Constable (1776–1837) and Joseph Turner (1775–1851) that English landscape painting freed itself from the dominance – though not the influence – of foreign models and classicism, as Romanticism encouraged a focus upon 'unmediated' nature (which could include the natural forces unlocked by industry) and native 'patriotic' locations.[47] It is also likely that the growing popularity of the domestic tour

---

[41] E. K. Waterhouse, *Painting in Britain, 1530–1790* (New Haven and London: Yale University Press, 1994), 154–60, 323–9.

[42] Brian Allen, 'Topography or Art', in *The Image of London: Views by Travellers and Emigrés, 1550–1920*, ed. Malcolm Warner et al. (London: Trefoil Books, 1987), 29–45; David Buttery, *Canaletto and Warwick Castle* (Chichester: Phillimore, 1992).

[43] Waterhouse, *Painting*, 159–60.

[44] Michael Rosenthal and Martin Myrone (eds.), *Gainsborough* (London: Tate Publishing, 2007), 49, 214; Patrick Conner, *Michael Angelo Rooker, 1746–1801* (London: Batsford, 1984), 53–4.

[45] David Solkin, *Richard Wilson: The Landscape of Reaction* (London: Tate Gallery, 1982), 11–21; Waterhouse, *Painting*, 232–41.

[46] Jakob Rosenberg et al., *Dutch Art and Architecture 1600–1800* (Harmondsworth: Penguin, 1966), 239–83.

[47] Peter M. Harman, *The Culture of Nature in Britain, 1680–1860* (New Haven and London: Yale University Press, 2009), 1–2, 148–9; Louis Hawes, *Presences of Nature: British Landscape, 1789–1830* (New Haven: Yale Centre for British Art, 1982).

and the rise of the seaside holiday (and the exposure to the power of coastline and sea) and with them the opening up and discovery of Britain played their part in this shift in perspective.[48]

Alongside more formal landscape painting, and subject to similar influences, a host of visual images, largely of the man-made landscape, were being produced – and reproduced through engraving and printing – in the form of topographical drawings and watercolours. Much of this output was associated with the antiquarian tradition reviewed in the previous chapter. Images of historic buildings and artefacts would often accompany written and printed texts, such as the fifty-six drawings engraved by Wenceslaus Hollar for William Dugdale's *Monasticon Anglicanum* (1655–73), or the 115 plates in Francis Drake's history of York, *Eboracum* (1736), the vast majority of Roman or medieval discoveries and survivals associated with the city.[49] Plates pushed up the price of publication, and this may initially have restricted the role of guides and histories as a platform for disseminating topographical illustrations. Such was their cost, Samuel and Nathaniel Buck's remarkable drawings and engravings of views and prospects of Britain, produced between the 1720s and 1750s, were issued initially individually or in groups, under a subscription system which guaranteed a financial return and secured a measure of exclusivity, but were collected together in three volumes as *Buck's Antiquities* (1774). The urban prospect included modern buildings and industrial processes, and this should remind us of the modernist and progressivist perspective of the Enlightenment. However, the introduction – and title – made clear the antiquarian basis of the Bucks' project, and points to the historical and often nostalgic content of much of the landscape imagery produced at this time. Their design, they wrote, was 'to rescue from the irresistible hand of time, and convey to futurity, those venerable piles of ancient grandeur, crumbling to dust, and hastening to their final dissolution; many of which are now no more; having been since intirely [*sic*.] demolished for modern structures, or perished by time or accident'.[50] Though this was a prestige publication, the growing market for topographical works lowered costs and expanded print runs, creating opportunities for cheaper series of illustrated works, replete with images of medieval churches and the like, such as John Britton and Edward Brayley's *Beauties of England and Wales* (1801–15), Britton's *Architectural Antiquities of Great Britain* (1805–18) and his *Cathedral Antiquities* (1814–35). This in turn paved the way for a mass market opened up by technical innovations in printing in the 1820s, permitting multiple reproduction of images, and based upon depictions of the 'olden time'.[51]

---

[48] Christiana Payne, *Where the Sea Meets the Land: Artists on the Coast in Nineteenth-Century Britain* (Bristol: Sanson & Co. 2007).

[49] Conner, *Michael Angelo Rooker*, 62; Francis Drake, *Eboracum: Or, the History and Antiquities of the City of York* (London: William Bowyer, 1736).

[50] Samuel and Nathaniel Buck, *Buck's Antiquities or Venerable Remains of above Four Hundred Castles, Monasteries, Palaces, &c. &c. in England and Wales*, 3 vols. (London: D. Bond, 1774), vol. 1, v.

[51] Patricia Anderson, *The Printed Image and the Transformation of Popular Culture, 1790–1860* (Oxford: Oxford University Press, 1991), 50–83; Ian Maxted, 'The Production and Publication of Topographical Prints in Devon, c. 1790–1870', in *Printing Places: Locations of Book Production & Distribution since 1500*, ed. John Hinks and Catherine Armstrong (London: British Library, 2005), 121–30.

Gilpin's *Observations*, with its precise and clear rules, and its didactic tone (he was a schoolmaster) supplied a toolkit for would-be tourists such as the fictional Catherine Morland, informing them how to look and how to construct some sort of visual record – in their memory and on paper – of their experiences. The guide opens by asserting the supposed novelty of the approach described, always a good selling point to those seeking to be fashionable: 'the following little work proposes a new object of pursuit; that of examining the face of a country *by the rules of picturesque beauty*'. It then proceeds to lay out the basic formulae for creating a picture of nature:

> The most perfect river-views ... are composed of four grand parts: the area, which is the river itself; the two *side-screens*, which are the opposite banks, and lead the perspective; and the *front-screen*, which points out the winding of the river. ... The views on the Wye, though composed only of these *simple parts*, are yet *exceedingly varied* first, by the *contrast of the screens* ... [second] by the *folding of the side-screens over each other* ... These *simple* variations admit still farther variety from becoming *complex* ... Besides these sources of variety, there are other circumstances, which, under the name of *ornaments*, still farther increase them. ... The *ornaments* of the Wye may be ranged under four heads; *ground, wood, rocks* and *buildings*.[52]

Here was a comprehensive and authoritative guide on how to envision and reproduce nature. By 1800 it had gone through five editions and prompted many other guidebook writers to jump on the Wye bandwagon. The Chepstow printer Mark Willett's *Excursion from the Source of the Wye, Descriptive of the Romantic and Picturesque Scenery of That Interesting River* (1810) deploys the picture-making language of Gilpin: 'at Coldwell the front-screen first appears as a woody hill, swelling to a point. In a few minutes it changes its shape, and the woody hill becomes a lofty side-screen on the right; while the front unfolds itself into a majestic piece of rock-scenery'.[53] Two years earlier Charles Heath, resident printer and bookseller in Monmouth, the midpoint of the Wye tour, published his own guide, in which he acknowledged that Gilpin's *Observations* 'have greatly increased the general desire for viewing the scenes his pen so charmingly describes'.[54] At about the same time Heath also published a *Descriptive Account of the Kymin, and Beaulieu Grove*.[55] The Kymin rises steeply above Monmouth and offers spectacular views of the Wye Valley and surrounding countryside. In the 1790s a summer house was constructed on its summit by a group of local gentlemen, a 'select party of friends' known as the Kymin Club, as a location for summer picnics.[56] It also served as a viewing tower and one that could be accessed by polite society undertaking the Wye tour. Heath structures his account

[52] Gilpin, *Observations*, 17, 25–6.
[53] Mark Willett, *An Excursion from the Source of the Wye* (Bristol: John Evans & Co., 1810), 44.
[54] Charles Heath, *The Excursion down the Wye* (Monmouth: Charles Heath, 1808), preface; Peter Borsay, 'New Approaches to Social History. Myth, Memory and Place: Monmouth and Bath, 1700–1900', *Journal of Social History* 39:3 (2006): 867–89.
[55] Borsay, 'New Approaches to Social History', esp. n. 6.
[56] Charles Heath, *Descriptive Account of the Kymin Pavilion and Beaulieu Grove* ([1809] repr. Monmouth, 2002), 5–6.

of the Kymin to service their aesthetic needs, providing detailed descriptions of the view from each of the five windows of the summer house – with each description divided into foreground, middle ground and background. To aid the observer, the upper room of the summer house was 'furnished with a Dolland Tellescope, whereby every object within the horizon may be correctly ascertained'.[57] The tower and its five window frames, aided by Heath's account, provided a series of frames through which to generate a picturesque view of the Wye. Ultimately the popularity of the picturesque may not have been so much its aesthetic, as its functional appeal to tourists keen to acquire the practical skills of how to look, consume and remember landscape. Malcolm Andrews argues that 'there is something of the big-game hunter' in the picturesque tourist, who 'pursued his prey with a Claude Glass rather than a gun'.[58] Rather like the Kymin tower, the Claude Glass – named after the painter – which used a mirror to create a miniaturized image of the landscape was a piece of technology to aid the tourist generate a picturesque view.[59] Other devices also existed, such as the camera lucida and camera obscura, which helped travellers with limited skills in drawing to make their own sketches of the landscape to act as aide-memoires. We are, of course, here on the edge of the invention of photography, whose origins lie not only in the market for cheap and accurate portraits but also in the requirements of the picturesque tourist. One of the factors that propelled Henry Fox Talbot (1800–77) to his discovery of photography in 1840 was his frustration at being unable to make an adequate drawing of Lake Como while on holiday in Italy in 1833; as he put it in the aptly titled *Pencil of Nature* (1844), his account of the discovery,

> I was amusing myself on the lovely shores of the Lake of Como, in Italy, taking sketches with Wollaston's Camera Lucida, or rather I should say, attempting to take them: but with the smallest possible amount of success ... this led me to reflect on the inimitable beauty of the pictures of nature's painting which the glass lens of the Camera throws upon the paper in its focus – fairy pictures, creations of a moment, and destined as rapidly to fade away. It was during these thoughts that the idea occurred to me ... how charming it would be if it were possible to cause these natural images to imprint themselves durably, and remain fixed upon the paper![60]

A key area where the notion of the picturesque and new attitudes to nature in general were pioneered, and which acted as the inter-face between the man-made and natural landscape, was gardening. It occupied this critical space because gardens could claim to be both a part of, and a representation of, nature. They deployed the elements of the natural world – plants, trees, rocks, water, etc. – and were a living phenomenon; yet they were interspersed with very man-made, inert artefacts like temples and statues and were modelled by human hands to create, it was often claimed, an analogue of nature. Gardens were therefore landscape laboratories, and changes

---

[57] Heath, *Descriptive Account*, 10.
[58] Andrews, *Search for the Picturesque*, 67–8.
[59] Malcolm Andrews, *Landscape and Western Art* (Oxford: Oxford University Press, 1999), 115–16.
[60] Aaron Scharf, *Pioneers of Photography: An Album of Pictures and Words* (London: BBC, 1975), 16.

in their design reflect and contribute to shifting perceptions of the landscape. The long-term developments between the late seventeenth and eighteenth centuries are clear enough – a general move away from formal schemes of gardening, based on straight lines, geometric shapes and parterres, to more informal modes of design using winding paths, curvaceous lines, undulating parkland, and artfully scattered clumps of trees and shrubs; and from enclosed spaces to ones that merged easily with the surrounding countryside and respected and utilized its local characteristics. All this was underpinned by a growing recourse to nature as a guide and inspiration.[61] Change was driven by an interaction of theory, conveyed in poems and prose treatises, and practice, the results of the latter disseminated through the pastime of garden visiting, itself part of the tourist circuit. Initial signs of the new attitudes can be seen in the early-eighteenth century in the writings of literary figures like Joseph Addison and Alexander Pope and in the laying out of some prominent gardens such as Stowe and Rousham. However, as Tom Williamson has made clear it was not until the middle of the eighteenth century that formal gardens began to be replaced on a widespread scale, promoted and serviced by professional practices such as that operated by Lancelot 'Capability' Brown. Williamson also demonstrates that the engines of change were not only aesthetic but involved matters of estate management directed at exploiting the buoyant market in timber and creating a recreational space suitable for hunting.[62]

But aesthetics did matter. The gardens and parks of the elite were highly sophisticated works of art fertilized, as John Dixon Hunt demonstrates, by their contact with other branches of polite culture. The extent to which the picturesque garden drew upon identifiable works of art can be exaggerated, but there is little doubt that creating a picture was central to its origins (as, for example, in the work of one of the innovators of the picturesque garden, William Kent)[63] or that a canon of foreign landscape artists and paintings evolved that provided general models for garden design, even if the landscapes of specific painting were rarely replicated in their entirety. From the 1740s at Stourhead in Wiltshire Henry Hoare II began to lay out a 'picturesque' garden on an impressive scale. The surviving garden suggests that the creation of pictorial views was on his mind from the beginning. When completed, he claimed, the view across the lake towards the village from the Pantheon 'will be a Charmg Gaspd picture at the end of the water', while the Pantheon itself closely mirrors architecturally that shown in several of Claude's paintings, such as *Aeneas at Delos*.[64] It would appear that the allusion to Virgil's *Aeneid* is more than just a pictorial one. Kenneth Woodbridge speculates that Hoare saw the walk along the side of the lake and in particular the path through the Grotto and on towards the Pantheon (with its mirroring of the hero's descent into and ascent from the underworld), as an allegory of Aeneas's journey.[65] This layering and interaction of images – literary, pictorial, architectural and

---

[61] David Jacques, *Georgian Gardens: The Reign of Nature* (London: Batsford, 1990); Michael Symes, *The English Landscape Garden: A Survey* (Swindon: Historic England, 2019); Tom Williamson, *Polite Landscapes: Gardens and Society in Eighteenth-Century England* (Stroud: Alan Sutton, 1995).
[62] Williamson, *Polite Landscapes*, 48–99, 124–40.
[63] John Dixon Hunt, *The Picturesque Garden in Europe* (London: Thames & Hudson, 2003), 28–30.
[64] Kenneth Woodbridge, *The Stourhead Landscape* (London: National Trust, 1974), 10–13.
[65] Woodbridge, *Landscape and Antiquity*, 33–6.

Ideas and Representations 47

Figure 3.2 Francis Nicholson, 'The Waterfall or Cascade falling into the Paddock Pond opposite Garden Lake', from 'Rural Scenery at Stourhead in the County of Wilts, the Seat of Sir Richard Hoare, Bt.' © The Trustees of the British Museum.

horticultural – demonstrates the extent to which representation influenced landscape gardening and it in its turn affected perceptions of the landscape. The images deployed at Stourhead were strikingly international ones, part of European high culture based on classical Greece and Rome. Yet the gardens landscaped by Hoare paradoxically also conform to Pope's exhortation to 'Consult the *Genius* of the *Place* in all'.

The gardens lie close to the watershed of three rivers and are built around a lake created by amalgamation and landscaping of a series of pools in the course of the River Stour, which has its springs in an adjacent valley (see Figure 3.2).[66] Hoare highlighted the significance of water by placing a statue of the water god in a rock arch under the Temple of Ceres [Flora], which was dedicated to the Mother Goddess and located on the edge of the lake, above a spring that was probably the village water supply. The Grotto – over whose entrance hung a plaque with the words in Latin, 'This was the home, the dwelling, the most secret haunt of the great river' – plunges those perambulating the gardens into a cavernous space below the level of the lake which contains a further statue to the River God.[67] It is clear that Hoare wished to celebrate the local association of the place with water and springs. In doing so there is a curious

---

[66] Woodbridge, *The Stourhead Landscape*, 5, 9.
[67] Ibid., 9–10.

reinvention of the 'localization of space' associated with the pre-Reformation world. Moreover, the multiple references to deities located in the natural world, allied to the absence of any allusion throughout the gardens to the Christian God, suggest a return to magical notions of landscape of which the Reformation and the Enlightenment had supposedly purged society. Other contemporary gardens pursue a similar theme. Croome Park in Worcestershire, sitting in the plain of the River Severn beneath the dramatic ridge of the Malvern Hills, was landscaped for George William Coventry 6th Earl of Coventry from the mid-eighteenth century, a process which included creating a river and lake, a dry arch bridge incorporating heads of river gods, and a grotto which accommodated a reclining figure of Sabrina, a water nymph who inhabited the River Severn.[68] It would be absurd to imply that landowners like Hoare and Coventry – or the host of country gentleman who decorated their gardens with the statues of classical gods – sought to undermine Christian theology. But the rich allusions in at least some landscape gardens to the 'genius of the place' and classical deities associated with elements of nature, such as rivers, and the absence of any obvious reference to conventional religious belief, flirted with a pantheism that was later reflected in the work of Romantic artists like Wordsworth; it betokens an attempt to invest nature with a new force and to re-enchant the landscape.

There are other ways of reading the eighteenth-century fascination with landscape gardening. Political messages were locked into many designs: Stowe, Stourhead and Croome Park were all coded at points to deliver a patriotic message. They were also profound expressions of a social order. The highly complex and sophisticated cultural allusions that they contained would have been incomprehensible to all but a tiny minority of the population. The gardens and the coded forms of representation that they deployed were a powerful tool of social exclusion. This also went for ideas like the picturesque, which must have meant little if anything to the majority of the population. It is likely that their perception of the cultural landscape remained tightly linked to notions of work, ordinary life, and religion though with some residual sense of a magical input. However, Gilpin's *Observations*, with its emphasis upon making pictures, and its practical 'toolkit' for tourists about how to look, had the potential to democratize landscape aesthetics (something which later theorists like Uvedale Price and Richard Payne Knight may have been reacting against with their more abstract concepts). In establishing the idea and practice of the picturesque, albeit at an elite level, the eighteenth century was reconfiguring the way landscape could be perceived and consumed as a recreational good, and doing so in a way that could reach a mass market once certain basic economic and social conditions had changed as they would do in the Victorian era.

---

[68] Oliver Garnet, *Croome Park* (Warrington: National Trust, 2008).

4

Reconfiguring the landscape

Ideas

By the late 1830s the landscape was already a recreational good subject to what John Urry has called the 'tourist gaze', a way of looking

> directed to features of landscape and townscape which separate them off from everyday experience ... [there is] a much greater sensitivity to visual elements ... than is normally found in everyday life. People linger over such a gaze which is then normally visually objectified or captured through postcards, films, models and so on. These enable the gaze to be endlessly reproduced and recaptured.[1]

This chapter is predominantly concerned with how, in the century before the Second World War, these forms of representation and reproduction expanded enormously to the point where it is possible to talk about them, and the recreational landscape and the tourist gaze that they underpinned, as mass commodities. But before discussing these texts we need to review the intellectual framework in which they were produced. The previous chapter showed how in the early modern period changes in ways of looking at and representing landscape were heavily influenced by the intellectual and aesthetic movements of the time: the Reformation, Enlightenment and Romanticism. The shock waves created by these movements continued to resonate during the Victorian and Edwardian periods. In the century after Victoria's accession, new movements emerged, such as democracy, socialism and nationalism, but these too can be traced back to the Enlightenment and Romanticism.

Victorianism is often associated with ideas such as progress and improvement, but the origins of these lie in the Enlightenment and were already fully fledged cultural concepts by the end of the eighteenth century.[2] John Ruskin's dictum that 'the representation of fact is the foundation of all art', and his injunction that 'from young artists nothing might be tolerated but simple *bona fide* imitation of nature', or the pre-Raphaelite emphasis upon a precision and richness of naturalistic detail in the

---

[1] John Urry, *The Tourist Gaze: Leisure and Travel in Contemporary Societies*, 2nd edn (London: Sage Publications, 2002), 3.
[2] Borsay, 'Culture of Improvement'.

landscape elements of their paintings can be related to Enlightenment empiricism.[3] Even such a quintessentially Victorian phenomenon as the Oxford Movement (originating in Oriel College in the 1820s)[4] had its architectural roots in the gothic revival of the mid-eighteenth century and can be seen as yet one more working out, albeit in a reactionary sense, of the 'long Reformation'.

Early gothic revival buildings were often described as picturesque, the concept emerged, as we have seen, in the eighteenth century as part of the embrace of Nature and an early manifestation of Romanticism. But the aesthetic of the picturesque did not quietly fade away as a more full-blooded version of Romanticism, such as that embodied in Turner's paintings, took hold. The language, and indeed the sensibility of the picturesque, became embedded in the tourist gaze and was arguably more significant in the popular perception of landscape than the wilder versions of Romantic gothicism. The term 'picturesque' continued to be widely used in guide literature throughout the Victorian era and deep into the twentieth century to describe aspects of both the natural and built environment. It does not, of course, follow that the meaning of the term remains the same; one would expect some change between say Gilpin's *Observations* of the 1780s and the Ward Lock guides of the 1920s. But the core concept remained remarkably similar. Even in 1938 William Beach Thomas could enthuse, '[W]hat an artistic pleasure [it is] to stop a car at a gap or low place in a hedge and to behold a view framed like a picture, composed like a picture, individual as a picture and endowed with the power of a great picture to engrave itself on the mind's eye.'[5] So, though it may be possible to identify something called 'Victorianism' or Edwardianism, what is being described is not an intellectual and aesthetic movement as such but a particular temporal amalgam – forged in the context of a specific set of economic and social forces – of often conflicting ideas and movements, many of which had been long in the making. Arguably it is only with the arrival of Modernism in the twentieth century that a genuinely new intellectual framework began to impose itself on perceptions of the landscape. However, how far this impacted on the mass market identified earlier is a matter of debate.

The Victorians may not have invented a movement as such, but it can hardly be argued that they did not witness major developments in the history of aesthetics and ideas – leaving aside for the moment technologies – that had the potential to change perceptions of the landscape. The architectural consensus that underpinned classicism in the eighteenth century gave way to a greater eclecticism, which affected the perception and valuation of both historic buildings and new ones. What characterized the shifts in architectural taste witnessed in the period was not only the variety of takes on classicism (mannerist, baroque, Palladian, Grecian) and the

---

[3] Lucinda Lambourne, *Victorian Painting* (London: Phaidon Press, 1999), 100, 105–9; Julian Treuherz, *Victorian Painting* (London: Thames & Hudson, 1993), 72, 82; Charles Hemming, *British Landscape Painters: A History and Gazetteer* (London: Victor Gollancz, 1989), 71; Heather Birchall, 'The Influence of John Ruskin', in *History of British Art, 1600–1870*, ed. David Bindman (London: Tate Publishing, 2008), 151.

[4] Boyd Hilton, *A Mad, Bad and Dangerous People? England, 1783–1846* (Oxford: Oxford University Press, 2006), 468.

[5] William Beach Thomas, *The English Landscape* (London: Country Life, 1938), 127–8.

gothic (Early English, Decorated, Perpendicular), or the tension that existed in the battle of the styles, but also the common resort to the past (and this went also for the vernacularism associated with the Arts and Crafts movement) as the source of inspiration. Only with the emergence of a Modernist aesthetic in the twentieth century was this hegemony of the past in architecture to be challenged. Victorian art also looked heavily to the past for its models and subject matter.[6] But – though fashions in painting are easily discernible – it is not quite so easy to identify the models as classical or gothic. Moreover the role of the visual image in reporting the contemporary, whether it be in portraiture or landscapes, meant the visual formats could hardly avoid engagement with the present, particularly once photography had established itself in the 1840s. As it happened the modernist movement impacted upon painting in England earlier than it did architecture, especially if one includes precursors like impressionism or, of course, Turner. But, significantly, it is possible in England in the 1930s and 1940s to identify a powerful body of 'romantic moderns' – the past could not be jettisoned that easily.[7]

We saw in Chapters 1 and 2 how under the impact of the Scientific Revolution and Enlightenment understanding of the material structure of the landscape and of the non-human living forms that inhabited its surface had changed rapidly. By the 1830s it was no longer easy for those who thought about it, and a growing if small minority did, to view the earth on which they perambulated, as a disorganized, undifferentiated mass of rocks. Nor, as the implications of identifying strata in the earth's crust sank in, was it easy to conceive that the geological landscape or the natural life that occupied its surface originated in one moment of time, in a single act of creation or destruction. The debate between catastrophism and uniformitarianism continued to rage, though with the outcome inevitably shifting in favour of the latter. Once the argument for gradualism, or the very slow process of change by forces still operating today, was accepted, attention turned to expanding and refining the stratigraphic column that delineated the various stages of the geological history of the earth, with the Cambrian (1835), Silurian (1835) and Devonian (1839) systems identified in the 1830s, and the Ordovician in 1879.[8] The establishment of the Geological Survey of Great Britain in 1835, under the Board of Ordnance and with its first director Henry Thomas de la Beche, Vice President of the Geological Society, and underpinned later by the Geological Survey Act of 1845, was a part of the process by which new geological knowledge was being extended and refined.

There was also a growing debate about the actual age of the earth, and of the nature of the forces that, over vast stretches of time, were able to dramatically remodel its appearance. Controversy, for example, existed over the impact of glaciations. There were also those who argued that the location of the earth's crust remained fixed over time; against them were ranged the drifters or mobilists, who literally saw place – as,

[6] Roy Strong, *And When Did You Last See Your Father? The Victorian Painter and British History* (London: Thames & Hudson, 1978).
[7] Alexandra Harris, *Romantic Moderns: English Writers, Artists and the Imagination from Virginia Woolf to John Piper* (London: Thames & Hudson, 2010).
[8] Nigel Woodcock and Rob Strachan (eds.), *Geological History of Britain and Ireland*, 2nd edn (Chichester: Wiley-Blackwell, 2012), 3.

for example, in the entity called England – as something fluid, in regular movement across the earth. Thus Charles Lyell argued that '[c]ontinents ... although permanent for whole geological epochs, shift their position entirely in the course of ages'.[9] By 1915, Arnold Wegener was propagating a full-blown theory of continental drift, though this was not widely accepted at the time, and its principles only became generally recognized with the development of plate tectonic theory in the 1960s.[10] Debate and controversy were the engines that drove the formation of new scientific knowledge, but the difficulties this caused for a lay audience in trying to arbitrate between different views, especially if presented in an increasingly specialized language, and the fluid nature of that knowledge, meant that its absorption into popular landscape literature, such as the guide book, was bound to be problematic. Paradoxically the difficulty of knowledge transference from the specialist to the generalist sphere was exacerbated by the nature of the knowledge itself. What was being argued for was inherently dramatic and in one sense might be seen to be appealing to minds, perhaps sensitized by gothicism, in search of an exciting and theatrical narrative in the landscape. But what was being suggested was so radical and flew so directly in the face of most people's experience – after all, very largely there was no observable change in the shape or location of the earth, and most English people did not experience the impact of an earthquake or volcano – that it was difficult for a lay audience to accept.

The first volume of Lyell's *Principles of Geology* was one of the books Charles Darwin took with him during the five-year explorative voyage in the *Beagle* (1831–6) – he picked up the newly published second volume while en route – and it had a deep influence on him. Lyell's advocacy of processes of slow but monumental change (and the way his volume also acted as a 'gateway' to Lamarck's theories of transmutation in life forms),[11] when interacting with Darwin's close observations of the very different environments and forms of life that he encountered, stimulated him to rethink the notion of fixed species (as suggested in the Linnaean system) and the traditional position of creationism and catastrophism in relation to the living world. The outcome was to be his theory of evolution by natural selection, articulated in *On the Origin of Species* (1859) and *The Descent of Man* (1871). All life originated in a common root, which over an unimaginably long period of time, and through an infinite amount of small variations prompted by mutation and a competitive advantage in nature, spread out into the huge tree of life, of which man was but one branch, but of which most branches have become extinct.[12] This theory, when combined – and the connections were clear enough – with the new ideas about the 'evolution' of the geological earth, constituted potentially a dramatic new way of perceiving the inorganic and living landscape. Whether in practice it had this effect for those engaged recreationally in

---

[9] Charles Lyell, *Principles of Geology, or, the Modern Changes of the Earth and Its Inhabitants Considered as Illustrative of Geology*, 12th edn (London: John Murray, 1875), 258.
[10] Andrew Goudie and Heather Viles, *Landscapes and Geomorphology. A Very Short Introduction* (Oxford: Oxford University Press, 2010), 32.
[11] Jonathan Conlin, *Evolution and the Victorians: Science, Culture and Politics in Darwin's Britain* (London: Bloomsbury, 2014), 70.
[12] Charles Darwin, *The Origin of Species* ([1859] London: Penguin, 1978), 457–9.

experiencing the landscape is less clear. Darwin himself recognized that what people could not see – and interaction with the landscape at the level of the tourist was very much about observation and 'gaze' – they were unlikely to believe: 'the chief cause of our natural unwillingness to admit that one species has given birth to other and distinct species, is that we are always slow in admitting any great change of which we do not see the intermediate steps'.[13]

Moreover, Darwin's theory of evolution, though hardly coming out of the blue, was of course highly controversial; it also fertilized, as Jonathan Conlin has shown, with a range of different Victorian evolutionary models which reflected very different religious, social and political perspectives. One of these models – what Conlin terms 'domestic evolution' – was concerned with the popular dissemination of new scientific ideas through gin palaces, pubs and clubs, improving Mechanics Institutes, rambles, popular scientific literature, zoos, exhibitions, music hall, museums and the like. There was undoubtedly widespread interest in the circulation of scientific ideas. Again, the extent to which the true nature and radical implications of these ideas were being absorbed by their popular audiences is less clear. There was a desire among an upper-working-class and middle-class public to be informed in a general sense about changing views of how the world operated, of which evolution would be one. But engagement with these ideas would usually be refracted through a conservative prism, retaining some role for God, and there is a strong sense that for many 'science' was as much a form of spectacle and entertainment as of education.[14]

One factor which further inhibited the impact of new scientific thinking on the minds of the general public was the growing professionalization and institutionalization of science, and indeed of all academic disciplines. In the early modern period knowledge was seen as a unified phenomenon: it was possible for and indeed expected that creative persons, such as architects like Christopher Wren, should embrace a range of what we today would call disciplines. But by the nineteenth century, the influence of the polymath was rapidly disappearing. Specialization in particular branches of science, paralleling the emergence of professional disciplines in the social sciences and humanities – such as history, geography, archaeology, anthropology and economics – may have accelerated the production of knowledge and increased its volume. However, there was a price to be paid for this. Professionalization and specialization made the language and methodologies of knowledge increasingly complex and opaque. They made it more and more difficult for any individual to straddle several disciplines and get the bigger picture, and they meant that science became less and less accessible and understandable for the lay public.

The word 'scientist', though coined in the 1830s, was in fact not commonly used until the 1880s,[15] but this was indicative of the fact that by now a gap was opening up between what might be broadly called the scientific and the aesthetic modes of discourse. The professionalization and institutionalization of the production and transmission of knowledge, on both sides of the divide, itself becoming systematized

---

[13] Ibid., 452.
[14] Conlin, *Evolution*, 172–94.
[15] Ibid., 220.

in the educational system, were creating a barrier that was increasingly difficult to penetrate, particularly by the end of the nineteenth century. And the evidence suggests that it was the aesthetic mode that came to dominate the forms of representation that governed the recreational use of the landscape. The conservative rural writer William Beach Thomas argued that

> the country scene is a department of art, not of science. The essential is the discovery of beauty, not of knowledge. Science comes second, and a bad second, to art. We do not listen to the nightingale in order to find out whether his song is erotic or polemic. We listen for the pleasure of the mood that the song and the scene engender. Flight matters more than its mechanics. The prime value of knowledge itself is to enlarge the circle of wonder. The chronicler does a better deed if he helps someone to enjoy the country more than if he botanises or ornithologises or entomologises or meteorologises.[16]

In 1883 M. J. B. Baddeley, one of the editors of the *Thorough Guide Series*, could cheerfully write in the Introduction to the Peak District guide under the section on 'Geology, &c.' that 'as in other volumes in our series, we only profess to handle the scientific bearings of our subjects in so far as they affect them from a picturesque point of view'.[17] This is not to argue that new scientific ideas were not to exert some influence over how the landscape was perceived by the layman and tourist. Nor is it to argue that the emergence of the divide was simply a product of the processes by which knowledge was produced and disseminated. In all likelihood the preference for the aesthetic mode was reinforced by the links that were felt to exist – rightly or wrongly – between science on the one hand, and work, industrialization, urbanization and modernity on the other. The recreational use of the landscape was for many all about escaping from the everyday world of modern living, into a world of Nature in which paradoxically the mechanics of Nature – in the sense that science was making dramatic advances in revealing the inner workings of Nature – played only a small part.

Cultural media

Chapter 3 argued that the processes and mechanisms of representation were critical to the way that ideas, and the movements that underpinned them, were transmitted and mediated to the public at large. For a material form like landscape, which had no inherent significance, to acquire or change its meaning and value, and for this to receive widespread and rapid acceptance, a likeness or analogue, embodying this new or reformed meaning, needed to be created and circulated. Towards the end of the early modern period, representations of landscape expanded considerably in volume and circulation. During the nineteenth and early-twentieth century under the forces of

---

[16] William Beach Thomas, 'Country Life', *The Spectator*, 14 Sep. 1950, 12.
[17] M. J. B. Baddeley, *The Peak District of Derbyshire and Neighbouring Counties*, 3rd edn (London: Dulau, 1884), xvii.

economic and technological change, complemented by a surge in consumer demand, this process was ratcheted up several notches. In *c*. 1900 W. H. Hudson, the naturalist and country writer, claimed that 'Guide-books are so many that it seems probable we have more than any other country – possibly more than all the universe together. Every county has a little library of its own.'[18] By the 1920s and 1930s representations of landscape were to be found across a wide range of cultural media and though the middle class was the principal target audience, such imagery was also increasingly accessible to the skilled and indeed broader working class.

Talk of a 'media revolution' at any point between 1840 and 1940 is always fatally flawed by the fact that it is plausible for similar claims to be made for eras before or after. There is also a clear risk in making easy assumptions about the relationship between volume of output, dissemination and impact. That said, it is difficult not to acknowledge the basic growth in the quantity and range of cultural media in the period or to speculate that this would have had a significant influence upon the way that the world was read by those who were exposed to this output. The remainder of this chapter will begin by mapping out the wide varieties of 'texts' and media through which landscape forms were represented – popular, scholarly, literary, iconic (or visual), musical and horticultural – and changes in this profile over the period. The discussion will then address the more elusive issues of production, performance and reception.

The proliferation of the printed word in the Victorian era and beyond is now well attested, and its impact – particularly in the forms of fictional literature and 'the press' – on the shaping of political and broader cultural attitudes has been the subject of much analysis.[19] The focus here is on the capacity of the printed word to transmit images of landscape. A distinction will be drawn between 'popular', 'scholarly' and 'literary' texts. By 'popular' is not meant texts intended to be read by those possessing limited literary skills or even necessarily those who were part of a 'mass' market, but texts for people who were generally highly educated but did not possess an expertise in the study of a particular aspect of the landscape. By 'scholarly' is meant texts produced by 'experts' – here defined as engaged, by no means necessarily professionally, in the production of knowledge about the landscape – intended to be read by other 'experts'. In practice the boundary between the two types of text is of course fuzzy, as is the distinction between these and 'literary' texts, but these distinctions have a real value in trying to understand the relationship between knowledge and perception.

The starting point for any discussion of popular texts aimed at revealing the meaning of the recreational landscape must be the guidebook. In its purest form it treated its user as an 'innocent', a stranger to the place described but, critically, not as 'innocent', in the sense of having no knowledge: all sorts of assumptions were made about the values, information sets and general intellectual skills of the reader. From a practical point of view the guidebook was also assumed to be portable, a pocket book or companion that could be easily carried around from place to place and used on

---

[18] W. H. Hudson, *Afoot in England* (London: Hutchinson & Co., 1909), 1.
[19] Raymond Williams, *Culture and Society, 1780–1950* (London: Vintage, 2017) and idem, *The Long Revolution* (London: Chatto, 1961).

the spot to make sense of a particular location. As suggested in the earlier chapters, guide literature was already a well-established genre of publication by the Victorian era. Daniel Defoe's *Tour* of the early-eighteenth century, for example, more or less met these requirements, even if its three volumes read more like a personal travel diary than a systematic guide. Perhaps more important in pioneering guidebook design were the volumes produced for individual locations, especially towns. London and the watering places had a key role to play here, precisely because they emerged – in the case of London, specifically, its West End – as early sites of concentrated tourism, where there was a need and a thirst to understand the locale.

Bath acquired its first guidebooks in the 1740s and 1750s, but it was from the early 1760s that it established a sequence of publications in which elements of continuity and regular updates, and in some cases annual editions, became the norm. In the 1920s *The Original Bath Guide* could claim, not without some credibility, descent from Cornelius Pope's *The New Bath Guide* of c. 1762.[20] Guidebooks abounded in nineteenth-century Bath (well over 150, including new editions, were published between 1740 and 1900),[21] as they did in the spas and seaside resorts of Kent. For the Thanet area, which includes the early resorts of Margate, Ramsgate and Broadstairs, R. J. Goulden has located 155 guides (many annual editions of the same guide) published between 1763 and 1900 and suggests that at least a further thirty remain unlocated: for Tunbridge Wells (1780–1900) the respective figures are 142 and four or five. Canterbury – a leading heritage town – with 126 and ten (1774–1900) shows that it was not just resorts that could provide fertile territory for the guidebook. However, significantly Maidstone, despite being the county town, could muster no more than five dedicated guides before 1900 and may be much more typical of provincial towns in England.[22] Town guidebooks would typically contain information about inns, carrying services, modes of transport, brief accounts of local charities and other institutions, details of local bye-laws and forms of government, some general history, and accounts of historic local heroes. A number of guides – such as *Matthews New History of Bristol or Complete Guide and Bristol Directory for the Year 1793-4* – also doubled as trade directories. But the town guidebooks also invariably contained a good deal of detail on the built and natural environment (such as churches and chapels, fortifications, antiquities, public buildings, private residences, walks, gardens and parks, and flora and fauna), increasingly contained a section on the local environs – often directed specifically at tourists using the town as a base – and frequently attached maps of the town and local area. Moreover, the general history element, though it might not be attached to specific material forms, rubbed off on the perception of the whole landscape.

The guide tailored to a particular location, and often the product of a local bookseller, printer or publisher, was joined in the later nineteenth century by the 'series'. Produced by a commercial – often metropolitan based – publisher, supported by an editorial team and list of house authors, this was to have a dynamic impact on the volume of guidebook output and its circulation and reflected a step change in the broadening of

---

[20] Borsay, *Image of Georgian Bath*, 209.
[21] *Bath: Guides, Newspapers, Directories*, 3rd edn (Bath: Bath Municipal Libraries, 1988).
[22] R. J. Goulden, *Kent Town Guides, 1763–1900* (London: British Library, 1995), 14–15.

Reconfiguring the Landscape 57

market demand. John Murray had published his first continental guide in 1836 (four years after Karl Baedeker's first guide), and Adam and Charles Black their first guide (to Scotland) in 1839, but it was the way Murray's and Black's, initially in 1850s and 1860s, and then alongside other publishers on an increasingly 'industrial' scale from the 1870s and 1880s, began to produce series-based guidebooks focusing on particular tourist localities and regions in England, that proved so dynamic. John Murray's guide to Devon and Cornwall, published in 1851, was the first of a sixty-volume series devoted to the British Isles that was finally completed in 1899. Although the Edinburgh firm Adam and Charles Black produced a guide to the English Lakes as early as 1841, its series only got fully under way in the 1850s and 1860s; the first editions of Derbyshire, Devonshire and Hampshire, for example, first came out in 1857.[23] The London firm Ward and Lock established by Ebenezer Ward and George Lock in 1854 began large-scale publishing of their so-called Red Guides in the 1880s; by the turn of the century they had produced over seventy separate volumes, the vast majority for locations in Britain.[24] Some were directed at a distinctive tourist region – such as the Cotswolds, the Thames, the Wye Valley and the Lake District – but most were associated with a particular town; however, these usually offered extensive coverage of the surrounding region. The Ward Lock guides were probably the most prolific of the 'series' guides, but they were joined by other series such as Stanford's 'Tourist Guides' (by 1882 it was already advertising over twenty, largely county-based guides),[25] the Baddeley 'Thorough Guides' (written by M. J. B. Baddeley, 1843–1906, and published by Thomas Nelson), the Methuen 'The Little Guides' – whose 'archaeological information' was said to be 'indispensable if you go in for the study of churches'[26] – the extensive guide output of the Homeland Association (an advert of 1910 lists over seventy guides in 'The Homeland Handbooks' series, almost wholly to places in southern England),[27] 'The Blue Guides' which first appeared in 1918 produced by the Scottish brothers James and Findlay Muirhead (both of whom had worked at Baedeker),[28] the 'Bell's Pocket Guides,'[29] the 'Penguin Guides' (already in production before the Second World War),[30] and the publications of provincial businesses, such as the West Country firm of E. J. Burrows. This last firm was initially established in Cheltenham in 1901, produced its first guide three years later and became famous for its 'Burrows Guides'. Allegedly, by the 1930s, guides were available for over 500 different locations from Shetland to Sicily.[31] In Norwich the publishing branch of Jarrold's produced a bewilderingly wide

---

[23] J. Vaughan, *The English Guidebook* (Newton Abbot: David & Charles, 1974), 47, 50, 141.
[24] On Ward Lock Red Guides, see https://wlrg.z33.web.core.windows.net/, accessed 16 Feb. 2022.
[25] G. Phillips Bevan, *Tourist's Guide to Warwickshire* (London: Stanford, 1882), adverts at rear.
[26] J. R. A. Hockin, *On Foot in Berkshire* (London: A. Maclehose & Co., 1934), 9.
[27] F. C. Elliston Erwood, *The Pilgrim's Road* (London: Frederick Warne & Co., 1910), adverts at rear, i–iv.
[28] 'History of the Blue Guides', https://www.blueguides.com/our-titles/history-of-the-blue-guides/, accessed 25 Oct. 2019.
[29] E.g., S. E. Winbolt, *The Chilterns and the Thames Valley* (London: G. Bell & Sons, 1932).
[30] E.g., S. E. Winbolt, *Kent, Sussex and Surrey* (London: Penguin, 1939).
[31] https://researchworcestershire.wordpress.com/2015/07/10/burrows-pointer-guide-map-of-worcester/, accessed 19 Oct. 2021.

range of cheap guide material for East Anglia.[32] If we add to these the series of guides produced for the railway companies or to service the needs of cyclists and motorists, all of which will be discussed later, then it will be clear that for those intent upon discovering the local landscapes of England, by the early-twentieth century, there was a surfeit of portable ciceroni to direct their travels.

However, literature of this sort represented only one way that the tourist might get to know the landscape. The guidebook, in its purest form, lay at the sharp end of the tourist's kit, something that could be taken into the field and deployed on the spot. There also existed a more illusive type of text, more literary and flowery in style, more directed at the sedentary tourist. Much of the popular travel literature has the air of the whimsical, armchair tourist about it, and it may be that the reader never got beyond his or her parlour – which would not of itself negate its significance, since what we are concerned with in this book is interaction with the virtual as well as the real landscape. John Hissey's *English Holiday with Car and Camera* (1908) rather gave the game away when he openly admitted that '[a]rmchair travel has the advantage of being costless, speedy, and is delightful by its absence of effort, inconvenience, noise, or bustle. With a suitable book you can travel thus, safely and at ease, the wide world over.'[33] In fact, much of this type of literature – including Hissey's volume – was organized along lines similar to that of a guide, with a notional journey undertaken, and many volumes could be carried in a knapsack, cycle bag or car pocket. Typical of this type of publication – though typicality was not part of the strategy – was Macmillan's *Highways and Byways* series, of which thirty-six largely county-based highly illustrated volumes were published between 1897 and 1948, and in which the various authors were given considerable leeway to adopt their own idiosyncratic approach to the subject.[34] Arthur Mee's *King's England* county-based series followed in this tradition, even if it had a stronger sense of direction. Begun in 1936, published by Hodder and Stoughton, based upon the work of a large team of writers, and claiming to be 'the first census of the ancient and beautiful and curious and historic possessions of England since the motor-car came to make it possible', over thirty volumes had been completed by the time of Mee's death in 1943.[35] It was a tradition that had its most lasting memorial in *The Shell County Guides*, the first of which appeared in 1934 (though the last was not published until 1984).[36]

At some point these types of popular guide shade into a more generalized type of tourist/travel literature, focused predominantly upon the historic and rural landscape. Some of this was in the form of loosely structured guide literature, one-off volumes that might cover a particular region or natural feature like a river, but might equally move from one spot to another, in a relatively disconnected fashion, such as C. J. Cornish's

---

[32] See, e.g., 'Jarrold's Holiday Series', in *The Handbook to the Rivers and Broads of Norfolk*, ed. G. Christopher Davies, 18th edn (London: Jarrold, 1891).

[33] J. John Hissey, *An English Holiday with Car and Camera* (London: Macmillan & Co., 1908), 66.

[34] David Milner (ed.), *The Highways and Byways of Britain* (Basingstoke: Macmillan, 2008), x.

[35] Arthur Mee, *Buckinghamshire: Country of the Chilterns* (London: Hodder & Hodder, 1947), rear cover; idem, *Warwickshire: Shakespeare's County* (London: Hodder & Stoughton, 1949), lists thirty-six volumes as 'now ready'.

[36] David Heathcote, *A Shell Eye on England: The Shell County Guides, 1934–84* (Faringdon: Libri Publishing, 2011).

Wild England of To-day and the Wild Life in It (1895). Cornish's volume merges easily into the general ruralist literature enjoying such a popularity from the late-nineteenth century, reaching a peak in the inter-war years, and seen in the work of figures like Richard Jefferies (1848–87), William Henry Hudson (1841–1922), and Harold John Massingham (1888–1952).[37] Many of those engaged in producing popular landscape literature of this type were also journalists. It is likely that much of their output first saw light of day in the expanding press and magazine sector of the publishing industry, whose products gained easy entry to people's homes, were consulted on a day-to-day basis, and may have proved less daunting to access than a formal book. In the preface to *Wild England*, Cornish notes that 'the greater number of the papers included in this book appeared in their first form in *The Spectator*', while John Prioleau records that in the case of his *Enchanted Ways* (1933) 'the greater part of the material of this book has appeared in the form of articles in *The Observer*'.[38]

In this generalized literature the natural and the man-made, at least that which was historic, blend into what can be called heritage, an umbrella concept, in which landscape plays a central role, that was gathering force among public and professionals alike from the later nineteenth century, and provided publishers with a market and strategy to exploit. Before the First World War Batsford's had been producing finely crafted, low print run, relatively highly priced books on art and architecture. During the 1920s they began to reduce their prices, and then from the 1930s, in response to the changing character of the market, the firm introduced, in the words of Charles Fry, who started work at Batsfords in 1924,

> an entirely new kind of book … the writing to be on subjects akin to our own … Britain, its churches, its houses and its landscape. But we planned to put more than a hundred illustrations in each book, to present them with Brian's [Cook's] attractive wrappers, and in editions so big that we could afford to sell the books for as little as seven shillings and sixpence each. We began our new type of publishing with *The British Heritage Series*, planning to tell thousands of people of the riches of the land in which they lived. Production prices were at a high level. … The only economic solution was to take the bull by the horns and print a first edition of 10,000 copies.[39]

This adventure into mass marketing on the part of Batsfords proved remarkably successful. The Heritage series was followed up by *The Face of Britain Series*, 'which treated the scenery and antiquities of the British Isles in a range of volumes devoted to their natural rather than geographical divisions', and *The Pilgrim's Library*, the three together generating sales of almost half a million copies in ten years.[40] British Heritage

---

[37] William Keith, *The Rural Tradition: A Study of the Non-Fiction Prose Writers of the English Countryside* (Toronto: University of Toronto Press, 1974).

[38] C. J. Cornish, *Wild England of Today and the Wild Life in It* (London: Seeley and Co., 1895), viii; John Prioleau, *Enchanted Ways* (London: J. M. Dent & Sons, 1933), viii.

[39] Hector Bolitho (ed.), *A Batsford Century. The Record of a Hundred Years of Publishing and Bookselling, 1843-1943* (London: Batsford, 1943), 65–6.

[40] Bolitho, *Batsford Century*, 66, 69–70.

series sported titles such as *English Church Craftsmanship*, *The Greater English Church*, *The English Country House*, *English Village Homes*, *The English Castle*, *The Old Towns of England*, *The English Garden*, or *The English Cottage*. In total, Batsford published 113 books describing the English countryside, of which more than half appeared between 1934 and 1940.[41] Batsford was only one of a group of publishers specializing in and capitalizing on this market in popular domestic heritage; these included national presses like Blackie, Simpkin Marshall, Methuen, Odhams, J. M. Dent and Robert Scott,[42] as well as local publishers such as Barnicott and Pearce in Taunton, Jarrold's in Norwich and Norman Sawyer in Cheltenham. The national presses were also producing the historical and geographical texts that were to influence the attitudes to the landscape of generations of young pupils. Collins's *County Geographies* (1872–4), though written by several authors, follows a standard format of 'natural features' (with some basic geology), 'industrial pursuits' (including agriculture), 'topographical details' (largely short accounts of individual towns) and 'historical notes' (with scarcely any post-1700 history).[43]

By and large the popular guide, heritage and educational literature described above were about transmitting rather than creating knowledge. This of course begs the question, where this knowledge came from, and raises the prospect that the surge of interest in the recreational landscape, and the remapping of the landscape that followed, was underpinned by, and indeed a response to, the rapidly changing intellectual framework of the period. These are issues that will be continuously returned to. The introduction to the chapter has made it clear that scholarly research, debate and publication – on an unprecedented scale – were underway on matters that impinged on an understanding of the landscape and had the potential to lead to dramatic new ways of reading it. The research was available to the public at large. Darwin's *Origins of Species* (1859) appears to have sold pretty well for a scientific work and there was clearly a market in popular science, serviced through lectures, exhibitions and publications.[44] There were also various other channels by which the lay public could get close to the 'coal face' of research. One might be by attendance at the annual meetings of the British Association for the Advancement of Science (founded in 1831 and located each year in a different provincial city) and reading its publications,[45] or by joining one of the extraordinary efflorescence of local natural history, scientific, historical and archaeological societies (the same society often embraced all these disciplines) that blossomed during the Victorian period. Their members were almost all amateurs, though the majority came from a professional background.[46] A perusal of their

---

[41] Catherine Brace, 'Publishing and Publishers: Towards an Historical Geography of Countryside Writing, c. 1930–1950', *Area* 33:3 (2001): 287–96.
[42] For Scott see Edric Holmes, *London's Countryside* (London: Robert Scott, 1927), rear pages adverts; Holmes's book was one of a series called 'The English Countryside Series'.
[43] Rex Walford, *Geography in British Schools 1850–2000: Making a World of Difference* (London: Woburn Press, 2001).
[44] Darwin, *Origin of Species*, 19; Conlin, *Evolution*, 178–83.
[45] Louise Miskell, *Meeting Places: Scientific Congresses and Urban Identity in Victorian Britain* (London: Routledge, 2016).
[46] Levine, *The Amateur and the Professional*, 54–9.

minute books and journals suggests a serious engagement with the national scientific and historical scene, and a dedication to a notion of locally based research, and the transmission of this knowledge through debate and publication. The studies contained in the societies' voluminous transactions were often highly detailed and descriptive in character, focusing on a particular archaeological, geological, biological or historical object, site or 'find'; they may not have been intellectually innovative, but they widened enormously the bank of local scientific and historical knowledge. It was a situation on the face of it tailored to meet the needs of the rapidly expanding guidebook sector with the need for each publication to stake its claim in an increasingly crowded marketplace by adding that extra bit of knowledge. Matters in this respect were facilitated by the fact that the compilers of popular guide literature were often highly educated men living in or close to the areas of their publications, who would also naturally be among the membership of their local scientific or historical societies.

Such a man was the Oxford-educated P. H. Ditchfield (1854–1930), rector (from 1886) of Barkham in Berkshire, and author or editor of over thirty volumes of history- and heritage-related works, much of it for the lay or popular market. In 1920, when he published *Byways in Berkshire and the Cotswolds*, he was editor of *Memorials of Old Gloucestershire and Oxfordshire* (1912) in the *Memorials of the Counties of England* series; joint editor of the authoritative *Victoria County History of Berkshire*; author of *Oxfordshire*; had been secretary of the Berkshire Archaeological Society for thirty years; and editor of the *Berks, Bucks, and Oxon Archaeological Journal* for twenty-three.[47] He must have had access to an enormous store of detailed local knowledge, much of it generated in the recent decades through research in the archives and the field. In the preface to *Byways* he explicitly cites these publications, among others, as his source material. What emerges, however, is a volume that wears its learning lightly, almost to the point of weightlessness. There is no significant scientific content (Darwin could as well not have existed). This may not be surprising given Ditchfield's historical leanings. More surprising are the limited references to archaeology, the anecdotal approach to history, and though churches are the subject of a good deal of attention, the architectural descriptions rarely contain much more than an intelligent stranger versed in architectural history could have arrived at. The account of Bisham Abbey finishes with the rather frustrating observation that '[t]here is much else to record about the place that cannot be told here', followed by a specific reference to the transactions of which Ditchfield is editor, which promises but then fails to add any other further information:

> Mr. Ernest Dormer has written of it in my *Archaeological Journal* ... 'It has all the beauties which the period and hand of time and nature and the old architects can give to it. Many indeed are the pleasure-seekers who rest upon their oars and gaze with thoughtful eyes towards one of the sweetest homes in the valley of the Thames. Long may it stand'.[48]

---

[47] P. H. Ditchfield, *Byways in Berkshire and the Cotswolds* (London: Robert Scott, 1920), vii–viii.
[48] Ditchfield, *Byways in Berkshire*, 101.

The Malverns was an area whose natural history was heavily researched in the nineteenth century chiefly because of what was perceived as its exceptional geological history: containing some of the oldest rocks in Britain, it was closely studied by many of the pioneers of British geology[49] and today, along with the Abberley Hills, has been constituted a 'geopark'.[50] It was also very well served by natural history societies, and their members' publications, with not only a specific Malvern Naturalists' Club servicing its interests but also a number of other clubs seeing it as within their sphere of interest: the Hereford-based Woolhope Club, the Cotteswold Naturalists' Field Club and the Worcestershire Naturalists' Club – all of which met on 12 June 1855 on Worcestershire Beacon to receive a 'geological lecture' from the renowned Sir Roderick Murchison, the formulator of the Silurian system.[51] Natural history was therefore potentially a major selling point for Malvern, a spa town which attracted large numbers of well-off and highly educated visitors, and there was a huge and ever-expanding body of knowledge to be mined for information by the prospective guide writer.

The general guides to the area pick up on this potential and usually offer some material on geology and botany, but this is invariably on the brief side and self-contained. *Cross's Illustrated Hand-Book to Malvern* (1872) notes that 'there are few districts in England that better repay the geologist for his time and attention' but confines its comments on 'geology, mineralogy and botany' to eight pages of a guide with over 170 pages.[52] Although *The Visitors' Guide to Malvern* [1862] acknowledges that 'the richly-fossiliferous Silurian beds ... afford a most interesting field of investigation to the geologist' and 'according to Mr Lees, there is no spot [the Malvern Plain] in the kingdom of a similar extent that contains so great a variety of lichens and fungi', the section on geology and flora receives only three pages in a guide stretching to over eighty.[53] This pattern continued into the twentieth century: the Homeland Association's *Malvern and District* [1933] handbook recognizes the exceptional geological interest of the Malvern district, 'affording unique opportunities for the study of the Silurian system', and acknowledges the dramatic history of the range of hills, 'Time was when these bold, blunt cones were lava-like rock deep within our slowly cooling planet, and long after the forces of Nature exalted them above all other eminences in England south of the Shropshire Highlands and north of Exmoor, a primeval sea filled the Severn Valley.'[54] But no additional scientific explanation was forthcoming, which is understandable since the aim of the series was to 'contain everything likely to interest the intelligent visitor regarding the History, Worthies, Antiquities and Literary Associations of the neighbourhood'.[55] In the preface to his guide to Malvern, Charles

---

[49] W. S. Symonds, *Old Stones: A Series of Geological Notes on the Plutonic, Volcanic, Laurentian, Cambrian, Silurian, and Devonian Rocks in the Neighbourhood of Malvern* (London: Simpkin, Marshal & Co., 1880), 17.

[50] *The Geopark Way* (Worcester: Herefordshire and Worcestershire Earth Heritage Trust, 2009).

[51] H. Cecil Moore (ed.), *Transactions of the Woolhope Naturalists' Field Club (TWNFC) 1852–65* (Hereford: Jakeman and Carver, 1907), 146.

[52] *Cross's Illustrated Hand-Book to Malvern: A Book for Visitors* (Malvern: H. Cross, 1872), 17.

[53] *The Visitor's Guide to Malvern* (Malvern: H.W. Lamb, 1862), 74–5.

[54] E. Maslin Kearsey, *Malvern and District* (London: Homeland Association, 1932), 7.

[55] Ibid., advert.

Grindrod admitted that since it was designed 'for those wishing to see the places of interest round Malvern, the scientific resources of the neighbourhood are only slightly treated'. The implication is that the general sightseer was unlikely to want to spend much time studying the scientific aspects of the landscape, a view reinforced by the fact that information on 'natural history' (geology, botany, entomology, ornithology and molluscs) is placed in a self-contained section of eighteen pages (out of 270) at the rear of the guide, clearly designed for the enthusiast.[56]

Publications with a seemingly populist scientific bent, compiled by key figures in the local natural history association networks, were available, however; such was Edwin Lees (1800–87), founder of the Worcestershire Naturalists' Club (1847), its first president, and a member of the Linnean Society, who prefaced his *Pictures of Nature in the Silurian Region* with the observation that 'I have always been of the opinion that Nature may be studied in a holiday fashion'; or William Symonds (1818–87), rector of Pendock in the shadow of the Malverns, founder of the Malverns Naturalists' Field Club, its president for eighteen years, and a fellow of the Geological Society. The origins of *Old Stones* (1880), he explained, lay in a railway journey between Worcester and Cheltenham in which he was asked to elucidate the nature of Plutonic rocks, and by implication the origins of the Malverns' oldest stones, to a bemused 'fellow traveller'.[57] Both were self-conscious efforts to reach a wider audience, but it is not evident from the guidebooks that this was the effect. The full title of Symonds's volume, *Old Stones: A Series of Geological Notes on the Plutonic, Volcanic, Laurentian, Cambrian, Silurian, and Devonian Rocks in the Neighbourhood of Malvern*, might suggest where the problem lay. But it was more than simply a question of language – more one of types of knowledge.

There are two key issues here. First, the successful guidebook was not one that delivered cutting-edge knowledge to its readers, other than in its description of practical details such as opening times, accommodation, etc. For their 'deep-knowledge' content most drew upon sources of information that had long been known, such as well-established antiquarian literature or other guide material. Their strength lay in the repetition of established knowledge; indeed, it was in this process of repetition, rather than in the processes of testing through evidence, as championed by Enlightenment experimental science or the Rankean history of the nineteenth century, that the 'veracity' of information was to be judged. Guide literature proves highly repetitive, recalling the same stories again and again, not just because of the laziness of their authors but because they dealt in a form of knowledge based on myth, in which the nature of the story recalled was more important than the evidence which supported it. Second, it is clear that guide literature did not handle scientific knowledge easily, whether of a natural or human historical kind. There was a strong inclination towards what might be called the aesthetic tendency. Grindrod's guide was as much about atmosphere and ambience as hard detail; at Little Malvern he found the 'ivy-veiled remains of the Priory church, artistically a ruin, though still used for the parish

---

[56] Charles F. Grindrod, *Malvern: What to See and Where to Go* (Malvern: Thompson, 1904).
[57] E. Lees, *Pictures of Nature in the Silurian Region and the Malvern Hills and Vale of Severn* (Malvern: H. W. Lamb, 1856), vi; Symonds, *Old Stones*, 1–2.

services. The whole scene breathes of calm, contented English landscape, deepened and spiritualized by the touch of mystery which thoughts of the Past can alone give.[58]

Arguably fictional or semi-fictional representations of landscape, and literary associations, have a much larger impact on guide literature, and generally public perceptions of landscape, than 'scientific' research. Poppy Land – 'a land where even in far-off fields the poppy flame shews in the grain' – was virtually created by the London theatre critic Clement Scott's heavily sentimentalized account of the 1880s of the countryside around the surviving church tower and 'Garden of Sleep', perched on the edge of a crumbling coastline, at Overstrand in Norfolk.[59] Ditchfield's *Byways in Berkshire*, in a way common in guidebooks, is replete with literary references and quotations: cited, for example, are William Shakespeare, Alexander Pope, Geoffrey Chaucer, Thomas Hughes, Charles Kingsley and Mary Russell Mitford.[60] In the case of the last two, Ditchfield went so far as to call the areas in which they lived a large part of their lives – Eversley in Hampshire where Kingsley was rector from 1846 until his death, and Three Mile Cross, south of Reading, to which Mitford moved with her father from 1820 – 'Kingsley country' and 'Miss Mitford's country'. This was not just a reflection of the kudos attached to literary figures in English culture, and the desire to turn their homes and surrounding environs into a sort of shrine, to be visited and worshipped at. Ditchfield's approach also pointed to the key role that fictional accounts of place increasingly played in defining geographical space. In this way the account of a place in a novel or poem (or group of novels and poems) gave shape and meaning to that place, creating an imagined location or region, and one that for the work's readers becomes the reality of the space described, and critically the reason for their visit as a tourist. Keith Snell has defined the developing tradition of the 'regional novel', as 'fiction that is set in a recognisable region, and which describes features distinguishing the life, social relations, customs, language, dialect, or other aspects of the culture of that area and its people'.[61] It was proving remarkably effective at remodelling the geography of England. In *How to See England* (1937) Edmund Vale considered the matter of such importance in the process of perception of the nation, that he included a 'list of regional novelists' as a brief appendix (in fact covering Wales as well as England).[62] Stated explicitly to be 'not exhaustive', it included forty-eight authors (the Brontes are counted here as one), and the place, region or county associated with them. Most were relatively recent authors – Theodore Francis Powys (1875–1953) and Llewelyn Powys (1881–1939) for 'Devon to Somerset, Gloucestershire' and D. H. Lawrence (1885–1930) for Nottingham – suggesting the modernity of the genre.

Although some of the more recent authors mentioned in Vale's list would have baulked at the epithet 'regional', it is almost certainly the case that several of them

---

[58] Grindrod, *Malvern: What to See*, 77.
[59] Clement Scott, *Poppy-Land: Papers Descriptive of Scenery on the East Coast* (London: Carson and Comeford, 1886); A. B. Osborne, *Old-World England: Impressions of a Stranger* (London: Nash and Grayson, 1924), 56–62.
[60] Ditchfield, *Byways in Berks*, 16, 20, 33–9, 124–30, 136–43, 220–4.
[61] K. D. M. Snell, 'The Regional Novel: Themes for Interdisciplinary Research', in *The Regional Novel in Britain and Ireland*, ed. K. D. M. Snell (Cambridge: Cambridge University Press, 1998), 1.
[62] H. E. T. Vale, *How to See England* (London: Methuen, 1937), 282–3.

intuited that there was a growing market for this type of place-specific imaginative literature and perhaps also sensed that in producing such material they were playing an influential part in reshaping the mental geography of the spaces described. Charles Kingsley's and R. D. Blackmore's novels – notably *Westward Ho!* (1855) and *Lorna Doone: A Romance of Exmoor* (1869) – were vital in nurturing, to quote Simon Trezise, a 'West Country consciousness'. This reached its zenith in the late Victorian and early Edwardian era, particularly in the novels and short stories of Thomas Hardy.[63] So powerful were these literary inventions that they proved capable of creating real places. Westward Ho was the name given to a newly created Devon resort in 1863, and Hardy created (or, strictly, re-invented) a whole region called Wessex around which a minor industry emerged among guidebook writers, trying to match Hardy's fictional locations with real ones. In 1894 Herman Lea, a bicycling and car touring companion of Hardy, published, with the author's permission, *A Handbook to the Wessex Country of Thomas Hardy's Novels and Poems*. This was followed a year later by B. C. A. Windle's *The Wessex of Thomas Hardy*, which was prefaced with the comment, 'Mr Hardy has annexed unto himself a small ... stretch of country, and has steadily, in novel after novel, proceeded to people it with a new population ... he has resuscitated, one even may say re-created, the old half-forgotten kingdom of Wessex.'[64] So effective was this process of re-invention that by the inter-war period *Burrows Guide to Wessex: The Hardy Country* claimed Hardy's recreation of the ancient kingdom of Wessex meant that the name 'has passed into currency as a popular designation of all England south of the Thames between Cornwall and the counties of Surrey and Sussex'.[65] By this stage any guide to Dorset would be wise from a market perspective to use Hardy and his fictional output as its organizing framework, for, as S. P. B. Mais put it, 'we come to Dorset, where all our thoughts are of Thomas Hardy'.[66]

In the twentieth century, Shropshire and the Border Country, like Devon and Dorset, were redefined by writers such as Mary Webb (1881–1927) – 'my guide [the vicar of Alberbury]', wrote Mais in 1939, 'seemed to take it for granted that I wanted to see the Border through Mary Webb's eyes only'[67] – and especially A. E. Housman (1859–1936). The latter is a reminder that the author did not have to be an inhabitant of the region since Housman was essentially a metropolitan voyeur, recreating an imaginary world from his studies in London and Cambridge. He is also a reminder that other forms of artistic output could act as representations of region and landscape and play a part in shaping perceptions of both. Housman's *Shropshire Lad* poems of 1896 had an extraordinary influence on fellow artists, and in particular composers – many of the key figures in the so-called English (important elements were in fact Celtic) musical renaissance, such as Somervell, Moeran, Gurney, Butterworth, and Vaughan Williams,

---

[63] Simon Trezise, *The West Country as a Literary Invention: Putting Fiction in Its Place* (Exeter: University of Exeter Press, 2000), 18.
[64] Peter Borsay, *A History of Leisure* (Palgrave: Houndmills, 2006), 212–3.
[65] A. D. Murray, *Burrows Guide to Wessex: The Hardy Country* (Cheltenham: E. J. Burrow, n.d.), 9; for 'Hardy Country'; see also H. Beresford Stevens, *Picturesque Towns and Villages of England and Wales* (London: J Burrow, 1928), 21–8 and Thomas, *English Landscape*, 80.
[66] Mais, *Round about England*, 147.
[67] S. P. B. Mais, *Highways and Byways in the Welsh Marches* (London: Macmillan, 1939), 99.

composed settings of the poems. Not all the texts are directly about landscape, but physical features such as Wenlock Edge (Shropshire) and Bredon Hill (Worcestershire) are prominent, and the poems as a whole are suffused with a sense of place.

Ivor Gurney and Herbert Howells were deeply influenced by the region surrounding their childhood homes in Gloucester – Howells, for example, composed a *Missa Sabrensis* or *Mass of the Severn* (1954) – but on the face of it the most important example of a 'regional' composer was Edward Elgar, who drew upon his area of birth and residence for inspiration. But here we encounter a number of problems. First, to what extent was Elgar a 'regional' composer, and one affected by a defined regional landscape? There can be little doubt that Elgar was deeply devoted to and inspired by the area of the West Midlands where he was born and lived most of his life. He occupied residences in Worcester, Hereford and the Malverns and spent a great deal of time cycling and later motoring its byways in pursuit of what may be broadly called landscape experiences. In many ways he was the archetypal late Victorian and Edwardian local landscape explorer and enthusiast. But whether he conceived of the area as a 'region' is difficult to say, and he also drew inspiration from other landscapes in England and indeed from various areas of Europe. Second, it is very difficult tying specific pieces of music to particular locations; there is nothing like the sort of 'topographical parallelism' between art and reality that can be found for example in Hardy. Connections can perhaps be drawn between the *Wand of Youth Suit* and the view from Elgar's birthplace outside Worcester or between his early oratorio/opera *Caractacus* and the British Camp in the Malverns, but any attempt to find a depiction of local West Midlands landscapes in canonical works such as the *Introduction and Allegro for Strings*, the *Enigma Variations*, the two symphonies, the violin and cello concertos, or the oratorios, is at best speculative (the theme for the *Introduction* was in fact a Welsh one and *Enigma* is people rather than place based).[68] Third, even if Elgar did draw inspiration for his music from the landscapes around him, and even if that music for him resonated with a sense of a particular landscape, it is difficult to demonstrate that his original audiences derived any clear sense of a regional identity from hearing it.

Many of Elgar's works did in his own time attract a significant popular audience, but the problem with much classical music is that it is a niche product whose influence on the public imagination, even if it can be demonstrated to convey notions of landscape and region, is likely to be very restricted. Ralph Vaughan Williams's (1872–1958) opera *Hugh the Drover* (first performed 1924) is set in the Cotswolds and was later drawn on by the composer for his cantata *A Cotswold Romance* (1951). Without ever being very place specific, its lyricism and subject reinforces the developing bucolic image of the Cotswolds as a pre-industrial locus of traditional English values (much the same could also be said of Gustav Holst's *Cotswold Symphony* of 1900).[69] Yet the opera was never a real success and 'reached only an esoteric minority'.[70] Given this and other problems of interpretation, it might be considered best to abandon the notion that

---

[68] Jerrold Northrop Moore, *Edward Elgar: A Creative Life* (Oxford: Oxford University Press, 1984), 451–5.
[69] Jane Bingham, *The Cotswolds: A Cultural History* (Oxford: Signal Books, 2009), 177–8.
[70] Meirion Hughes and Robert Stradling, *The English Musical Renaissance, 1860-1940: Construction and Deconstruction* (London and New York: Routledge, 1993), 234.

music constituted a way of representing landscape that was influential in the period. But this may be taking it too far. Rutland Boughton (1878–1960) was one of the key figures behind the establishment of the Glastonbury Festival, which ran from 1914 to 1926, and was seen as an English answer to Wagner's Bayreuth. Boughton's fairy-tale opera *The Immortal Hour*, which opened the first festival and achieved considerable popularity, was vague in topographical detail but must have drawn on and reinforced the general ambience of mystery that surrounded the town and its purported location as the legendary Isle of Avalon.[71] Moreover, it is surely significant that many composers did see landscape and place as a stimulus to their music and sought to represent these elements in their output. In this respect they reinforce the notion that for creative artists as a whole in the period landscape was a critical resource.

One medium of representation which undoubtedly did play a key role in shaping public perceptions of landscape was the visual. Chapter 2 showed how during the eighteenth and early-nineteenth century the pictorial representation of landscape was transformed with a rise in its status as a branch of painting, changes in printing technologies that allowed images to be reproduced more easily and cheaply, the development of a theory of the picturesque which made the visualisation of landscape forms potentially more accessible and more of a consumer and recreational good, and – at the very beginning of the Victorian era – the discovery of photography. The following century built heavily on these developments. Spearheaded by Turner's extensive output and reputation, and encouraged by an expanding and lucrative market reflecting rising public demand for images, landscape painting largely shed its inferior status and attracted growing numbers of professional artists. The greater prestige of landscape painting, and the money to be made from it, gave the artist potentially more freedom to dictate the sort of images produced, but in practice the majority of artists were still constrained by the expectations and requirements of the market they operated in. Individual wealthy patrons could of course set their own standards and go out on a limb, though at the risk of failing to obtain critical recognition, and the cultural capital – a pressing motivation for the growing numbers of well-off businessmen – derived from this. Artists were also free to forge their own path but at the even more debilitating risk of penury. For these reasons, added perhaps to a certain nationalist perspective, modernist trends from the later nineteenth century, such as Impressionism and later Cubism, were slow to embed themselves in artistic practice and had relatively limited impact on the mass market in landscape images.[72] What was required by the vast majority of those consuming landscape as a recreational good was naturalistic, realistic and easily intelligible images, but also images that were different from those encountered in their everyday life, that played upon the sentiments, and were morally uplifting; that could shape the viewers' responses to landscape in a stimulating and pleasurable manner but were not ultimately challenging

---

[71] Patrick Benham, *The Avalonians* (Glastonbury: Gothic Image, 1993), 169–96; Mervyn Cooke (ed.), *The Cambridge Companion to Twentieth-Century Opera* (Cambridge: Cambridge University Press, 2005), 212–13; H. Antcliffe, 'A British School of Music-Drama: The Work of Rutland Boughton', *Musical Quarterly* 4:1 (1918): 117–27.

[72] Michael Rosenthal, *British Landscape Painting* (Oxford: Phaidon Press, 1982), 146; Hemming, *British Landscape Painters*, 24–6.

and disturbing. What this meant in practice was an emphasis – and it was a matter of emphasis rather than exclusivity, as we shall see in the case of the seaside resort and the town park – upon the rural rather than urban, and the old rather than the new.

This encouraged many artists to celebrate the local, regional and provincial, and for some to abandon London for locations in the perceived remoter areas of Britain, and occasionally to form 'colonies' there; and to focus on specific features of the traditional rural landscape like rivers, hills, trees, cottages and churches. A number of the London-based Camden Town Group vacated the metropolis to spend time at the Applehayes Estate, Clayhidon, bought by Harold Harrison in 1909 in the secluded Blackdown Hills on the Devon/Somerset border. Artists such as Robert Bevan, Charles Ginner and Spencer Gore produced stylized, highly coloured pastoral landscapes influenced by French post-impressionism.[73] A less sophisticated and more traditionalist late Victorian manifestation of the ruralist trend was the so-called Idyllist group of populist painters, such as Helen Allingham (1848–1926), who illustrated Hardy's *Far from the Madding Crowd* but is best known for her florid and deeply nostalgic images of the 'cottage idyll', as in her best-known books, *Happy England* (1903) and *The Cottage Homes of England* (1909) (see Figure 4.1).[74]

Figure 4.1 Helen Allingham, 'At the Cottage Gate' (1900). © Getty Images.

[73] 'The Camden Group in Context', https://www.tate.org.uk/art/research-publications/camden-town-group/robert-bevan-haze-over-the-valley-r1139230, accessed 22 Jun. 2022.
[74] Treuherz, *Victorian Painting*, 187–9; Christopher Wood, *Paradise Lost: Paintings of English Country Life and Landscape, 1850–1914* (London: Barrie & Jenkins, 1988), 129–31; Hemming, *British Landscape Painters*, 80.

Allingham's cottage paintings also include images of their inhabitants, as do many rural landscapes. Indeed, it may be misleading to talk of an exclusive genre of landscape painting, since natural features and built forms appear in a wide variety of types of art, including genres such as animal and sporting painting, while much pre-Raphaelite art frequently contains striking landscape elements.[75] The rise, and during the nineteenth and early-twentieth century, maturation and popularization of the seaside resort, however, created a potentially novel genre of marine and coastal painting. The new significance given to 'nature', the sea and coastline – previously perceived in negative terms, as a dangerous place only to be visited out of economic necessity, a location to avoid rather than seek out – provided artists with a huge, largely unexplored and inherently dramatic landscape resource to investigate the picturesque and sublime.[76] At the same time beach and promenade offered artists engaged in social commentary with rich examples of human action and interaction. The result was, as Christiana Payne has shown, a surge of interest in painting sea and coastline. Resorts and their vicinities became an important focus of attention for major and minor artists, many of whom specialized in coastal views and visited particular resorts on a regular basis to gather material to supply a growing market.[77] Some artists resided (permanently or for a portion of each year) in popular resorts to service this market, such as Anthony Vandyke Copley Fielding (1787–1855), Richard Henry Nibbs (1816–93), W. J. Leathem (fl.1840–55) and W. E. Bates (1812–72) in Brighton and Hove.[78] By the later part of the nineteenth century artists' colonies were emerging in some of the smaller, remoter and more 'untouched' coastal settlements, such as Walberswick in Suffolk and Newlyn and St Ives in Cornwall.[79]

The 1840s saw the arrival of the new visual mode of representation of photography which was custom-built to meet the needs of resorts and their clientele. In Tenby, for example, during the period before the First World War eight different professional photographers have been identified operating out of permanent or seasonal studios. This excludes individual peripatetic photographers and large-scale businesses like that of Francis Frith making an occasional visit to collect material.[80] Worthing and its local area likewise supported a corpus of professional photographers, who from the 1870s were producing single view *cartes de visite*, albums and stereoscopic cards of the resort. In neighbouring Brighton, everything would have been on a grander scale. A directory of 1886 lists thirty-two photographers working in the town.[81] Photography's most immediate and dramatic impact was on portraiture – traditionally the most important

---

[75] Lambourne, *Victorian Painting*, 209–55.
[76] Alain Corbin, *The Lure of the Sea: The Discovery of the Seaside in the Western World* (Cambridge: Cambridge University Press, 1994).
[77] Payne, *Where the Sea Meets the Land*; David Blayney Brown, Sarah Skinner and Ian Warrell, *Coasting: Turner and Bonington on the Shores of the Channel* (Nottingham: Nottingham City Council Museums and Galleries, 2008).
[78] Charles Hemming, *British Painters of the Coast and Sea: A History and Gazetteer* (London: Victor Gollancz, 1988), 109–11.
[79] Joanna Mattingly, *Cornwall and the Coast: Mousehole and Newlyn* (Chichester: Phillimore, 2009), 133–46; David Tovey, *St Ives Art Pre-1890* (Tewkesbury: Wilson, 2008); Tom Cross, *The Shining Sands: Artists in Newlyn and St Ives 1880-1930* (Tiverton: West Country Books, 1994).
[80] Mark Lewis (ed.), *Tenby in Camera: A History of Photography and Tenby Photographers* (Tenby: Tenby Museum and Art Gallery, 2002), 1–11.
[81] Geoffrey Godden, *Collecting Picture Postcards* (Chichester: Phillimore, 1996), 14–20; *Robinson's Popular Brighton Directory* (Brighton: A. M. Robinson and Son, 1886), 500.

sector of the art market. However, landscape was also an object of attention: the medium's capacity to capture and archive accurately the visual experience of the holiday ensured that it would have, over the longer term, played a major role in the 'authentic' representation of landscape as it did in portraiture. The development of less cumbersome and cheaper technologies, in particular dry plates from the 1870s and then roll film and the 'pocket' camera by the very end of the century, increased enormously the potential of photography, both for the professional and the amateur, giving those with little or no skill in drawing, the opportunity to capture an instantaneous image of a selected scene.[82]

The seaside and its surrounding environment provided an obvious target for such attention, but photography was used across the spectrum of touristic spaces. Professional, semi-professional and committed amateur Victorian photographers – such as John Wheeley Gough Gutch (1808–61) in (among other places) the Malverns, the West Country and the Lake District; Benjamin Brecknell Turner (1815–94) in Worcestershire, the South East and Yorkshire; Francis Bedford (1816–94) in Wales, Devon and Warwickshire; Alfred Watkins (1821–1935) in Herefordshire, Worcestershire and the Border country; John Thomas (1838–1905) in Wales; and Francis Frith (1822–98), founder of the largest photographic business in England, throughout Britain, zealously recorded the natural and built environment, with a particular emphasis upon the natural and historic heritage (see Figure 4.2).

They also often included the human inhabitants; and though the 'natives' were usually treated with respect and even admiration for their engagement in traditional crafts, and embodiment of a sort of primitive authenticity uncorrupted by the city, there is no escaping their ornamental role in building the touristic landscape. The rugged and primitive qualities of farm labourers and fishermen seemed to parallel the starkness and antiquity of the physical landscape.[83] Alfred Watkins was an enthusiastic member of the Herefordshire Woolhope Club, and the members of these societies along with those joining the proliferating numbers of photographic clubs – many of them urban based – often felt a duty to record what was perceived as a rapidly vanishing landscape and way of life. This could result in a formal photographic survey, such as that established for Warwickshire in 1890 (by 1896 it possessed over 3,000 prints), which foreshadowed the formation of the National Photographic Record Association in 1897 and the nationwide survey that it oversaw until it was disbanded in 1910.[84]

---

[82] Helmut Gernsheim, *The History of Photography from the Earliest Use of the Camera Obscura in the Eleventh Century up to 1914* (London: Oxford University Press, 1955); I. Jeffrey, 'Photography', in *The Oxford History of Western Art*, ed. Martin Kemp (Oxford: Oxford University Press, 2002), 366–79.

[83] Ian Sumner, *In Search of the Picturesque: The English Photographs of J.W.G. Gutch* (Bristol: Westcliffe Books, 2010); Martin Barnes, *Benjamin Brecknell Turner: Rural England through a Victorian Lens* (London: V&A Publishing, 2001); R. Shoesmith, *Alfred Watkins: A Herefordshire Man* (Little Logaston: Logaston Press, 1990), 87–106; Hilary Woollen and Alistair Crawford, *John Thomas, 1838–1905: Photographer* (Lladysull: Gomer Press, 1977); Martin Barnes, 'Facts and Emotions: A Photographic Survey', in *Recording Britain*, ed. Gill Saunders (London: V&A Publishing, 2011), 106–29.

[84] John Taylor, *A Dream of England: Landscape, Photography and the Tourist's Imagination* (Manchester: Manchester University Press, 1994), 55–60; Barnes, 'Facts and Emotions', 112; Elizabeth Edwards, *The Camera as Historian. Amateur Photographers and Historical Imagination, 1885–1918* (Durham and London: Duke University Press, 2012).

Figure 4.2 John Wheely Gough Gutch, 'View of Tenby from the Croft' (1857). © Getty Images.

One of the guiding lights behind the Warwickshire project was W. Jerome Harrison, a citizen of Coventry and passionate advocate of photography, who from 1881 had spent his summers exploring the Warwickshire countryside by foot, bicycle and railway. In 1907, as part of a complete edition of Shakespeare's works, he published a guide to 'Shakespeare-Land', illustrated with his own photographs. Harrison uses his images of sites associated with the poet and his county (many of decaying timber-framed cottages and houses that seem to have been erected at some vague point in Tudorbethan times) to prove, as John Taylor has argued, 'the continuing existence of the past'.[85]

Photographic views contributed to the same process of constructing an imaginary region in the Broads (see Figure 4.3); in the 1880s Jarrold's was advertising 100 'artistic photographs of the rivers and broads of Norfolk and Suffolk, by Payne Jennings, as seen in the Great Eastern Railway Carriages', available singly or as a bound set at four guineas.[86] By the inter-war years it was implied by some that extensive use of the camera was beginning to de-sensitize the tourist image, S. P. B. Mais asserting in 1928 that 'Clovelly has been overphotographed' (see Figure 4.4).[87]

---

[85] Thomas, *Dream of England*, 79; W. Jerome Harrison, *Shakespeare-Land*, ed. A. Crosby (Warwick: Warwickshire Books, 1995).

[86] G. Christopher Davies, *The Handbook to the Rivers and Broads of Norfolk and Suffolk*, 11th edn (London: Jarrold & Sons, 1888), adverts at rear.

[87] S. P. B. Mais, *Glorious Devon* (London: Great Western Railway Co., 1928), 139.

Figure 4.3 Whitlingham Vale from Postwick, *c.* 1883 from *The Scenery of the Broads and Rivers of Norfolk and Suffolk* (Norwich: Jarrold & Sons, 1883). © Getty Images.

Figure 4.4 'Over-photographed' Clovelly: Clovelly, Harbour and Red Lion Hotel 1930. © The Francis Frith Collection.

The notion of the 'artistic photograph' raises important questions about the relationship between the new medium and traditional forms of art. By the early-twentieth century photographs were being increasingly deployed in guidebooks and topographical literature (the Ward Lock guides appear to have adopted the medium from early on in their production). In terms of shaping the 'tourist gaze' of equal and perhaps greater importance was their use in postcards. Photography, once cards without the pre-paid printed stamp (1894), of a larger size (1899) and with full-sided images (1902) were permitted, greatly added to the appeal of the postcard. Its 'golden age' has been dated 1902-18 and it became the form of tourist communication par excellence, with its ideal combination of the visual image and brief textual message.[88] If the aim was to reproduce an image as faithful as possible to nature – a good Enlightenment goal – then the photographic, once the suitable technologies were in place, should have swept all before it. However, photographs did not force out the handcrafted image on cards, with the prolific Alfred Quinton (1853–1934) producing his popular picturesque views, primarily for the Kent firm of J. R. Salmon, and of course the rise of the comic seaside postcard.[89] Similarly in guide literature the line drawing and painting continued to be widely used, treated as a key selling point of many volumes, with the artist named on the title page and advertising blurb. Clive Holland's *Warwickshire* (1906), for example, is accompanied by thirty-two paintings by the Leamington-born artist Fred Whitehead (1853–1938), who later moved to Dorset and was a friend of Thomas Hardy; A. G. Bradley's *Avon and Shakespeare's Country* (1910) has reproductions of thirty paintings in colour by Alfred Quinton, and Walter Jerrold's *Shakespeare-Land* (1910) twelve colour paintings by Ernest William Haslehurst, all deeply evocative in character and straight out of the Idyllist school (see Figure 4.5). Haslehurst (1866–1949), Slade educated, illustrated thirty-six volumes in the Blackie and Son's series in which Jerrold's volume appeared. Despite its textual content, Henry Thornhill Timmins's *Nooks and Corners of Herefordshire* (1892) was effectively 'a vehicle for his drawings', with almost a hundred monochrome illustrations of romanticized castles, churches, and timber-framed buildings.[90]

One of the principal attractions of the *Highways and Byways* series was the striking monochrome drawings of the illustrator and etcher Frederick Griggs (1876–1938). Living in the arts and crafts centre of Chipping Campden from 1903, he illustrated twelve volumes with evocative images of churches, manor houses, villages, rural scenes, 'which demonstrate his technical virtuosity as well as his visionary talents'.[91] In some cases there was a mixture of mediums; Harper's *Summer Days* included the

---

[88] E. J. Evans and J. Richards, *A Social History of Britain in Postcards 1870–1930* (London: Longman, 1980), 1–5, 125–46.
[89] C. W. Hill, *Picture Postcards* (Princes Risborough: Shire, 1987), 4–14; Godden, *Collecting Picture Postcards*.
[90] Henry Thornill Timmins, *Nooks and Corners of Herefordshire* ([1892] Hereford: Lapridge Publications, 1992), introduction by Peter Latcham.
[91] Justine Hopkins, 'Griggs, Frederick Landseer Maur (1876–1938), Etcher, Illustrator, and Architect', *Oxford Dictionary of National Biography*, 23 Sep. 2004, https://www.oxforddnb.com/view/10.1093/ref:odnb/9780198614128.001.0001/odnb-9780198614128-e-59283, accessed 29 Jul. 2022; Christopher Neve, *Unquiet Landscape: Places and Ideas in Twentieth-Century English Painting* (London: Faber & Faber, 1990), 39–44.

ANNE HATHAWAY'S COTTAGE, STRATFORD-ON-AVON

Figure 4.5 Ernest William Haslehurst, 'Anne Hathaway's Cottage', from Walter Jerrold, *Shakespeare-land* (London: Blackie, 1910). Reproduced by kind permission of the David Wilson Library, University of Leicester.

author's own pen drawings alongside the photographs. Issues relating to the cost of reproduction might play a part here, but perhaps of greater significance was the need to reinforce the prevailing *Zeitgeist* of the genre by avoiding over-dependence on machine as opposed to handmade images and by emphasizing the aesthetic mode of discourse. The need to produce and advertise 'artistic' photographs was in many respects a response to these pressures.

The Jarrold's advert, as well as emphasizing the aesthetic quality of the Broads photographs, also alluded to their display in railway carriages. The place of transport in the development of the touristic landscape is something to be addressed later in this book, but the role of the railway carriage as a mobile gallery shaping travellers' perceptions of the landscape, not to mention the interplay between the image within and the image without as the train sped through the countryside, is an important one. The railway companies soon recognized their power to shape their customers' gaze with guidebooks directed specifically at those occupying their trains.[92] But what they came increasingly to realize was that leisure, and not just industry and commerce, was a lucrative line of business, and that in order to exploit this they needed to promote the idea of tourist destinations, and specifically the landscapes that made these spaces attractive to holidaymakers and travellers. In doing this it is significant that they turned not only to the photographer but also to the artist.[93] From the 1890s, taking advantage of technical developments in colour lithography which reduced its cost, the companies began to produce posters to be displayed both on their own premises and suitable public sites in the towns such as telephone kiosks. All this was supported by growing investment in professional advertising staff and offices and by working with other interested partners. The Great Western Railway (GWR) and London, Midland and Scottish Railway (LMS), for example, co-operated with the council in Bath in the inter-war years, sharing the costs of production, to create a unified image that could be deployed on both the railway poster and the cover of the city's official guide.[94] Early posters were fussy in their presentation, trying to cram in too much detail and too many images, but after the First World War the approach became more sophisticated with imagery that was bolder and more direct. The content varies a good deal with some posters focusing on sports, holidaymakers or just the railways themselves, but representations of landscapes – and landscape as source of pleasure, whether in built or natural form – are a major element. Those employed to produce the posters were among the top commercial artists of the day, and there was a consciousness in the companies of the significance of 'style' and the need for an aesthetic element for the advertising to reach its market and be effective.[95] This meant that although the posters needed to be instantaneously intelligible to the

---

[92] See, for example, G. H. Martin, 'Sir George Samuel Measom and His Railway Guides', in *The Impact of the Railway on Society in Britain: Essays in Honour of Jack Simmons*, ed. A. K. B. Evans and J. V. Gough (Aldershot: Ashgate, 2003), 225–40.

[93] Beverley Cole and Richard Durack, *Happy as a Sand-Boy: Early Railway Posters* (London: HMSO, 1990); eidem, *Railway Posters, 1923–47* (York: Laurence King, 1992); Aldo Delicata and Beverley Cole, *Speed to the West. Great Western Publicity and Posters, 1923–1947* (Harrow Weald: Capital Transport, 2000); Tony Hillman and Beverley Cole, *South for Sunshine* (Harrow Weald: Capital Transport, 1999).

[94] Borsay, *Image of Georgian Bath*, 221–2.

[95] See especially Cole and Durack, *Railway Posters 1923–47*, 17–21.

public, and much of the imagery produced promoted a ruralist idyll,[96] there was also scope for elements of modernism as well alongside more traditional aesthetics, more so than perhaps would be found in much of the illustrative material that accompanied the general guide and topographical literature. This is a reminder that the touristic landscape was not entirely locked in the past or rural, and particularly in the case of the seaside and coast, the public were willing to celebrate the contemporary and the urban.[97]

In one particular form of visual representation of the landscape the aesthetic might seem to have little part to play, the map. With its emphasis upon observation of the natural world, measurement and evidence-based description, modern cartography dovetailed closely with the Enlightenment project. As such, there would seem little space for artistic licence. The shift from the three-dimensional or bird's-eye perspective that had characterized early modern maps to the flatter two-dimensional image would seem to confirm this more 'scientific' and 'neutral' approach. But maps are no less filtered through the human eye than drawings. What they include and exclude, and what they encourage the observer to see and ignore, is a matter of human decision-making. They are, in other words, icons. For the leisured traveller in early modern England the printed county maps, which begin to appear from the late-sixteenth century, may have provided some sort of guide, but more directly useful were the

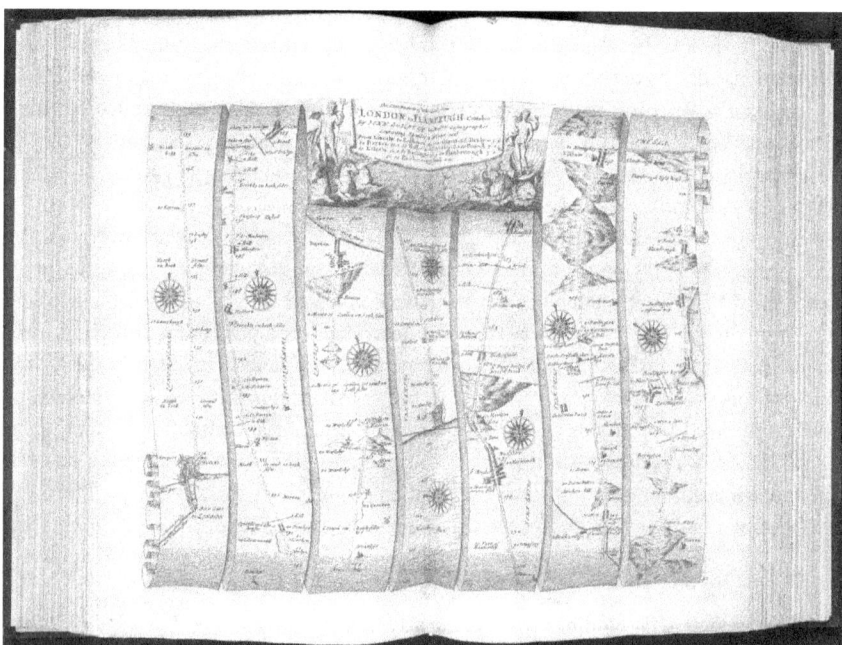

Figure 4.6 Strip map from John Ogilby, *Britannia* (London: John Ogilby, 1675). © British Library Creative Commons.

---

[96] Hemming, *British Landscape Painters*, 112; Rosenthal, *British Landscape Painting*, 164–6.
[97] Lara Feigel and Alexandra Harris (eds.), *Modernism on Sea: Art and Culture at the British Seaside* (Oxford: Peter Lang, 2009).

printed road maps and route planners, notable among which were the strip maps in John Ogilby's *Britannia* (1675) (see Figure 4.6).[98]

Landscape features (such as hills and churches) are shown, but these are presented in largely symbolic forms. How far the maps were much more than a practical tool for travelling is a matter of doubt; there seems little sense of an agenda to create tourist space as such around the road. The case for the towns is stronger, or at least those likely to attract fashionable visitors; during the eighteenth century, a range of overtly tourist maps were produced for London and Bath.[99]

The establishment of the Ordnance Survey (OS) at the end of the eighteenth century was stimulated by the exigencies of war, but the project – to provide a survey and map of the nation, of unprecedented detail and comprehensiveness – opened up the potential for a large-scale mapping of Britain for recreational purposes.[100] It is unlikely that this motive was in the minds of those who established the survey, but for the growing numbers of the public bent upon exploring their native localities and the country at large the individually published sheets of the one-inch scale maps were a godsend. Reductions in price meant that by the 1840s they could no longer be considered luxury purchases, a pricing policy which suggests that the OS itself recognized the potential of the popular market. By 1870, with the first survey completed, 'English and Welsh citizens', in the words of Rachel Hewitt, 'owned a lifelike cartographical mirror of their countries', by which point in time a new survey and series was underway with the first use of colour from 1897.[101] The year 1919 saw the first publication in the Popular Series. This recognized the explosive growth in recreational travel as a consequence of the emergence of new modes of transport (cycle and motor car) and rising real incomes. The new policy to target the recreational market was most strikingly demonstrated by the decision to front the Popular Series with attractive illustrated covers in a way that parallels developments in the railway poster. A talented commercial artist, Ellis Martin, was recruited and, working alongside an existing member of the survey staff, Arthur Palmer, produced a series of appealing covers. These made heavy use of landscape elements, and seem to promise that the map within would provide access to the experience portrayed (both the Chilterns and the Cotswolds depicted rolling hills and hikers, Exmoor a brooding moorland and a huntsman). The titles on several of the illustrated covers – 'New Forest', 'Deeside', 'Lake District', 'Scott's Country', 'Burn's Country', 'Exmoor', 'Dartmoor', 'South Downs', 'Thames', 'Peak District', 'Norfolk Broads', 'Wye Valley', 'Cotswolds', 'Chilterns' – show the extent to which the maps were playing to and reinforcing the notion of imagined regions.[102]

---

[98] Catherine Delano-Smith and Roger Kain, *English Maps: A History* (London: British Library, 1999), 49–111, 142–78.

[99] Peter Barber, *London: A History in Maps* (London: London Topographical Society in association with the British Library, 2012), 86–95; Borsay, *Image of Georgian Bath*, 225–7.

[100] For the origins and history of the OS see Rachel Hewitt, *Map of a Nation: A Biography of the Ordnance Survey* (London: Granta Books, 2010); Nicholas Alfrey, 'Landscape', in *Mapping and Landscape: Essays on Art and Cartography*, ed. Nicholas Alfrey and Stephen Daniels (Nottingham: University Art Gallery, 1990), 23–7; Stephen Daniels, 'Mapping National Identity: The Culture of Cartography with Special Reference to the Ordnance Survey', in *Imagining Nations*, ed. Geoff Cubitt (Manchester: Manchester University Press, 1998), 112–31.

[101] Hewitt, *Map of a Nation*, 296–7, 306.

[102] J. P. Browne, *Map Cover Art: A Pictorial History of Ordnance Survey Cover Illustrations* (Southampton: Ordnance Survey, 1991).

Early OS maps had contained limited information that was of a specifically tourist nature (though details on road systems and landscape relief must have been invaluable). This began to change over time. From the 1880s a key was introduced for the first time and footpaths and bridleways were specifically indicated. Antiquities and archaeology were originally recorded in a rather sporadic and unsystematic fashion. Sheet 14 published in 1817, and covering Wiltshire, was able to contain a good deal of archaeological data because of access to the recent research of Sir Richard Colt Hoare and other local antiquaries,[103] but from 1920 and the appointment of a full-time archaeology officer at the Survey the recording improved in coverage and quality.[104] From the 1920s specialist archaeological and history maps were also published, such as *Neolithic Wessex*, *Roman Britain* (which indicated *municipia* and *coloniae*, towns, villages, villas, fortresses, marching camps, signal stations and roads, and also included inhabited caves, potteries, mining sites and woodland, along with a substantial explanatory text and place name index), and *XVII Century England*.[105] In 1892 Henry Timmins's guide to Herefordshire had referred to 'the indispensable Ordnance map, with whose unfailing aid we steer a course', but by the inter-war years the OS map had acquired a totemic place in any tourist's and rambler's kit. 'The best picture of England ever devised', declared Edmund Vale in 1931, 'is the ordnance map', and four years later S. P. B. Mais exhorted his readers 'to take down your ordnance survey maps of the English counties and stuff your pockets first with them as you stuff your mind full of the English scenery'.[106] It has to be said that the OS's popularization policy was also a reaction to the fact that it was lagging behind private competitors (like Bartholmew),[107] who – sometimes plagiarizing the OS surveys – were producing a plethora of general and specialist maps, including for cycling and motoring, in response to the surge in demand for the means to navigate the recreational landscape. Indeed, few guidebooks by the later nineteenth century were being printed without some sort of map. It was recognized that maps and recreation had become closely bound together and that the cartographic icon played a critical part in what David Matless has called 'the ordering of leisure'.[108]

Production and performance

Representations of the landscape, particularly its natural and historic aspects, were being produced in growing numbers and variety during the nineteenth century, with a particular acceleration in the later part of the century, reaching something of a peak in the inter-war years. These were geared to presenting the landscape as essentially a place of leisure rather than one of work – a location in which to pursue the 'tourist gaze' which they constructed. But what do we mean by constructed? And what impact

[103] Alfrey, 'Landscape', 26.
[104] Richard Oliver, *Ordnance Survey Maps* (London: The Historical Association, 1994), 71–3, 95–7.
[105] Browne, *Map Cover Art*, 52–9, 130–3.
[106] Timmins, *Nooks and Corners of Herefordshire*, 54; Vale, *How to See England*, 1; S. P. B. Mais, *See England First* (London: Richards, 1933), 24.
[107] Browne, *Map Cover Art*, 18.
[108] David Matless, 'The English Outlook', in *Mapping the Landscape*, ed. Alfrey and Daniels, 28.

did the images have on the 'public'? Much of the remainder of the book will be taken up with answering these questions, but at this point we need to consider briefly the key issues of production, reception and performance.

When economic historians have considered the processes of production, attention has inevitably focused on the classic material products of the Industrial Revolution like textiles, ceramics and ironwares. The notion that something as impressionistic and vague as a 'gaze' or 'view', or even the material forms such as books, paintings, photographs and maps that acted as vehicles for these, could be a product is difficult to grasp. Yet they are subject to processes of production, and indeed of industrialization, as much as their more studied counterparts. The raw materials for a product like a 'gaze' are phenomena such as ideas, values and taste, what might broadly be called the intellectual framework. This was constantly in the process of change, with inputs from a wide range of parties (from novelists to geologists), with often conflicting perspectives, such as the controversies over interpretations of the picturesque or evolution. But despite the variety of inputs we should not lose sight of the fact that a transformation did take place in the way the landscape was perceived, and without suggesting that any single gaze was the outcome, there were measures of consensus. Those contributing to the changing intellectual framework often had little obvious commercial interest in the outcome of their deliberations; many (such as the members of the natural history/local history societies) would have been proud of their status as gentleman amateurs, and their disinterested pursuit of the truth. Particularly important in this respect were the landed gentry, or those of independent means; and professionals, especially clergymen, who were disinclined to conceive of their income as a 'wage' derived from labour. In conceiving of the 'gaze' as a product, we are therefore forced to acknowledge that some of the process of production occurred outside the economic nexus normally associated with manufacture. That may account for at least some of the difficulty in transferring new scientific knowledge into the popular guidebooks. Those creating the knowledge had no real sense of, or interest in, a market. However, there can be little doubt that the commercial imperative impinged closely on the intellectual framework, and even more so on the way that it was communicated to the public – not that the message and the medium can be easily separated. Artists, painters and writers of fictional and non-fictional literature often depended upon their labour for their livelihoods; they simply could not afford to be insensitive to the market. That did not necessarily mean 'playing it safe'; there was always scope for innovation and reshaping the nature of the market. But innovators though Turner and Hardy were in representations of the landscape, they had also to be businessmen with an acute eye to what the public wanted or would accept and to the processes of production (or reproduction) and marketing. As we have seen, the OS was an interesting example of an organization creating knowledge with a series of remits (such as servicing military needs), not necessarily of a commercial nature. Nonetheless, the Survey clearly felt under pressure in the early-twentieth century to respond to the market and popularize its product.

Between the public and those who shaped the intellectual framework was the 'industry' responsible for delivering the product. The most obvious example of this would be the publisher, printer and their networks of distribution. They constituted the most immediate interface with the market. Some topographical literature was supported by subscription, a traditional mode of publication for prestigious antiquarian material (such as Francis Drake's 1736 history of York, *Eboracum*) that guaranteed a market prior to publication. Henry Timmins's *Nooks and Corners of Herefordshire* (1892), published by Elliot Stock of London, fell into this category, with interestingly, in terms of the geography of demand, subscribers drawn from predominantly urban locations, including eighteen of the 200 or so listed from Birmingham and Edgbaston alone.[109] But the majority of tourist literature was wholly commercially produced. The organizational and technological changes that allow publishers and printers to expand the volume and character of their output are as remarkable a story, and as much a part of the Industrial Revolution, as say the textile industry. What becomes noticeable by the late-nineteenth century, if not before, is the emergence of a sector within the industry – Black's, Ward Lock, Bartholomew, Jarrold's, Burrow and Batsford spring immediately to mind – that specialized in tourist-type material, whether it be maps, photographs, guidebooks or general travel literature. It was during this period that the guidebook 'series' emerged as a marketing strategy – it had of course been foreshadowed by multi-volume tomes like Britton and Brayley's *Beauties of England and Wales* (1801–15) – proliferating the quantity of material available. The surging demand for 'copy' also led at this time to the development of specialist writers of guide literature, such as A. G. Bradley, P. H. Ditchfield, C. G. Harper (a 1912 guide of his lists over thirty tourist volumes by him),[110] H. V. Morton, H. J. Massingham (who published over fifty books, the majority with some connection to landscape and travel)[111] and S. P. B. Mais. Some worked effectively in-house for particular publishers. Their output is difficult to quantify effectively because, alongside books, many were also writing a huge amount of articles for newspapers and magazines. To be successful, and to find publishers who would use their services, they had to possess a good nose for the market and develop a literary style that appealed to it. That said, their very skill and success in accessing the market helped to mould and expand it. In some of the more freely composed tourist texts there develops a style of writing, mixing anecdotes, humour, snippets of conversation, factual detail and florid passages that reach an almost mystical intensity, that is highly engaging, and suited in particular to the armchair traveller. The 'market' was of course not a homogeneous one; different writers and publishers would appeal to different sectors within it. Alongside stay-at-home or virtual tourists were real walkers, rail travellers, cyclists and motorists, who could be supplied with their own practically orientated guide. Not all tourists like to be considered tourists. Some writers adopted a critical, and occasionally cynical, tone when addressing the more popular hotspots. It is disconcerting to open the pages of Dixon Scott's guide to *Stratford-on-Avon* to hear him describe the ticket office to Shakespeare's birthplace as

> really a box-office where you book for the whole Stratford entertainment. It is a kind of toll-gate to the town, and the shilling you part with there, like a coin

---

[109] Timmins, *Nooks and Corners of Herefordshire*.
[110] C. G. Harper, *Summer Days in Shakespeare Land* (London: Chapman & Hall, 1912), inside cover.
[111] Edward Abelson (ed.), *A Mirror of England: An Anthology of the Writings of H. J. Massingham (1888–1952)* (Bideford: Green Books, 1988), 195–6.

dropped into a slot, sets in motion an elaborate machine which will enable you later to rotate easily from point to point among the tangle of memorials – finding all the relics popping out, nicely polished and labelled, and all the venerated sites certified and beautifully scrubbed.

However, this would appeal to readers and visitors who like to consider themselves too sophisticated to be taken in by the Shakespeare 'machine'. Significantly, nonetheless, Scott goes on to find 'the real thing'; 'behind the tea-rooms and the relics and the shops … a vivid and lovable life still beats and burns capriciously … There is romance'.[112] Tourists also had values and political views which could vary a good deal. That gave writers on rural affairs, for example, scope to take up different positions in their reading of the countryside, some encouraging change and innovation, others regretting it, some adopting a deeply conservative position, others a more liberal or socialist perspective.

The specialist writers of guide literature were paralleled by the dedicated landscape artists. Some of these were working as illustrators of guide literature, some were working as commercial artists for organizations like the rail companies or the OS, but many were one-man businesses, producing unique images, depending upon exhibitions and galleries to sell their works. Photographers, though many must have worked for publishers, also appear in general to have been small-scale businesses (Frith's office was an obvious exception) interfacing directly with the public through studios and shops. Many of these were located in seaside towns, and this is a reminder that the 'tourist gaze' was not only about representations but also about physical engineering (supported by public and private investment) to create viewing platforms like promenades, piers and walks, to capture the best view of the landscape. That said, the view acquired much of its resonance from the fact that it was readily available on a postcard, poster or in a guidebook.

What did a guidebook, poster or postcard – or for that matter a novel or a painting – do for a tourist? It conveyed information, but it also provided, tacitly or otherwise, a performative framework within which that information could be deployed. Tourism is a form of theatre, and tourists are actors. They invariably follow collectively established routines and codes, whether in dress, speech, travel, dining or forms of recreation such as bathing, walking and sightseeing. How well they perform their roles will have a considerable impact on how successful the experience is. Christopher Davies, in his *Handbook to the Norfolk Broads*, warned his readers to

> bathe only before eight o'clock in the morning, if in sight of other vessels or moored in a frequented part of the river. Ladies are not expected to turn out before eight, but after that time they are entitled to be free from any annoyance. Young men who lounge in a nude state on boats while ladies are passing (and I have known Norwich youths do this) may be saluted with dust shot, or the end of a quant.[113]

---

[112] J. Dixon Scott, *Stratford on Avon with Leamington and Warwick* (London: A. & C. Black, 1923), 6, 39.
[113] Davies, *Handbook to the Rivers and Broads* … 11th edn, xv.

The Ward Lock guide to Oxford advised non-Oxonians (by which was, of course, meant non-university men), as late as *c.* 1950, not to visit during Eights Week and Commemoration, as they would be 'a superfluity at such times'. It warned that it was 'desirable to impress on the visitor, if he wishes to retain his self-respect and the regard of others, that for him New College is New College and not "New"; that Undergraduates are Undergraduates and not "Undergrads"; and, first and last and every time, that "Varsity" is an atrocious solecism'.[114] Etiquette manuals of the inter-war years, framed in specifically gendered terms like Davies's *Handbook*, contain 'travel tips', and advice on 'boarding houses and hotels', 'tipping', 'travelling by train' and 'motoring manners'. In the last of these new norms were being established. One author warns 'the average motorist ... will be aware of the discourtesy to other road users – apart from the danger – in such actions as cutting in, overtaking at corners or bends, in leaving his car where it inconveniences other traffic'.[115] The distinct impression is that it is the 'discourtesy' rather than the 'danger' that matters and that driving a car is not that different from attending a dinner or playing cricket; it is an opportunity to display the qualities of a gentleman. Such indeed might be said for the whole business of being a tourist. Get the performance wrong and the whole investment could be wasted. A. G. Bradley said as much when he mused in 1905 that

> the tourist who rambles mainly in bricks and mortar is about in Hereford, too, by the end of July. He comes by train, stops a night at an hotel, and you will see him inspecting the terracotta front of the town hall with his wife on one arm, an umbrella under the other, and open guide-book in hand. After lunch he will do the cathedral; after tea call a cab and drive around the outskirts of the town, when his attention will be called to the jail, the race-course, the water works and the union; so home and to bed – that is, after dinner, of course. The next day he will proceed to Shrewsbury, Gloucester or Lichfield, and will repeat the process for which there may be much to be said. This concentrated form of touring, however, is not the sort to which England would seem most readily to lend itself, where the country is so rich, and the towns, with a few notable exceptions, so lacking in objects of interest to the intelligent stranger. It is a method, however, that might be highly commended for practical reasons to a town councillor.[116]

The sarcasm, anti-urbanism and snobbishness are clear enough. This form of 'municipal' tourism will only reveal the social flaws of its adherents. The 'town councillor' does have recourse to a guidebook, but it is a matter of choosing the correct one or at least reading the lines from it correctly. Bradley's guidebook, deliberately framed in the form of companionable and meandering journey through the *March and Borderland of Wales*, offers an altogether different style of tourism, more geared to the discerning and superior traveller, but one no less prescriptive about the nature of the performance.

[114] *A New Pictorial Guide to Oxford and District*, 4th edn (London: Ward Lock, 1949), 21–2.
[115] I. Davison, *Etiquette for Women: A Book of Modern Manners and Customs* (London: C. Arthur Pearson, 1928), 78–81; G. R. M. Devereux, *Etiquette for Men* (London: C. Arthur Pearson, 1902), 53–8, 93–102.
[116] A. G. Bradley, *In the March and Borderland of Wales* (London: Constable, 1905), 128.

Reception

The commercialization of the tourist gaze and the representations that underpinned it are clear enough, as is the fact that they also implied a certain type of performance. What is much more difficult to establish is how the tourist actually responded to the images that he or she was fed. Some tourists may simply have ignored the media altogether, put off by its didacticism, choosing to be free spirits. Herbert Tompkins advised those visiting Stratford-on-Avon 'to ramble among the surrounding villages at random, as inclination prompts ... ignore the guide-books and follow where the sweet Warwickshire lanes and bypaths lead you'.[117] However, the fact that this was written in a guidebook and by a professional author who contributed several works to the genre seems ingenuous at the least. Reception is problematic because the general public do not readily leave historical records of precisely how guide material impacted on their behaviour and patterns of perception. Book reviews are one possible means of gauging opinion; publishers were understandably keen to quote favourable elements from them. In 1922 the *Times*, under the heading 'By English Roads', reviewed jointly Charles Harper's *The Great North Road* and *Burrows Guide to Devon and Cornwall*. The review very largely tells us what could be gleaned from the book itself; Harper's text 'proceeds to beguile the traveller with many an anecdote and tale of the road ... [he] is more interested in the road than in the places through which it passes,' Burrows guide 'gives in a condensed form the information needed by the average tourist'.[118] The American man of letters William Dean Howells (1837–1920), in a series of articles that began life in *Harper's Magazine* and were later published as *Certain Delightful English Towns* (1905), wrote that

> I always liked to believe everything that I read in guide-books ... In Chester you can believe not only the blunt Baedeker, with its stern adherence to fact, but anything that anybody tells you; and in my turn I ask the unquestioning faith of the reader when I assure him that he will find nothing so medieval-looking as that street – I think it is called Eastgate Street – with its Rows, or two-story sidewalks, and its timber-gabled shops.[119]

This may all be a little tongue-in-cheek, but the deeper point may be that there is little point in tourists buying and reading guide literature unless they believe its contents and that in the final analysis they depend on such literature to invest the sites they gaze on with any sort of meaning.

Records of tourists using guides, especially in England, are difficult to pin down. One set of diaries does survive for Henry Peerless (1866–1930), a seemingly well-off timber merchant and solid middle-class businessman from Sussex. For Peerless it is clear that a regular annual family holiday represented an important part of his lifestyle,

---

[117] H. W. Tompkins, *Stratford-on-Avon* (London: J. M. Dent & Co., 1904), 54.
[118] 'By English Roads', *Times*, 14 Jun. 1922, 16.
[119] W. D. Howells, *London Films and Certain Delightful English Towns* (London: Harper & Brothers, 1905), 459.

and his diaries record visits to various destinations in Britain and Europe, though predominantly England, between 1891 and 1920. He was not the sort of holidaymaker who stayed chained to his hotel or resort but used these as a base to explore the surrounding area, visiting typical middle-class tourist sites like churches and ruined abbeys, and natural landscape features like rivers, lakes and mountains. The diaries reveal a knowledge of not only where to go, and how to get there, but also of what to see and how to interpret a site. While staying in Ross on Wye, he visited Wilton Bridge, just outside the town, and recalled the story of how one of its arches had to be rebuilt after it was destroyed by Royalists in the Civil War, and while holidaying in Windermere he went on 'the Round of the Langdale ride – 21 miles through such scenery as a southerner never dreams of' and then paid threepence 'to see the Stock Gill Face … a waterfall renowned for its beauty'.[120] Such tourist information could, of course, be picked up by word of mouth after arrival. However, there are tantalizing glimpses of the role played by guide material. On arrival in Malvern in August 1894 'we put the little boy to bed and then go out to reconnoitre … we buy a guide to Malvern' and later in Worcester he 'purchase[s] some views'; when considering a holiday destination in the following year 'Weston-super-Mare, "finely situated on the Somersetshire coast of the Bristol Channel, open to the invigorating breezes of the Atlantic Ocean," … as the advertisement says, finally secures our patronage'; while on a visit to Torquay in 1912 he turned 'into Fleet Street and buy[s] in a stationer's shop, kept by a very angular quaint female, a guide to Torquay and some postcards'; and on a stay in Ross in 1914 he declared himself 'very fond of maps'.[121] In 1909, after prevaricating over whether to take a holiday, in part because of the poor state of business, he took the plunge and obtained a copy of Cook's 'Holiday Tours', at which point his wife 'went to Beal's, East Street [Brighton], and bought me a guide-book to Lynton and Lynmouth'.[122] We can never know to what extent his interaction with the landscape at the North Devon resorts was affected by what he read in the guide, but purchasing it prior to arrival suggests a desire and perhaps a need to obtain a vision of the place in advance if he was going to maximize the benefits of the visit. After a visit to Glen Lyn (the gorge near Lynton) he recorded in his diary that it was 'perhaps the prettiest spot we have ever been to. The guide-book says: "No words can do this paradise justice. Its charms are inexhaustible."'[123] We should remain open-minded, however, about how closely guide material reflected the behaviour and feelings of the tourists, who were usually well aware of the often inflated pretensions of the medium. After visiting the Cow and Calf Rocks on Ilkley Moor, Peerless commented in his diary:

> Whyever these rocks were christened 'Cow and Calf' I am at a loss to understand. Even the guide-book says, "The rocks have not the slightest resemblance to the animals whose name they bear" – and that is a pretty admission for a guide-book to

---

[120] Edward Fenton (ed.), *A Brief Jolly Change: The Diaries of Henry Peerless, 1891–1920* (Charlbury: Day Books, 2003), 67, 177.
[121] Fenton, *Brief Jolly Change*, 13, 17, 20, 168, 174.
[122] Ibid., 127–8.
[123] Ibid., 134.

make, as their general mission in life is to puff up everything, and have you believe that the district they are dealing with is the most charming in the whole world.[124]

As a purchaser of 'dear old *Ally Sloper's Half Holiday*' – the weekly illustrated comic that ran from 1884 to 1923, delineating the 'outrageous picaresque adventures' of its hero in 'a conflation of high and low life', in many ways the model of the anti-tourist – it is unlikely that Peerless would have been dictated to by any guidebook.[125] But Peerless's holiday routines do have a distinctive pattern to them which involve a good deal of educated and earnest engagement with landscape features. And what is beyond dispute is that guide material sold. No amount of market manipulation could have generated the escalating levels of sales experienced across the period without a public eager to consume the product. This is perhaps the strongest evidence that the representations of landscape to be found in such material both reflected and shaped, in some measure, popular perceptions.

---

[124] Ibid., 248.
[125] Peter Bailey, 'Ally Sloper's Half Day Holiday: Comic Art in the 1880s', *History Workshop Journal* 16:1 (1983): 4–31, especially 4, 24.

5

New geographies and topographies

Imagined spaces

The growing volume of texts devoted to creating representations of the landscape was indicative of a rising public demand to treat the environment as a recreational good and redefine it in ways that made sense of its new function. Changing patterns of leisure were therefore leading to a major reconfiguration of the topography and geography of England. It was a process long in the making, as we saw in the earlier chapters, but over the century from about 1840, and particularly from the 1870s, such was the pace of change, it transformed the way that the majority of Englishmen saw their country, or at least parts of it, since it was a highly selective process. In 1934 J. R. A. Hockin opined,

> How much of England is parcelled out, neatly ticketed, into convenient guide-book 'Countries'! The Shakespeare Country, The Thames, The West Country, Hardy's, Constable's, Milton's Countries – the list has no end … This labelling is but a symptom of the modern, ill-regulated, undiscerning but wistful and desperately well-meaning attitude towards the country. … We are in danger of forgetting that the countryside is the background of work, of regarding it solely in terms of leisure and pleasure and prettiness.[1]

What was being created was a variegated recreational map on which some places and spaces were tourist hotspots, subject to intensive treatment, while others were very largely ignored. In some respects the 'black holes' – the places, and places within places (such as the modern parts of a historic town), that were not envisioned, where tourists were not taken to – did as much to define this map as the chosen places. The black holes might indeed form a map of their own. The migrant worker would in all likelihood have a map that tracked potential places of employment, such as industrial centres, which looked very different from the map discussed here, though it would overlap if work within the burgeoning tourist industry was a consideration. There was of course nothing new about the notion of mental maps as such or about different individuals and classes possessing different or multiple maps. What was new was the introduction of a map based on the tourist gaze, which involved the reconfiguring

---

[1] Hockin, *On Foot in Berkshire*, ix–x.

of familiar spaces and places, and a new way of looking, driven by the forces of leisure. Superficially it might seem much the same as one of the old mental maps. The New Forest, the Forest of Dean, and Malvern Chase were historic entities, long discernible on paper maps, and the mental economic and legal maps to which local people operated. In the new tourist maps, these locations remain nominally the same. But infused with the leisure function, they were perceived and mapped in a new sort of way, not necessarily unrelated to prior economic and legal ways – particularly if these could be given a heritage value – but one that treated the area as touristic by emphasizing its historic and/or natural elements. Over time, as these spaces lost much of their traditional economic function and legal status and as they become increasingly recreational spaces, so – as Paul Readman has argued on the New Forest – the new ways of reading their landscapes became the dominant one and their topographies redefined.[2] Arguably what we are seeing is simply a new sort of economic map; only the nature of the work has changed. This is to some degree true. The Forest of Dean no longer produces timber, iron and wood, but a tourist experience. But the critical differences are that this space is not the source of a product but the product itself. Although work has to be undertaken to generate this product it is fundamentally a space devoted to non-work or leisure, and in redefining the topography, imaginative processes of representation are at work which did not operate when the space was an agrarian and industrial site.

The discussion that follows begins by looking at the way that the meaning of generic types of space – grey (urban), green (rural), blue (water) – was redefined under the tourist gaze. Though each is treated separately, it will be seen that there was a close interaction between them. It is clear from the autobiography of the English nature mystic Richard Jefferies, often portrayed as a ruralist, that he drew as much inspiration from the sea as from the countryside. He finishes his account at a spot where the downs meets the sea, the countryside the ocean:

> sometimes I stay on the wet sands as the tide rises, listening to the rush of the lines of foam in layer upon layer; the wash swells and circles about my feet, I lave my hands in it, I lift a little in my hollow palm, I take the life of the sea to me. ... Leaving the shore I walk among the trees ... Beautiful it is, in summer days, to see the wheat wave, and the long grass foam-flecked of flowers yield and return to the wind. ... I have found in the hills another valley grooved in prehistoric times, where, climbing to the top of the hollow, I can see the sea.[3]

Though generic types of spaces are identifiable, one of the key facets of redefining these spaces was the emphasis upon specificity and localization; the tourist did not just go to see a town, forest or seascape in general but a specific town, forest and resort. Tourism is usually associated with exploring unfamiliar lands. But for the vast majority of Englishmen, international recreational travel was either financially unfeasible or at

---

[2] Readman, *Storied Ground*, 154–91.
[3] Richard Jefferies, *The Story of My Heart: My Autobiography* (London: Longmans, 1891), 205.

the margin of their resources and they looked to Britain (which did of course include Wales, Scotland and Ireland) instead. Tourism involved exploring the domestic (though not necessarily familiar) scene, and this stimulated a great adventure in local discovery that in many ways paralleled that underway by Europeans on their own and other continents at the time. Englishmen were exploring and finding out about their native land. This focus on and celebration of the local led to the 'discovery' – though creation would be nearer the truth – of a series of zones, regions, or imagined spaces, sometimes defined by being given invented names (though these usually had some sort of historic dimension), in which landscape was often a key part of their touristic character. These will be examined in the latter part of the chapter.

Town: Grey space

Much of the recreational travel, as we saw in Chapter 1 associated with the Grand Tour and the British tour, was focused on towns, and many of the representations of landscapes produced in the eighteenth century depicted urban scenes. This was in line with the long-held belief, accentuated during the Renaissance and the Enlightenment, that towns were the centres of civilization. They were the places where man demonstrated his powers of reason, order, organization and beauty and by implication used these powers to keep at bay and master the forces of uncultivated nature that lay outside the urban boundaries.[4] There are good grounds for arguing that the appeal of the English town for the eighteenth-century polite tourist was growing. First, under the influence of an 'urban renaissance' the town was becoming an increasingly commodious and attractive location to visit and live in with the development of a range of fashionable leisure facilities and activities such as assemblies, theatre, concerts, libraries, walks, and sports, and growing investment in upmarket accommodation and improvements to the urban environment (from street widening and lighting to water supplies).[5] Such was the impact of these developments that a category of towns emerged – spas and seaside resorts – that catered specifically for the needs of the health and leisure tourist. Second, towns were sites of dynamic commercial and industrial growth, and this was itself an attraction to many educated tourists who found the signs of economic activity – a busy market, a quay bristling with ships' masts or a new industrial process – inherently fascinating. When this is added to the cultural changes afoot, towns became locations to admire and revel in the forces of improvement, progress and modernity. The urban landscape became an object of the tourist gaze either because it housed and facilitated the new economic and cultural processes or because it was in its own right a manifestation of these. In London and Bath, for example, the proliferating classical squares and terraces were considered tourist attractions in themselves, at the cutting edge of architectural development.

---

[4] Peter Borsay, 'Fat Sources and Big Ideas: Society, Enlightenment, and the Town', *Journal of Urban History* 24:5 (1998): 647–52.
[5] Borsay, *English Urban Renaissance*.

This notion of the town as a locus of civilization and modernity, and as a tourist phenomenon because of this, continued in the nineteenth and twentieth centuries. Paul Readman has argued that despite increasing sensitivity to poverty, dirty and disease 'the industrial landscape of Manchester excited more wonder and awe than it did disapprobation' throughout the nineteenth century while its landscape was valued for its association with 'change, progress and national greatness'.[6] London's image as the wonder city of the early modern era was sustained and even strengthened in the Victorian and Edwardian age, bolstered by the explosive growth of Britain and its Empire, attracting visitors to enjoy its dazzling range of cultural and consumer facilities and view its spectacular buildings.[7] Bradshaw's *Handbook* of 1863 pulls no punches: 'The British metropolis, if we include its suburban districts, contains the largest mass of human life, arts, science, wealth, power, and architectural splendour that exists, or, in almost all these particulars that ever has existed in the known annals of mankind.'[8] It was, in short, the capital of the civilized world. Precisely what sights the tourist was expected to take in to reflect this embarrassment of riches becomes clearer in the detail, where the emphasis is on churches, public buildings and structures (like bridges), museums and galleries, gardens, and the West End.[9] Docks and the Arsenal at Woolwich do receive some attention, but, even though London was the largest manufacturing centre in Britain, there is little mention of industry. Baedeker's comment in 1894 probably sums up the situation: 'The manufacturing quarters on the right bank of the Thames, and also the outlying districts to the N. and E. are comparatively uninteresting to strangers.'[10]

In the more purely industrial cites of England, however, tourists were invited to visit industrial plant. Bradshaw (1863) recommended visits to Messrs Elkington, Mason and Co. (electro-plate and silver) and Messrs Gillott and Son (steel pens) in Birmingham. In Manchester 'among the factories, notice Birley's, at Chorlton, and Dewhurst's, in the Adelphi, Salford, with its tall stone chimney, 243 feet high. ...'[11] Thirty years later Baedeker was still recommending Gillott and Son among Birmingham's 'most interesting manufactories' and declared that 'no traveller should quit Manchester without having seen one at least of its great manufactories. A letter of introduction is desirable.'[12] Locally based guides might contain more detail of manufacturing, but far more space was devoted to non-industrial locations like public buildings, churches and charity institutions.[13] During his ten-day Lakes holiday in 1903, Henry Peerless managed to fit in two nights in Liverpool. What impressed him most – although we do not know which guidebook, if any, he was using – were the public facilities: notably St George's Hall, the Walker Art Gallery, the Exchange, the Town Hall, the Custom

---

[6] Readman, *Storied Ground*, 206, 220, 248–9.
[7] Felix Driver, 'Heart of Empire? Landscape, Space and Performance in Imperial London', *Environment and Planning D: Society and Space* 16 (1989): 11–28.
[8] *Bradshaw's Descriptive Railway Handbook* ([1863] Oxford: Old House, 2012), sections 1, 5.
[9] Bradshaw, section 1, 1–23.
[10] K. Baedeker, *Great Britain: A Handbook for Travellers*, 3rd edn (Leipzig: Baedeker, 1894), 5.
[11] Bradshaw, section 3, 20, 38.
[12] Baedeker, *Great Britain*, 256, 335.
[13] *Black's Guide to Warwickshire*, 6th edn (Edinburgh: A. & C. Black, 1881), 9–38.

House and 'some very fine theatres'. Significantly he added, 'like all shipping ports it appears to have a deep lower stratum of squalid poverty', highlighting one of the problems that faced port cities as tourist destinations.[14]

Many of the public buildings in Liverpool, and the ports and industrial towns as a whole, were of recent erection and were a bold statement of the wealth, progress and cultural achievements of Britain's commercial cities and their governing classes. They were also a celebration of modernity. Yet, paradoxically, they were constructed in a historic style. The great town halls and public buildings of early Victorian England – such as those in Liverpool or Birmingham town hall (1832–4) – were generally built in monumental neoclassical or neo-Grecian style. Partly this was because the city fathers got caught up in a fevered cycle of emulation, but it also reflected a desire to tap the Roman and Grecian notions of civic government and virtue. A later shift to Italian Renaissance models only reinforced the notion of civic independence when it drew upon the ideal of the city republic. In this context Manchester's adoption of a full-blown early English gothic style for its spectacular town hall, designed by Alfred Waterhouse, begun in 1867 and opened a decade later, might seem curious and problematic.[15] But by this time the gothic revival was in full flood, infiltrating sacred and secular buildings alike. Developed by architects and theorists like Augustus Pugin and John Ruskin as a reaction to the materialism and degraded lifestyle of the modern industrial city, Victorian gothic provided the ideal camouflage for Manchester's city fathers.[16] It allowed them to assert their prosperity, modernity and status, at the same time as cleansing the city of its image of Mammon by drawing upon the historic, religious and political associations of the gothic style.

Urban modernity was then being refracted through the lens of the past during the Victorian period and beyond. Even factories, warehouses and offices were being constructed to look like a Venetian or Florentine *palazzo*.[17] In these circumstances, with the past exerting such a powerful influence on contemporary design, it is hardly surprising that the genuinely historic building was a target of the tourist gaze in towns. Despite the fact that Defoe in his *Tour* could be so dismissive about antiquities, there were early signs in the eighteenth century that certain towns were being visited for their historic buildings.[18] In the nineteenth century this emerged as a major and growing – in some respects the most important – strand of urban tourism. Paradoxically, given the levels of industrialization and urbanization underway, towns were increasingly being valued as much as repositories of the past as showcases of the present. It was

---

[14] Fenton, *Brief Jolly Change*, 72.
[15] Tristram Hunt, *Building Jerusalem: The Rise and Fall of the Victorian City* (London: Weidenfeld and Nicolson, 2004), 169–92; Brooks, *Gothic Revival*, 233–8, 303–5; Charles Dellheim, *The Face of the Past* (Cambridge: Cambridge University Press, 1982), 131–75.
[16] Phoebe Stanton, *Pugin* (London: Thames & Hudson, 1971), 85–92; Rosemary Hill, *God's Architect: Pugin and the Building of Romantic Britain* (Harmondsworth: Penguin, 2008), 153–9; M. H. Lang, *Designing Utopia: John Ruskin's Urban Vision for Britain and America* (Montreal: Black Rose Books, 1990).
[17] H. R. Hitchcock, *Architecture: Nineteenth and Twentieth Centuries* (Harmondsworth: Penguin, 1958), 327–34.
[18] Rosemary Sweet, *The Writing of Urban Histories in Eighteenth-Century England* (Oxford: Oxford University Press, 1997), 100–41.

not only the medieval cathedral and monastic towns that could be drawn into the net, or the historic county towns, but by the later nineteenth many smaller towns – seemingly left behind by the economic expansion of the period, such as those in the Cotswolds – were being 'discovered' as uniquely preserved landscapes of the past. The development of the old or heritage town will be explored in the following chapter on timescapes. But part of the process involved turning a blind eye to the impact of the present and progress.

In the late medieval period Coventry was one of the most prosperous towns in England, with its woollen textile industry generating the wealth to produce a rich private and public fabric. After its 'glory days' the city underwent a series of economic ups and downs, enough to sustain the importance of the place without obliterating its historic fabric. By the late-nineteenth century, Coventry was entering a period of sustained economic growth and modernization based on engineering and particularly the cycle and motorized vehicle industries.[19] In the accounts of the city in *Collins' County Geographies ... Warwickshire* (1872–4) and *Black's Guide to Warwickshire* (1881), there is little hint of this; rather the emphasis is on the medieval history and landscape. Nor does the pre-modern focus change in later accounts, even while acknowledging the changing economic fortunes of the city. In 1914 W. H. Hutton acknowledged that '[t]here are few towns which at the centre of modern business retain so much of what is ancient' but then almost wholly ignored the 'modern business'. In a similar vein, in *Warwickshire: the Land of Shakespeare*, Clive Holland declared that 'seen from a little distance ... Coventry still possesses a strange old-world charm, and the more modern elements of its present-day life seem to fade away, leaving a picture of elegant spires rising from amid a sea of indistinct and even picturesquely disposed roofs'.[20] Only the bombs of the Luftwaffe would make this vision of Coventry no longer credible.

The tendency of urban tourism to focus on the historic rather than contemporary landscape reflected, to some degree, a rejection of the modern city. This shaded into something more profound, a reaction against city urbanism per se. However, it did not extend to the smaller country and market towns – even in 1901 there were some 641 country and market towns in England with populations of under 10,000 – whose close functional relationship with their surrounding areas meant that they were often presented as an extension of the countryside.[21] Anti-urbanism and pro-ruralism had a long history. At the same time as the civilizing qualities of the city and boorishness of the country were being adumbrated, there was a parallel discourse which highlighted the city's degeneracy and extolled the healthy and honest virtues of the country.[22]

---

[19] *Victoria County History of Warwickshire*, vol. 8, ed. W. B. Stephens (London: Victoria County History, 1969), 151–89.

[20] William Fretton, *Geography of the County of Warwickshire* (London: Collins, 1872-4), 17–21; *Black's Guide to Warwickshire*, 49–69; W. H. Hutton, *Highways and Byways in Shakespeare's Country* (London: Macmillan, 1914), 400; William Andrews and Elsie Lang, *Old English Towns* (London: Werner Laurie, 1931), 126; F. Whitehead and C. Holland, *Warwickshire: The Land of Shakespeare*, 2nd edn (London: A. & C. Black, 1922), 125.

[21] Stephen A. Royle, 'The Development of Small Towns in Britain', in *The Cambridge Urban History of Britain. Vol. III*, ed. Martin Daunton (Cambridge: Cambridge University Press, 2000), 159.

[22] Penelope Corfield, *The Impact of English Towns, 1700–1800* (Oxford: Oxford University Press, 1982), 2–4.

During the early modern period much of the dialogue centred upon London because of its size – already by 1700 it was a metropolis of half a million, and sixteen times the size of its nearest rival Norwich with 30,000 inhabitants – but with urban growth in Georgian and particularly Victorian England, and the development of large industrial cities and conurbations, the debate widened into a broader analysis of town and country in general, with the voices of the urban critics and rural enthusiasts strengthening. By the 1920s town and country were being characterized as two entirely separate worlds. When H. V. Morton stood on the top of Pendle Hill in Lancashire what lay before him were, as he perceived it, entirely contrasting landscapes:

> In the valley of smoke I could see little gasworks, little streets of houses, mills, high stacks, now and then a puff of smoke from the railway … A grim panorama of effort … And the other side of this picture? To the left of me was old Lancashire – old England! This lovely green valley of the Ribble, bounded by the wild fells of Lancashire and the blue moors of Yorkshire, lay comfortably, little field against little field, bridges, white threads that were roads, little white farms, church spires among trees. To the right, industrial England; to the left, rural England.[23]

In truth, however, for the majority of rural tourists it was not so much a matter of rejecting the city as simply wanting to experience something different in their leisure time.

One way in which the town responded to the growing interest in the rural, and countered some of the anti-urban discourse, was by developing its own green agenda. Again, this had a long history with the development of public walks, pleasure gardens and parks initially in London, and later in many provincial towns, from the seventeenth century.[24] From early on these landscape features became one of the key tourist attractions of the town and were commented on by travellers. During the nineteenth century, as the pressure on recreational space grew with the rapid growth in urban population, and as associated concerns about issues of pollution, health, moral well-being and public order mounted, a movement for public (often municipal) parks developed, initiated by the report to parliament presented by the Select Committee on Public Walks in 1833. The resultant spaces and facilities (parks might include, for example, a botanic garden or arboretum) were undoubtedly a tourist attraction – the Royal Victoria Park in Bath, founded as early as 1830 and arguably the first of the new breed of parks, though not a municipal one at this stage, attracted widespread coverage in the spa's guidebooks – but in many of the cities where public parks were established they were directed at the needs of the inhabitants – operating as the 'lungs' of the city – rather than visitors.[25]

---

[23] H. V. Morton, *The Call of England*, 9th edn (London: Methuen, 1932), 140.

[24] Borsay, *English Urban Renaissance*, 162–72, 350–4; Mark Girouard, 'The Georgian Promenade', in *Life in the Georgian Town. Papers Given at the Georgian Group Annual Symposium 1985* (London: The Georgian Group, 1986), 26–53; Mark Girouard, *The English Town* (New Haven and London: Yale University Press, 1990), 145–54.

[25] R. Whalley, 'The Royal Victoria Park', *Bath History* 5 (1994): 147–69; Hazel Conway, *People's Parks: The Development and Design of Victorian Parks in Britain* (Cambridge: Cambridge University Press, 1991); eadem, *Public Parks* (Princes Riseborough: Shire, 1996); Douglas A Reid, 'Praying and Playing', in *Cambridge Urban History of Britain. Vol. III*, ed. Daunton, 762–6.

As we saw in Chapter 1, many of the early formal walks and promenades were laid out on the edge of towns, often taking advantage of the space made available by abandoned walls and fortifications or following the contours of a naturally raised terrace or a river bank. Lined with trees or shrubs, and sometimes part of a garden ensemble, they were ornamental landscape features in their own right. But they also often acted as access points to, or viewing platforms for, the surrounding countryside, sometimes offering a spectacular panoramic perspective, as in the case of the Park Walk (1753) at Shaftesbury with its views over the Vale of Blackmore, and Northern Hay Exeter (pre-Civil War, replanted 1664) of a distant Dartmoor.[26] In this capacity they provided a connection between town and country and offered a deliberate attempt to blur the traditional boundaries that had been drawn between the civilized town and the primitive country. The widespread dismantling of town walls, which had provided a physical and symbolic barrier, in the eighteenth century and the construction of walks on the foundations – as at Dorchester – reinforced this process. The country was no longer seen as threatening but as a positive force to be welcomed into the town. The development in Bath and other resorts of an urban architecture of terrace and crescent, located on elevated urban sites and designed to provide views of the natural world beyond the town, encouraged and facilitated this green agenda. It was to achieve its culmination in the garden city movement in the early-twentieth century.[27]

The formal walks and perambulating culture established in the eighteenth century were by the reign of Victoria beginning to burst out of the town and into the surrounding countryside. Preceded at first by informal strolling in the fields immediately surrounding the town, and by longer-distance riding in horse and carriage, there later emerged – as can be seen in the section on walking in Chapter 8 – a complex network of semi-formal paths that laced around the urban edge and penetrated deep into its penumbra. This reconfiguration of the rural periphery surrounding the town as recreational space for visitors and citizens alike was reinforced by an ever more fundamental remodelling of the interface between town and country. In the medieval and early modern town the general pattern was for the well-off to occupy the central streets and the poor the periphery, sometimes in small suburban extensions. From at least the late-eighteenth century in the provinces, and substantially earlier in London, this social geography began to be reversed, with the rich townsmen seeking to live on the urban edge and their less wealthy fellow citizens congregating in the urban centre. The rise of middle-class suburbia hardly created new touristic landscapes for visitors, but it did represent for those inhabitants who made the journey to the ever-shifting urban edge a sort of recreational space since it usually involved the separation of work and living space.

Where housing remained relatively low density, with villas supporting large private gardens, thoroughfares lined by trees, and with good access to open spaces, the new

---

[26] Peter Borsay, 'The Rise of the Promenade: The Social and Cultural Use of Space in the English Provincial Town', *British Journal for Eighteenth-Century Studies* 9 (1986): 125–40; idem, *English Urban Renaissance*, 352–3.

[27] Helen Meller, *Towns, Plans, and Society in Modern Britain* (Cambridge: Cambridge University Press, 1997), 35–8.

suburbs could be seen as a type of semi-rural world, a fantasy countryside – a process reinforced by the fact that suburban expansion often involved the absorption of once real villages, some of whose character remained (often encouraged by new residents' bucolic aspirations) even after they had been drawn into the urban body. Areas such as these shaded into something even more rural in character but umbilically linked to the town, what might be called deep suburbia. These were satellite developments of spacious up-market architect-designed (often influenced by the arts and craft fashion) residential properties, which might involve the colonization of an adjacent village, heathland or forest. Though distinct from the neighbouring town or city, due to developments in transport they were within close reach of it, and provided prosperous citizens with the environment in which to play at being country lads/squires and lasses/ladies.

Hampstead and Solihull in their earlier manifestations, before they became more fully absorbed into the London and Birmingham metropolises, would be an example as, on a much smaller scale, would Boars Hill, three miles south west of Oxford. Until the late-nineteenth century it was a tiny and isolated hamlet, a part of the predominantly agricultural parish of Wootton. A genteel invasion by dons, painters, and poets – John Masefield moved there in 1917 but left for the Cotswolds in 1933 when apparently he found it too suburban – transformed it into an urban Arcady. Sustained by poetical myth in the form of Matthew Arnold's deeply nostalgic threnodies to rural England, 'The Scholar Gypsy' and 'Thyrsis', it was also home to the curious Jarn Mound, erected in 1929–31 as a viewing platform by another resident, the Oxford archaeologist Sir Arthur Evans.[28] The area was the focal point of much of the early attention of the Oxford Preservation Trust, founded in 1927, which confirmed its green agenda by purchasing property on Boars Hill in the late 1920s to protect the area from possible development and 'secure for the enjoyment of the public the views commemorated' in Arnold's poems.[29] This trend towards deep suburbia was not confined to the great cities; Playden outside Rye and Cusop on the English side of Hay on Wye are also products of it.

Country: Green space

However tenuous, there was a link between the urban park and deep suburbia. They were both part of the town, its green agenda and the appropriation of a version of nature. But beyond the urban edge, and beyond deep suburbia, there was a 'real' countryside. How 'real' this was is of course a matter of debate. One interpretation of

---

[28] *Reaching Back: Aspects of Local History from the Villages of Wootton and Dry Sandford Oxfordshire* (Wootton: Wootton, Dry Sandford and District History Society, 2000), 33–5, 40–2; M. B. Rix, *Boars Hill Oxford* ([1941] Abingdon: the Abbey Press, *c*. 1970); Margaret Aldiss and Patricia Simms (eds.), *A Boars Hill Anthology: Containing a Little History and Many Memories* (Faringdon: Boars Hill Association, 1998); Arthur Evans, *Jarn Mound with Its Panorama and Wild Garden of British Plants* (Oxford: J. Vincent, 1933).

[29] *Oxford Preservation Trust, 3rd Annual Report, 1928–9* (Oxford, 1929), 5. The early activities of the Trust on Boars Hill can be followed in the printed annual reports for 1927–8 and 1928–9 and the manuscript Minute Book of the Trustees and General Meeting (1927–35) located at the Trust's office in Oxford. I am grateful to the Trust for permission to consult these.

real might be a working rural landscape of agriculture. However, there are problems with this. First, it would also have to include industry since quarrying and mining have remained persistent features of the rural environment to the present day, and manufacturing processes continued to take place in the countryside throughout the nineteenth century, even if there was a tendency for these to concentrate in the towns. Second, for a growing majority of the population the working rural landscape could never be a 'real' landscape in the sense that it was for the agricultural worker; the urban worker's perspective was always going to be fundamentally different. For them the real countryside was essentially a recreational one (though many urban workers in the nineteenth century and twentieth century temporarily relocated into the rural environs to participate in the various harvests). The real recreational countryside was then in one sense always an imaginary one, but it was a perceived as a different sort of green space to that in the town.

Agriculture did of course play a crucial part in defining the recreational countryside. In a practical sense it raised critical issues over access, but the sort of agriculture engaged in was also vital in determining the visual appearance and symbolic meaning of the landscape. Three types of broad agricultural regime operated historically in England: arable, pastoral and mixed farming. Because of climatic factors and soil types these regimes can be very roughly mapped on to the basic geological distinction that divides England (and Britain), that between lowlands and highlands/uplands. It was one that early-twentieth-century geographers and archaeologists, such as Halford J. Mackinder (1902), Cyril Sharp (1932), Cyril Fox (1932) Laurence Dudley Stamp (1946) and H. J. Fleure (1951), made much of.[30] The lowlands lay to the east of a line that runs from the mouth of the Tees in the North East to the mouth of the Exe or Weymouth in the South West, the highlands to the west.[31] Because this line is a slanting one, sloping from east to west, it reinforced the other great division in England – perhaps more psychological than geological – that between north and south, with the north falling predominantly in the highland and the south in the lowland zone. In the lowlands arable and mixed farming was possible; in the highlands only pastoral farming was generally feasible. This, together with the obvious physical differences such as the presence of mountains and moorland, created two contrasting types of landscape: the one highly cultivated and domesticated, the other sparse and wild. Though exaggerated, the distinction has a certain force when it comes to types of recreational landscape. For those seeking the more 'civilized' countryside the lowland and southern half of England was likely to deliver the requisite product; for those in pursuit of the 'unspoiled' and primitive countryside the highland and northern half was more conducive. S. P. B. Mais captured this when he wrote how the 'homeliness' of London's countryside 'grips you', whereas the Pennines is 'a land of open moors and deep dales … It is not soft as the South

---

[30] H. J. Mackinder, *Britain and the British Seas* (London: William Heinemann, 1902), 41–62; Cyril Fox, *The Personality of Britain: Its Influence on Inhabitant and Invader in Prehistoric and Early Historic Times* (Cardiff: National Museum of Wales, 1932); Laurence Dudley Stamp, *Britain's Structure and Scenery* (London: Collins, 1946), 5–9; H. J. Fleure, *A Natural History of Man in Britain* (London: Collins, 1951), 1–2.

[31] Joan Thirsk, *The Agrarian History of England and Wales* (Cambridge: Cambridge University Press, 1985), vol. 5 pt.1.

of England. It is at times a little grey and grim and dour, but it is impressive, and it is beautiful.'[32] H. V. Morton claimed that on Dartmoor, 'the green Sahara of England, a wilderness of hills and heather', a man 'drops the mask of his civilization and is humbled and afraid. ... Here are no cosy acres'.[33] This divided profile of England's landscape is reinforced by the fact that historically lowland settlements tended to be nucleated, with a manor house and church (inhabited by a resident gentlemen and clergyman) – the classic picture of an English village – whereas upland settlements were more dispersed, often no more than a hamlet of a few houses and part of a huge parish in which the nearest church and manor house might be miles distant. Tourists then had two types of countryside to explore, the civilized and the primitive. Both appealed to the urban imagination, and choice was to some extent determined by accessibility. Because of its easterly location those living in the huge population centre that was London were more likely to visit the civilized countryside of the lowlands, accessible on a daily excursion basis. But it is arguable that the hectic, compressed and mechanized character of life in the Metropolis, and the divorce from nature, led to a particularly strong yearning for a countryside whose landscape seemed very largely untouched by mankind and moulded by natural forces. In this light it is significant that the first ten national parks established in the wake of the legislation that set up the National Parks Commission in 1949 were all located in the highland zone of England and Wales.[34] The notion that 'the west' was in some way a more primitive and ancient land than the east, one closer to pristine nature, would prove increasingly powerful in the nineteenth and early-twentieth century, not least among artists and writers who were creating the representations of landscape that shaped the public imagination. The idea was strengthened by the inclusion of the Celtic 'nations' of Britain, seen as repositories of a more ancient landscape and of an older British race before invasion. The political implications of this bifurcation of the tourist landscape into civilized and primitive, east and west, core and periphery, are ones we will explore later in the book.

The lowland-highland divide was in many respects more an idea than a reality. In practice there were hills in the east and low-lying land in the west. *Bell's Pocket Guide* to the Chiltern district (1932) could describe – in an area between Luton and Stevenage, scarcely 30 miles from London – 'a delightful out-of-the-way route – no folk, no cars; one remote hamlet succeeds another', 'we have a block of hill country ... which retains a remarkable privacy, and is perhaps the least violated territory of the whole of the Chiltern range'.[35] Moreover, as areas in the highlands of England and Britain experienced some of the highest levels of urbanization and industrialization the notion of an ancient, sparsely populated west, untrammelled by modernity and closer to nature, was difficult to maintain (though the Cornish and the Welsh came close to sustaining the paradox). Close examination of any region or county, in west or east, revealed wide varieties of landscape, some of which could be said to be more or less civilized or primitive. The geographer Laurence Dudley Stamp stressed that neither of the highland/lowland zones

---

[32] Mais, *Round about England*, 137, 161.
[33] Morton, *In Search of England*, 108–9, 111.
[34] Borsay, *Leisure*, 189–90.
[35] Winbolt, *The Chilterns and Thames Valley*, 43–4.

'forms a homogenous whole' and drew up a regional map for Britain, highlighting not only inter- but also intra-regional variations, noting that it was 'important to emphasise the wide differences which are possible from one locality ... to another'.[36] Devon lay in the west, but there was a world of difference between the undulating bosky lanes and chequered fields of the south and east and the wastelands of Dartmoor, Exmoor and the north. As Methuen's *Little Guide* to the county puts it:

> Devon is hilly. ... It is dominated by two lofty and waste tracts of country – Dartmoor ... and Exmoor ... Between these the country is broken up into irregular ranges of hills, very much like a chopping sea suddenly consolidated. As a general rule, excepting the elevated moors, the country is fertile, and merits the name given it of 'The Garden of England'; but this does not apply to the large tract to the N. ... This district is one of clay, cold and unproductive.[37]

Dorset is a county that straddles the highland/lowland divide. Perhaps surprisingly, no mention of this as such is made in the Dorset volume of 'County landscapes' published by Blacks in 1935. The Introduction is explicit about the touristic function of the series: it was hoped the volume would 'prove both interesting and useful to the growing body of English men and women who are turning to the English countryside for recreation after the turmoil of modern town life'.[38] The authors, Geoffrey Clark and W. Harding Thompson, distinguish eight distinct landscape regions to be found in the county; the chalk uplands, the heathlands, the Isle of Purbeck, Portland and the Chesil Beach, West Dorset, Blackmoor Vale, East Dorset and the Rivers. The text is accompanied by a highly illustrated pull-out map that plots these specific landscapes and – through the use of colouring and symbols – helps to identify certain other generic landscape formations, such as 'river valleys', 'woodlands', 'important heights' (i.e. hills) and something intriguingly titled, 'normal country'. Text and map demonstrated the intricate mixture of physical elements that were felt by the authors to make up the natural landscape in Dorset. In a companion volume published in the same year the same authors carried out a similar exercise for Sussex, in this instance compartmentalizing the landscape into the South Down, the Weald, the Sandy Hills, the Forest Range, the Coastal Flats of West Sussex, the Marshes and Levels, and the Rivers.[39] In one sense they were simply revealing what was there. But in another sense they were constructing a picture, highlighting features that could have been viewed in other ways or simply ignored. They were, in other words, creating material for the tourist imagination to work on: 'The Weald is no place for the motorist in search of speedways. On the other hand, there is a wealth of material to be found by those with leisure on a long summer's day, either on foot or by car.'[40]

Several of the landscape types described in the Dorset and Sussex volumes, such as heathland and woodland/forest, shared many of the characteristics of the highland

---

[36] Stamp, *Britain's Structure and Scenery*, 172, 174, 189.
[37] Sabine Baring-Gould, *Devon* (London: Methuen, 1907), 2.
[38] Geoffrey Clark and W. Harding Thompson, *The Dorset Landscape* (London: A. & C. Black, 1935), viii.
[39] Geoffrey Clark and W. Harding Thompson, *The Sussex Landscape* (London: A. & C. Black, 1935).
[40] Clark and Thompson, *Sussex*, 32.

areas. But they also had a rich history and symbolic meaning of their own, which those building representations of the countryside were keen to develop. The history of wooded landscapes is a complicated one, about which misinterpretations and myths abound, as Oliver Rackham and others have demonstrated.[41] No prehistoric 'natural' wildwood survives in England; almost all woods have been man-managed, often intensively, for centuries. As early as the mid-fourteenth century, woodland covered only 10 per cent of England and forests ('an unfenced area where deer were kept') frequently consisted primarily of moorland, heath or fen rather than trees (such as Dartmoor or Sherwood). As a physical form Royal Forests covered less than 3 per cent of England (though forest law operated in larger areas) rather than the third that is sometimes claimed.[42] Such hard realities were not allowed, as Simon Schama has demonstrated at a general level, to obstruct the cultural envisioning of the forest and trees – as sites of age and antiquity, continuity, nature, the primitive, fear, legends, liberty but also royal despotism – developed in art, literature and the like.[43]

The Forest of Arden in north Warwickshire was a heavily wooded area, though never a royal forest. Already by Domesday it contained many clearings and was not continuously wooded, and between the mid-eleventh and mid-fourteenth century 'experienced vigorous colonization' and clearance, so that it 'became no more wooded than the rest of the country'.[44] Nineteenth- and twentieth-century observers and guide writers, though generally acknowledging the decline of the forest by the sixteenth century, were loath to give up on the *idea* of the forest. In 1912 Charles Harper recounted how:

> All the surrounding district north of the Avon was woodland, the great Forest of Arden; ... The travellers who came this way in early Saxon times, and perhaps even later, came to close grips with the true inwardness of things. ... The wild things in the forest menaced them, floods obscured the fords, lawless men no less fierce than the animals which roamed the tangled brakes lurked and slew.[45]

W. H. Hutton could observe of the village of Coughton that:

> It stands at the south-west entrance, as it once was, of the forest of Arden, that woody district, not strictly a forest, which stretched from the Avon over most of North Warwickshire. Warwickshire, one may here interject with the late Mr. Charles Eaton, is the most wooded of shires, and 'a squirrel might leap from tree to tree for nearly the whole length of the county.'[46]

---

[41] Oliver Rackham, *The History of the Countryside* (London: Dent, 1986), 62–247.
[42] Ibid., 64–5, 88, 130,133.
[43] Schama, *Landscape and Memory*, 23–242.
[44] H. C. Darby and I. B. Terrett (eds.), *The Domesday Geography of Medieval England*, 2nd edn (Cambridge: Cambridge University Press, 1971), 296–7; B. K. Roberts, 'A Study of Medieval Colonization in the Forest of Arden in Warwickshire', *Agricultural History Review* 16:2 (1968): 102; Rackham, *History of the Countryside*, 88.
[45] Harper, *Summer Days in Shakespeare Land*, 2.
[46] W. H. Hutton, *Highways and Byways Shakespeare's Country* (London: Macmillan, 1914), 350.

The 'myth of the wide unbroken forest', replete with ancient gnarled trees, was perpetuated by the paintings of Frederick Henry Henshaw, with his 'Forest Glade, Arden, Warwickshire' (1844–5) and 'An Old Oak, Forest of Arden' (1850) (see Figure 5.1).[47] Clive Holland noted that

> anciently the town [Stratford-on-Avon] stood almost on the edge of the Wooland or Woodland district ... At even so late a period as the times of the poet [Shakespeare] Camden speaks of the greater part of the district as thickly wooded, although possessing tracts of pasture and land given over to corn. Probably the immediate neighbourhood very closely resembled the more thickly wooded portions of the New Forest of the present day.[48]

The allusion to Shakespeare's Forest of Arden, and the need to demonstrate its impact, and by implication of its wild nature, on the nation's iconic poet, was a powerful reason for sustaining the longevity and myth of the forest. John Hannett's study *The Forest of*

Figure 5.1 Frederick Henry Henshaw, 'A Forest Glade, Arden' (1844–5), photo by Birmingham Museums Trust.

[47] Della Hooke, *The West Midlands* (London: Collins, 2006), 233.
[48] Holland and Whitehead, *Warwickshire*, 203.

Arden (1894) acknowledged that even in Elizabethan times it was likely that much of the woodland would have disappeared to be replaced by 'covert and champaign'. Nonetheless, he suggested, '[W]e may, without any very large drafts upon imagination, suppose Shakespeare to have studied the originals of many of his most exquisite descriptions of rural scenery; ... the beautifully wooded neighbourhood of Henley-in-Arden, within easy reach of ... Stratford ... would furnish him with an ample store of images.'[49]

Guidebook writers of the later nineteenth and early-twentieth century adopted a similarly imaginative approach, frequently invoking the medieval associations of forests, as when P. H. Ditchfield opened his guide to Berkshire and the Cotswolds (1920) declaring that '[t]here is no forest in England like unto Windsor Forest, none so steeped in romance and legend, in old story of kings and queens and mighty hunters, in love of lords and ladies'.[50] For A. G. Bradley the historical resonances invoked by the wooded lower Wye gorge were even older, more illusive and primitive: 'Looking down the rugged, mossy steeps, under the tangled foliage and through the gnarled and twisted trunks that bear it ... the thought of fauns and satyrs, and all the uncanny shapes with which immemorial fancy loves to people the untamed, untrodden forest, comes up here irresistibly.'[51] Writing for *The Graphic* in 1874 Richard Jefferies described Savernake or Marlborough Forest as 'this wild solitude, utterly separated from civilization'. The forest, set apart from civilization, offered an escape route to another world where, according to *The Open-Air Guide* (c. 1927), '[o]nce inside, the foliage shuts us off from the outer world and we feel that here is being lived a life quite remote from our own'.[52]

The allure of the forest stretched to a keen interest in individual trees that seemed more than simply scientific. The King Charles or Royal Oak and its successors (near Boscobel House in Shropshire), in which Charles II is supposed to have hid after the battle of Worcester in 1651, was long a point of pilgrimage and myth-making, and the Knightwood Oak in the New Forest achieved celebrity status during the Victorian era.[53] At Bowshot Wood, near Wellesbourne in Warwickshire, George Bevan reminded the tourist of the presence of 'the Bowshott oak, a giant of unexceptional proportions'. Charles G. Harper discovered a particularly large and handsome yew tree in the churchyard at Wixford, Warwickshire, 'whose spreading branches, perhaps more symmetrical than those of any other yew of its size in this country, are supported at regular intervals by timber struts, forming a curious and notable site'.[54] Naturalist and scientific societies shared this fascination: the Worcestershire Naturalists' Club were forever arranging excursions to forests and woods in the county and region – such

---

[49] John Hannett, *The Forest of Arden, Its Towns, Villages and Hamlets* (London: Simpkin, Marshall and Co., 1863), 18.
[50] P. H. Ditchfield, *Byways in Berkshire and the Cotswolds* (London: R. Scott, 1920), 3.
[51] A. G. Bradley, *The Wye* (London: A. & C. Black, 1910), 125.
[52] Richard Jefferies, *The Hills and the Vale* (London: Duckworth, 1909), xxii, 30; Edward Hutton, *Highways and Byways in Gloucestershire* (London: Macmillan, 1932), 417; J. R. Ashton and F. A. Stocks, *The Open Air Guide* (Manchester and London: John Heywood Ltd., 1928), 109.
[53] W. W. Watts, *Shropshire: The Geography of the County*, 2nd edn (Shrewsbury: Wilding & Son, 1939), 65; Jerome de Groot, 'The Royal Oak', https://www.historytoday.com/royal-oak, accessed 6 Feb. 2020; Readman, *Storied Ground*, 176.
[54] Bevan, *Warwickshire*, 118; Harper, *Summer Days in Shakespeare Land*, 160.

as Wyre, Wychwood, Shrawley, Hartelbury, Ockeridge, Charlbury and Doderhill Common (a remnant of the old Forest of Feckenham).[55] On an excursion in May 1864 the Woolhope Club (Herefordshire) walked from Kingsland station to Croft Castle, 'where a Sweet Chestnut was measured 21 feet in girth and one of its boughs 9 feet, and several others 18 & 19 feet. An oak opposite the house 35 feet in girth'.[56] The Worcestershire club had a particular interest in the Sorb Tree or Whitty Pear of Wyre Forest, visiting it on several excursions. Edwin Lees's account after one such visit in 1853 suggests interest in the Sorb was of more than a purely scientific nature:

> [C]ertain is it that the hard fruit of the Sorb Tree had used formerly to be hung up in the foresters' houses as a security 'from the witch', an honest wood-cutter, met with on the present occasion, who admitted a habit of carrying a piece of the common 'Witchen' or mountain ash in his pocket 'to be on the safe side' even in these unromantic times, thought that the Whitty Pear Tree, and especially its fruit, might be *rather stronger* in the way of protection![57]

When 'ruffian hands' destroyed it by fire in 1862, the 'relics that were left of the limbs of the old veteran' were turned into artefacts, including four cups or chalices, two of which were presented as tokens of gratitude to honorary secretaries of the club in 1864 and 1902,[58] its cultural meaning clearly outweighing its botanical value.

In 1856 Edwin Lees prefaced his *Pictures of Nature in the Silurian Region* with the observation that

> I have always been of opinion that Nature may be studied in a holiday fashion; and that pleasure is derivable from the exploration of the woods and fields, whether the object be strictly confined to scientific purposes, or joined with an earnest regard to the mental tinting that makes a picture from each out-of-doors study on every excursional occasion, and 'looks on Nature with a poet's eye'.[59]

Lees's recognition of the recreational potential of the natural landscape, and of its cultural and not just scientific meaning, underpinned representations of the forest. What applied to woodland also operated for other generic types of green scape such as common land, fenland, hills, mountains, heath, moorland, wold and downland. Downland was considered to contain 'the oldest traces of cultivation' and was therefore particularly saturated with the past.[60] Its spirit was captured in 1883 by Richard Jefferies – born on Coate Farm on the outskirts of Swindon but the edge of the Marlborough/Lambourn Downs – in his mystical 'On the Downs' and his autobiographical account of his regular walks as a teenager to Liddington Hill near the Ridgeway, three miles

---

[55] M. M. Jones, *The Lookers-Out of Worcestershire* (Trowbridge: The Worcestershire Naturalists' Club, 1980), 63–8, 139–40, 190, 199.
[56] Herefordshire Record Office (HRO), BH70/2, 26 May 1864.
[57] Jones, *The Lookers-Out*, 71–2.
[58] Ibid., 74; Edwin Lees, *The Botany of Worcestershire* (Worcester: H.W. Lamb, 1867), xci.
[59] Lees, *Pictures of Nature*, vi.
[60] J. A. Scott Watson, *The Farming Year* (London: Longmans, 1943), 36.

from Coate Farm.⁶¹ Jefferies was a guiding spirit for the poet Edward Thomas (1878–1917), who published a biography of Jefferies in 1909, the first chapter of which was titled 'The country of Richard Jefferies'. In the same year Thomas published his own *South Country*, the core of which – and perhaps, by implication, the core landscape of England – were the downs of Kent, Sussex, Surrey, Hampshire, Berkshire, Wiltshire and parts of Somerset. One chapter, based on a summer excursion in Sussex, opens '[f]ar up on the Downs the air of day and night is flavoured by honeysuckle and new hay. It is good to walk, it is good to lie still'.⁶² It was the likes of Thomas and especially Jefferies that inspired Harold Timperley (1890–1964) to compile his *Ridge Way Country* (1935), a series of walks, rich in natural description with a tinge of mysticism, based on a portion of the Ridge Way running across the Berkshire and Wiltshire Downs.⁶³ As the urge to explore these different 'countries' grew, and with it representations of them, many were transformed into places of leisure (and not just work), and in the guidebooks and imaginative literature and art, they became as much symbolic as real spaces.

The worship of mountains is well attested with the rise of the Lake District as a national playground, but there were many smaller groups of hills and individual heights that attracted attention. Edward Hutton – no doubt encouraged by the Wordsworth and Coleridge connections – managed to describe the Quantock Hills in Somerset, despite never reaching more than 1,300 feet, as 'those romantic and beautiful mountains'.⁶⁴ In the view of Walter White, the Breidden Hills, an isolated volcanic group of three peaks that rise above the Severn floodplain and straddle the Welsh/English border, were of only 'moderate elevation'. But, he continued, 'their effect in the landscape is mountainlike…'.⁶⁵ Shropshire was described in the 1930s as 'almost mountainous', the Long Mynd as a 'mountain in character with a Cymric character in its dark heights' and 'a huge, smooth whale without a dorsal fin', and the Wrekin as 'a shape [that] fills the eye and remains in the memory as clearly as Table Mountain'.⁶⁶ In *Hills of the South* (1939), a guide published by the Southern Railway Company, S. P. B. Mais defended the hills from the condescension of north country men who did not realize there were any hills in the south, firstly because 'few North country men' recognize anything under a thousand feet as a hill and secondly because, unlike the hills of the north which are 'bold and striking … the hills of the South country are shy as fawns and lie behind clusters of pines or clumps of beeches … Luckily', he concluded, '[T]here are still at least a thousand … hills within fifty miles of London where no motorist can penetrate and man can be alone with Nature.'⁶⁷ W. D. Hudson, however, took issue with the orthodoxy that pleasure in a prospect was dependent upon a high vantage point, as he reflected on the attractions of the South Downs in Sussex: 'The fact is, once we have

---

⁶¹ Jefferies, *The Hills and the Vale*, 270–9; idem, *Story of My Heart*, 2–8.
⁶² Edward Thomas, *Richard Jefferies; His Life and Work* (Boston: Little, Brown and Co., 1909), 1; idem, *The South Country* (London: J. M. Dent & Co., 1909), 1, 180.
⁶³ Harold W. Timperley, *Ridge Way Country* (London: J. M. Dent & Sons, 1935), for references to Jefferies and Thomas see 33–4, 47, 52, 191–2.
⁶⁴ Edward Hutton, *Highways and Byways in Somerset* (London: Macmillan, 1912), 328.
⁶⁵ Walter White, *All Round the Wrekin* (London: Chapman and Hall, 1860), 45.
⁶⁶ Thomas, *English Landscape*, 114–16; Vale, *How to See England*, 99.
⁶⁷ S. P. B. Mais, *Hills of the South* (London: Southern Railway Company, 1939), 4–5.

got above this world, and have an unobstructed view all round, whether the height above the surrounding countryside be 500 or 5000 feet, then we at once experience all that sense of freedom, triumph, and elation which the mind is capable of.'[68]

The Sinodun Hills and Wittenham Clumps, which overlook the Thames and historic town of Dorchester, are less than 400 feet in height yet exert a huge presence in the landscape, as C. Fox Smith acknowledged in 1931, they were 'not large hills: but there is about them something strangely compelling – something which renders them more imposing in a way than many a twenty-thousand-foot peak in some great mountain range'. Three years later J. R. Hockin declared that

> the [Berkshire] downs, like the Thames, are haunted by the Sinodun Hills ... you will sense a profound and stimulating mystery in the Wittenham Clumps ... And so you come to a mystery as impenetrable as those of Stonehenge or Avebury. Who raised these tremendous ramparts no man knows, and the guesses fill pages of guide-books; ... You must stay silent for a while ... and wonder at the silver splendour of the Thames below and the pageant of hills round the horizon. Perhaps you will come to the conclusion that the secret of Sinodun is poetical rather than archaeological, to be felt not comprehended.[69]

Wittenham Clumps were also a favourite scene for painters such as Paul Nash, who completed the first of many painting and drawings of the Clumps in 1912 (see Figure 5.2).[70] Yet Peter Howard's analysis of the subject matter of a large sample of British landscape paintings suggests that trees became increasingly important during the 'romantic period' 1830–70, whereas 1870–1910, the 'heroic period', saw the rise of the 'dreary landscape' of marsh, field, fen, heath and moorland.[71] It was during the latter of these periods that highly influential literary images of heath and moorland appeared, elemental and rich in symbolic meaning, such as Richard Doddridge Blackmore's *Lorna Doone: A Romance of Exmoor* (1869) – for which it is said the author 'made a prolonged stay on Exmoor, in order to equip himself more perfectly'[72] – Thomas Hardy's depiction of Egdon Heath in *The Return of the Native* (1878) and Conan Doyle's of Dartmoor in the *Hound of the Baskervilles* (1901–2). A new sort of desolate, deeply anti-urban, anti-social sublime was being created that celebrated unpeopled landscapes.[73] In 1912 Edward Hutton could write,

> The loneliness of the Mendips is a real loneliness. A man turns to the sky because he must; he is shut away from the great and fruitful world he knows, the towns,

---

[68] W. H. Hudson, *Nature in Downland* (London: Longmans, Green and Co., 1900), 23.
[69] C. Fox Smith, *The Thames* (London: Methuen, 1931), 5; Hockin, *On Foot in Berkshire*, 51, 61–2.
[70] http://www.nashclumps.org/paintings.html, accessed 9 May 2014.
[71] Peter Howard, *Landscapes: The Artist's Vision* (London and New York: Routledge, 1991), 56–101; for an account of the fens see G. Home, *Through the Chilterns to the Fens* (London: J. M. Dent & Sons, 1925), 148.
[72] F. J. Snell, *A Book of Exmoor* ([1923] Tiverton: Halsgrove, 2002), 53.
[73] Readman, *Storied Ground*, 54–5.

Figure 5.2 Paul Nash, 'The Wood on the Hill' (Wittenham Clumps) (1912). © Ashmolean Museum.

the villages, the plough-lands, and the steadings beneath him, not only by the height, but also by the breadth and flatness of the great plateau which the roads, purposeless for the most part, shepherded by their loose walls of grey stone, traverse so swiftly, anxious only to pass on their endless ways. One is caught as it were in an empty space, a featureless desolation, a solitude that is like no other solitude.[74]

The western peripheries of England were particularly prone to being depicted as wild, lonely and primitive, and by implication as an opportunity to escape from the day-to-day pressures, to be found especially in the cities, of other humans' presence. In 1924 Albert Osborne could write of the 'bare, bleak passes over the summits of naked hills' in the Lake District, 'where nothing indicates that man has ever been, except the road and the great stone circles of the sheepfolds', and of the 'wild and

---

[74] Hutton, *Highways and Byways in Somerset*, 106.

solitary scene' at Land's End in Cornwall, 'bleaker and bleaker grows the way, and finally, where a handful of houses guard the steep, England plunges into the sea'.[75] Four years later S. P. B. Mais intoned of Dartmoor, 'Look where you will, north, south, east, or west, you will see no trace of human habitation … Its inhumanity is more than a little awe-inspiring.'[76]

Water: Blue space

Green space is heavily moulded, over many millennia, by the action of water, and it is hard to conceive of any rural scene that does not include a river, stream, rill or rivulet – not to mention the drains and dykes of the fens – with the attendant depressions, gullies, combes, vales and valleys. In this sense blue space and green space are closely integrated both in the real and imagined landscape. Water features were something that the early landscape gardeners, such as Henry Hoare II at Stourhead or Capability Brown at Croome Court, and artists were always keen to incorporate in their designs and depictions. But blue space needs to be considered as a force of nature in its own right and as a powerful imaginative resource for those engaged in reconfiguring the landscape. As such it was able to draw upon a long tradition of the association between water on the one hand and magic, the sacred and spiritual on the other.[77] Inland water systems, as they increasingly lost much of their economic rationale as arteries of communication, fisheries, and sites of industrial and agricultural production, developed more and more into what were essentially recreational spaces. Paul Readman has shown how in the case of the upper Thames (though not the lower, which may have experienced increased industrialization) there was an 'explosion' in the 'popularity of the landscape' from the 1880s as 'seemingly ever-increasing numbers of people took to the river for their holiday and weekend recreation'.[78] Between 1879 and 1887 lock receipts for pleasure boats on the Thames more than doubled, overtaking those for barges, and the Thames Preservation Act of 1885 defined more clearly the rights of different river users and duties of the Thames Conservancy (founded in 1857), so as to protect the Thames for recreational purposes.[79] The Thames below Reading was described in 1908 as '"the playground of London." All the summer long its bosom is dotted with boats, and the lawns upon its banks are filled with people who have fled from "town" to rest their eyes on green fields and shining stretches of cool running water, so delightful after the heat and glare of London'.[80] Boulter's Lock

---

[75] A. B. Osborne, *Old World England: Impressions of a Stranger* (London: E. Nash & Grayson, 1924), 28, 255.

[76] Mais, *Glorious Devon*, 90.

[77] Sue Owen et al. (eds.), *Rivers and the British Landscape* (Lancaster: Carnegie Publishing, 2005), 137–68; Nick Middleton, *Rivers: A Very Short Introduction* (Oxford: Oxford University Press, 2012), 30–46; Schama, *Landscape and Memory*, 243–382.

[78] Readman, *Storied Ground*, 265.

[79] Simon Wenham, 'The History of Boating on the Thames', 31 Dec. 2018, http://simonwenham.com/history-boating-thames/#_ftn55, accessed 7 Nov. 2019.

[80] J. Finnemore, *Peeps at Many Lands: England*, 2nd edn (London: A. & C. Black, 1912), 18.

north east of Maidenhead, to judge from Edward John Gregory's painting *Boulter's Lock, Sunday Afternoon* (1882–97), was crowded with leisure craft at the weekend. In 1912 it 'was rebuilt in double size ... to cope with the great number of pleasure-boats which pass here, especially on Sundays'.[81] The Arun in Sussex was described by H. V. Morton in 1942 as 'a river which has retired from business and now amuses itself with punts and young men who row boats'.[82] Firms such as Salters Brothers in Oxford developed highly successful businesses based on rowing, pleasure craft and passenger excursions.[83] In this role rivers became the focus of a tourist literature aimed at reshaping their cultural meanings and identities, as elegiac and mythic spaces, often invested with anthropomorphic qualities. In his *Little Guide* to the River Thames, C. Fox Smith could muse that 'it will not, I think, be disputed that a river, perhaps more than any other work of nature, has a definite and distinctive character – one might, indeed, almost call it a personality – of its own'.[84]

Specific guides were published to rivers such as the Thames, Wye, Severn and Avon but also for water-based and wetland landscapes such as the Lake District, Romney Marsh, the Fenlands, the Isle of Ely, the Somerset levels and the Norfolk Broads. The shallow lakes that constitute the Broads had been created (a fact only discovered in the 1950s) from a series of flooded peat diggings that were largely medieval in origin.[85] Though recreational boating on the rivers and lakes of Broadland dates back at least to the late-eighteenth century, it was only in the late-nineteenth century, as Tom Williamson, Brian Moss and David Matless have shown, that a major tourist industry based on the area began to emerge. Thirty-three books on the Broads were received by the British Library between 1880 and 1900: 'surely', reported *Nature* magazine in 1897 'no spot in the British Isles has been so "be-guided" as the Norfolk Broads'. A new landscape of leisure craft, boatyards (there were thirty-seven yards hiring boats by 1891) and picturesque chalets began to materialize.[86] Already by 1892 Arthur Henry Patterson (pen name John Knowlittle, born in the Rows of Yarmouth in 1857) could claim that

> ten years ago a book on Broadland would have needed a lengthy introduction – the likeness of its spreading lagoons, their whereabouts, attractions, and delights would have required treatment in detail to have become intelligible to many who live outside the county ... Now everybody knows them ... In summer crowds of yachting folk, and excursionists by rail, steamer, and road, visit these reed-surrounded, coot-haunted waters.[87]

---

[81] Winbolt, *Chilterns and the Thames Valley*, 269; Edward John Gregory, 'Boulter's Lock, Sunday Afternoon, 1882–97', Lady Lever Art Gallery.
[82] H. V. Morton, *I Saw Two Englands* (London: Methuen, 1942), 121.
[83] Simon Wenham, 'Oxford, the Thames and Leisure: A History of Salter Bros, 1858–2010' (DPhil thesis, University of Oxford, 2013).
[84] Smith, *The Thames*, 1.
[85] David Matless, *In the Nature of Landscape: Cultural Geography on the Norfolk Broads* (Chichester: Wiley Blackwell, 2014), 39–54.
[86] Tom Williamson, *The Norfolk Broads: A Landscape History* (Manchester: Manchester University Press, 1997), 84–91, 154–60; Matless, *Nature of Landscape*, 57–64; Brian Moss, *The Broads: The People's Wetland* (London: HarperCollins, 2001), 174–6.
[87] Patterson quoted in David Clarke, *The Broads in Print* (Norwich: Joy and David Clarke, 2010), 51.

Many of the guidebooks adopted the format of a travel journal, describing a boating holiday. There were good practical reasons for this – it could provide visitors with limited knowledge of the area with an itinerary – but it also played to the metaphor of a journey and often implicitly a journey through life. This is a theme introduced by George Christopher Davies into one of the earliest and most influential guides to the Broads – first published in 1882, by 1899 it had reached twenty-nine editions, and fifty editions by its final appearance in the 1930s[88] – highlighting especially the virtues of rivers over other modes of man-made transport in this symbolic role:

> [I]n a journey through it [the Broads] by rail, you see nothing but its flatness; walk along its roads, you see the dullest side of it; but take to its water-highways, and the glamour of its detail steals over you, if you have aught of the love of nature, the angler or artist in you. One reason may be that the rivers are highways. From them you view things from a different stand-point; along them flows a current of life differing from that of either rail or road: the wind is your servant, sometimes your master; there is an uncertainty in the issue of the day's proceedings, which to an idle holiday-maker is most delightful, and the slowly-moving water is more like a living companion than any other inanimate thing can be.[89]

A similar metaphorical voyage along the Thames lay behind the huge success of Jerome K. Jerome's *Three Men in a Boat* (1889), which despite – or perhaps because of – its humour has an underlying serious message, revealed in the occasional lapse into sentimental reflection:

> I ... crept under the canvas on to the bank. It was a glorious night. The moon had sunk and left the quiet earth alone with the stars. It seemed as if, in the silence and the hush, while we her children slept, they were talking with her, their sister – conversing of mighty mysteries in voices too vast and deep for childish human ears to catch the sound.[90]

In addition to its symbolic meaning, water had been held in the ancient and medieval worlds to have therapeutic qualities, a consequence of the magical or sacred powers with which it was imbued. One impact of this on the landscape was the widespread presence of holy wells and springs.[91] For many ordinary people these would have continued to function in their traditional capacity in the early modern period, but in post-Reformation and Enlightenment England it was difficult for the well-off and educated to continue – at least explicitly – to see these waters effecting cures through divinely mediated influence. As we saw in Chapter 3, a new 'scientific' paradigm of the relationship between water and health emerged based on the chemical composition

---

[88] Clarke, *Broads in Print*, 17.
[89] Davies, *Handbook to the Rivers and Broads*, 18th edn, 17–18.
[90] Jerome K. Jerome, *Three Men in a Boat* (Harmondsworth: Penguin, 1957), 96.
[91] F. Jones, *The Holy Wells of Wales* (Cardiff: University of Wales, 1954); Walsham, *Reformation of the Landscape*, 398–414.

of the waters, and it was this that underpinned the rise and proliferation, especially from the late-seventeenth century, of fashionable spas such as Bath and Tunbridge Wells.[92] The springs, wells and baths that formed the medical infrastructure of the spas were rarely particularly impressive features in themselves, but the places where they were located were frequently highly ruralized, and sometimes hilly and wild. The natural setting became a key selling feature – arguably the key feature – for many spas and something that they exploited in their marketing, services and architecture.[93] The spa towns blazed the trail, shaping demand and providing the model for what was to become the most important of all the recreational and therapeutic forms of blue space, the sea and coast. Blessed with an extensive and accessible coastline, Britain pioneered the notion of the seaside resort.[94] From the early-eighteenth-century ports and fishing villages, especially in the south east of England in close proximity to London, began to re-orientate their economies, and built environments and cultures to service a visitor population bent on engaging with the sea. By 1790 resorts were emerging around virtually the entirety of the English coastline, prompting Horace Walpole to observe, 'one would think that the English were ducks, they are for ever waddling to the waters'.[95] As John Walton has shown resort growth in the first half of the nineteenth century did not proceed in a linear progression but increased rapidly from the 1860s to enjoy a golden age in the late Victorian and Edwardian era when prices of holidaying fell and real incomes grew, and visiting the seaside percolated down the social scale. By 1911 Walton identifies 145 resorts in England and Wales, though one guide of 1900–1 could list 251 'holiday resorts on the coasts of England and Wales'.[96] Of course many visitors to the seaside went for reasons other than simply to interact with Nature. Recuperation and relaxation, voyeurism, sexual flirtation, display and gratification, courting, family interaction, socializing and showing off, gambling, sport, fantasy and fun were among the multiple pleasures to be enjoyed at resorts. But landscape tourism and the consumption of Nature were also a key part of the seaside experience for visitors. Perceived as something to be feared and avoided before the eighteenth century, the sea became the very embodiment of unbridled Nature, even less subject to human control than inland landscapes, a force to embrace and immerse oneself in.[97] Quite apart from bathing and boating, sea and coast provided rich opportunities to engage with Nature by perambulating promenades, beaches and cliffs; by collecting and recording fossils, rocks, shells and flowers; and most striking of all by the apparently

[92] Hembry, *The English Spa*, 79–98; Borsay, 'Health and Leisure Resorts', 775–804; idem, 'Le développement des villes balnéaires dans l'Angleterre géorgienne', in *Les villes Balnéaires d'Europe occidentale du XVIIIe siècle à nos jours*, ed. Yves Pettert-Gentil, A. Lottin and Jean-Pierre Poussin (Paris: PUPS 2008), 13–34.
[93] Peter Borsay, 'Town or Country? British Spas and the Urban-Rural Interface', *Journal of Tourism History* 4:2 (2012): 155–69.
[94] John Walton, *The English Seaside Resort: A Social History, 1750–1914* (Leicester: Leicester University Press, 1983); Borsay, 'Health and Leisure Resorts'; Brodie and Winter, *England's Seaside Resorts*.
[95] J. A. R. Pimlott, *The Englishman's Holiday: A Social History* (London: Faber & Faber, 1947), 35–6.
[96] Walton, *English Seaside Resort*, 59, 66; Anon, *Seaside Watering Places. Being a Guide to Strangers in Search of a Suitable Place in Which to Spend Their Holidays* (London: L. Upcott Gill, 1900–1).
[97] Corbin, *Lure of the Sea*.

simple act of viewing sea and coast, a process which involved the observer in a complex psychological interaction between their own minds, conditioned by literary and visual accounts, and the external landscape.[98]

Frameworks of spaces

Among the most powerful factors in determining the meaning of landscape are the geographical boxes or frames in which it is placed. In 1972 the country writer Aubrey Seymour published an amusing and affectionate account of the farm on the Warwickshire/Worcestershire/Gloucestershire border that he had bought, built up and worked as a young man in the early-twentieth century until he sold out during the agricultural crisis of the inter-war years.[99] The text is shot through with personal anecdote and highly detailed descriptions of fields and wildlife and is accompanied by hand-drawn illustrations. His quirky and evocative map of the farm includes field names like 'Far Nedge', 'Middle Nedge', and 'Little Nedge', and asides such as 'Where bullock got stuck in the mud & broke its leg', and 'Gorsefield where I shot my first woodcock'. Neighbrook Farm was for Seymour a highly personalized and localized space, one defined by his experiences and memories of it; it was a working space but also an imaginative one, perhaps even more so after he had left it. Seymour's account is a reminder that a person and their immediate locality form one way of framing space (the writings of the eighteenth-century curate and naturalist Gilbert White deliver a similar message). The title of Seymour's recollections, *A Square Mile of Old England*, reflects this perspective. Space is personal and local. This is *his* square mile and he will share it with us. But the title of course contains another frame, that of England. This merging of personal and collective, local and national frames is at the heart of the reconfiguring of the landscape during the years 1840 to 1939. The opening up of England and the English countryside as a site for recreational exploration and travel encouraged the turning of what had been highly personal and local – and effectively hidden for the majority – spaces into something accessible to a potentially national audience. It also involved the discovery – for indigenous people and tourists – of new types of local knowledge, particularly relating to the natural world and the past. It was these needs that provided the impetus behind the growth in the study and publication of local natural and human histories, the formation of clubs and societies to facilitate this, and above all the proliferation of guide literature to make all this new and old local knowledge available to a national market. What sort of frames were being constructed in which to deliver this?

One of the most powerful and persistent vehicles for presenting local knowledge was the county or shire. In many respects this was perfectly understandable since these were local units of long historic standing. The word 'county' is of French origin, but all the counties south of the Humber except Rutland were pre-Conquest based on Anglo-Saxon shires, some of which themselves reflected ancient tribal divisions.[100] The importance of

---

[98] Peter Borsay, 'A Room with a View: Visualizing the Seaside, *c*. 1750–1914', *Transactions of the Royal Historical Society* 6th ser., vol. 23 (2013): 175–201.
[99] Aubrey Seymour, *A Square Mile of Old England* (Kineton: Roundwood Press, 1972).
[100] Hey, *Oxford Companion to Local and Family History*, 113–14.

the county as the principal unit of local administration – and in some respects identity – was strengthened in the early modern period by the growing volume of business passed down to it by a central government keen to expand its remit but possessing only limited means to intervene directly in local affairs. This was due not only to the restricted financial resources available to the state but also to resistance from a landowning elite suspicious of central government and reluctant to surrender their local powers. The significance of the county as an administrative and political unit underpinned its broader role as a 'community' in which the local elite recreated and socialized together, notably during the eighteenth century in the county town at events like assize and race week.[101] As interest grew from the late-sixteenth century among the better off in antiquarianism, topography and natural history, county society became one of the key vehicles through which investigation and dissemination were facilitated. The result was that so many of the early publications on local human and natural history were county-based – the first county history was William Lambarde's *A Perambulation of Kent* (1576) – and when societies were established to further studies of local landscapes in the mid-nineteenth century, these also generally conformed to a county frame. Though the lumbering multi-volumed county history may have faltered a little during the Victorian period, the county continued to exert a remarkable influence over the way that notions of the local were framed and transmitted. Geography and history school texts, such as the Collins and the Cambridge University Press *County Geographies*, or the Oxford University Press's *County History* series, published in the late nineteenth and early twentieth centuries, were rigidly organized around county units. That these were considered much more than dry administrative spaces, possessing a certain emotive power, was reflected in the description of Shropshire in the latter series, as having 'always been a genial and desirable home-land, inhabited by a peace-loving and landed population'.[102] When a great national local history of England was established in 1899 under the auspices of *The Victoria History of the Counties of England* its volumes were county-based – a nice example of the merging of local and national frames – as were those of the Royal Commission on Historical Monuments founded in 1906.[103] The county remained a key unit for the production of commercial guides, and it is a practice that continued through the twentieth century with *The Little Guides*, Arthur Mee's popular King's England guides, introduced in the inter-war years (the first volume appeared in 1936), and the two most influential post-war guides, the Shell guides and the Pevsner *Buildings of England* series.

J. D. Newth could claim in 1922 that 'of all the English counties there are few that have not some outstanding feature which serves to disclose the character of the whole; the fens of Lincolnshire, the Sussex downs, the Devon moors, the lakes and fells of

---

[101] Alan Everitt, *The Community of Kent and the Great Rebellion, 1640–60* (Leicester: Leicester University Press, 1966); Andrew Hopper and Jacqueline Eales (eds.), 'Introduction: The Impact of the County Community Hypothesis' in *The County Community in Seventeenth-Century England and Wales* (Hatfield: University of Hertfordshire Press, 2012), 1–13; David Eastwood, *Government and Community in the English Provinces, 1700–1870* (London: Macmillan, 1997), 91–116.

[102] Watts, *Shropshire*, 1.

[103] M. W. Greenslade, 'Introduction: County History', in *English County Histories: A Guide*, ed. C. R. J. Currie and C. P. Lewis (Stroud: Alan Sutton, 1994), 9–25; Jack Simmons, 'The Writing of English County History', in *English County Historians*, ed. Jack Simmons (Wakefield: EP Publishing, 1978), 1–21; Beckett, *Writing Local History*, 15–24, 35–48.

Westmorland'.[104] But much as these counties became defined for touristic purposes in terms of a single landscape feature, all of them possessed more than one physical environment. As *The Little Guide* (1910) to Sussex recorded, 'here is the fine range of the Downs ... Then there is the bright, irregular Weald, with the high forest-clad ridge traversing its centre. Lastly there is the sea-coast, with its brilliant, health-giving watering-places ... and its lines of chalk and sandstone cliff'.[105] For counties in general diversity rather than homogeneity was the typical profile. When Jack Simmons, reviewing the county history tradition in 1978, declared 'the county is itself, in some ways, an unsatisfactory unit. Of the forty historic English counties ... only one, Cornwall, can properly be regarded as a separate physical entity', he was stating the obvious.[106] Why then should the human and natural landscape, particularly the latter, be viewed through a county frame? Very largely it was the power of a political and cultural tradition rooted in a landowning elite and of that tradition's influence over the production of knowledge that accounts for the continuing significance of the county as a way of framing the notion of the local. Crucially it also reflected the willingness of the middle class in the nineteenth and twentieth centuries, in their pursuit of status, to buy into this tradition. P. H. Ditchfield recognized this when directing his *Memorials of Old Gloucestershire* (1911) towards a fictional market of seventeenth-century landed squires rather the real one of twentieth-century professional and business men – 'the importance and dignity of the Shire of Gloucestershire have long demanded that it should be included in this series of the Memorials of the Counties of England. ... We doubt not that the gentlemen of Gloucestershire will be equally eager to possess themselves of such a work'.[107]

If the county constituted a rather uncomfortable, if influential, frame through which to see the landscape, the village and town would appear a more natural fit, particularly in the case of the built environment. We saw earlier how town guides, such as those to resort towns like Bath and Leamington Spa, were a developing genre, and many guides, even if organized around the unit of the county, took the form of a gazetteer, progressing – usually alphabetically – from one town to the next. Some major guide series appear to have eschewed the county format altogether. The *Ward Lock Red Guides* were typically named after a headline town, though sometimes with the suffix 'and district', as in 'Oxford and District'. Perusal of the title page of a Ward Lock 'town' guide reveals that in reality it was directed at a larger geographical unit, so *Cromer* covers 'Cromer, Sheringham, Norwich and North Norfolk', and *Bath*, 'Bath with excursions to Cheddar, Wells, Glastonbury, Bristol, Frome, etc'.[108] These were essentially regional guides, in which the region was determined by proximity to an urban tourist base. There were good practical reasons for this; towns provided precisely the sort of services – comfortable accommodation, shops, entertainments, etc. – that the modern tourist required, and with the arrival of new, more flexible forms of transport, accessing locations some distance from the base was becoming easier. As

---

[104] J. D. Newth, *Gloucestershire* (London: A. & C. Black, 1927), 1.
[105] F. G. Brabant, *Sussex*, 3rd edn (London: Methuen, 1910), 2.
[106] Simmons, 'Writing of English County History', 2.
[107] P. H. Ditchfield (ed.), *Memorials of Old Gloucestershire* (London: George Allen, 1911), vii.
[108] *Pictorial and Descriptive Guide to Cromer*, 10th edn (London: Ward, Lock & Co., 1939); *Pictorial and Descriptive Guide to Bath*, 8th edn (London: Ward, Lock & Co., 1922).

S. P. B. Mais claimed, 'the best thing about Brighton is the ease with which you can get out of it'.[109] But it also reflected the growing power of towns in defining the tourist region and the frames through which the landscape was perceived.

A number of the Ward Lock guides were directed not at a town but a topographically defined feature, such as the 'English Lake District', the 'Thames', the 'Broads', the 'Wye Valley', the 'Cotswolds', the 'Malverns', the 'New Forest' and Dartmoor. In these cases, unlike the county or town, the frame is clearly that determined by the landscape itself. All are part of the historic 'natural' environment, though ones heavily modelled by human intervention. Critically, in a touristic as opposed to working sense – and it is the touristic sense in which the vast majority of the population came to know them – they only came into existence late in the day. The earliest were the Lake District and the Wye Valley, eighteenth-century hotspots of the Romantic Movement. But it was in the nineteenth century, and particularly the latter part of the century, that these landscapes really began to crystallize in the public imagination. It was at this time that the Lake District experienced a new phase of invention, stimulated by the arrival of the influential art critic and public intellectual John Ruskin to live at Brantwood on Coniston Water in 1872 and of Hardwicke Rawnsley, one of the three 'founders' of the National Trust, to take up the post of Vicar of Wray near Hawkshead in 1878.[110] Both were intrepid conservationist campaigners, and it is notable that the Lake District Defence Society was founded in 1883, the same year as the formation of the Dartmoor Preservation Association.[111] Campaigning and pressure groups of this sort were – albeit perhaps unconsciously – vital in reframing the landscape. Newly formed official bodies, charged with a specific remit to protect and foster the recreational functions of their landscapes, also played an important part. From the outset the Malvern Hills Act of 1884 made it clear that one of the responsibilities of the organization established to oversee the hills, the Malvern Hills Conservators, was their protection and development for public leisure, while the Thames Preservation Act of 1885, as we have seen, enshrined the principle that the river should be preserved for public recreation.[112]

The Cotswolds Conservation Board was not established until 2004 to administer the Area of Outstanding National Beauty (ANOB) designated in 1966, but the Cotswolds is an upland region long recognized to have distinctive landscape characteristics.[113] In 1779 Samuel Rudder's *A New History of Gloucestershire* identified it as one of the three environmental divisions of the county: 'under the denomination of the Coteswold, I now include all the high country on the south-east side of the beforementioned range of hills [Cotswold escarpment] which runs through the county. It is a noble champain country ... Within the last forty years, prodigious improvements have been made here'.[114]

---

[109] Mais, *See England First*, 236.
[110] John Walton and Jason Wood, *The Making of a Cultural Landscape: The English Lake District as Tourist Destination, 1750–2010* (Farnham: Ashgate, 2013), 16–17, 43.
[111] Milton, *Discovery of Dartmoor*, 139.
[112] Pamela Hurle, *The Malvern Hills. A Hundred Years of Conservation* (Chichester: Phillimore, 1984), 14–45; F. S. Thacker, *The Thames Highway*, 2 vols. (London: Fred S. Thacker, 1914 and 1920), vol. 1, 252.
[113] For changing perceptions of the Cotswolds see Bingham, *The Cotswolds*, xviii–xxii.
[114] Rudder, *New History of Gloucestershire*, 21.

'Within the last hundred years', confirmed William Rudge in 1803, 'a total change has taken place on these hills. Furze and some dry and scanty blades of grass were all their produce, but now with few exceptions the downs are converted into arable inclosed fields'.[115] The Cotswolds was recognized by contemporaries to be in the vanguard of the 'agricultural revolution'. However, this had little appeal to William Gilpin in his pursuit of the picturesque, as he was forced to traverse the area on his journey to undertake his now famous tour of the Wye gorge in 1770. He was impressed by the view from the Cotswold escarpment across the Severn valley, especially of the Forest of Dean, but was less appreciative of the road (now the A40) that ran across the Cotswold uplands: 'about North-leach the road grows very disagreeable. Nothing appears but downs on each side; and these often divided by stone-walls [the means of enclosure], the most offensive separation of property'.[116] William Cobbett shared these feelings when he passed though the Cotswolds in 1821. After leaving Cirencester on the road for Gloucester he 'came up hill into a country, apparently formerly a down or common, but now divided into large fields by stone walls. Anything so ugly I have never seen before', while he found the road (A40) from Cheltenham to Oxford 'very poor, dull, and uninteresting country'.[117] There is no hint at this stage, or indeed for much of the nineteenth century, in the guide literature of the imagined space that the Cotswolds was to become. Murray's *Handbook for Travellers in Gloucestershire* (1895) notes of the 'Wolds' that 'the general features are pleasing – a succession of hill and valley relieving the landscape, whilst villages, farms and mansion-houses afford an agreeable variety in the route', but there is little to suggest that the location is a *special* place with its own touristic identity. The account however does point to an important economic change that was to lay the foundations for its future role. The late Victorian agricultural depression was forcing a reversion of land use from arable back to sheep pasture so that 'a large area is being restored to its original state'.[118] The scene was set for the Cotswolds' emergence as a place lost in time, an area valued not for its economic progress and modernity but its preservation of an ancient way of life. With an agricultural landscape – not least the stone walls which so upset Gilpin and Cobbett – now an object of growing admiration, it became a destination in its own right rather than a place merely to pass through.

A harbinger of change was William Morris's decision in 1871 to rent the Tudor manor house at Kelmscott in 1871 as a retreat from London.[119] In the mid-1880s a small group of American painters and friends 'discovered' Broadway, situated under the Cotswold escarpment conveniently close to Shakespeareland, and for a number of years established a summer holiday home there, some returning to New York for the winter. Whereas Morris retained his residential and business base in the English metropolis, Ernest Gimson and Sidney Barnsley (joined by his brother Ernest) left London for the hamlet of Ewen near Cirencester in 1893, once the Bloomsbury furniture company of which they were part was disbanded, moving on to Pinbury later – eight years later.

---

[115] Thomas Rudge, *The History of the County of Gloucester*, 2 vols. (Gloucester, 1803), vol. 1, xviii–xix.
[116] William Gilpin, *Observations on the River Wye*, 5th edn (London: A. Strahan, 1800), 6.
[117] William Cobbett, *Rural Rides in the Counties of Surrey, Kent, Sussex etc.* (London: A. Cobbett, 1853), 18, 33.
[118] *A Handbook for Travellers in Gloucestershire*, 4th edn (London: John Murray, 1895), 1–3.
[119] Fiona McCarthy, *William Morris: A Life for Our Time* (London: Faber & Faber, 1994), 311–47.

Charles Ashbee similarly relocated his London-based Guild of Craftsmen (established in 1888) to Chipping Campden.[120] As part of the intricate network that constituted the Arts and Crafts Movement, and in the vanguard of aesthetic taste, figures of this sort – for whom relocation was a journey of discovery – were important in redefining the character of the Cotswolds as a rural area that appeared miraculously to have escaped the impact of industrialization and to have managed to preserve the spirit of traditional English craftsmanship.

However, more influential in this process of geographic remodelling were the Cotswold publicists. In *Harper's New Monthly Magazine* in 1889 Henry James had written that Broadway, where he had joined the set of American aesthetes, 'and much of the land about it are … the perfection of the old English rural tradition'.[121] However, the first writer to have presented the *idea* of the Cotswolds in a concerted fashion seems to have been J. Arthur Gibbs (1867–99), the Eton and Christ Church educated cricketer and writer from a banking family, who settled in the Elizabethan manor house at Ablington near Bibury, where he played the role of the village squire and, in 1898, published *A Cotswold Village*. Combining a sense of deep rural nostalgia with a feeling of discovery akin to that of an African explorer – at one point he calls the indigenous 'labouring classes … a primitive people' – Gibbs's volume set the tone for the travel and guide literature that soon followed.[122] By 1905 Macmillan was able to issue a volume in the 'Highways and Byways' series on *Oxford and the Cotswolds* that boldly asserted the special identity of the area:

> Few natural districts have their frontier more clearly defined. … from whatever side he enters it the traveller who penetrates into the Cotswolds proper is conscious of having passed into a new region. The long stretches of upland, the winding valleys, the clear trout-streams, and the grey venerable hamlets dotted along their banks, the very vegetation, the weather-beaten ashes of the hills, the sheep-downs fragrant with wild thyme and burnet, and the deep rich water-meadows below, with here and there a thick covert of oak and hazel, are all marks of a strange land, marked off by its peculiar genius from the outside everyday world.[123]

Three years later John Hissey during a tour briefly took in 'the Cotswold country – a region of repose and peacefulness', and then in 1910 in what seems a more extensive visit described how, in his

> reliable little motor car … [he] deserted the high road and turned down a lane that led us into the heart of a sequestered and hilly country. … what a delightful

---

[120] Mary Greensted, *Gimson and the Barnsleys* (London: Evans Brothers Ltd., 1980), 67–80; Fiona McCarthy, *The Simple Life: C. R. Ashbee in the Cotswolds* (London: Lund Humphries, 1981); H. A. Evans, *Highways and Byways in Oxford and the Cotswolds* (London: Macmillan, 1908), 187–91; Alan Crawford, *Arts and Crafts Walks in Broadway and Chipping Campden* (Chipping Camden: Guild of Handicraft Trust, 2002), 4–22.

[121] Henry James, 'Our Artists in Europe', *Harper's New Monthly Magazine* 79 (1889): 50.

[122] J. A. Gibbs, *A Cotswold Village, or, Country Life and Pursuits in Gloucestershire* (London: Murray, 1898), 44–5.

[123] Evans, *Oxford and the Cotswolds*, 146.

Columbus-like thrill of pleasure comes over you when you do chance to make an interesting discovery in, to you, an unknown world. ... It was a pleasant land that we passed through, a bit of genuine old England; there, in the very heart of the Cotswolds, we chanced upon many an ancient stone-built home of the Jacobean days.[124]

Many more specialist or general guides were to follow that defined the region and its character; the 1930s was a particularly rich decade, notably with the works of H. J. Massingham (1888–1952), the Westminster School and Queen's College Oxford educated ruralist and country writer, who 'discovered Cotswold by accident'[125] and went on to live there for nearly two years between 1930 and 1932 at Blockley near Chipping Campden.[126] *Wold without End* (1932) is a deeply personal month-by-month account of his year from December 1930 to November 1931 in which he explores what it is 'which gives to Cotswold a place unique in English country'.[127] His emphasis upon the key role played by the limestone geology of the area, 'the bones of the land',[128] led later to *Cotswold Country* (1937), in which he extended his geological determinism to deal with the whole of the oolitic limestone belt from Dorset to Stamford, claiming that 'the rock rules every living thing upon its surface'.[129] Stone – 'the inimitable Cotswold stone' – plays a prominent part in almost all accounts that attempt to distil the essence of the Cotswolds.[130] When J. B. Priestley visited during his English journey of autumn of 1933 he recorded 'the luminous old stone' and reinforced the impression of being able, at a mere turn of the wheel, to enter a mythical country – of which those once offensive limestone walls were now an integral part – where time and space were collapsed: 'you have only to take a turn or two from a main road ... into one of these enchanted little valleys, these misty cups of verdure and grey walls, and you are gone and lost, somewhere at the end of space and dubiously situated in even time, with all four dimensions wrecked behind you'.[131] Did he have in his glove box W. H. Hutton's *By Thames and Cotswold*? 'In the Cotswolds there are certainly many byways. ... One way there is that seems quite outside the common world. It is worth travelling by, for it takes you into a land where the nineteenth century seems not to have begun.'[132]

---

[124] Hissey, *English Holiday*, 339; idem, *The Charm of the Road. England and Wales* (London: Macmillan and Co., 1910), 2, 170–1.
[125] H. J. Massingham, *Wold without End* (London: Cobden-Sanderson, 1932), 13.
[126] Abelson (ed.), *Mirror of England*, 1–10.
[127] Massingham, *Wold without End*, 287.
[128] Ibid.
[129] J. A. Gibbs, *Cotswold Country: A Survey of Limestone England from the Dorset Coast to Lincolnshire* (London: Batsford, 1937), 3.
[130] K. H. Green, *The Cotswolds: An Introduction* (Bristol: Garland Press, 1947), 7; see also Clough Williams-Ellis's account of 'Cotswold Architecture', in *Guide to the Cotswolds*, 2nd edn (London: Ward Lock, 1948), 18–19.
[131] J. B. Priestley, *English Journey* (London: William Heinemann Ltd., 1934), 57–8.
[132] W. H. Hutton, *By Thames and Cotswold: Sketches of the Country*, 2nd edn (Westminster: A. Constable, 1908), 156.

6

Timescapes

When J. B. Priestley visited one of the 'enchanted little valleys' in the Cotswolds, it looked, he said, 'as if it had decided to detach itself from the rest of England about the time of the Civil War'.[1] The notion that landscape allowed special access to a period of time, usually a past period of time, that in William Beach Thomas's phrase 'landscape is history in a picture', was central to its appeal.[2] Imagined regions were like time machines, able to transport the visitors so inclined, and many were, to another age. Paul Readman has written of the 'late Victorian and Edwardian historicisation of the Lake District', and this was indicative of a wider process by which certain landscapes were being invested with past associations.[3] But such associations were rarely just with some vague and indeterminate point in the past; in the case of the Lakes the Viking era was particularly drawn upon. Priestley's reference to 'about the time of the Civil War' reflected not only the particular period in which it was assumed that the Cotswolds, decoupled from the engine of change, was marooned, but for much of the Victorian and Edwardian period also represented the watershed at which the past started to cease being of historic interest for most observers. When in 1910 John E. Morris and Humfrey Jordan published their *Introduction to the Study of Local History and Antiquities* seven of the ten chapters focused exclusively on ancient and medieval Britain; two general chapters on 'Commercial and Industrial England' and 'Domestic England' mixed medieval and early modern content. Only the final chapter, 'Tudor and Stuart and Later England', dealt specifically with the post-medieval era.[4]

This chapter begins by exploring the relationship between landscape, memory and myth. In the following three sections three different types of history, and their relationship to the landscape, will be explored: deep history, pre-history and 'recent' history. The emphasis here is upon the way that landscape was invested with historical meaning between *c.* 1837 and 1940 for the recreational – in the broadest

---

[1] Priestley, *English Journey*, 58.
[2] Beach Thomas, *English Landscape*, 72.
[3] Readman, *Storied Ground*, 131, 135–43.
[4] John E. Morris and Humfrey Jordan, *An Introduction to the Study of Local History and Antiquities* (London: George Routledge and Sons, 1910).

sense – interests in particular of visitors and tourists. One aspect of this was the way certain places became seen as especially historic, locations in which it was possible to breach the membrane of the present, and literally to step back in time. We have seen already that this was often the case with the imagined regions, but in the next section the focus is on what was often a critical element in the tourist package, the old town and village. In the case of the town this is an important point to make, given that elsewhere this book argues that urbanization, and the negative response to it, was probably the single most important factor in reconfiguring the meaning of the landscape and its rise as a recreational resource. Towns were not per se modern or places from which people sought to escape. There were many parts of or whole towns which were defined as historic, and whose landscapes were part of the tourist itinerary. Finally, and to emphasize the point that timescapes were not exclusively about past time, the last section will explore those parts of the urban and rural landscape that were perceived as modern or futuristic and attracted the tourist gaze precisely because they allowed contact with some notion of modernity.

Landscapes of memory and myth; stories and landscape

Landscape, by its very nature, is moulded by past events and is a record of these. Time is built into its very fabric. As W. G. Hoskins wrote in his *Midland England* (1949) for the Batsford Face of England series: 'I am not much interested in surface impressions. The three visible dimensions of a building or a landscape are not enough: they may entrance for the moment but they make no abiding impression on the mind. One needs the fourth dimension of time to give depth to the scene.'[5] Hoskins had a particular conception of time, which treated it as an essentially factual dimension. Yet as suggested in the Introduction there is another way of reading the past in the landscape, not as reality but *representation*. As Simon Schama, writing of the natural landscape (something Hoskins was not primarily concerned with), argues, nature and human perception – far from being separate entities – are indivisible. 'Before it can ever be a repose for the senses, landscape is the work of the mind. Its scenery is built up as much from strata of memory as from layers of rock.'[6] Here the emphasis is upon the landscape as a repository of memory and myth – that is a narrative, generally about the past, whose robustness lies in its internal logic, common acceptance and capacity to address the psychological needs and beliefs of its recipients, rather than empirical verification, to whose modes of analysis it is often immune. 'Truth' or otherwise is not the central issue.

Though guides can contain straightforward empirical data, on topics such as accommodation and travel, one of their key tasks is to invest items of landscape with memory and myth. Central to the operation of myths are narratives, stories and – though the modern discipline would reject this use of the term in this context – histories. The effectiveness of guide literature largely depends on its capacity to re-tell

---

[5] Hoskins, *Midland England*, v.
[6] Schama, *Landscape and Memory*, 6–7.

familiar stories – they rarely invent new stories, not least because the strength of a myth lies in its repetition – and to couple those stories with the physical world to which the tourist's gaze is directed. In their guide to the Thames, published in 1859 and among the first guides to the river, the Halls noted that

> its associations are closely linked with heroic men and glorious achievements. … There is scarcely a mile of its borders which may not give birth to some happy thought in association with its past: … Sites and memorials of famous battles – king with baron, lord with serf, ancient owners of the soil with its invaders, those who warred for despotism or fought for liberty, for feudal rights or freedom.[7]

It is to these sort of *mythical* timescapes that the majority of this chapter will be directed.

Deep history: Geology and natural history

Chapter 4 described the changing intellectual framework that confronted those who lived in Victorian England. Scientific discoveries of a truly paradigm-changing nature were shaking the foundations of how the world was viewed. New knowledge of the earth's geological and natural history was transforming understanding of how the natural landscape and its inhabitants evolved, and in a way that hugely expanded the age of the earth and the period over which change was taken to have occurred. From a traditional scenario in which the earth's entire history had been compressed into a few thousand years, its past would now appear to stretch back millennia, into what may be called 'deep history'. On the face of it, this turned the landscape into a timescape of infinitely greater potential. Moreover, though paradoxically the new thinking emphasized the slowness of change and uniformitarianism (as opposed to catastrophism), nonetheless dramatic changes in the character and occupants of the landscape were being revealed, such as the existence of seas where there was now dry land, of volcanic activity where there was now a placid hillside, and of strange creatures such as dinosaurs. For those who cared to explore it, the landscape now offered a whole new realm of historic possibilities and recreational opportunities.

One such pastime open to the gentleman amateur was observing the hidden structure of the landscape and reflecting on what this meant in terms of the earth's history. This was not any easy pastime to engage in since by its very nature the evidence was largely concealed. But there were two locations where the character of the earth's crust was particularly exposed: quarries and coastal cliffs. Of these two the latter was always going to be the most attractive. Quarries were industrial sites, but the coastline – though by no means free of quarrying and industrial activity – contained long stretches of wild and picturesque scenery with spectacular views. This advantage would be reinforced if nearby was a comfortable seaside resort to act as a base from which to access the cliffs, permitting geology to be added to the range of pastimes open

---

[7] S. C. and A. M. Hall, *The Book of the Thames from Its Rise to Its Fall* (London: James S. Virtue, 1859), 1–2.

to the middle-class male holidaymaker. But mere observation of the earth's strata was unlikely to be satisfying in itself. What was needed was an added recreational element, something that provided an opportunity to make a discovery, and – above all – to acquire an artefact that could be added to one's 'collection'. In this respect certain strata, and the cliffs where these were located, were more attractive than others. In particular it was the fossil-bearing strata – especially the Jurassic – with their evidence of exotic but extinct forms of life that were most appealing.

The collection and study of fossils dates back to the 'Scientific Revolution' of the late-seventeenth century, with fossils forming a part of a gentleman's cabinet of curiosities, but it was from about the 1790s that the practice entered its heroic age and became a pastime that both experts and the middle-class layman could engage in.[8] The epicentre of discovery was the fashionable seaside resort of Lyme Regis in Dorset, which was patronized by many who visited Bath. Here the presence of rich strata of Jurassic rocks allied to highly unstable cliffs provided a constantly replenished supply of fossils to entice the would-be geologist. Already by 1817 an early guide to Lyme could record that 'the eastern Clifts … are celebrated for the number of fossils found in them … Many … have been sent to Bullock's Museum; particularly a large Crocodile, about two years since'.[9] The creature referred to here was almost certainly the ichthyosaur discovered by Mary Anning (1799–1847) in 1811, which was eventually deposited in William Bullock's London Museum of Natural History in Piccadilly. By 1834, when George Roberts published his history of and guide to Lyme, Anning, though only the daughter of a poor cabinet-maker, had become something of a local celebrity through her exploits in recovering and selling fossils.[10] Her inclusion, though still alive, by Roberts among the town's 'worthies' was indicative of how important the fossils had become to Lyme's appeal.[11] For the aspirant scientist Roberts's volume included – alongside accounts of the assembly rooms and walks – H. T. L. De la Beche's geological map of the area, which made reference to the location of elephant and rhinoceros 'remains in gravel' and an extensive 'Geological Notice, with a Description of Our fossils'.[12]

To what extent clambering around cliffs and acquiring fossils was motivated by much more than a simple sense of adventure and a desire to collect souvenirs, whether it led to deeper thinking about the history of the landscape and the origins of life itself, is difficult to tell. But Roberts did remind his readers that 'to gaze on fossil remains without indulging in any consideration of the state of the world at the earliest periods, when these animals had life, and without being carried back to the infancy of creation, would be very unprofitable'.[13] Five years after the publication of Roberts's history there

---

[8] P. J. Whybrow, 'A History of Fossil Collecting and Preparation Techniques', *Curator* 28:1 (1985): 1–26.
[9] *Picture of Lyme-Regis and Environs* (Lyme Regis: Tucker and Toms, 1817), 15.
[10] Patricia Pierce, *Jurassic Mary: Mary Anning and the Primeval Monsters* (Stroud: The History Press, 2014); Deborah Cadbury, *The Dinosaur Hunters: A Story of Scientific Rivalry and the Discovery of the Prehistoric World* (London: Fourth Estate, 2000).
[11] George Roberts, *The History and Antiquities of the Borough of Lyme Regis and Charmouth* (London: Samuel Bagster, 1834), 284–90.
[12] Roberts, *Lyme Regis*, 316–35.
[13] Ibid., 330.

occurred on the cliffs west of Lyme, according to William Conybeare, writing in the *Edinburgh New Philosophical Journal*, 'a convulsion so remarkable, from the extent, magnitude and picturesque change it has produced ... that I cannot conceive that some account of it cannot fail to be acceptable'.[14] Such was the cataclysmic scale of the Great Bindon and Dowlands Landslip of Christmas 1839[15] that it was reported widely in the national press, attracted great numbers of sightseers, and prompted speculation on the forces of nature:

> an immense portion of the top cliffs, consisting of between forty and fifty acres of arable and pasture land, with their crops, together with the common below, sunk to a depth varying from 50 to 200 feet; two of the above tenements being completely buried, whilst the other two are shattered to their very foundations. The scene presents a spectacle not easily described – gigantic rocks having been rent asunder, lofty trees buried beneath the mighty mass, with only their tops visible; large fields with their crops, separated, one part here and another there – immense precipices formed, awful chasms which appear bottomless, the whole of which strike the beholder with terror and amazement and present a striking view of the Almighty power of Him 'who holds the mountains in the scales and the hills in a balance.' The length of cliffs affected by this shock is more than two miles, and perhaps in breadth about one, encompassing about a thousand acres. But perhaps the most remarkable phenomenon of the whole is, that immense and ponderous rocks in front of this scene of action have been forced by the concussion from their beds, where they have reposed for ages, under the bed of the ocean beyond low water mark, and made their appearance in pyramids and different forms – in some places 40 or 50 feet above the sand, and have wonderfully formed a sort of harbour, while the beach adjoining the land remains unmoved. Boats have entered this naturally formed harbour on the eastern side, which is shallow, and found in the middle three fathoms of water. Outside the rocks thus formed, towards the sea, is about five fathoms at high water. Thousands of persons have already been to visit this extraordinary scene. No doubt but it will attract numbers of the nobility and gentry to Lyme Regis.[16]

Later William Buckland and William Conybeare published a richly illustrated account of the event which must have spread its fame even further and attracted more sightseers (see Figure 6.1).[17]

George Roberts also got in on the act, publishing an extensive account of the event and speculating on its causes. By the time this appeared it is clear that the resultant

---

[14] Donald Campbell, *Exploring the Undercliffs: The Axmouth to Lyme Regis National Nature Reserve* (Wareham: Coastal Publishing, 2006), 18–19.
[15] R. W. Gallois, 'The Failure Mechanism of the 1839 Bindon Landslide, Devon, UK: Almost Right First Time', *Geo-Science in South-West England* 12 (2010): 188–97.
[16] 'Supposed Earthquake in Dorsetshire', *The Hull Packet*, 10 Jan. 1840, 4.
[17] William Buckland and William Daniel Conybeare, *Ten Plates Comprising a Plan, Sections, and Views, Representing the Changes Produced on the Coast of East Devon, between Axmouth and Lyme Regis by the Subsidence of the Land and Elevation of the Bottom of the Sea, on the 26th December, 1839, and 3rd of February, 1840* (London: John Murray, 1840).

Figure 6.1 'A view of the landslip from Great Bindon, looking westward to the Sidmouth hills and estuary of the Exe', from W. D. Conybeare and William Buckland, *Ten Plates Comprising a Plan, Sections, and Views, Representing the Changes Produced on the Coast of East Devon, between Axmouth and Lyme Regis* (London: John Murray, 1840). Reproduced by kind permission of the Geological Society of London.

landscape had been turned into a commercial attraction: 'upon entering the farm yard of Dowlands, persons are ready to take charge of horses, and dinners are prepared on reasonable terms at the house, where Lemonade and Soda water can be procured, as well as tea made for parties'. To get full access to the landslip two payments of sixpence were required, but it was money well spent, 'many are breathless and bewildered at the sight'.[18] The landscape observed was of course of recent origin, but the huge chasms opened up by the landslip allowed a view of the earth's interior and must have prompted thoughts about its history.

Pre-history

Because of its underlying geology, Lyme Regis was particularly favoured by tourists seeking to explore the deep past. The same could also be said for the resort of Lynton in North Devon with its spectacular cliffs and the Valley of the Rocks, or the inland spa of Great Malvern with its access to some of the oldest rock formations in Britain

---

[18] George Roberts, *An Account of the Mighty Landslip of Downlands and Bindon* (Lyme: Daniel Dunster, 1840), 6–7.

in the hills that rise steeply above the town.[19] However, not all those who visited geological sites were tourists in the strict sense. An important group were drawn from the gentry and middle class, especially the professions, keen to recover the past of their *local* society. From about the 1840s they were coalescing into clubs and societies, many as we have seen based on counties, to visit sites, collect data, deliver and publish papers, and – perhaps most importantly – to socialize together. Among the first was the Berwickshire Naturalists' Field Club founded in 1831, with many more established in the 1840s and 1850s.[20] They were the work horses of the local past, and though their endeavour was a serious one, and they did much to expand the knowledge base, their study of the landscape was essentially recreational – secondary to their principal jobs. Their interest in the past was remarkably eclectic and to a degree depended on local circumstances. The Woolhope Naturalists' Field Club, founded in 1852, was based at Hereford, drew many of its members from the city (twelve of the original thirty-two members were listed with Hereford addresses), and was in effect the county field society.[21] The club took its name from a hilly geological feature the Woolhope valley of elevation or Dome that rises sharply above the flood plain of the River Wye to the east of Hereford. Earth movements some 250 million years ago created a dome-like feature which subsequent weathering and landslips turned into an enclosed landscape of ridges and valleys.[22] It was made famous by Sir Roderick Murchison (an honorary founder member of the club), who described it as 'a most remarkable example of these phenomena [valleys of elevation] which occur within the Silurian system', a geological phase *c*. 409–39-million-year old that he was responsible for discovering and naming (after an ancient Welsh tribe).[23] The club's very first field visit on 18 May 1852 was to the Dome, and it was subsequently visited on several other occasions (1857, 1861, 1867, 1868, 1876), suggesting that it represented a space with a special significance for members.[24]

The distinctive character of the Dome continued to attract the attention of observers. In 1892 Henry Timmins called it the 'ground classic to the geological mind', and in the early-twentieth century A. G. Bradley described it as 'famous among geologists as a strange Silurian upcast of fantastic formation, and of an obviously strange geological history among the all-prevailing red sandstone of Herefordshire'.[25] The geological

---

[19] Peter Keene and Brian Pearce, *The Valley of the Rocks, Lynton* (Oxford: Thematic Trails, 1993); Hurle, *The Malvern Hills*, 67–98.
[20] Kenneth Hudson, *A Social History of Archaeology* (London: Macmillan, 1981), 15–20; N. Hewitt, 'Encountering Nature: The Tyneside Naturalists' Field Club and the North East, 1846–1900' (M. Res thesis, Northumbria University, 2008).
[21] HRO BH70 (Minutes of the Woolhope Naturalists' Field Club), 1 (1852–9), 13 April 1852; F. C. Morgan, 'An Outline of the History of the Woolhope Club, 1851 to 1951', in *Herefordshire: Its Natural History, Archaeology and History* ([1954] East Ardsley: S. R. Publishing, 1971), 1–9; J. H. Ross, 'Founders of the Woolhope Club', in *A Herefordshire Miscellany: Commemorating 150 Years of the Woolhope Club*, ed. David Whitehead and John Eisel (Hereford: Lapidge Publications, 2000), 17–26.
[22] *Exploring Woolhope Dome* (Worcester: Hereford and Worcestershire Earth Heritage Trust, 2004).
[23] Roderick Murchison, *The Silurian System ... in Two Parts. Part I* (London: John Murray, 1839), 427–37 on the Woolhope Dome, 428; Peter Toghill, *The Geology of Britain* (Marlborough: Airlife, 2006), 65–81.
[24] *TWNFC, 1852–65* (1907) and *TWNFC 1874–6* (1880).
[25] Timmins, *Nooks and Corners of Herefordshire*, 24; Bradley, *The Wye*, 87.

conditions combined to make the Dome a special natural environment that appeared to outsiders as curious, secluded and remote – the product of titanic forces from a deep past – a lost world waiting to be discovered, yet it lay scarcely 4 miles from the centre of Hereford.

Unsurprisingly – given the presence of the Jurassic Coast – an important area of interest, to judge from their transactions, for the Dorset Natural History and Antiquarian Field Club (founded 1875), was geology and fossils, and in particular for its first president, J. C. Mansell-Pleydell (1817–1902), a member of the Geological and Linnean Society. His obituary not only recorded that he 'always held geology in especial favour' but also added more pointedly that he was 'almost the last of the race of country gentlemen of high social position who took any deep interest in geology'.[26] This may be indicative of the fact that geology and the deep past were by this time losing something of their cachet for the county amateur, as professional scientists took more and more control of the subject. The early meetings and field trips of the Woolhope Club appear to have been dominated by geology and natural history, but though these continued to be subjects of interest, by the late-nineteenth century they were joined by extensive coverage of the historic built environment, including archaeological sites. In 1882, for example, visits were made to and/or papers read on 'Credenhill Camp – Magna Castra [Kenchester] – and the Roman stations and towns of Herefordshire', 'the site of the last battle of Caractacus', Roman villas, Ivington Camp, and Arthur's Stone (Dorstone) (see Figure 6.2).

The last (in fact a Neolithic burial chamber) was described as 'one of the most perfect Druidic structures in our Island', though it was acknowledged that it had little to do with the 'the Great Pendragon' since it was constructed more than 500 years before his birth 'at Tintagel about the year, 501'.[27] The romantic character of much of the archaeological interest of the time was brought out in another account of Arthur's Stone of 1892: 'to trace the history of the great cromlech … leads one back into the mists of a prehistoric era, when the mystic rights of the Druids were enacted amidst the silent solitudes of this bleak hill-top'.[28]

The 'archaeological turn' was something experienced by many field societies.[29] The Dorset Field Club itself merged with the Dorset County Museum (f. 1845) to form the Dorset Natural History and Archaeological Society in 1928. The passing of the Ancient Monuments Protection Act and the appointment of General Pitt-Rivers as Inspector of Ancient Monuments in 1882 represented the first attempt to list and preserve sites deemed of national importance and pointed to the growing significance of archaeology and pre-history. Pitt-Rivers was a key figure in pioneering a more scientific and systematic approach to archaeology working on his estates in Cranborne Chase in Dorset. He seems to have influenced the remarkable Heywood Sumner (1853–1940),

---

[26] *Geological Magazine* 9 (1902): 335–6.
[27] G. H. Piper, 'Arthur's Stone, Dorstone', *TWNFC 1881–2* (1882): 175–80.
[28] Timmins, *Nooks and Corners of Herefordshire*, 118.
[29] Hudson, *Social History of Archaeology*, 16; Stuart Piggott, 'The Origins of the English County Archaeological Societies', *Transactions of the Birmingham and Warwickshire Archaeological Society* 86 (1974): 1–15.

Figure 6.2 Members of the Woolhope Naturalists' Field Club viewing Arthur's Stone from *Transactions of the Woolhope Naturalists' Field Club 1881–82* (1882). Reproduced by kind permission of the David Wilson Library, University of Leicester.

who at the age of forty-seven effectively retired from his life as a commercial artist in London (1897) and settled in Bournemouth and then the New Forest, and pursued a life as an amateur topographer and archaeologist, surveying and drawing the ancient earthworks of Cranborne Chase, the New Forest and the Bournemouth District and excavating – largely on a solitary basis – a range of local sites.[30] Undoubtedly Sumner took his work seriously, but in the final analysis it was a recreation – it is unlikely that he made much, if any, money from the publications derived from what was in reality his 'hobby'.

It is difficult to know how far Sumner's passion, or indeed the appetite of those who frequented the county field societies for archaeological timescapes, was shared by the more general tourist. Maps provided one potential way of disseminating knowledge to a wider public. From their origins OS maps identified antiquities, though this depended on visibility, the knowledge available and the predilections of the surveyor involved; moreover the terms that were often deployed to describe sites, such as 'camp', 'tumulus', and 'castle', conveyed little specific information about the date, nature or function of the feature. However, the maps did alert cyclists, motorists, and hikers to the presence and location of antiquities, and from the 1920s – just as the Popular Series kicked in – matters improved with the appointment of a full time OS archaeology officer and the publication of specialist 'period' maps, notably the popular *Map of Roman Britain* (first edition 1923).[31] Guide literature was another way of alerting the public to the pre-history of the landscape. Iconic sites like Stonehenge had long been on the tourist itinerary, but the development of the transport network increased accessibility. Stonehenge – by this point a scheduled monument under the 1882 Act – features as 'an interesting excursion' in the Baedeker guide to Great Britain in 1894. From Salisbury, accessible by rail from the late 1840s, a carriage could be hired, 'there and back', with one horse for 13–15 shillings and two horses 21 shillings; in addition 'excursion-brakes sometimes make the trip in summer, fare 5s'. The account is largely descriptive, falling back on *Chambers Encyclopedia* when it came to interpretation – 'it has been called a temple of the sun, and of serpent-worship, a shrine of Buddha, a planetarium, a gigantic gallows' – adding briefly 'now it is most generally classed as a sepulchral stone-circle, perhaps exceptionally developed under some religious influence, and is referred to the Bronze Age'.[32] Visitor numbers in 1901, when admissions charges were formally instituted, were 3,770 and by the 1920s – it came into public ownership in 1918 – around 20,000.[33] Other monuments, such as the Rollright Stones in Oxfordshire – also a scheduled monument – received only limited attention, described simply as 'the scanty remains of stone circle like Stonehenge'.[34]

The Little Guides of the early-twentieth century, more likely to be consulted by the serious local explorer, have separate introductions on antiquities and more

---

[30] Barry Cunliffe, *Heywood Sumner's Wessex* (Wimborne: Roy Gasson, 1985), 9–13, 73–4, 117–19.
[31] Richard Oliver, *Ordnance Survey Maps: A Concise Guide for Historians* (London: Charles Close Society, 1993), 71–3; Brian Harley, *Ordnance Survey Maps: A Descriptive Manual* (Southampton: Ordnance Survey, 1975), 145–58.
[32] Baedeker, *Great Britain*, 100–1.
[33] Ousby, *Englishman's England*, 98.
[34] Baedeker, *Great Britain*, 186.

extensive accounts. The introduction to the Devon volume, originally compiled by Sabine Baring-Gould (1834–1924), a key figure in the 'creation' of Dartmoor, proudly declares 'excepting Cornwall and Wiltshire, there is probably no county in England so rich in primaeval antiquities as Devonshire, and no part of Devon so rich as Dartmoor'. The account which followed no doubt drew much on the large-scale excavations by the Dartmoor Exploration Committee between 1894 and 1905.[35] Other accounts are less obviously informative. The Herefordshire volume's entry on Arthur's Stone is wholly descriptive, as is the one of the Rollright Stones in the Oxfordshire volume. The latter occupies almost two pages, but – in the absence of any attempt at an archaeological interpretation – half of this is taken up with rehearsing 'the quaint legend' of bewitchment associated with the stones.[36] H. A. Evans's more extensive account in his *Highways and Byways* (1905) Oxfordshire volume of 'the spell-bound circle of the Rowldrich' suggests that the stones 'were all sepulchral in intention' but is largely engaged with the folkloric associations.[37] A similar 'country story' of the ossification of miscreants is recounted of the standing stones at Stanton Drew in the Somerset *Little Guide*, which offered limited analysis by way of 'rational' interpretation other than 'these mystic rings probably had the same origin (whatever that may be) as the more celebrated circle at Avebury'.[38] At this stage the line between archaeology and mythology was still thin with the systematic scientific exploration of sites, and an empirically derived interpretative framework of analysis, still to establish itself. It was a period in which a real Arthur could be believed in, in which it could be claimed that a British hero (Caractacus) took his last stand against the invading Romans at the British Camp on the Malverns (and Edward Elgar could construct a rousing opera around the story line).[39]

Not only were old mythologies harnessed to inject the past into the landscape, but new ones were created, such as that constructed by Alfred Watkins (1855–1935), member of the Woolhope Club (from 1888), intrepid local explorer, enthusiastic photographer, and inventor and passionate advocate of the idea of ley lines. *The Old Straight Track* (1925) finished with a guide to the pastime of 'ley hunting', a form of landscape recreation for which 'field work is essential', as is the use of 'Government Ordnance maps', with the popular editions being 'the most convenient' and 'cheapest'.[40]

---

[35] Baring-Gould, *Devon*, 50–1; Sandy Gerrard, *Book of Dartmoor* (London: Batsford, 1997), 15–17.
[36] G. W. Wade and J. H. Wade, *Herefordshire* (London: Methuen, 1917), 128–9; F. G. Brabant, *Oxfordshire*, 3rd edn (London: Methuen, 1919), 201–3; Jennifer Westwood and Jacqueline Simpson, *The Lore of the Land: A Guide to England's Legends, from Spring-Heeled Jack to the Witches of Warboys* (London: Penguin, 2005), 593, 596.
[37] Evans, *Highways and Byways in Oxford*, 137–40.
[38] G. W. Wade and J. H. Wade, *Somerset*, 7th edn (London: Methuen, 1926), 224–5.
[39] Mark Bowden, *The Malvern Hills: An Ancient Landscape* (London: English Heritage, 2009), 8. The Caractacus story was invented by a nineteenth-century vicar of Great Malvern: see B. S. Smith, *A History of Malvern* (Leicester: Leicester University Press, 1964), 10; Baedeker, *Great Britain*, 188: 'According to tradition, this [Herefordshire Beacon] was the scene of the capture of Caractacus by the Romans in A.D. 75.' Matthew Riley, *Edward Elgar and the Nostalgic Imagination* (Cambridge: Cambridge University Press, 2009), 83, 161–4.
[40] Shoesmith, *Alfred Watkins*, 125–36; Alfred Watkins, *The Old Straight Track: Its Mounds, Beacons, Moats, Sites, and Markstones*, 3rd edn (London: Methuen, 1945), 219–26.

One source of evidence that Watkins deployed to support his theory was 'folk-lore tales' which 'almost always contain some germ of prehistoric fact, mixed with much accumulated imaginings'.[41] The grooved Queen Stone, Huntsham, located in a loop of the Wye near Symonds Yat, may not have attracted the folklore of other standing stones, but it gave Watkins an opportunity to invent some new lore.

In 1933 Watkins gave a talk to a Woodcraft Folk camp, assembled around the stone, looked on by two sacrificial victims ensconced in a wicker cage, constructed according to Watkins' directions, and attached to the stone – an early, if one assumes only partially executed, example of experimental archaeology (see Figure 6.3).[42] The rich heritage of associations between landscape features and folklore, and the late-nineteenth- and early-twentieth-century folklore revival reinforced the notion that objects like standing stones and tumuli could place those who visited them into direct contact with a prehistoric past, however ill-defined and romanticized that might have been.[43]

Figure 6.3 Mr Alfred Watkins addressing a meeting at the Woodcraft Folk Camp at the Queen Stone, Huntsham, 9 August 1933. Herefordshire County Library Service, www.herefordshirehistory.org.uk.

---

[41] Watkins, *Old Straight Track*, 168.
[42] Shoesmith, *Alfred Watkins*, 126–30.
[43] Jacqueline Simpson, *Folklore of the Welsh Border* (Stroud: Tempus, 2003), 17–30; Westwood and Simpson, *Lore of the Land*, passim.

Recent pasts and competing pasts

Many of the camps, tumuli and the like recorded on the OS maps must have been overgrown, damaged or inaccessible. Rights of public access to even the few monuments scheduled under the 1882 act were not guaranteed until 1900.[44] In 1917 the ramparts of Ivington Camp in Herefordshire were reported 'much impaired by quarrying operations', and of the Roman town of *Magnis* at Kenchester it was said 'it is deplorable that that there is practically nothing to be seen of the remains above ground', with most of the finds located in Hereford Museum.[45] Without carefully planned and executed excavations, on-going conservation, accessibility, and some form of display, archaeological sites had limited tourist value. That was why Mortimer Wheeler's excavations at Maiden Castle in Dorset 1934-7, during which the public were invited to visit the site and the press were well briefed, and the work done to reveal and present the Roman baths at Bath – as we shall see – were so important.[46] But these were the exception. In practice it was the more visible, better preserved and accessed remains of the relatively recent past – such as castles, churches and monastic sites, public buildings and houses – that were to prove the most popular timescapes. In understanding how these features in the landscape were valued and interpreted, and how this changed over time, we need to take into account a number of factors: competing pasts, access, architectural fashion, politics, and story-telling.

Not all pasts are equally valued, and how they are valued changes over time. In 1937 Edmund Vale claimed that 'Roman remains have always had a strong appeal to Englishmen',[47] and there is little doubt that the influence of the Renaissance, the Grand Tour and a classical education on elite taste have historically placed Roman archaeology on a pedestal. As we saw in Chapter 2, for much of the early modern period the medieval past and its remains – characterized by its backwardness, barbarism, and distorted and corrupt religious beliefs – were problematic territory for many Britons. By the time Victoria ascended the throne, much of this antipathy had dissipated. Since the mid-eighteenth century, the intellectual and religious stigma attached to the medieval period had begun to be replaced by a growing enthusiasm and passion for it. It was a process which for some at least was to be accentuated by the high church and Catholic revival of the nineteenth century. This opened up a huge touristic resource of military and sacred fabric. Domestic architecture was less well represented – simply because of the problem of survival – but this was compensated by the inclusion of Tudor and early Stuart era, the so-called olden time, in the Victorian vision of the nation's past.[48]

---

[44] John Delafons, *Politics and Preservation: A Policy History of the Built Environment* (London: E & F.N. Spon, 1997), 29.

[45] Wade and Wade, *Herefordshire*, 173, 242; R. Shoesmith, *Hereford: History and Guide* (Stroud: Alan Sutton, 1992), 3-6.

[46] *Making History: Antiquaries in Britain* (London: Royal Academy, 2006), 186.

[47] Vale, *How to See England*, 110.

[48] Tinniswood, *Polite Tourist*, 171-2; Peter Mandler, '"In the Olden Time": Romantic History and English National Identity', in *A Union of Multiple Identities. The British Isles, c. 1750-1850*, ed. Laurence Brockliss and David Eastwood (Manchester: Manchester University Press, 1997), 78-92; idem, *Stately Home*, 21-51.

What becomes clear from surveying the guide and topographical literature of the later nineteenth and early-twentieth century is that the Stuarts, and very largely the Civil Wars, is where history hit the buffers. Medieval and military architecture are the largest element in the section on 'buildings' in the Cambridge University Press county geography of Shropshire (first edition 1919), with the treatment of 'domestic architecture' almost wholly focused on the sixteenth and seventeenth centuries.[49] In Oxford University Press's county history of Gloucestershire, intended for schools, almost 90 per cent of the substantive text is devoted to the years before 1714 with the conclusion proclaiming that 'some of us, at least, rejoice that the fair face of our county is not disfigured by the squalid evidences of rapid commercial progress'.[50] If this was a highly dubious claim to make for Gloucestershire, it was an impossible one for Warwickshire. Yet guides to the county are dominated by accounts of castles, battles and the bard – Warwick and Kenilworth castles received by far the most extensive accounts of any single building in Black's 1881 guide, about thirty pages between them, while the description of Stratford-on-Avon and the surrounding area (*c.* thirty-five pages) is shot through with Shakespeare and his associations.[51] Though the growth of modern Birmingham does receive some recognition, Bevan's 1881 guide to the county makes clear the focus of the tourist gaze: 'so numerous were the events that happened in Warwickshire during the different wars and troubles of the Middle Ages, that a history of Warwickshire would be a microcosm of that of England'.[52] In fact, the wars and troubles of the seventeenth century – notably the Gunpowder Plot and the Civil Wars – are frequently cited in the rail and road 'excursions' described in Bevan, but here the history largely stops.[53] Elsewhere, the Civil Wars also feature prominently in *The Tourist's Guide to Bridgnorth* (1875), as they do in *Black's Guide to Dorsetshire* (1872), to which is added Monmouth's rebellion (1685), and a description of the obelisk erected at Charlborough Park to commemorate 'the secret council held in a small adjacent building in 1686, when the great whig [*sic*] lords determined to invite the aid of William of Orange', but again after this the history largely peters out.[54] The country writer, folklorist and novelist Walter Raymond's (1852–1931) *Short History of Somerset*, infused with a strong whiff of myth and medievalism, finishes its chronological survey of the county's history with the Bloody Assizes of Judge Jeffries at Taunton and Wells (1685).[55]

It is of course difficult to know to what extent tourists were influenced by this take on the past, but when four University College, London, students undertook a camping holiday on the Wye in 1892, the illustrated diary of one of their number

---

[49] Watts, *Shropshire*, 139–71.
[50] W. H. Weston, *Gloucestershire* (Oxford: Clarendon Press, 1912), 252.
[51] *Black's Guide to Warwickshire*.
[52] G. P. Bevan, *Tourist's Guide to Warwickshire* (London: Stanford, 1882), 3.
[53] Bevan, *Warwickshire*, 1.
[54] J. Randall *The Tourist's Guide to Bridgnorth* (Bridgnorth: Evan, Edkins & McMichael, 1875); *Black's Guide to Dorsetshire*, 6th edn (Edinburgh: A. & C. Black, 1872), 52.
[55] Walter Raymond, *A Short History of Somerset*, 3rd edn (London: Methuen, 1923); B. Osborn, 'Walter Raymond Regional Author and Poet', http://www.yeovilhistory.info/raymond-walter.htm, accessed 12 Nov. 2019.

suggests – albeit a little tongue-in-cheek – a measure of engagement with the guidebooks' romantic vision. At Little Doward they visited 'Arthur's Cave, Arthur's Hall etc.', an earthworks 'said to be the camp of Caractacus' (appending a drawing of 'Caractacus on guard'), and at Goodrich Castle recreated an 'unctuous feast' in the ruins of the medieval Banqueting Hall, and 'the rage of hunger now appeased', sat back to absorb the atmosphere: 'No sound but the "night winds whispering low" the ghosts of knights and ladies, the Lords of Goodrich and of that brave garrison which in King Charles' reign held out for five months against Cromwell's Roundheads, passed before us peopling the ruined courts.'[56]

In many respects the Stuart threshold on England's history and timescapes continued up to the Second World War. This was reflected in the popularity of castles, medieval moated houses, Tudor black and white, Elizabethan and Jacobean prodigy houses and the like in the guide literature. In practical terms – that is the actual properties visited, as opposed to simply read about from the comfort of an armchair – a great deal depended upon accessibility and location. The vast majority of properties were in private ownership, and often situated on large estates and behind belts of trees that reduced their visibility from public spaces. Many might also be located in areas of the country remote from the centres of urban population where most tourists lived. Having said this there was a long tradition of allowing a measure of public access to the houses of royalty, the aristocracy and gentry. Country house visiting dates back at least to the sixteenth century, and by the eighteenth century, was fully incorporated in the domestic British tour, by which point guidebooks were being published for some of the more prestigious properties, such as Stowe and Wilton. Owners permitted and facilitated access to their houses and gardens because, despite the inconvenience and potential threat to privacy, a key rationale behind the magnificent properties they built, the sumptuous interiors they decorated and the glittering collections of paintings, antiquities and *objets d'art* they collected, was display. It was only by exhibiting to the wider world the material manifestations of wealth that status could be asserted and recognized, and to achieve this end a measure of public access was necessary. However, it is clear that until the nineteenth century it was a *polite* public that was targeted and allowed access.[57] This changed in the nineteenth century, as Peter Mandler has shown, as the notion of 'the olden time' was popularized in print, and many of the great historic castles and mansions opened their doors to a growing urban middle class and skilled working-class excursionist market.[58] Hampton Court had set the tone of this new wave of 'popular' country house visiting by permitting free public access in 1839, followed by Windsor Castle in 1850. A range of developments – such as improvements in transport (explored in Chapter 8), the rise of tourist societies arranging excursions, and proximity to major urban centres, where most tourists lived – facilitated the process.[59] It is clear that

---

[56] S. K. Baker (ed.), *Camping on the Wye: The Tale of a Trip along the Wye from Whitney in Herefordshire to Chepstow in 1892* (Almeley: Logaston Press, 2003), 32–3, 40–1.
[57] Tinniswood, *Polite Tourist*, 1–112; Jocelyn Anderson, *Touring and Publicizing England's Country Houses in the Long Eighteenth Century* (London: Bloomsbury, 2018).
[58] Mandler, *Stately Home*, 21–106.
[59] Tinniswood, *Polite Tourist*, 136–58.

the popularity of Warwick Castle and Aston Hall owed much to their closeness to Birmingham, as did that of Shakespeareland as a whole.

From the 1880s, however, Mandler argues that this trend went into reverse, with country house owners – responding to various economic and social pressures – closing their doors (and often abandoning their houses and estates), and the general public turning more to the natural than the historic landscape. That said, on the eve of the Second World War, as Morton's account of a journey in summer 1939 makes clear, country houses were still accessible; in Kent there was a measure of public access, at least during the season, to Quebec House at Westerham (three days a week), Penshurst Place (two or three days a week), Igtham Motte (every Friday), Leeds Castle (once or twice a year), Knole (two or three days a week), and Walmer Castle (every Thursday). However, it was only after the Second World War and the National Trust's campaign to include country houses in its portfolio that the great house once again, and on an ever-expanding scale, became the national leisure resource that it had been.[60]

Whatever the fate of country house visiting in the early-twentieth century, during the 1920s over 230 abbeys, castles, gardens and country houses were regularly open to the public and charged an admission price.[61] Perhaps the most accessible and numerous of all historic properties were not houses but religious buildings: cathedrals, ruined abbeys, and above all the humble parish church – of which thousands existed, often packed with rich historic features, and to which entrance was free. In this context it might not seem surprising that churches constitute the bread and butter of many guidebooks. That this is the case in respect of Dent's early-twentieth-century 'Cathedrals, Abbeys and Famous Churches series' is to be expected. However, for Ernest Suffling's 1892 guide to the Norfolk Broads to declare that 'pains have been taken to point out the chief ecclesiastical features' of the area, and to advise on such matters as brass rubbing and 'epitaph-hunting', may seem a little odd in a guide to the boating fraternity.[62] But this reflects the centrality of ecclesiology to the tourist gaze of the period. *The Little Guides* and *Bell's Pocket Guides* often read like an itinerary for a church crawl. This may of course simply reflect the predilections of a particular type of educated, respectable middle-class tourist, and indeed of the authors themselves, quite a number of whom were clergymen and might be heavily involved in the antiquarian researches of county field and archaeological societies.

However, it was certainly also possible to produce a guide relatively free from churchiness. J. R. Hockin's *On Foot in Berkshire* (1934), for example, is very much an open-air walker's guide, in which accounts of churches are kept to an absolute minimum. But in the generality of guides that consciously address the human as opposed to natural landscape – such as Macmillan's *Highways and Byways* series, the *Ward Lock Red Guides*, the popular Arthur Mee's county guides, and early Shell and Penguin guides – churches feature prominently. The 1939 Penguin guide to *Kent, Surrey and Sussex* defended the emphasis on churches in guidebooks on the grounds that 'the parish churches of England are a ready-made history book, and no

---

[60] Mandler, *Stately Home*, 193–263; Morton, *Two Englands*, 7, 38, 57, 87.
[61] Tinniswood, *Polite Tourist*, 164.
[62] Ernest R. Suffling, *The Land of the Broads* (Stratford: B. Perry, 1895), iv, 4–7.

one who is at all interested in the story of this country can afford to neglect them.'[63] It was an approach continued in the most prestigious of the post-war architectural guides, the Pevsner county-based *Buildings of England* series, in which – for reasons never explained but simply assumed – religious buildings always head the accounts of individual locations. There was a notion of architectural and functional hierarchy here – these were the places that had to be visited first, and whose fabric was to be most valued – that impacted deeply on recreational travel and tourism.

Deerhurst in Gloucestershire was a church very well known to church cognoscenti because of its extensive surviving Saxon features. Its inclusion in the Ward Lock guide to Malvern (1907) is indicative of how spa towns were used as centres from which to explore the surrounding locality.[64] The accounts in this and *The Little Guide* (*Gloucestershire* 1914) focus on identifying the pre-conquest elements, and distinguishing later stages in the evolution of the medieval fabric, in this case early English and fifteenth century, and both referenced learned journals. The notion of an architectural stratigraphy is reminiscent of the geologist's concern to establish and locate landscapes in a chronologically ordered framework and underpins most accounts of churches, especially the more serious ones. Like much of tourism, visiting becomes an exercise in identifying and logging. *The Little Guide's* account of Burford church (*Oxfordshire* 1919) enhances this sense of a special church spotters' language by deploying abbreviations to describe the different phases of medieval style to be found in the building – in an account of three pages there is one reference to 'Saxon', two to 'Norman', eight to 'E.E.' (Early English), one to 'Dec.' (Decorated) and thirteen to 'Perp.' (Perpendicular). A plethora of manuals appeared to guide readers through the intricacies of the subject so that even before they set foot in a church they were already aware of what to look out for and how to structure their observations. Cyril Power's *English Medieval Architecture* (1912), comprehensive and authoritative (Power was declared to be a Soane medallist of the RIBA), but also accessible with 424 illustrations, and easily portable in two pocket-size volumes, was neatly divided into a chronological or historical section, describing the various phases, and a section on the elements of construction (doorways, mouldings, etc.). For those contemplating including Europe in their travels there was George Herbert West's *Gothic Architecture in England and France* (1911), similarly arranged under historical and construction sections. West claimed to be appealing to the wider market by 'making clear in a brief and popular form the causes and principles which underlie the wonderful history and development of medieval art', but Charles Budden's Batsford *English Gothic Churches* (1927), whose frontispiece was a photograph of Burford church, more obviously made a pitch for this market, eschewing the historical approach for what he saw as the more user-friendly constructional or features approach, declaring 'this little volume' to be written 'to assist the tourist in his rambles round these relics of bygone England'.[65]

---

[63] Winbolt, *Kent, Surrey and Sussex*, 9.
[64] *A Pictorial and Descriptive Guide to Malvern and District* (London: Ward Lock, 1907), 125.
[65] George Herbert West, *Gothic Architecture in England and France* (London: G. Bell & Sons, 1911), ix; Charles W. Budden, *English Gothic Churches* (London: Batsford, 1927), v.

The manuals were written to inform and guide their readers, to add to their body of useful knowledge, and – overtly in the case of West – to develop their aesthetic taste. But it is clear from the accounts that a visit to a parish church, and here the manuals are more explicit than the guidebooks, was about more than aesthetics. There was seen to be something peculiarly English about the parish church. Budden proclaimed 'it is safe to say that no country in the world can vie with England in its wealth of parochial buildings', while Power declared England's 'Parish Churches, the glory of the country; not erected as the appendage of a class, or the private property of a corporate body, be it monastic community or secular ecclesiastic, but the very heritage of the people themselves'.[66] This patriotic mode of analysis carries through to issues of style. Perpendicular (from the mid-fourteenth century) was seen as a peculiarly English version of gothic, when the nation broke from its dependence on continental (and especially French) tradition. Power considered the perpendicular

> the most interesting portion of the Gothic story of these islands. Firstly, from the democratic quality of its art, no longer that of a class, – monk, ecclesiastic, king, or noble, – but more widely representative of the nation as a whole; secondly, arising from its oft, almost unambitious, homely character of the religious aspirations of the people, and typified in the Parish Church.[67]

West, committed to comparisons with France, was even more explicit about the divergence in approaches, and national characteristic, brought about by the arrival of Perpendicular in England: 'While French art becomes more and more rigidly logical … more and more the expression of a system, English art becomes more and more individual … an English building is the record of the facts of its history, often of the history of the nation, a French one of the ideal of the builder or of the race.'[68] None of this explicit political interpretation is conveyed in the *Little Guide's* account of Burford church, but the thirteen references to 'Perp.', compared with eleven to all other periods, carry a subliminal national message.

The Victorian enthusiasm for gothic should not hide the fact that classical style continued to have an appeal. But it was generally muted, occupying a lower spot in the architectural pecking order, behind that of the medieval period and 'olden time'. The *Bell's Pocket Guides* 'Glossary of architectural terms' simply ignores the classical orders, concentrating largely on such features as the broach spire, crocket, lancet, ogee, and squint – 'opening in a church wall, through which the altar can be seen'.[69] When Charles G. Harper visited Warwick in *c*. 1912 he found 'for dullness and pretentious ugliness combined … [it] would be difficult to match'. This remarkable judgement was not due to some early-twentieth-century architectural carbuncles but was a response to the simple classical style in which the town centre had been rebuilt following a

---

[66] Budden, *English Gothic Churches*, 1; Charles Power, *English Medieval Architecture in Two Parts* (London: Talbot & Co., 1912), vol. 2, 489.
[67] Power, *English Medieval Architecture*, vol. 2, 273.
[68] Ibid.; West, *Gothic Architecture*, 285–6.
[69] Winbolt, *Chilterns and the Thames Valley*, xiii–xiv.

large-scale fire in 1694, 'at a time when architects were obsessed with the idea of designing "stately" buildings. What they considered stately we nowadays look upon with a shudder and style heavy and unimaginative'.[70] The contrast with the glories of medieval gothic Warwick would have made the classical additions seem even more distressing. Even the baroque splendour of a Blenheim (c. 1705–25) could elicit only an ambivalent response in the *Little Guide*: 'That the palace is heavy and ungraceful its admirers will hardly deny, but it may lay claim to a massive dignity and skilful combination of its parts'.[71] The problem was that classical was seen as a foreign style, that Blenheim was all too reminiscent of Versailles and French absolutism, and that its building crossed the 1714 threshold when the British monarchy became Germanic (not a happy association in the run-up to the First World War) and continental.

In this lack of interest in the post-Stuart era, architectural fashion mirrored that of history – as we saw earlier – in general. A sign of the prevailing taste was the fact that the newly founded (1908) Royal Commission on Historical Monuments recorded only buildings constructed before 1700, a date advanced to – but not beyond – 1714 in 1922, and only to 1850 in 1946.[72] Pre-1714 versions of classicism, particularly of the more domestic sort, could be accommodated in the lexicon of taste – as was evident in the so-called Queen Anne revival of the turn of the century, or the Arts and Crafts interest in 'vernacular' classical features – but the full on Palladian classicism of the Georgian era was not yet appreciated. However, attitudes began to change in the early-twentieth century, with – perhaps unsurprisingly – Bath among the first places to incorporate an appreciation of post-baroque classicism into its tourist agenda and conservation landscape. The founding of the Georgian Group in 1937 marked a recognition that the tectonic plates of architectural fashion had started to shift.[73] By this point there was also a developing reaction against Victorian design and the gothic revival. Richard Wyndham in 1939, for example, warned his readers of All Saints (Kent), a Giles Gilbert Scott creation of 1861, that 'it has all the horror of a late Victorian billiard room – and exactly the same smell'.[74] However, even in the same year guides such as Edmund Vale's *How to See England* were published with plenty on churches, monasteries and castles and ignoring the post-medieval period in its entirety.

Architectural aesthetics was only one factor that determined touristic interest in the built environment. S. P. B. Mais, that prolific writer of guidebooks, freely admitted his ignorance of architectural history, explaining, 'I am inclined to judge sacred buildings quickly by the general atmosphere that permeates them'.[75] For all the emphasis in serious literature and guides on the informed understanding and appreciation of architecture, it is clear that another mode of interpretation was at work: biography, romance and story. In 1939 visitors to Dover were reminded that 'a pageant of history has passed below these castle walls', with various momentous occasions referenced such as the

---

[70] Harper, *Summer Days in Shakespeare Land*, 245.
[71] Brabant, *Oxfordshire*, 265.
[72] Borsay, *Image of Georgian Bath*, 354–8.
[73] Ibid., 72–7, 150–67; Peter Borsay, 'The Georgian House: The Making of a Heritage Icon', in *Valuing Historic Environments*, ed. Lisanne Gibson and John Pendlebury (Farnham: Ashgate, 2009), 157–77.
[74] Richard Wyndham, *Sussex, Kent and Surrey* (London: Batsford, 1939), 16; see also 59, 112.
[75] S. P. B. Mais, *Highways and Byways in the Welsh Marches* (London: Macmillan & Co., 1939), 212.

Roman invasion, the Norman Conquest and the Armada. The allusion to a 'pageant' may owe much to the pageant movement of the early-twentieth century when many historic urban centres, including Dover in 1908, staged spectacular events comprising a series of tableaux intended to represent the history of their towns.[76] In this mode, locations and buildings were appreciated as much for their human associations as their architecture. The material fabric was often a convenient hook on which to hang the story of a noble or ignominious life, a bloody battle, a romantic attachment, or simply retell a ripping yarn.

Warwickshire guides invariably retold the legend of Guy of Warwick in their account of Guy's Cliff and its medieval chapel and caves, of Shakespeare's supposed venture into deer poaching at Charlecote House near Stratford, and of the tragic demise of the devoted Amy Robsart in the description of Kenilworth Castle, the possession of her celebrated husband Robert Dudley, Earl of Leicester and favourite of Queen Elizabeth I.[77] The last of these stories has all the ingredients of a romantic thriller – intrigue, loyalty, betrayal, royalty and aristocracy, vaulting ambition, love and a highly suspicious death – and indeed provided the story line for Walter Scott's hugely popular if factually distorted novel *Kenilworth* (1821). It was *Kenilworth* that introduced the dramatic scene of Elizabeth I meeting Amy during her famous visit to Kenilworth in 1575, an encounter that could not have taken place since Amy had died fifteen years earlier but nonetheless is recorded regularly in the guidebooks. As the author of *Historic Warwickshire: Its Legendary Lore, Traditionary Stories, and Romantic Episodes* (1876) made clear, truth mattered less than fiction when it came to the touristic landscape:

> It seems a sacrilege to tear away this veil of fiction, so attractively woven by the great Wizard of the North ... Not one in a hundred ever dream of questioning the accuracy of Scott's great romance. Not one in fifty would be willing to have a glorious dream of love, loyalty, and devotion dispelled.[78]

Amy's death from a fall – whether by accident, suicide, or murder (perhaps at Dudley's behest in his pursuit of the Queen's hand) remains tantalizingly unresolved, as all good mysteries should – took place at Cumnor House (now in Oxfordshire, but until 1974 in Berkshire). Though the residence – originally a medieval grange – was demolished around 1810 the story is regularly included in accounts of Cumnor, together with the obligatory haunting.[79] Amy's ghost also strayed further afield to

---

[76] Angela Bartie, Linda Fleming, Mark Freeman, Tom Hulme, Alexander Hutton and Paul Readman, 'Historical Pageants and the Medieval Past in Twentieth-Century England', *English Historical Review* 133 (2018): 865–902.
[77] *Black's Guide to Warwickshire*, 92, 165–7, 183, 200, 202–3, 208–11; Bevan, *Warwickshire*, 39, 53–4, 91, 112, 118; Holland, *Warwickshire*, 67–8, 135–6, 252–3.
[78] J. Tom Burgess, *Historic Warwickshire: Its Legendary Lore, Traditionary Stories, and Romantic Episodes* (London: Simpkin Marshall & Co., 1873), 121.
[79] E. K. W. Ryan, *The Thames from the Towpath* (London: The Saint Catherine Press, 1938), 201–2; John H. Ingram, *The Haunted Homes and Family Traditions of Great Britain*, 3rd edn (London: W. H. Allen & Co., 1886), 409–12; Morton, *Two Englands*, 156–60; C. Fox Smith, *The Thames* (London: Methuen, 1931), 80–1.

Cornbury Park near Charlbury in Oxfordshire, where she appeared before Dudley to warn him of his impending death ('according to the story', by poisoning at the hand of his third wife, Lettice),[80] and though the *Little Guide* treats this with humorous scepticism, it does recount the 'story' and warns that 'the ghost was believed still to walk and to be a message of death to those unlucky enough to meet it'.[81]

Castles and country houses were one hook on which to hang an intriguing human story, but in some respects even more convenient were churches. As the location of the major rites of passage where the soul could be said to enter and exit the world, of the resting place of the bodily remains of local individuals and families, and – from the early modern period – the site of increasingly numerous and elaborate memorials to commemorate their lives, it is unsurprising that accounts of churches and churchyards often became an exercise in local biography. Arguably, indeed, until architectural history developed and disseminated a specific mode and language of aesthetic analysis in the later nineteenth century it was life stories rather than material fabric per se that predominated in the descriptions of cathedrals and churches. The Beauchamp Chapel in St Mary's Warwick is one of the richest examples of late medieval art in Britain. Most accounts recognize its special architectural qualities, but it is the occupants of the chapel, and their tombs, which generally receive the most extensive descriptions. Among the celebrities buried in the chapel is Robert Dudley, whose presence often draws a censorious comment: 'a Latin inscription gives him the credit for virtues which history refuses to associate with his name. He died September 4, 1558, from the effects, it is said, of poison he had himself prepared for others', claims Black's 1881 guide. Comparing Dudley's memorial to the 'quiet and chaste altar tombs' erected to the other occupants of the chapel, Bradley's guide of 1910 described it as the 'gorgeous erection reared by a decadent taste to a person for whom such a florid departure was not wholly inappropriate', while having described how '[Sir Walter] Scott's "heart thrilled" at the sight of its [the chapel's] monuments'. Wade in 1932 peremptorily dismisses the 'infamous Robert Dudley' as 'a man without courage, talent, or virtue'.[82]

Touring the landscape of West Midland castles, houses and churches, it is not difficult to reconstruct a villains – and heroes – history of England, that is a curious mixture of patriotic and morality tale. The propensity of guides – even the more serious ones such as *The Little Guides* – to use landscape elements as a scaffold on which to build historical stories, in which the borderline between fact and fiction is frequently blurred, suggests that landscape is being deployed much in the manner of a theme park or even a soap opera, in which the myths and beliefs by which a society lives are being rehearsed and reinforced. It is an issue that we will return to later in the book.

---

[80] Since Amy's death he had secretly married Lady Sheffield in 1573 and then Lettice Knollys in 1578. See Simon Adams, 'Dudley [née Robsart], Amy, Lady Dudley (1532–1560), gentlewoman', *Oxford Dictionary of National Biography*. 23 Sep. 2004, https://www.oxforddnb.com/view/10.1093/ref:odnb/9780198614128.001.0001/odnb-9780198614128-e-8144, accessed 30 Jul. 2022.

[81] Brabant, *Oxfordshire*, 108–9.

[82] *Black's Guide to Warwickshire*, 193; A. G. Bradley, *Avon and Shakespeare's Country* (London: Methuen, 1910), 324–5; J. H. Wade, *Rambles in Shakespeare's Country* (London: Methuen, 1932), 159–60.

Old towns and villages

It is tempting to characterize the whole touristic turn in English culture as the pursuit of a past rural Arcadia. However, the examples cited above – Warwick, Kenilworth, Stratford, Burford, Bridgnorth – make it clear that the discovery of England included towns as well as villages. As Chapter 5 showed, cities and towns have always been a key part of the tourist itinerary, something which was accentuated by the urban renaissance, and the rise of the spa and seaside resort. Tourists were drawn to the urban environment for a range of reasons, such as its social life, natural assets, and health and consumer facilities, but history and the historic landscape became from at least the eighteenth century an important part of the package. Any one town could service several and indeed all of these attractions. London, particularly if we include the spas on its periphery, comfortably met all of these requirements. However, industrialization and modernization were making it increasingly difficult, though by no means impossible, to play this multi-faceted touristic role. Industry, commerce and history did not sit easily together in the same location. Economic activity was becoming increasingly focused on those towns favourably located close to mineral resources, transport nodes, and large concentrations of population. For such places the drive to industrialize and modernize was threatening whatever historic fabric they possessed. A series of dynamic industrial and commercial urban centres was also developing – such as Birmingham, Manchester and Liverpool – which, though often medieval in origin, were effectively 'new towns' with limited inherited fabric and, despite adopting gothic and classical styles for their business premises and public buildings, could in no way be said to be 'historic'. At the same time towns outside the zones of economic growth, some of which had been major centres of industrial and commercial activity in the medieval and early modern eras, and may even have benefited from the early stages of the Industrial Revolution, by the mid- and later Victorian periods found it difficult to compete in the new economic order. Their principal commercial asset was now their history, historic fabric, timescapes and tourism. Out of this changing economic context, a category of touristic and residential urban centre began to crystallize that became known as 'old towns'.

By the late Victorian period articles were appearing in popular magazines and newspapers on the subject of old towns. In the mid-1870s *Bow Bells* carried a series of pieces on 'The history and tradition of old English towns' by George Wall, which included accounts of the cathedral cities of Winchester, Hereford and Exeter, and in the 1890s the *National Observer* printed an item on 'Old English towns'.[83] The essays in Henry James's *English Hours*, published in 1905, but largely penned in the 1870s and 1880s, are full of accounts of 'picturesque old towns', including Lichfield, Warwick, Wells, Salisbury and Chester – 'an American strolling in Chester streets finds a perfect feast of crookedness'.[84] P. H. Ditchfield's *The Story of Our English Towns* (1897) is very

---

[83] *Bow Bells: A Weekly Magazine of General Literature and Arts*, vol. 22, 555 (1875): 25–2; vol. 23, 572 (1875): 34–6; vol. 23, 581 (1875): 250–5; *The National Observer* vol. 11, 283 (1894): 586–7.

[84] Henry James, *English Hours* ([1905] Oxford: Oxford University Press, 1981), 37, 102.

much a tale of *old* English towns, scarcely making it beyond the Civil Wars threshold. Only by the final chapter (eighteen), 'Modern changes and survivals', is there any attempt to address the world beyond the seventeenth century, and then it is primarily about 'survivals' of a prior age. The reasons for his attachment to a pre-modern notion of the town are made clear enough:

> A great gulf yawns between the England of to-day and that strange, vigorous, youthful England which is so far removed from us, not so much by the lapse of years, but by the mighty changes, social and political, which time has wrought. ... We see the vast commercial towns and cities of the North ... We see the countless factories, with their tall chimneys belching forth their clouds of smoke ... But in spite of all these changes ... there are still some old features left of our ancient towns, and these it behoves us to protect from injury and destruction.[85]

Much of Ditchfield's *Vanishing England* (1910) is taken up with towns, as fears mounted about the impact of urban development on the historic townscape. At the turn of the century a volume of town vignettes, compiled originally by William Andrews and added to by Elsie Lang, was published by T. Werner Laurie under the title of *Old English Towns*, which went through several editions during the inter-war period.[86] This was joined in 1936 by Batsford's contribution to the genre, Clive Rouse's *The Old Towns of England*, which on its opening page appealed to patriotic tourists, 'We may not have a Carcassonne, a Toledo, a Venice or an Athens. But, on the other hand, where else will you find a York, a Canterbury, a Lincoln, a Norwich; or, on smaller scale, a Bath, a Warwick, a Chipping Campden or a Ludlow?'[87] A glance at the forty-three towns described in Andrews and Lang should warn against any simple stereotyping; they include, for example, Manchester, Liverpool and Leeds. But the accounts of these places, probably included simply because of their size, reinforce the impression that industry, commerce and history did not mix easily: in Manchester '[t]owering warehouses are seen on every hand, and the ruins of ancient strongholds and old religious houses which we usually associate with an old-time town are missing'; Leeds 'has a past as well as a modern glory, but its early history is lost in the mists of antiquity'; it 'is certainly not an attractive place; it has many fine buildings, but in not a few instances the mean surroundings completely mar their beauty', while Liverpool 'has its medieval memories, although its antiquities may have been swept away by a practical and ruthless corporation'.[88] Such accounts were unlikely to attract the tourist in pursuit of the past.

In fact over half the towns pictured in the Andrews and Lang list are either traditional cathedral towns, or county towns, or both, and almost two-thirds are located south of Birmingham. Though some of these were heavily industrialized, such

---

[85] P. H. Ditchfield, *The Story of Our English Towns* (London: Methuen, 1897), 290–1, 293.
[86] Ditchfield, *Story of Our English Towns*; William Andrews and Elsie M. Lang, *Old English Towns* (London: T.W. Laurie, 1923).
[87] Clive Rouse, *The Old Towns of England* (London: Batsford, 1936), 1.
[88] Andrews and Lang, *Old English Towns*, 160, 167, 281.

as Leicester or Northampton, the vast majority were not, and we can see in them the basic characteristics that came to define old towns – a significant medieval profile with a surviving built heritage of religious (such as a cathedral, major abbey or impressive parish church) and secular (such as a castle or fortifications) fabric, and an apparent absence of modernizing influences. It was an image that comfortably suited places such as Winchester and York. Albert Osborne claimed of the former that 'among the smaller towns I know none … that possesses in more marked degree the very atmosphere of the past', and H. V. Morton described the latter as 'England's last real anchor to the Middle Ages'.[89] Warwick, dominated by its historic castle and great collegiate church, also fitted the historic profile like a glove; 'commercially the town is of little importance', 'an old world town, all the more refreshing from the contrast with its gay and modern neighbour Leamington … few places in England have so much to offer in the shape of architectural interest and historical associations'.[90] Arthur Mee summed it all up when in 1936 he described the town as a place that 'almost defied the spirit of Change. Time comes and goes, but she remains'.[91]

As the reach of domestic tourism spread in the later nineteenth and early-twentieth century so the definition of the classic old town broadened beyond the cathedral and shire town to include the 'country town'. In 1935 R. H. Mottram created an archetypal version of this, which he dubbed 'Slowdon-in-the-Soke':

> the stresses of the nineteenth century have passed it by. The febrile activities of the twentieth century have rendered it at once more accessible and more desirable. … Slowdon belongs to an older, pre-Victorian, almost pre-Elizabethan England. It was, and largely still is, a town of the old, self-contained island that cared nothing for Montreal, and was not affected in its politics by Bombay. Europe even was a long way off, and its older inhabitants still speak of its younger ones as having 'gone foreign' when they go to London.[92]

Medieval character represented the gold standard, but the term 'medieval' came to encompass any buildings and streets believed to be constructed during the 'olden time', of vernacular materials, in a broadly vernacular style. An ancient fabric of some sort was a prerequisite, but in this broadening definition of an old town anywhere might qualify which appeared to have been bypassed by the Industrial Revolution and the forces of modernization. This opened the door to hundreds of small towns, located outside the core zones of industrial growth and off the main arteries of communication, often situated in districts that in the medieval and early modern eras were heavily engaged in manufacture, which had endowed them with a rich heritage of buildings but were now concentrating on agricultural production – such as in Wiltshire, Dorset, East Devon, Suffolk and Norfolk – many now hovering on the border between urban and village status. There was Thomas Hardy's 1886 fictional account of early-nineteenth-century

---

[89] Osborne, *Old-World England*, 166; Morton, *Call of England*, 31.
[90] *Black's Guide to Warwickshire*, 186; Bevan, *Warwickshire*, 47, 50.
[91] Mee, *Warwickshire*, 272.
[92] R. H. Mottram, 'The Country Town', in *The Legacy of England* (London: Batsford, 1935), 132, 143–4.

Casterbridge (in reality Dorchester in Dorset) as 'untouched by the faintest sprinkle of modernism'.[93] The Cotswold towns, such as Burford, Chipping Campden, Northleach, Broadway, and Stow on the Wold, seemingly detached at some point from the flow of modern life – Burford, literally cut adrift from the communications network when the railway bypassed it, and called in 1908 the 'forgotten town', or Chipping Campden described in 1905 as 'outwardly but little changed for some three hundred years, a silent yet eloquent witness of the past', and in 1935 as a place which 'seems to have stood still ... since the sixteenth century' – were particular subjects of nostalgic reverie.[94]

The Sussex hilltop 'port' – port is something of a historicism since the sea vacated it in the sixteenth century – of Rye in Sussex was another quaint town that seemed to fit the 'forgotten' category. In 1918 Bradley could write, '[M]any things have happened in the last two decades since Rye was "discovered" ... Most of the strangers who have taken up their abode in the town have possessed themselves of one or other of its many alluring little old houses, Tudor, Jacobean or Georgian.'[95] Dating the discovery and colonization of Rye to *c*. 1900 reinforces the view that it was at the very end of Victoria's reign that the notion of the old town was expanding to include smaller places but also that such places were beginning to attract, alongside visitors, a permanent residential class, fleeing the pressures of the modern city and seeking to immerse themselves in the past. Henry James arrived in 1897 to occupy Lamb House, which offered 'every promise of yielding me an indispensable retreat from May to October', returning to his London rooms in the Reform Club over winter. Its next resident from 1919 was E. F. Benson, whose *Mapp and Lucia* novels were in part based on Rye (known in the novels as Tilling). Though affectionately mocking the polite and snobbish life of the town, the popular novels helped to reinforce the archetype of the old town: 'There is not in all England a town so blatantly picturesque as Tilling. ... The hill on which it is built rises steeply from the level land, and, crowned by the great grave church ... positively consists of quaint corners, rough-cast and timber cottages, and mellow Georgian fronts.'[96]

Lamb House (see Figure 6.4), also occupied by Miss Mapp in the novel, was not medieval, Tudor, or Jacobean but an elegant red brick classical construction of the 1720s. Bradley's and Benson's inclusion of such buildings in their accounts recognized the shift in taste, referred to earlier, underway at the turn of the century, which began to incorporate Georgian in the notion of the 'old'. This had the advantage of reflecting the reality of the situation since Rye, like Ludlow, Burford, Tewkesbury, Warwick, Bridgnorth and many other 'historic' towns, was, visually at least, much more Georgian than medieval, the product of an eighteenth-century architectural 'renaissance'.[97] But

---

[93] Thomas Hardy, *The Life and Death of the Mayor of Casterbridge: A Story of a Man of Character* ([1886] London: Macmillan, 1966), 31–2.
[94] Hutton, *By Thames and Cotswold*, 105; Evans, *Highways and Byways in Oxford*, 182; Mais, *Round about England*, 181.
[95] A. G. Bradley, *The Old Gate of England. Rye, Romney Marsh, and the Western Cinque Ports* (London: Robert Scott, 1918), 23.
[96] Oliver Garnett, *Henry James and Lamb House* (London: National Trust, 1999); E. F. Benson, '*Miss Mapp*' [1922], in *The Complete Mapp and Lucia*, ed. Keith Carabine, 2 vols. (London: Wordsworth Editions, 2011), vol. 1, 258.
[97] Borsay, *English Urban Renaissance*.

58   AN OLD GATE OF ENGLAND

living seems fairly chronic. They never fail, moreover, to remind the powers that be, that if Rye suffers, whether through its indispensable church spire beacon, or its refractory harbour,

LAMB HOUSE, FROM THE GARDEN.

or its confounded French fish poachers, the nation suffers. Indeed it would be almost unnatural if its self-importance had not out-lived the days when the ships of Devon and Norfolk

Figure 6.4 Lamb House from A. G. Bradley, *An Old Gate of England. Rye, Romney Marsh, and the Western Cinque Ports* (London: Robert Scott, 1918). Reproduced by kind permission of the David Wilson Library, University of Leicester.

this did not threaten the overall concept of the old town since it was still possible to conceive of the Georgian era as part of the pre-industrial, pre-modern world. Moreover, it also had the advantage of bringing into the fold of the 'old' a whole series of spa and resort towns that were self-evidently recent-ish creations. Bath fell into this category since though it was a medieval town the vast majority of its fabric from that era had been swept away by the reconstruction and expansion that occurred during the eighteenth century.

By the time that John Betjeman published his contribution to the Collins Britain in Pictures series on *English Cities and Small Towns* in 1943, Georgian and even Regency architecture had been fully incorporated into the old town model. He began his chapter on 'Spas and watering places': 'The great ages of town building in England were the late eighteenth and early nineteenth centuries. There was a sense of planning, not of a single house, as there is to-day, and as there was before the eighteenth century, but of whole streets and towns.' This reflected a new thirst for town planning to counter the perceived impact of unregulated urban expansion during the nineteenth and early-twentieth century, and for which the spas of Bath, Cheltenham, Leamington and Clifton might serve as historic models. Betjeman also famously proved, at least in later years, to be a passionate advocate of Victorian architecture, and in this book includes a chapter on 'Industrial towns'. His comments, however, were unlikely to draw in the tourists: 'Except for connoisseurs of architecture, the industrial towns of England are more interesting for their people than their buildings.' The archetype of the old town, unblemished by industrialization, remains essentially intact.[98]

Two years before the publication of Betjeman's volume, another poet, Edmund Blunden, produced a parallel contribution in the same Collins series, this time on *English Villages*. It is an unsurprisingly elegiac account and one that places the village at the moral centre of a national identity: 'I am profoundly persuaded ... that to the man or woman who is desirous of finding the best in this country I recommend the English village.'[99] In 1935 S. P. B. Mais declared that 'no other country has anything to show more fair than the average English village', and James Bradley Ford that

> The harmony of the village is in part an inward harmony, based on the Englishman's love of his soil and the house he has built upon it. Such freedom and content as have flourished in this country do still, notwithstanding many reverses, find their best material expression in the quiet beauty of many English villages.[100]

These authors' accounts were very largely descriptions of the *old* English village. At one point Blunden refers to the 'many dreary and imprisoned villages ... under the shadow of huge industrial organisation', and S. E. Winbolt warned the readers of his 1930s guidebook to give Wheatley and Horspath, on the eastern outskirts of Oxford, a wide berth, 'there is little to see, the roads are villainous, and the villages have become

---

[98] John Betjeman, *English Cities and Small Cities* (London: Collins, 1943), 32, 34, 41.
[99] Edmund Blunden, *English Villages* (London: Collins, 1941), 8.
[100] Mais, *Round about England*, 179; C. Bradley Ford, 'The Village', in *Legacy of England*, 100.

sordidly suburbanised'.[101] These are not the archetype that Blunden models in his description, where the emphasis is upon an identikit village with key historic features: the local inn 'with its nooks and corners answering no particular scheme of architecture', the medieval bridge; the church and tower, which rises 'well above the mixed group of shops and dwellings and inns and alleys, [and] which seem like its brood under its protection';[102] the grammar school 'that gabled, rosy building';[103] the windmill; the village green, the site of 'our great game … cricket, our summer is incomplete without its encounters… the entire scene within this zone of woods and pastures, with the pigeons flying over or the cuckoos calling across, and now and then the church clock measuring out the hour with deep and slow notes';[104] and the cosy domestic architecture:

> The chief style of the houses on the street is still eighteenth-century, an easy, balanced prose style of glowing but not glaring brick, and high roofs with attic windows, and sometimes an ornamental facing of semicircular tiles. The cottages are apt to be built of wood, in this district – weatherboard, a pleasant, simple material which seems to last forever.[105]

Blunden's account is based on the Kent villages of Twyford and Yalding in Kent. He acknowledges that 'the English village is a very numerous creation'[106] and later introduces 'an English village of decidedly different aspect to that we have left in the Home Counties'.[107] But the difference here is largely one of building materials (stone) and its apparent even older (medieval) appearance. The shift in geographical location is merely to the region around Oxford and the Cotswolds. Significantly Blunden strayed no further north in search of the English village.

In shaping his village archetype, Blunden drew upon a well-established literary and pictorial tradition. This was by no means wholly positive, as Blunden acknowledged,[108] but by the later Victorian and Edwardian period a deeply evocative and nostalgic 'touristic' archetype was crystallizing, embedded in a broader picture of a rural Arcadia, that contrasted with the modern industrial city. William Morris set a model for this in his account and woodcut of his country retreat of Kelmscott in his post-industrial utopian view of England, *News from Nowhere* (1890):

> [T]he garden between the wall and the house was redolent of the June flowers, and the roses were rolling over one another with that delicious superabundance of small well-tended gardens … this many-gabled old house built by the simple country-folk of the long-past times, regardless of all the turmoil that was going on in cities and courts, is lovely still … We went into the church, which was a

---

[101] Blunden, *English Villages*, 43; Winbolt, *Chilterns and the Thames Valley*, 182.
[102] Blunden, *English Villages*, 14.
[103] Ibid., 16.
[104] Ibid., 17.
[105] Ibid., 13.
[106] Ibid., 8.
[107] Ibid., 25.
[108] Ibid., 46.

simple little building with one little aisle divided from the nave by three round arches, a chancel, and a rather roomy transept ... the windows were of the graceful Oxfordshire fourteenth-century type.[109]

In the 'old-world village' of Lacock in Wiltshire 'the modern world', according to John Hissey, 'vanishes from mind as though it were but a dream of ugliness, and you look upon a reality of beauty' and H. V. Morton considered Alfriston in Sussex 'the ideal village which most Englishmen keep in their hearts'.[110] S. E. Winbolt recommended Aldbury in Hertfordshire as his ideal: 'Lying under wooded hills, it is grouped about a broad green, a presiding elm and a pond, and the church and its old houses form part of the compact little scene. No wonder that artists wishful to paint a complete English village consort here.'[111]

The village and its landscape were the themes of much of the art of the period and a focus of attention for many of the early photographers. The thatched, half-timbered cottage appears again and again in drawings and paintings of the countryside,[112] as Christopher Wood puts it, 'a cherished symbol of an innocence they felt they had lost', and the epitome of a way of life that they knew to be disappearing'.[113] A key artist was Helen Allingham, whose sentimentalized depictions of cottages have been characterized as 'old-fashioned objects ... forms of public remembering whose goal was not to reclaim a verifiable version of past labor, but to promote the building into a national icon'.[114] The idealized and nostalgic image of the cottage is likewise there in the guide and general topographical literature, such as the prolific publications of P. H. Ditchfield. In the two or so decades before the First World War he produced at least five books on the English village and cottage, many running through several editions.[115] Ditchfield's view was that the humble village cottage, largely unaffected by imported foreign fashions (by which read classicism), had acted like a time capsule, preserving the essence of an English architecture:

> At a time when the craft of building among Anglo-Saxon races had reached the nadir of its fall ... reaching at last at the end of the XVIIIth century, a point below which there seemed no pit of further fall, the discovery of the English cottage was almost ... like the finding of a precious manuscript preserved by faithful monks from the wreck of the ancient world.[116]

[109] William Morris, *News from Nowhere* ([1890] Oxford: Oxford University Press, 2009), 173, 179.
[110] Hissey, *Charm of the Road*, 340; Morton, *Two Englands*, 101; see also Fox Smith, *The Thames*, 93.
[111] Winbolt, *Chilterns and the Thames Valley*, 100.
[112] See, e.g., Timmins, *Nooks and Corners of Herefordshire*, 75–84 for half-timbered houses.
[113] Wood, *Paradise Lost*, 129.
[114] Linda M. Austin, *Nostalgia in Transition, 1780–1917* (Charlottesville and London: University of Virginia Press, 2007), 145.
[115] P. H. Ditchfield, *Our English Villages: Their Stories and Antiquities* (London: Methuen, 1889); idem, *English Villages* (London: Methuen, 1901); idem, *Picturesque English Cottages and Their Doorway Gardens* (Philadelphia: John C. Winston, 1905); idem, *The Charm of the English Village* (London: Batsford, 1908); idem, *The Village Church* (London: Methuen, 1914). See also idem, *Old Village Life; or, Glimpses of Village Life through all the Ages* (London: Methuen, 1920).
[116] Ditchfield, *Picturesque English Cottages*, prefatory note; see Austin, *Nostalgia in Transition*, 136–43 on Ditchfield.

A focal point of Ditchfield's account was the cottage garden, which seemed to mix the natural and historic agendas:

> [O]n the outskirts of Dorking there is a beautiful cottage garden. A small stream separates it from the road on which the Romans marched, and the pilgrims wended their way to the Shrine of St Thomas at Canterbury. In the front of the house, which is a half-timbered structure, with a beautiful tiled roof, and tile-covered porch and a graceful clustered chimney-stack, is the flower garden, while behind it useful vegetables grow.[117]

Luxuriant and heavily perfumed gardens feature in many literary and pictorial accounts, with the fabric of the cottage – invariably constructed of 'natural' materials such as wood and thatch – seeming to grow organically out of the old-fashioned flowers and vegetation surrounding it.[118] E. M. Forster's Howard's End – the mystical house that forms the spiritual heart of his novel of the same name (1910) – was surrounded by a luxuriant garden, as Margaret described it on her visit:

> Lent lilies … advanced in battalions over the grass. Tulips were a tray of jewels. She could not see the wych-elm tree, but a branch of the celebrated vine, studded with velvet knobs, had covered the porch. She was struck by the fertility of the soil; she had seldom seen a garden where the flowers looked so well, and even the weeds she was idly plucking out of the porch were intensely green.[119]

It was a model also deeply affecting elite garden design at the time with the more 'natural' and English approach advocated by William Robinson and Gertrude Jekyll in reaction to the formality of what was stigmatized as 'carpet bedding' and 'stereotyped gardens'.[120]

To discover the 'authentic' villager's dwelling and to tap into that stream of building tradition that embodied the national spirit, there was no alternative but to scour the nooks and crannies of the countryside for survivals from the medieval past and olden time. This was where the domestic travel literature of the later nineteenth and early-twentieth century was so helpful. Moreover, by this period specific villages were being identified as tourist locations in their own right, relatively untouched by modernization, replete with cottages of an indeterminate but obviously historic date, and ornamented by a sprinkling of suitably aged inhabitants, looking like the survivals of an ancient peasantry. Visitors to Bath were always looking for activities to fill their leisure time. During the eighteenth century walking and riding in the immediate vicinity of the city was an option, and an increasingly attractive one as the picturesque and romantic turn took a grip towards the end of the century. A section specifically describing the

---

[117] Ditchfield, *Picturesque English Cottages*, 48.
[118] Wood, *Paradise Lost*, 143–52; Blunden, *English Villages*, 45–6.
[119] E. M. Forster, *Howards' End* ([1910] Harmondsworth: Penguin, 1975), 200.
[120] William Robinson, *The English Flower Garden*, 13th edn (New York: Charles Scribner, 1921), 6–7, 16; Patrick Taylor (ed.), *The Oxford Companion to Gardens* (Oxford: Oxford University Press, 2006), 128–9.

'Environs' began to appear in the city guidebooks[121] and expanded considerably under the early Victorians, as visitors turned their attention further and further afield.[122] At this stage the emphasis was on antiquities (such as castles and cathedrals), picturesque views and natural features, and especially country seats. By the 1870s villages are beginning to be included as objects of interest in their own right, and locations are appearing that in later years would be seen as archetypal English villages and become leading tourist attractions.

The role of artists in promoting this model is clear from an 1884 account of a village in the Peak District of Derbyshire: 'we know not how better to describe Tissington than by saying that it looks more like the fount from which that artist [Myles Birket Foster (1825–1899), a celebrated painter of rural scenes] drew his inspiration than any other village we have ever seen. Its essence is rustic simplicity and undersigned picturesqueness.'[123] At Lacock the Abbey (converted at the Reformation into a residence but preserving substantial elements of the medieval nunnery) was the focus of attention, but visitors were also reminded that 'many of the houses in the village are very picturesque, preserving as they do their antique appearance'.[124] Lacock gets no mention in the Ward Lock guide of 1909, but Castle Combe is very briefly referred to (though on account of its castle and manor house, not cottages) and included in a cycle tour.[125] By the 1920s, however, both villages are depicted in the guide as significant tourist destinations:

> Lacock village, with its many fifteenth- and sixteenth-century houses, has been described as 'unique in Wiltshire and not easily matched in England': its [Castle Combe] attractions have been thus aptly summed up by Mr. Edward Hutton (*Highways and Byways in Wilts*) ... 'in its own way it is as unique as Clovelly' ... The village ... is a place in which to linger and to which to return – flower-covered cottages and delightful old houses clustering round the market cross to make up a picture that would be difficult to match.[126]

The old English village archetype had come of age. Villages which met the necessary criteria, located in invented historic regions in southern England such as Wessex, the Wiltshire Downs or the Cotswolds, but also now including picturesque fishing settlements such as Clovelly, 'England's loveliest village', 'an English Amalfi rising sheer from the bay',[127] joined the tourist itinerary. The Ward Lock guide's tendency to quote from other sources – Hutton in the case of Castle Combe, unidentified in the case of Lacock – demonstrates the essentially self-referential and self-reinforcing process by which the village had become a national icon.

---

[121] See, e.g., *Improved Bath Guide*, 33–40.
[122] *The Original Bath Guide* (Bath: Meyler & Son, 1840), 135–62.
[123] M. J. B. Baddeley, *The Peak District of Derbyshire and Surrounding Counties*, 3rd edn (London: Dulau, 1884), 49.
[124] *The Original Bath Guide, Historical and Descriptive* (Bath: William Lewis, 1876), 141.
[125] *Pictorial and Descriptive Guide to Bath* (London: Ward Lock, 1909–10), 148, 169.
[126] Ibid., 122–3.
[127] Mais, *Glorious Devon*, 136; Morton, *In Search of England*, 115.

Landscape as modernism; the modernist seaside and countryside

It is probably true that the majority of guidebook writers adopted a predominantly nostalgic perspective. The sight of the 'romantic many-gabled manor-house in a deep-wooded combe' at Owlpen in Gloucestershire prompted Edward Hutton to reflect in 1932 that 'the disaster of modern England can almost be forgotten, since England here is not modern, but enduring'.[128] However, landscapes embody not only the past but also the present, and even the future. There is plenty of evidence that domestic tourists were interested in not only the historic but also the modern content of the landscapes that they visited. Paul Readman has argued that 'English cultural nationalism went with the grain of modernity, integrating the contemporary with the traditional, the past with the present'.[129] We saw in Chapter 5 how travel guides highlighted, and their readers sought out, contemporary urban industrial and public buildings as places to visit. As Andy Croll has pointed out, one of the appeals for the working class trippers flooding into the resort of Barry Island in South Wales in the 1880s was 'industrial tourism', notably a sight of the construction of the impressive coal docks complex.[130] For tourists timescapes could thus embrace past and present, even if it would seem that it was increasingly the former that predominated. A central problem in interpreting tourists' temporal responses to the built environment – where they placed a structure on the spectrum between past and present – is the issue of style. In 1881 *Black's Guide to Warwickshire* described the county town as 'mostly modern, the fire of 1694 having swept away the great majority of its old houses'.[131] The failure to recognize the pretty post-fire classically designed houses lining the central streets of Warwick, even two centuries after their construction, as anything other than 'modern' speaks volumes for the reluctance at the time to incorporate anything after *c.* 1700 – and more broadly anything classical – in the notion of 'old'. Classicism, specifically Palladianism and neoclassicism (what we today associate with the Georgian style), was equated in effect with modernity. But there was of course a problem here. Classicism was self-evidently a *historic* style. Its roots were firmly planted in the Graeco-Roman past and in the revival of this during the European Renaissance. When Lord Burlington designed the new Assembly Rooms in York in the early-eighteenth century he was engaged in what he would have conceived of as an act of archaeological reconstruction, bringing back to life the so-called Egyptian Hall described by the Roman architectural theorist Vitruvius.[132] The same process of authentic mimicry can be argued for Joseph Hansom's Birmingham Town Hall of the 1830s, closely modelled on the Temple of Castor and Pollux in the Roman Forum.[133] And of course the same line of argument

---

[128] Hutton, *Highways and Byways in Gloucestershire*, 243.
[129] Readman, *Storied Ground*, 310.
[130] Andy Croll, *Barry Island: The Making of a Seaside Playground, c. 1795–c. 1960* (Cardiff: University of Wales Press, 2020), 79–80, 84–7.
[131] *Black's Guide to Warwickshire*, 187.
[132] Rudolf Wittkower, 'Burlington and His Work in York', in idem, *Palladio and English Palladianism* (London: Thames & Hudson, 1974), 134–44.
[133] Andy Foster, *Birmingham* (London: Yale University Press, 2005), 58–9.

can be developed about the whole Gothic Revival. Until the early-twentieth century, it was impossible to build in any formal style that did not in some way hark back to a past tradition. However, it is perfectly clear that contemporary classical – and by the nineteenth-century gothic – buildings were considered 'modern' at the cutting edge of change and style. In this sense all new construction was fundamentally ambivalent, conveying mixed messages about the past and the present. We cannot easily say then that tourists who took in the reconstructed Houses of Parliament, the great new town halls – or even the factories and warehouses – of England's industrial cities, were in pursuit of the past or present. It was probably a mixture of both. By the late-nineteenth century this potentially unsettling ambivalence, allied to the pace of construction and threats to surviving 'historic' buildings (including their 'restoration'), led to a need to define more clearly what was, and what was not, 'old'. It became the aim of the conservation movements founded at this time, notably the Society for the Protection of Ancient Buildings (established in 1877), to prescribe, protect and preserve what they conceived of as genuinely old. It was an approach which the guide literature largely followed because authors and publishers realized that it was what their readers wanted when they took to the roads, a clearer demarcation between the historic and the modern so that it was possible to access an 'authentic' past on their travels.

But it would be wrong to underrate the appeal of modernity, even as a tourist attraction. The well-off middle classes in the late-nineteenth and early-twentieth century were occupying new, large, comfortable, architect-designed arts and crafts and neo-Georgian houses, fitted with cutting-edge domestic technology, happy to live with the mixed messages of past and present. There was a widespread recognition that in towns particularly there existed large pockets of poor-quality housing, ripe for demolition and replacement. Edmund Vale ends his *How to Look at Old Buildings*: 'the great slum-clearances of the last decade (1930–40) indicate a public consciousness of rapidly changing conditions and a desire to meet the future half way by making daring experiments. ... Vandals must be let loose sometimes or our rubbish dumps would never be cleared.'[134]

The products of the emerging town planning movement attracted generally favourable press. Bournville was developed from the 1890s as a model factory village on the edge of Birmingham by the paternalist Quaker chocolate manufacturer, George Cadbury. Constructed in an Arts and Crafts style, and incorporating plenty of green space, it was commended by Arthur Mee in his *King's England* volume on Warwickshire, as a 'shining example to the world'. J. B. Priestley was a little more ambivalent: he admired it as 'one of the small outposts of civilization, still ringed round with barbarism' but 'I would prefer houses arranged in small courts and squares. I do not understand this passion for being detached or semi-detached'.[135] Bournville was a forerunner of the Ebenezer Howard-inspired Garden City Movement, the earliest examples of which were Letchworth (from 1903) and Welwyn Garden City (from 1919). In 1935 Marjorie and Charles Quennell in *The Good New Days* – a future-centred, modernist counterpart to their four-volume *History of Everyday Things in England* (1918–24), all supposedly directed at the country's children – declared that

---

[134] Vale, *How to Look at Old Buildings*, 88.
[135] Foster, *Birmingham*, 68; Mee, *Warwickshire*, 63; Priestley, *English Journey*, 92.

'Letchworth should be visited'.[136] However, adult guidebook writers do not appear generally to have accepted the invitation.

More significant in terms of the tourist circuit, and in many respects modernism, were the seaside resorts – one guide of the 1920s referred to the 'gay modernity of Bournemouth'[137] – to which a sizeable chunk of the holidaying population headed in growing numbers by the early-twentieth century. Containing limited historic building fabric, many were effectively new towns. In the Victorian and Edwardian periods seaside architecture could be among the most innovative and enterprising, mixing metal, glass and electric technologies in structures like piers, towers and pleasure palaces. The design of these drew predominantly on the vernacular, classical and gothic traditions but they also could look to more exotic influences such as Indian architecture, which, though it had imperial resonances for the English, had little historical meaning.

It is also clear that during the inter-war years the international Modernist Movement (pioneered by figures like le Corbusier) began to affect seaside architecture, and though its influence should not be exaggerated at this stage (it could be seen in some hotels, lidos and pleasure facilities, but primarily in one-off houses for the trend-setting rich), here was an architecture that appeared to celebrate its divorce from the past, and from an English past, and that found a receptive home in the seaside.[138] In the Introduction to their edited collection, *Modernism on Sea*, Lara Feigel and Alexandra Harris put 'the case for a new geography of avant-gardism' that embraces resorts, arguing that 'the most intriguing cultural hubs of modern times include Swanage, Margate, Morecambe and Hythe'.[139] They might have included Bournemouth, described in 1938 as 'the king of the modern towns',[140] and Blackpool. During the 1930s the latter acquired the strikingly modern Lion Hotel, Casino (at the Pleasure Beach), Odeon, Woolworth's department store and Talbot Road Bus Station and Car Park.[141] As part of his *English Journey*, Priestley visited the resort in 1933:

> Compared with this huge mad place, with its miles and miles of promenades, its three piers, its gigantic dance-halls, its variety shows, its switch-backs and helter-skelters, its array of wine bars and oyster saloons and cheap restaurants and tea houses and shops piled high and glittering with trash; its army of pierrots, bandsmen, clowns, fortune-tellers, auctioneers, dancing partners, animal trainers, itinerant singers, hawkers; its seventy special trains a day, its hundreds and hundreds of thousands of trippers; places like Brighton and Margate and Yarmouth are merely playing at being popular seaside resorts. Blackpool has them all licked.

The blatant modernity of Blackpool, the raucous celebration of the here and now, was obvious enough (see Figure 6.5).

[136] Marjorie and Charles H. B. Quennell, *The Good New Days* (London: Batsford, 1935), 36.
[137] Stevens, *Picturesque Towns*, 27.
[138] Fred Gray, *Designing the Seaside* (London: Reaktion, 2006), 47–53, et seq; Brodie and Winter, *England's Seaside Resorts*, 62–92.
[139] Feigel and Harris, *Modernism on Sea*, 1.
[140] Beach Thomas, *English Landscape*, 79.
[141] Allan Brodie and Matthew Whitfield, *Blackpool's Seaside Heritage* (Swindon: English Heritage, 2014), 99–112.

Figure 6.5 South Shore Blackpool, contemporary postcard, c. 1933.

But for Priestley it all came at a price; 'That is Blackpool. It is a complete and essential product of industrial democracy. If you do not like industrial democracy, you will not like Blackpool.' Here was a clear warning – a sort of anti-tourism – to his middle-class readership to keep away. There was also a message for those among the working class who aspired to respectability:

> One section of it [the working class] ... does not want the new Blackpool ... it does not care for mass entertainment and prefers to spend its leisure in quieter places, cycling and walking and playing games in the sun. There are plenty of young working-class people of that quality now in the North. The rest of them, the less intelligent and enterprising, are, I feel, fit patrons of the new Blackpool, which knows what to do with the passive and listless.[142]

Like Priestley, Bernard Newman, conducting his British journey towards the end of the Second World War, had a sort of grudging admiration for the unapologetic, present-centred superficiality of Blackpool; 'there will be hundreds of thousands ... who will prefer the charm of the countryside or the beauty of the hills: yet the taste of the mass, until it can be raised, favours the blatant artificiality which Blackpool provides so magnificently, and which some other resorts try to imitate'.[143] Priestley and Newman

---

[142] Priestley, *English Journey*, 265–7.
[143] Bernard Newman, *British Journey* (London: R. Hale, 1945), 132–3.

portray the tourists' interaction with landscape as something class driven; for the middle and aspiring working class, it involved visiting the old and rural; for the mass working class it was the urban and new that they sought out. In such circumstances it is not surprising that much of the tourist and topographical literature, aimed at a middle-class market, focused on the countryside and the past.

Not that those who took to their feet and cycles (not to mention motor cars) to explore Arcadia always found it inhabited by the past. It is clear that by the inter-war years there were a series of initiatives underway aimed at modernizing and regenerating the countryside. Among these are increasing levels of agricultural mechanization, the modernization of parts of the craft sector, the growth of rural and agricultural education, the village hall and theatre movements, and innovative large-scale projects such as at Leckford, a Hampshire estate bought and completely re-organized by the retail magnet John Lewis in 1929, or Dartington Hall in south Devon, an iconic initiative begun in 1925, whose moving spirit, Leonard Elmhirst, believed that the country house estate provide 'a programme of social and economic regeneration that would be a model for the nation'.[144] On top of this there was the impact of the burgeoning town and country planning movement, which argued that through centrally directed planning it was possible both to preserve and modernize the countryside, 'a particular form of modernism' that David Matless has dubbed 'a moral modernity'.[145] Quite what all this

Figure 6.6 'Mousehole, Penzance' (1932), poster design for Shell by Alexander Stuart-Hill. © Shell Heritage Art Collection.

---

[144] Paul Brassley, Jeremy Burchardt and Lynne Thompson (eds.), *The English Countryside between the Wars: Regeneration or Decline* (Woodbridge: Boydell & Brewer, 2006), 117 et seq; Quennell, *Good New Days*, 7–26.

[145] David Matless, *Landscape and Englishness* (London: Reaktion, 1998), 51, 25–61.

meant for those whose interest in the countryside was purely recreational is difficult to say. It is unlikely that they would have been interested in, or even registered, the processes of agricultural innovation. However, the physical exercise associated with a visit to the countryside could be seen as a wider international and modern movement towards improving bodily health. The use of new technologies and infrastructures – such as rail, cycles, motor cars, improved roads, petrol stations, etc. – to access the countryside could also be said to reinforce the notion that a visit to the countryside was a modernizing experience.

Inter-war advertising and publicity directed at domestic tourists, such as that by the major rail companies or the Shell oil company, cleverly married notions of the modern and the historic, in a way that moved on from the more overtly sentimental images of pre-war guide literature and art (see Figure 6.6).[146] Indeed, landscape painting as a whole – town, sea and country – was responding to the radical changes in the European art scene since the late-nineteenth century, incorporating and transmitting a modernist aesthetic.[147] So the case for the countryside representing modernity, albeit often as part of a mixed message that spliced together the rural past and present, is a persuasive one by the inter-war years. That said, it is difficult to read the bulk of tourist literature without gaining the impression that much as modernism had permeated practice and theorizing about the rural world, and access to it was dependent on modern means, for the majority of rural tourists, it was the opportunity to experience the past that primarily drove them to vacate their urban homes.

---

[146] Harris, *Romantic Moderns*, 214–21; Cole and Durack, *Railway Posters*, 9, 18, 23; Heathcote, *A Shell Eye on England*, 112–33.
[147] Ysanne Holt, *British Artists and the Modernist Landscape* (Abingdon: Routledge, 2018).

7

Economic and social change

One of the great appeals of landscape, or of certain sorts of landscape, is its apparent timelessness. Its seeming immutability provided a psychological antidote to the forces of change. As Thomas Hardy described Egdon Heath (the fictional name he gave to the heathland close to his birthplace in Dorset) in the opening to *The Return of the Native* (1878), 'to know that everything around and underneath has been from prehistoric times as unaltered as the stars overhead, gave ballast to the mind adrift on change, and harassed by the irrepressible New'.[1] This was surely one of the principal attractions of the natural landscape to the late Victorian rural tourist, whose world was altering so rapidly under the combined forces of economic and social change. This chapter seeks to describe these forces, in part to explain why so many turned to 'great inviolate place[s]'[2] as a source of solace but also in part to explore the reasons why *attitudes* to landscape changed quite fundamentally in the period. Far from being unaltered, landscape as a physical reality, but even more so as a mental concept, was undergoing radical change.

Industrialization

We start with the industrialization, and more specifically the Industrial Revolution. It now seems something of an historical cliché to turn to the Industrial Revolution as an explanation of anything and everything in nineteenth-century history. It is not just a question of it being an over-worked idea, but ever since the Victorian era historians have regularly debated the veracity and value of the concept itself. Is there sufficient quantitative data to support the notion? Was the impact of industrialization more a gradual than a revolutionary process, and one heavily focused on a narrow economic sector and very specific regions?[3] In addressing these questions, and the legitimate doubts that they raise, there is the risk of throwing the baby out with the bath water. A process of industrialization was underway, whether that is termed 'a revolution' or not, that over the longer term – and here one might be looking at a span of a century and

---

[1] Thomas Hardy, *The Return of the Native* ([1878] Harmondsworth: Penguin, 1985), 56.
[2] Ibid.
[3] Pat Hudson, *The Industrial Revolution* (London: Edward Arnold, 1992), 9–36; Charles More, *The Industrial Age: Economy and Society in Britain* (London and New York: Longman, 1989), 72–84.

a half – radically changed the economic and social structures, alongside the political and cultural ones, in which people lived. To attribute all this to industrialization in a narrow sense of factories and machinery – to ignore, for example, the closely related but distinctive roles of urbanization and the 'leisure revolution'[4] – would be a mistake, and these will be examined later in this chapter. But industrialization in its own right deserves attention, not least because contemporaries were themselves very conscious of what W. S. Shears in the 1930s called 'the deluge of the Industrial Revolution',[5] and its impact on their reading of the landscape.

Industry was nothing new in the late-eighteenth century. Manufacturing, mining and quarrying were major and – especially from the late-seventeenth century – growing sectors of the early modern economy and left a substantial imprint on the landscape. Much of this economic activity was located in the countryside, and the vast majority took place in people's homes or in small-scale industrial units with limited technology. When observers recorded the presence of industry, it was generally in positive terms, as evidence of enterprise and a working population, able to cater for itself rather than depending on poor relief. In the 1720s Defoe noted that the houses of Sheffield were 'dark and black, occasioned by the continued smoke of the forges, which are always at work', but there is little hint here of the pollution narrative of later generations of writers; the more smoke, the more evidence of economic prosperity.[6]

This positive attitude was challenged but by no means banished by the developments in the early stages of the Industrial Revolution. In 1791 William Gilpin, the theorist of the picturesque, could complain of the salterns facing the Solent at Lymington (Hampshire), that 'the square, bounded receptacles to receive the brine, are a glaring injury to the beauty of the shore', and a decade earlier of how the Stroudwater Valley (Gloucestershire) 'one of the most beautiful of these [rural] scenes, has been deformed lately not only by a number of buildings', associated with the textile industry, 'but by a canal cut though the middle of it'. However, in his famous description of his tour along the River Wye, he drew on the language of the sublime to describe how 'many of the furnaces on the banks of the river consume charcoal, which is manufactured on the spot; and the smoke, which is frequently seen issuing from the sides of the hills; and spreading its thin veil over a part of them, beautifully breaks their lines, and unites them with the sky'.[7] As large-scale industrial plant began to be developed it was usually treated as an object of wonder rather than distaste and could be easily accommodated in the tourist itinerary and narrative.[8] Iron works, mines and factories – the early manifestations of the Industrial Revolution – were at this point in time usually located in the countryside, and frequently, for ease of access to power and mineral resources, in dramatic natural locations. The construction of

---

[4] W. J. Baker, 'A Leisure Revolution in Victorian England: A Review of Recent Literature', *Journal of Sporting History* 6:3 (1979): 16–87.

[5] W. S. Shears, *This England: A Book of the Shires and Counties*, 2nd edn (London: Right Book Club, 1938), 31.

[6] Defoe, *Tour*, vol. 3, 81; see Morton, *Call of England*, 172–4.

[7] William Gilpin, *Remarks on Forest Scenery and Other Woodland Views*, 2 vols. (London: R. Blamire, 1791), vol. 2, 88; idem, *Observations on the River Wye*, 12.

[8] Scarfe (ed.), *Innocent Espionage*, 90–100; Lord, *Industrial Society*, 13–50.

such plant coincided with the rise of the picturesque and romantic movements, and it was possible for observers to see industrialization and romanticism as part of a similar process, both releasing the potential of natural resources and contributing to a notion of the sublime. The sheer scale of the copper mines at Parys Mountain on Anglesey – the dramatic landscape gorged out by the extensive workings – attracted the attention of late-eighteenth- and early-nineteenth-century painters such as John Warwick Smith (who also captured the Hafod Estate in Ceredigion), Julius Caesar Ibbetson, Edward Pugh and William Havell.[9] The deep cut and wooded valleys, furnaces and forges of Coalbrookdale and the Ironbridge Gorge of the River Severn drew numerous tourists and painters to this early seat of the Industrial Revolution, the artists constructing images in which the smoke and flames belching from the industrial plant enhanced the awesome character of the natural landscape. It was something captured at its most extreme in Philip James de Loutherbourg's famous *Coalbrookdale by Night* (1801) with its 'magnificently sublime representation of the furnaces at Bedlam' (see Figure 7.1).[10]

In Joseph Wright's paintings by night (1782–3) and day (*c.* 1795–6) of Richard Arkwright's textile spinning mill at Cromford in Derbyshire – with its innovative water frame technology – the factory is at one with the romantic natural landscape of the Derwent Gorge. In 1774 Wright was touring Italy and witnessed the eruption

Figure 7.1 Philip James de Loutherbourg, 'Coalbrookdale by Night' (1801). © The Science Museum Group.

---

[9] Peter Lord, *Industrial Society* (Cardiff: University of Wales Press, 1998), 23–8.
[10] Stuart Smith, *A View from the Iron Bridge* (Ironbridge: Ironbridge Gorge Museum Trust, 1979), 46; Barrie Trinder, *The Most Extraordinary District in the World: Ironbridge and Coalbrookdale* (London: Phillimore, 1977).

of Vesuvius, then in one of its highly active phases, and on his return to England produced a series of spectacular canvases depicting the awe-inspiring character of what he described as 'the most wonderful sight in Nature'.[11] What appealed to Wright was the glimpse the eruption provided of the immense concealed forces of nature. In a similar fashion industry also revealed these forces, though at the same time harnessing them to productive ends, through water or mineral derived power. There was therefore no contradiction between industry and nature. Joseph Turner also took in Vesuvius during a tour of Italy in 1819, and though his depictions of the mountain's eruptions are fabrications – the volcano was inconveniently quiet when he visited – there is the same depiction of the release of huge natural energy.[12] On occasions Turner also illustrated advanced industrial technology, notably in the tug in *The Fighting Temeraire* (1839) and the railway engine in *Railway, Steam and Speed – the Great Western Railway* (1846). Turner is normally associated with his highly dramatic paintings of natural coastal or rural landscapes, both of which are to a degree incorporated into these paintings. The presence of the steam engine – perhaps the most innovative of all the technologies of the Industrial Revolution – in the form of the tug and the railway engine, thrusting and blazing with energy, might be seen as an implicit criticism of the impact of industrialization on nature. But it is equally possible to interpret Turner's depiction of the steam engine as a celebration of the capacity of industrialization to unlock the forces of nature, in a similar fashion to the volcano, and therefore within the tradition of the sublime in which he had been nurtured: a tradition that could view industry and nature as complementary rather than contradictory.

By the late-nineteenth century, if not before, for many observers the relationship between nature and industry had soured. This was not of course a universal response – as we have seen, there were many who would celebrate all facets of modernity – but a powerful anti-industrial strand of thought began to emerge among artists and commentators, in which nature and technology, and past and present became decoupled. Peter Lord has described how for Welsh artists – to the limited extent that they continued to engage with the world of manufacture – 'industrial gloom emerged from the industrial sublime. The observers were alienated from what they saw'.[13] This was a consequence of what was seen as the damaging physical and human impact of industrialization that was occurring at a pace to which it was difficult for society to adjust, at least in the immediate – and perhaps even in the longer – term. Leading public intellectuals like Thomas Carlyle, John Ruskin and William Morris developed an anti-mechanization narrative of the deleterious effects of machinery and mass production. Both, as they saw it, had damaging consequences for the physical and psychological well-being of the human capital bound to the new technology and industries, but it also had negative ramifications for the landscape that accommodated working people.

---

[11] Amina Wright, *Joseph Wright of Derby: Bath and Beyond* (London: Philip Wilson Publishers, 2014), 51–69; James Hamilton, *Volcano* (London: Reaktion, 2012), 78–81.
[12] Hamilton, *Volcano*, 90–3.
[13] Lord, *Industrial Society*, 136.

In *The Two Paths* (1859) Ruskin portrayed an apocalyptic vision of a future in which industrialization had triumphed absolutely:

> [F]rom shore to shore the whole island is to be set as thick with chimneys as the masts stand on the docks in Liverpool; ... there shall be no meadows in it; no trees; no gardens; only a little corn grown up on the house tops, reaped and threshed by steam: ... no acre of English ground shall be without its shaft and its engine; and therefore, no spot of English ground left on which it will be possible to stand without a definite and calculable chance of being blown off it, at any moment, into small pieces.[14]

In such accounts the battle lines between industry and nature are starkly delineated. It is also a conflict articulated by writers of fiction. The steam thresher, alluded to by Ruskin, makes a powerful symbolic appearance in Thomas Hardy's *Tess of the d'Urbevilles* (1891), where Tess becomes the slave of the machine, with its 'despotic demand', and where the engineer, the 'sooty and grimy embodiment of tallness' (surely the human metaphor for a factory chimney), who 'spoke in a strange northern accent', was completely at odds with the natural landscape of the south into which he had intruded: 'What he looked he felt. He was in the agricultural world, but not of it. He served fire and smoke: these denizens of the fields served vegetation, weather, frost, and sun.'[15] The conflict dramatized here between industry and nature – the disregard of the former for the seasons and the natural world – was played out even more depressingly in Charles Dicken's fictional northern factory town, Coketown, based on a visit to Preston (*Hard Times*, 1854):

> The whole town seemed to be frying in oil. ... The steam-engines shone with it ... Their wearisome heads went up and down at the same rate, in hot weather and cold, wet weather and dry, fair weather and foul. The measured motion of their shadows on the walls, was the substitute Coketown had to show for the shadows of rustling woods; while, for the summer hum of insects, it could offer, all the year round, from the dawn of Monday to the night of Saturday, the whirr of shafts and wheels.[16]

Much of the plant associated with the early Industrial Revolution, as we have seen, was located in the countryside. The development of steam power and more effective modes of transport, taken together with the gains in efficiency through the concentration of factors of production, drew manufacturing into the towns. However, there was one area of the economy where industry had an ever-growing impact on the rural landscape. Mining and quarrying enterprises expanded hugely, as demand for metal ores, coal, china clay, limestone and building materials generally, including for

---

[14] John Ruskin, *The Two Paths: Being Lectures on Art and Its Application to Decoration and Manufacture, Delivered 1858–9* (London: George Allen, 1890), 118–19.
[15] Thomas Hardy, *Tess of the D'Urbervilles*, ed. Simon Gatrell and Juliet Grindle ([1891] Oxford: Oxford University Press, 2005), 345.
[16] Charles Dickens, *Hard Times*, ed. Kate Flint ([1854] London: Penguin, 1995), 112.

canal, rail and road construction, escalated as a consequence of economic growth. This left a clear imprint on the largely upland countryside. What could once be celebrated as an improvement to the landscape, transforming barren and wild hillsides and mountains into a productive environment, was being perceived as a scar on the natural landscape by the later nineteenth century.

As early as 1898 Baedeker warned those visiting the Cornish coast in the vicinity of St Austell that '[t]he beauty of the district now traversed is marred by numerous mines and the white refuse of kaolin, or china-clay, which is found here in great abundance', a formula repeated by Muirhead's *Blue Guide* in 1930 when it recorded the 'refuse-heaps ... which mar the adjoining district'. In the mid-1930s – with unemployment high on the economic and social agenda – R. A. J. Walling's account of *The West Country* was inclined to take a more sympathetic view of the damage but was forced to admit that 'neither china clay works nor tin mines improve the character of the landscape where they exist in great extent' while also acknowledging that they formed 'an integral part of Cornish life and help to sustain the fabric of beauty and amenity which the visitor to Cornwall enjoys'.[17] In 1945 Bernard Newman called quarries 'huge white gashes on the landscape ... ugly but useful'.[18]

The tension between the aesthetic expectations of the tourist and the economic needs of the indigenous population identified by Walling remained a constant issue. Dartmoor, emerging during the nineteenth century as one of the most powerful imagined wild regions in Britain, was also the site of considerable industrial activity.[19] In 1912 the Geological Survey listed sixty or more mines in the area.[20] Between 1770 and 1940, at least 100 sites on or in the vicinity of the Moor were mined for tin.[21] There was also extensive stone quarrying across the Moor.[22] By the 1870s tin and copper production were declining, due to the opening up of overseas sources, but the thirst for granite – to meet the needs of road construction and urban growth – and china clay grew.[23] William Crossing, a key figure behind the re-mapping of Dartmoor as a recreational space, in *Amid Devonia's Alps* (1888) acknowledged the economic benefits of quarrying at the same time as bemoaning its damaging effects:

> The granite quarries are of some magnitude ... The true lover of the moor, while fully realising that works of this sort which afford employment for so many, are in themselves desirable, will, however, scarcely be able to help regretting that the face which it wore in the old time, is, around the scene of such operations, being entirely spoiled. Still, sentiment must bow before the welfare of the community.[24]

[17] Baedeker, *Great Britain* (1898), 142; Findlay Muirhead, *England*, 3rd edn (London: Macmillan & Co., 1930), 182; R. A. J. Walling, *The West Country* (London: Blackie & Son, 1935), 31–2; see also H. A. Piehler, *England for Everyman* (London: J. M. Dent & Sons, 1933), 92.
[18] Newman, *British Journey*, 16.
[19] Ian Mercer, *Dartmoor: A Statement of Its Time* (London: Collins, 2009), 255–76.
[20] L. A. Harvey and D. St Leger-Gordon, *Dartmoor* (London: Collins, 1953), 57.
[21] Roger Kain (ed.), *The South West: England's Landscape* (London: Collins, 2006), 140–2.
[22] Kain (ed.), *The South West*, 148: Milton, *Discovery of Dartmoor*, 99.
[23] Milton, *Discovery of Dartmoor*, 130–1.
[24] William Crossing, *Amid Devonia's Alps: Or, Wanderings & Adventures on Dartmoor* (London: Simpkin, Marshall & Co., 1888), 24; Matthew Kelly, *Quartz and Feldspar: Dartmoor – a British Landscape in Modern Times* (London: Vintage, 2016), 193–211.

The Malvern Hills, like their Dartmoor counterpart, were an excellent source of plutonic rock (granite and diorite) used as a building stone but especially as aggregate.[25] When the Malvern Hill Conservators were established under Act of Parliament in 1884, quarrying was not at the forefront of their concerns. It was probably accepted that this represented a necessary exploitation of the environment, and landowners, who saw the Conservators as endangering their economic interests, needed to be appeased. Moreover, quarries could be said to be a tourist attraction for amateur geologists.[26] However, the rising demand for building and especially aggregate for road construction in the later nineteenth and early twentieth centuries, allied to growing public use of the hills for recreation, meant that the threat presented by the quarries to the natural environment loomed more and more into prominence. The extent of quarrying was scarring the appearance of the hills and disrupting its amenity for visitors. The quarries were regularly reported by the Conservators' chief ranger as a risk to ramblers and measures were taken to fence off dangerous spaces.[27] In 1890 he recorded that the footpath at Eacock's quarry had been seriously encroached upon and undermined by the quarrymen 'and I know that a gentleman from the Wells has fallen into the quarry in consequence'. Three years later the ranger found the same quarry still in a 'dangerous condition … As I was passing there last night a young foal was precipitated into the quarry, it was walking upon the outer edge of the path when the ground gave way under it'.[28]

However, probably more important than safety issues over the longer term was the sense of physical and aesthetic damage quarrying was doing to the appearance of the hills. By 1909 the level of concern had reached the point where the Conservators established a special committee to address the 'quarrying and disfigurement of the hills', whose report noted that Mr Whinnery, the Secretary of the Board of Agriculture, had visited and 'inspected the quarries and saw the terrible depredations in progress and was of the opinion that immediate action should be taken to prevent these disfigurements'.[29] A new Act of Parliament introduced in 1909 did little to tackle the problem, largely because of opposition from local landowners and quarry owners. For the Conservators, and the residents and tradesmen of Malvern, quarrying continued to constitute a major and growing blot on their immediate landscape and a serious threat to what had become the spa's most important recreational and tourist asset. George Bernard Shaw wrote to the *Times*, 'The approach to Malvern from the great plain of the Severn … has always had a peculiar charm. It now has a peculiar horror. Visitors from Worcester used to see the unspoiled North Hill with an indescribable pleasure. They now see it hideously disfigured by three gigantic scoops.'[30] A long battle ensued to curtail industrial activity on the hills, but by the 1920s the forces representing leisure

---

[25] *Explaining Aggregates along the Geopark Way* (Worcester: Herefordshire and Worcestershire Earth Heritage Trust, 2012).
[26] Grindrod, *Malvern: What to See*, 261–3.
[27] See, e.g., MHC, Committee (1886–9, 1889–1909), 20 Aug. 1988, 11 Oct. 1899, 13 Feb. and 8 May 1901.
[28] MHC Ranger's Report Book (1887–91, 1891–96), 7 May 1890, 10 May 1893.
[29] MHC, Minute Book of the Quarrying and Disfigurement of the Hills Committee (1907–9)
[30] *Times*, 8 Oct. 1929, 17.

and tourism were winning the day with new legislation and policies to restrict and eventually reverse the impact of quarrying on the Malverns.[31] A new act obtained by the Conservators in 1924 recognized that the Hills had become 'a centre of attraction to the inhabitants of the counties of Worcester and Hereford and visitors from all parts of the country for purposes of health, recreation and enjoyment', but at the same time acknowledged that 'in recent years the amenities of Malvern Hills have been seriously interfered with by quarrying operations … [which] are being extended in such manner as to threaten to destroy the value of Malvern Hills as objects of public interest'.[32] The act gave the Conservators powers to regulate and subsequently prevent quarrying on the Hills, but the carefully modulated language conceals years of struggle and negotiation to obtain these powers. Its passage in part reflects the growing industrial pressures on the environment, but in all probability, even more important was the rising urban demand for rural recreational space, the emergence of an ethos and policy in which tightly controlled reserves of green space were to be created and protected from the ravages of economic development and above all the developing sense – proselytized by Ruskin et al. – that industry and the countryside (and by implication Nature) were incompatible.

The reality of industry's impact on the urban and rural landscape is inescapable. But the extent to which that impact is by definition negative is less obvious. The physical scar left by mining and quarrying, the pollution belching out of the factory chimney, and the monotony and risks to health and safety of the work place are real enough, but how the damage is perceived depends a good deal on the observer. As we saw earlier, at the turn of the nineteenth century industrial activity could be accommodated positively in Enlightenment and Romantic narratives under the guise of improvement and the picturesque. Moreover, though artisan groups certainly took to their feet, and later bicycles, to explore the countryside,[33] the most assiduous and wealthy domestic tourists for much of our period were the urban middle class, whose direct experience of the worst aspects of industrialization would be limited by the nature of their jobs (or in the case of women, lack of employment) and their suburban residences. What was critical was not so much the reality or otherwise of industrialization, as the narrative in which it was framed. This is where the anti-industrial themes developed by Dickens, Ruskin and Morris – not to mention official and semi-official reports on the Condition of England question – were so important in re-modelling public perceptions. However, from a perspective of tourism and the landscape, perhaps even more important was the way the writers of guidebooks took on board the grand narrative of the public intellectuals and used it to shape their accounts of the landscape of old and rural England.

In 1944 W. H. Godfrey opined that '[w]ith the rapid expanse of industry and the increases of population we began to be indifferent to the hitherto familiar art of building'.[34] This sense of transformation and alienation, as a consequence of industrialization,

---

[31] Hurle, *The Malvern Hills*, 67–98.
[32] Malvern Hills Act (1924), 3.
[33] Chad Bryant, Arthur Burns and Paul Readman, *Walking Histories, 1800–1914* (Basingstoke: Palgrave, 2016), 8.
[34] W. H. Godfrey, *Our Building Inheritance* (London: Faber & Faber, 1944), 15.

of the human disconnect with nature and the past, and of the need to reconnect through travel, permeates much of the guide literature. Locations to be avoided in the quest for reconnection are clearly identified. The *Contour Roadbook* (1909) advised of Lancashire that '[a]s a county for touring scarcely any but the northern portion [distant from the industrial towns of the south] can be recommended. ... Few of the towns have much beauty'. Two years earlier the *Contour Motoring Map of the British Isles* had an inset map indicating 'industrial area to avoid'.[35] In the 1920s the Dunlop-sponsored *Picturesque Towns and Villages* comforted tourists to the West Country that 'it is hardly touched by industrialism of the kind that the motorist on a pleasure tour is anxious to avoid' but warned those that ventured into the North East that 'Durham Cathedral stands like an oasis of art in a desert of coal mining'.[36] In 1927 H. V. Morton cautioned those sharing his search for England of the 'startling' 'change of country' at the Cheshire-Lancashire border, 'here was New England: an England of crowded towns, of tall chimneys, of great mill walls, of canals of slow, black water; an England of grey, hard-looking little houses in interminable rows; the England of coal and chemicals; of cotton, glass, and iron'.[37] H. A. Piehler's *England for Everyman* (1933) was unabashed about its omission of 'the great manufacturing cities' and 'all predominantly industrial districts' and cautioned that 'South Lancashire, with its numberless cotton mills and its strings of smoky manufacturing towns, is no place for the average tourist'.[38] 'Newcastle is not very pretty', warned Bernard Newman, and Gateshead was 'a depressing town', it being 'difficult to make a slag-heap beautiful, or to camouflage the smoke from a factory chimney'. 'Perhaps', he mused, 'it is the regional consciousness and pride of the Geordie which made him so long oblivious to the ugliness of his region'.[39] William Beach Thomas held a more nuanced view. He went further than many in recognizing that the north contained 'country spaces that are among the wildest, the least spoiled, and the most thinly populated within this island'. But it was in the south that he found 'a sense of quiet and unhampered space. Joy is unconfined. As you reach the northern counties the feeling of the country is utterly and entirely different. ... The [physical] contraction of England in the north is enhanced by the influence of its industries. Scores of big industrial towns are wedged into the narrow space'. Astutely he observed, '[S]uch industrial ante-chambers are crowded with men and women who thirst for the wildness, the romance, the poetry of unsullied country', such as that provided by the Lake District and the Pennines.[40]

It was not just 'the North' that suffered from industrial blight. In his short text on *How to See the Country* (1940) Harry Batsford warned that 'not all or most villages are really beautiful ... some are just dreadfully repellent. North Buckinghamshire can

---

[35] *Contour Road Book of England* (London: Gall and Inglis, 1906), xxiv; Sean O'Connell, *The Car in British Society: Class, Gender and Motoring, 1896-1939* (Manchester: Manchester University Press, 1998), 81, quoted in Joe Moran, *On Roads: A Hidden History* (London: Profile, 2010), 57.
[36] Stevens, *Picturesque Towns and Villages*, 29, 117.
[37] Morton, *In Search of England*, 185-6.
[38] Piehler, *England for Everyman*, vii, 208.
[39] Newman, *British Journey*, 207, 209, 211.
[40] Thomas, *The English Landscape*, 158-60.

show quite a few, while the Nene Valley settlements are a dismal example of the effects of Victorian industrialisation'.[41] Visitors to the Forest of Dean were advised by John Prioleau in *Car and Country* (1929) to 'avoid Coleford and Cinderford', and though no explanation is given it was clearly because of the industrial character of the area.[42] Some tourists might have been attracted to the Severn Gorge near Ironbridge, a key site of early industrialization because of its rural location, but the message for such visitors from *Seeing Shropshire* (1937) was, to say the least, ambivalent: 'Before man spoiled it, this must have been of unique loveliness and even to-day, gashed and scarred and wreathed in foul smoke, there is always beauty round the corner.'[43] Round the corner is the message of much of the guide literature, though usually it was industry rather than rural beauty that loomed in the background and defined the appeal of the countryside: the Wye Valley 'generally is fortunately singularly free from industrialisation … but it will have to be watched, as it is rather near to the industrial area of South Wales'.[44] The close proximity of the South Wales industrial conurbation accentuated the rural character of the Wye valley, but even where industry was not nearby its remote presence, in towns as well as the countryside, still defined the landscape. Ludlow was described as an 'excellent example' of a small provincial English town unsoiled or disfigured by industry: 'it exhibits no tall chimneys and smoke-streamers, no attendant purlieus and slums'. Likewise at Tewkesbury 'there is no expanding industrial prospect whatever', Warwick had 'no besmirching industry', and in Dorset '[i]ndustry has not marred the landscape … with that black pall of smoke and grime which has devastated so much of the northern countryside'.[45] W. H. Auden's subversive travelogue 'Letter to Lord Byron' might claim, 'Tramlines and slagheaps, pieces of machinery, / That was, and still is, my ideal scenery', but its very contrariness proves it was the exception to the prevailing orthodoxy.[46] Industrialization – whether in reality or through the narratives it gave rise to – had changed the meaning of town and countryside and transformed their appeal for tourists.

Urbanization

However, probably more important than the impact of industrialization in shifting perceptions of the landscape was urbanization. The two processes are closely interlinked. The economic logic of coal-fuelled industrialization encouraged the

---

[41] Batsford, *How to See the Country*, 27. On the Nene Valley see also Hoskins, *Midland England*, 8.
[42] John Prioleau, *Car and Country: Week-End Signpost to the Open Road* (London: J. M. Dent & Sons, 1929), 126.
[43] E. Moore Darling, *Seeing Shropshire* (Shrewsbury: Adnitt & Naunton Ltd., 1937), 6.
[44] H. E. Page, *Rambles and Walking Tours in the Wye Valley* (London: Great Western Railway, 1938), 10.
[45] James, *English Hours*, 137; Bradley, *Avon and Shakespeare's Country*, 4–5, 310; Clark and Thompson, *The Dorset Landscape*, 23.
[46] 'Letter to Lord Byron', in *Letters from Iceland*, ed. W. H. Auden and Louis MacNeice (London: Faber & Faber, 1937), 51. I owe this reference to John Hirst. See also Tim Youngs, 'Auden's Travel Writing', in *The Cambridge Companion to W.H. Auden*, ed. Stan Smith (Cambridge: Cambridge University Press, 2004), 73–4.

concentration of working populations in towns, as well as remodelling the real and perceived urban landscape. But urbanization also needs to be treated as a phenomenon in its own right.

Demographic urbanization – the increase in the proportion of the population living in towns – was a long-term process that had started in the sixteenth century, and accelerated rapidly from the late-eighteenth century, and not only was a growing proportion of the population living in towns but in large towns and cities. Whereas at the beginning of the nineteenth century 20 per cent of the inhabitants of England and Wales occupied towns of over 10,000 people, by the end of the century the figure had trebled to 60 per cent: for cities of over 100,000 inhabitants the rise across the same period was from 10 to 40 per cent. The latter point about the growth in large towns and cities is critical. It was these locations that because of their size were most likely to insulate their populations from the countryside and accentuate among them an urban life style. The trend towards urbanization, and *deep urbanization*, was consolidated in the early-twentieth century by the growth of cities of over 500,000 inhabitants, some of which merged effectively into conurbations – so that by 1950 they contained almost 40 per cent of the population. Britain as a whole was the most urbanized nation in Europe and probably in the world by the end of the nineteenth century and was arguably not only the 'first industrial nation' but also the first urbanized one.[47]

What was happening in England during the course of the nineteenth and early-twentieth century could justifiably be called an urban revolution, though one with long roots. Although using the same demographic measure of a town across long periods of time and highly varied societies is problematic, there is little disguising the fact that a major shift had occurred in the profile of England's population. From being a predominantly rural society, England was transformed, and over what is historically a comparatively short period of time, into a predominantly urban one. This great demographic reversal had huge social, political and – most importantly in respect of this book – cultural implications. There was a growing proportion of the population whose residences and livelihoods were disconnected from the countryside and land.

This change did not happen overnight, however. In important respects it had already been anticipated with the remarkable early modern growth of London from a city of about 75,000 inhabitants in 1500, to half a million in 1700 (becoming the largest city in western Europe having overtaken Paris), to almost a million in 1800, by which point it was probably among the largest three cities in the world.[48] As a consequence, well before the nineteenth century London developed a pastoral counter-culture that presaged and laid the foundations for much that was to come later.[49] Indeed, arguably

---

[47] Peter Clark (ed.), *The Oxford Handbook of Cities in World History* (Oxford: Oxford University Press, 2013), 668–9.

[48] Peter Clark (ed.), *The Cambridge Urban History of Britain. Volume II. 1540–1840* (Cambridge: Cambridge University Press, 2000), 316, 650.

[49] Laura Williams, 'To Recreate and Refresh', in *Imagining Early Modern London: Perceptions and Portrayals of the City from Stow to Strype, 1598–1720*, ed. Julia Merritt (Cambridge: Cambridge University Press, 2001), 185–213; Elizabeth McKellar, 'Peripheral Visions', in *The Metropolis and Its Image: Constructing Identities for London, c. 1750–1950*, ed. Dana Arnold (Oxford: Blackwell, 1999), 29–47.

it was the growth of the Metropolis that was the primary force behind the revolution in English landscape gardening, and more broadly the cultural shift towards the celebration of Nature, in the eighteenth century.

We should also remember that disconnection was not absolute. Though it is convenient statistically to divide the nation into town- and country-dwellers, these are not absolute categories. Many of the growing towns' inhabitants lived on the urban edge and could easily interact with the surrounding countryside. On the face of it, the rise of suburbia encouraged this process. However, in the case of suburbia the crucial point is that interaction, to the extent that it occurred, was essentially recreational. Suburbanites worked in the city but played in the country. That said, the expansion of suburbia did not necessarily trap the urban working class in the inner city. Many of them migrated on a seasonal basis to work in the countryside when there was a high demand for labour, such as during harvest time. But even here there was an element of the recreational about it. As Rider Haggard observed of the hop-pickers 'who in the autumn of the year flock in thousands from the great towns' to Kent, it was their 'annual holiday ... to them, indeed, what the autumn visit to sea or countryside is to other classes of town dwellers'.[50] Working and living in the city was not the same as working and living on the land. Country-dwellers of course enjoyed rural recreations, but the country could never – except for the great landowners whose wealth permitted them not to work – be primarily a place of leisure. The hard realities of their working relationship with the rural landscape prevented that. For the town-dweller, quite the opposite was the case. For those inhabiting one of the great cities, and agglomerations of towns and cities, emerging in London, the West Midlands, and across the Lancashire/Yorkshire conurbation, the countryside became one of their playgrounds.

Why was this the case? In part it reflected a reaction against the deterioration of the urban environment. Cities and their authorities responded sluggishly to the mounting pressures placed on the environment by unprecedented levels of urbanization and industrialization, leading to poor-quality housing, overcrowding, inadequate water supplies and waste disposal systems, and high levels of water, street and air pollution. Early modern London foreshadowed the problems which spread to many towns during the late eighteenth and nineteenth centuries where, in Bill Luckin's words, 'systems of local self-government were incapable of reacting rapidly to socially and epidemiologically debilitating pollution of air and water'.[51] The consequences were environmental disasters such as the cholera pandemic of 1831–2 or the 'Great Stink' of London in 1858, when MPs were driven from the House of Commons to escape the noxious fumes.[52] Against this backdrop it is understandable that the countryside and seaside seemed increasingly attractive.

---

[50] Peter Keating (ed.), *Into Unknown England, 1866–193. Selections from the Social Explorers* (Glasgow: Fontana, 1976), 203, 205.

[51] William M. Cavert, *The Smoke of London: Energy and Environment in the Early Modern City* (Cambridge: Cambridge University Press, 2016); Bill Luckin, 'Pollution in the City, 1840–1950', in *Cambridge Urban History of Britain. Vol. III*, ed. Daunton, 226.

[52] Rosemary Ashton, *One Hot Summer: Dickens, Darwin, Disraeli and the Great Stink of 1858* (New Haven: Yale University Press, 2017).

But, against this, it must be remembered that living conditions in the countryside were also very poor and, in the later nineteenth century, deteriorating for some as the agricultural depression began to bite (just as effective action began to be taken to tackle the urban problem).[53] Moreover, the consistent trend for residential (as opposed to recreational) migration was from country to town. The appeal may have been largely one of jobs and earning capacity rather than environment, but living conditions must not have been so poor as to put off newcomers. A further problem with the urban deterioration argument is that the middle classes, who were at the forefront in developing the idea of, and demand for the recreational countryside, had limited experience of the problems of inner city life: indeed – as slum and suburb became increasingly physically defined and mentally conceptualized, so that, as Richard Rodger has put it, 'the suburb inoculated its middle-class residents against the harsh realities of downtown life'[54] any middle-class contact with the working-class environment was probably confined to the view from the railway carriage and the media. It was the latter that was perhaps most important in structuring negative perceptions of the city and, since one inevitably impacted on the other, positive perceptions of the countryside.

During the second half of the nineteenth century, there was a media-driven onslaught on the image of the city from which it has never entirely recovered. Industrially driven urbanization underpinned much of what Thomas Carlyle in 1839 dubbed the 'Condition-of-England question', formulated as a consequence of a clutch of investigations, reports and accounts, such as those published by James Kay, Peter Gaskell and Andrew Ure in the early 1830s, all of which featured Manchester.[55] Significantly Friedrich Engels' *The Condition of the Working Class in England* (1845), with its graphic account of the slums of 'the great towns', especially Manchester, was initially published in Germany, and only appeared in English in 1886 (in the United States), and was not published in England until 1892.[56]

By this point a new and, in some ways, darker wave of concern about urban decline was in full flow, like that in the 1830s and 1840s prompted by anxieties about political insurgency and instability. The harbinger of this new wave was the early investigative journalism of Henry Mayhew, whose forensic exploration of London's low life – 'information concerning a large body of persons, of whom the public has less knowledge than of the most distant tribes of the earth'[57] – was published in three volumes in 1851 as *London Labour and the London Poor*, with a fourth volume added in 1861. During the latter decades of the nineteenth century, and with growing frequency, accounts and reports were published in newspapers, popular magazines and books, based on early forms of social and ethnographic investigation, which revealed in lurid detail to a middle class increasingly isolated in suburbia the physical and human landscape of

---

[53] Newby, *Country Life*, 76–137.
[54] Richard Rodger, 'Slums and Suburbs: The Persistence of Residential Apartheid', in *The English Urban Landscape*, ed. Philip J. Waller (Oxford: Oxford University Press, 2000), 243.
[55] Hilton, *Mad, Bad and Dangerous People?*, 573, 578; Friedrich Engels, *The Condition of the Working Class in England*, ed. V.G. Kiernan ([1892] London: Penguin, 1987), 11.
[56] Ibid., 34–46, 68–110.
[57] Keating, *Unknown England*, 13.

Figure 7.2 Gustave Doré, 'Dudley Street in the Seven Dials' (1872). © Getty Images.

the inner city, especially in London. Studies such as Charles Booth's *Life and Labour of the People in London* (1889), which had reached seventeen volumes by 1902–3, and Benjamin Seebohm Rowntree's *Poverty: A Study of Town Life* (1901), centred on York, carried weight because of their social-scientific approach, but it is the titles of the more impressionistic and emotive studies – like Blanchard Jerrold's *London: A Pilgrimage* (1872) and illustrated with Gustave Doré's striking engravings (see Figure 7.2); Andrew Mearns's *The Bitter Cry of Outcast London* (1883); George Sims's *How the Poor Live and Horrible London* (1889); William Booth's *In Darkest England and the Way Out* (1890); and Jack London's *People of the Abyss* (1903) – which revealed the underlying anxieties and probably did more to shape public perceptions.

Mearns could write of the 'pestilential human rookeries', where 'no form of vice and sensuality causes surprise or attracts attention',[58] Sims of the 'great evil which lies like a cankerworm in the heart of this fair city [London]',[59] and William Booth of the 'colonies of heathens and savages in the heart of our capital'.[60] There was a curious inversion here. In the early modern period it had been the barbarous Gubbins living on the edge of Dartmoor and Celtic peoples occupying the wild peripheries of Britain,

---

[58] Ibid., 94, 97.
[59] Ibid., 68.
[60] Ibid., 19.

who represented the primitive forms of humanity;[61] whereas it was the civilizing environment of the city that promoted the advance of the human race.[62] Now that had been reversed. The city was rapidly becoming the seat of barbarity rather than civility and as such endangered the long-term progress of the nation. This line of argument took a more sinister turn when allied to Darwinian notions of evolution and late Victorian ideologies of race. William Booth wrote of a 'submerged class', with a 'heredity of incapacity',[63] and Masterman of a 'population bred in the Abyss', giving rise to 'this new city race'.[64] There were fears that such was the nature of the inner city environment that it was effectively putting evolution into reverse gear in a way that could threaten the genetic stock of England as a whole. These types of arguments underpinned much of the thrust towards urban improvement in the late nineteenth and early-twentieth century, as well as the eugenicist movement. It also had its echoes in the world of fiction, a powerful medium for shaping public attitudes. *The Hound of the Baskervilles* (1901-2) was Conan Doyle's comeback novel. Set largely on Dartmoor, it was seemingly a tale of modern enlightenment, of how the super-rational and metropolitan Sherlock Holmes defeated the dark forces of superstition and violence that lurked on the Moor. Yet the triumph of urbane reason over rural ignorance looks less clear when we discover that one of the 'beasts' occupying the Moor is the escaped convict 'Selden, the Notting Hill [at that time largely a working class area of London] murderer'.[65] In reality no individual was ever prosecuted, but a publication of 1865 described the crimes as 'almost too horrible to contemplate', and in the novel Selden is described as a 'man of violence, half animal and half demon', possessing 'an evil yellow face, a terrible animal face, all seamed and scored with vile passions'.[66] Selden is characterized as a genetic throwback to a pre-human, animal form, and it could not have escaped the notice of readers that it was the slums of London that had nurtured this animal-human hybrid. In fact the real beast of the Moor is not Selden, and not even the hound, but the respectable Stapleton who deploys the hound to execute his murderous deeds. Tellingly it is not Holmes who puts an end to Stapleton but the Moor itself, as he is sucked into the bog at its mysterious centre. Thus the Moor restores the natural order. The true quagmire is now an urban one: as William Booth declares, 'The foul and fetid breath of our slums is almost as poisonous as that of an African swamp.'[67] The implication would seem to be that culture now is to be found in the wild, and that the wild is necessary to counter the corrupting effects of the barbarous city.

A process of social investigation, parallel to that in the town, was also underway in the countryside, and it did not escape the notice of those involved that the problems

---

[61] Milton, *Discovery of Dartmoor*, 25–8; Murray Pittock, *Celtic Identity and the British Image* (Manchester: Manchester University Press, 1999), 20–60.
[62] Peter Borsay, 'Urban Life and Culture', in *A Companion to Eighteenth-Century Britain*, ed. H. T. Dickinson (Oxford: Blackwell, 2002), 203–4.
[63] Ibid., 158, 172.
[64] Ibid., 242.
[65] Arthur Conan Doyle, *The Hound of the Baskervilles*, ed. F. O'Gorman ([1902] Peterborough, OT: Broadview Press, 2006), 106.
[66] Ibid., 106, 143, 179.
[67] Keating, *Unknown England*, 148.

of poverty, hygiene and poor housing that besmirched the city were also to be found in villages and small towns.[68] But at least the country had the presence of the open air and nature. As Simms put it, 'God made the country, they say, and man made the town; and wretched as is the lot of the agricultural labourer the handiwork of Heaven still remains to give some relief to the surroundings of his miserable life'.[69] Or, as Rider Haggard argued of the temporary accommodation provided for the London hop pickers, 'around these crowded insanitary hovels breathes the sweet fresh air, and above them stretches the blue sky of English summer. In the festering slums of London such blessings are absent'.[70]

This valorization of the rural was reflected in the rise of suburbia, which allowed the middle class to escape the corrupting environment of the inner city and inject green scape and village values – or at least the appearance of these – into their urban lives. However, the unregulated growth of the outer city, what Patrick Abercrombie described in 1945 as 'the cancer of ribbon development and urban sprawl',[71] was itself proving as big a threat to the urban image as that of the inner city. A character in Edward Thomas's *South Country* (1909), an alienated Londoner who annually abandons his job to go haymaking and sleep in the open air, reflects that 'I realize that I belong to the suburbs still. I belong to no class or race, and have no tradition. We of the suburbs are a muddy, confused, hesitating mass, of small courage though much endurance.'[72] In 1929 H. J. Massingham could write how 'the mongrel suburb has destroyed the particularity of division between town and country', and in 1940 how Suburbia has 'deserted the town in order to betray the country'.[73] Thomas Sharp went so far as to argue that the whole notion of the fusion of Town and Country, which underpinned the idea of suburbia, and was promoted by Ebenezer Howard's Garden City concept, simply added to the problem, 'semi-detached houses in a sham-rural street in a wilderness of semi-detached houses in sham-rural streets ... the physical expression of the prime social evil of their time'.[74]

As 'deep' urbanization set in, a swelling chorus of complaints emerged during the early-twentieth century – prefigured in criticisms of nineteenth-century London – castigating the impact of unregulated urban sprawl. This was not simply a matter of the expanding edges of major cities but also of smaller towns and even villages. In 1934 J. R. A. Hockin's angst at the fate of a 'once ... perfect village' at the foot of the Berkshire Downs is palpable: 'Alas! Blewbury' has 'swollen horribly in the last twelve years. Staring red clots and dribbles of the most revolting villas are beginning to creep out along the open roads; in a century, no trees, even if they were planted, could screen

---

[68] Mark Freeman, *Social Investigation and Rural England, 1870–1914* (Woodbridge: Boydell Press, 2003).
[69] Keating, *Unknown England*, 78.
[70] Ibid., 205.
[71] Patrick Abercrombie quoted in Gilbert and Elizabeth Glen McAllister (eds.), *Homes, Towns and Countryside: A Practical Plan for Britain* (London: Batsford, 1945), 9.
[72] Thomas, *South Country*, 85.
[73] H. J. Massingham, *Heritage of Man* (London: Jonathan Cape, 1929), 294–301; idem, *Chiltern Country*, 2nd edn (London: Batsford, 1943), 99.
[74] Thomas Sharp, *English Panorama* (London: Architectural Press, 1950), 95.

them from the downs above.'[75] In Surrey the blight had even spread on to the downs itself, with Eric Holmes in 1928 describing how the Hog's Back, an elongated ridge on the North Downs, 'has been caught in the tentacles of the estate agent, and the northern slopes of the uplands which sink to the Leatherhead road have been made hideous by hundreds of flimsy week-end bungalows that appear to have been sprinkled anyhow out of a giant castor on to the bare sward'.[76] In 1939 Richard Wyndham highlighted what he and many other observers saw – with a scarcely concealed social disdain – as the despoliation of the coast by cheap and unregulated ribbon development:

> [T]he coast from Rottingdean to Newhaven [in Sussex] is probably the nastiest mess in the British Isles: first Saltdean, an unplanned outcrop of concrete and gaudy red and green tiles; then Peacehaven, where bungalows like hen-coops, half-timbered cinemas and garages, ye olde tea shops, and ye old smugglers dens stand (and in some cases fall) between lines of washing, notices of plots for sale, and avenues bearing important-sounding names.[77]

By the end of the Second World War, the depth of anxiety had reached a new level. In the case of the country town, warned Ruth Cobb, 'there are the modern "Estates", just outside the town, creeping up the hillside in an aimless way … If care is not taken there may be more and more of this mushroom growth outside the towns … they will indeed become "Wens" on a hillside'.[78]

The threat of deep suburbanization to the countryside was particularly acute on the barren heath lands in striking distance of London. Relatively uncultivated, they were now seen as vestiges of wild England. However, because of their low land values they were cheap to build on and therefore vulnerable to metropolitan overspill and unregulated development. Already by 1895 in *Wild England*, the naturalist and schoolmaster Charles John Cornish (1858–1906) was arguing that the 'transference of capital from the suburbs not only of London, but of the great towns of the Midlands and the North, to the heaths of Berkshire, Surrey, and Western Hampshire, is assuming the dimensions of an urban exodus'.[79] Fifteen years later in *Howard's End* E. M. Forster, from the vantage point of the Purbeck Hills, observed that 'Bournemouth's ignoble coast cowers to the right, heralding the pine trees that mean, for all their beauty, red houses, and the Stock Exchange, and extend to the gates of London itself. So tremendous is the City's trail!' It was all summed up in Helen's *cri de coeur*, 'London's creeping'.[80]

The anti-metropolitan, anti-urban refrain was taken up by Cornish's geographer brother Vaughan (1862–1948) writing in 1932 (in a volume published by the Council for the Preservation of Rural England), 'the great towns grew radially, flinging out

---

[75] Hockin, *On Foot in Berkshire*, 57–8.
[76] Holmes, *London's Countryside*, 281.
[77] Wyndham, *Sussex, Kent and Surrey*, 83–4.
[78] Ibid., 44.
[79] Cornish, *Wild England*, 76.
[80] Forster, *Howard's End*, 170, 329.

hideous tentacles like those of an octopus, which enfolded country towns and villages, crushing out the corporate life of rustic communities'.[81] In their 1935 study of the Dorset landscape, Geoffrey Clark and W. Harding Thompson likewise observed how 'the urban tentacles of Weymouth have pushed out their red and white villas almost to the foothills'.[82] The metaphor of the city as a sea monster, its suburban tentacles strangling the life out of the surrounding countryside, had acquired notoriety in Clough Williams-Ellis's *England and the Octopus* (1928) and was repeated by the public intellectual and controversialist C. E. M. Joad in *The Untutored Townsman's Invasion of the Country* (1946). Here he argued that, driven by the urban-dweller's yearning for rural life, 'the towns shot out their arms into the country as though they were telescopes, and octopus-like yearly engulfed fresh areas of green with their tentacles of builders' pink'.[83]

There was of course a reality to all this. Suburban sprawl and ribbon development were not figments of the imagination. But it was also – as in the case of the demise of the inner city – a matter of language, discourse and perception, though even more so in respect of the suburbs. The slums were demonstrably unhealthy, overcrowded, polluted, and poorly constructed and maintained: the same could not easily be argued of the suburbs. Their sin was ultimately an aesthetic one. The repetitive uniformity of their terraces or villas, the ubiquitous use of machine-made red brick and roof tiles, the rectilinear regularity of their layout and the ribbon development intruding into the countryside were all seen as signs of a monotonous and invasive modernity. They represented a travesty of taste; as Williams-Ellis declared in the *Octopus*, 'it is chiefly the spate of mean building all over the country that is shrivelling up the old England – mean and perky little houses that surely none but mean and perky little souls should inhabit with satisfaction'.[84] It was the regular repetition by writers and publicists of the view that suburbs were ugly that made them disagreeable, rather than any inherent quality of ugliness that they possessed.

In a broader sense it was the negative picture painted of the city as a whole – its inner and outer manifestations – that made it appear a damaged and dangerous environment and that made the countryside in comparison so attractive. Guidebook writers and those producing popular topographical literature, though their focus might be on the countryside and old towns, subtly exploited the anti-urban discourse, weaving it into their accounts, with the aim of making their subjects seem more seductive. In 1937 the Labour politician Oliver Baldwin (son of the Conservative Prime Minster Stanley), who lived at Little Stoke in Oxfordshire, could write in the foreword to J. H. Baker's guide to the southern Chilterns, 'In these days when so many of us are forced by economic reasons to live the artificial life of townsfolk, it is good to be reminded of the country districts from which our forbears come, and to absorb

---

[81] Vaughan Cornish, *The Scenery of England. A Study of Harmonious Grouping in Town and Country* (London: Council for the Preservation of Rural England, 1932), 21.
[82] Clark and Thompson, *Dorset Landscape*, 79, 83.
[83] C. E. M. Joad, *The Untutored Townsman's Invasion of the Country* (London: Faber & Faber, 1946), 16.
[84] Clough Williams-Ellis, *England and the Octopus* (London: Geoffrey Bles, 1928), 15.

something of the calm and beauty which the country alone can give.'[85] In a similar vein in 1940 the publisher Harry Batsford produced his pocket-sized guide, *How to See the Country*, in which he declared that 'England is more than an aggregation of urban wens' and that 'for most of us, however urbanised and sophisticated, there is an instinctive reaching of our souls towards the fields and woods, the streams and hamlets of the land around us'.[86]

It was that 'instinctive reaching' that may have played some part in the partial relocation of Batsford's business from London to Malvern during the Second World War. Fear of bomb damage played a part in this decision, but there is no doubt that Harry Batsford enjoyed the move to the countryside and could write of how 'we publish and illustrate our work, with the country coming generously right up to our doorstep' and how 'when their work is finished, the staff sometimes walk over the hill ridges to the west'.[87] There were echoes here of the decision of Charles Ashbee and the Guild of Handicraft in 1901 to exchange Whitechapel and the East End of London for Chipping Campden and the Cotswolds, 'to leave Babylon and go home to the land'.[88] Whether the pull of the countryside was due to its instinctive appeal, or even an instinctive reaction against urbanization – or, as has been argued here, the construction of a discourse that stigmatized the city and valorized the country and old towns – there is little doubt that growing numbers of townspeople sought some contact with old and rural England. A. G. Bradley, for example, recorded the magnetic appeal of the Avon, and its historic riverine communities, to the inhabitants of the West Midlands conurbation: at Tewkesbury was to be found 'the merry tripper, who comes in shoals from the Midland towns ... in his active season'; at Cleeve 'half a dozen well-armed and prosperous-looking anglers down for the day from Birmingham', and at Bidford '[a] hotel on the river, a beer garden, and every accommodation, including boats for giving the Joes and Jills of Birmingham a happy day'.[89] In the late 1920s John R. Ashton and F. Arnold Stocks, both heavily involved in the rambling movement, observed in their *Open-Air Guide* how 'modern easy transit' gives the 'average townsman ... the power to visit nature more often than before and every year sees greater numbers leaving the towns for a half-day or day'.[90] It was the modern myth of the escape from the city, and to the country, that underpinned the invention of the English countryside, a point S. P. B. Mais acknowledged as he evoked the scene around Leith Hill in Surrey, 'The smell of the pines, the sight of the great yellow seas of gorse, the bewildering maze of tracks over the heath commons, all combine to make you feel a thousand miles away from the city streets.'[91]

---

[85] J. H. Baker, *Land of 'The Gap'* (Oxford: Basil Blackwell, 1937), xi.
[86] Thomas Burke, *The English Townsman: As He Was and as He Is* (London: Batsford, 1946), 136; Batsford, *How to See the Country*, 44, 50.
[87] Bolitho, *Batsford Century*, 96–7.
[88] Allan Warmington, *Campden a New History* (Chipping Campden: Campden & District Historical & Archaeological Society, 2005), 224.
[89] Bradley, *Avon*, 4, 48–9, 85.
[90] Ashton and Stocks, *Open-Air Guide*, 5.
[91] Mais, *Round about England*, 112.

Leisure

Accounts of the flight to the country often emphasize, alongside the negative aspects of town life, the recreational nature of the experience. The foreword to the Penguin guide to *Kent, Sussex and Surrey* (1939) called the three counties 'one of the great playgrounds of London'.[92] Central to understanding new attitudes to the landscape was the growth of a consumer-driven, leisure economy, and the role of landscape as a recreational good within this. Leisure in some form, though it may be described in terms different to those we use today (accommodating, for example, events associated with the festive calendar), had long been a feature of most people's lives. However, the rapid economic and social change experienced in Britain between the late-seventeenth and early-twentieth century initiated a transformation in the volume and nature of leisure available. Three phases of change can be suggested. The first, from the late-seventeenth century, witnessed the 'commercialization of leisure', involving the placing of high-status pastimes into the marketplace and their reshaping along more public, enlightened and polite lines. During this phase heritage and nature were already being incorporated into the new leisure portfolio with the growth in touring, the 'invention' of Nature and growing interest in antiquities (an early sign of the heritage industry), but this ran in parallel with a growth in modern urban-based leisure. The second phase, the period of the so-called Industrial Revolution, initiated at some point between the late eighteenth and early-nineteenth century, saw an acceleration of the trends in the first phase with the old and the natural playing an increasingly prominent part as the pace of industrialization and urbanization picked up, and the romantic movement gained momentum. The third phase, beginning in the later nineteenth century, emerged as the impact of large-scale industrialization and particularly urbanization, led to a quantitative and qualitative change in leisure for the generality of the population. This paved the way for a transformation in the nature of urban leisure, as exemplified in the sporting revolution or the rise of the music hall and later the cinema, but also in the mass turn to nature and heritage, and the development of the recreational landscape.[93]

Underpinning all three phases are changes in the volume and distribution of wealth. During the first phase an increasingly commercialized agrarian and industrial economy generated growing volumes of wealth among the aristocracy, gentry and the middling orders. Because the vast majority of this was 'surplus' to meeting the basic necessities of life, it spilled over into the conspicuous consumption of 'luxury' products, some of which took the form of leisure (as in spa visiting or landscape gardening). During the second phase the benefits of rapid industrialization were diffused more widely among an increasingly diversified middle class and underpinned, for example, the rapid spread of the seaside resort. The middle class continued to enjoy the fruits of surplus wealth during the third phase – the rapid expansion of golf courses and suburban tennis from the 1890s are an example of their affluence – but they were joined by significant sections of the working class (generally the higher-paid workers, such as

---

[92] Winbolt, *Kent, Surrey and Sussex*, 7.
[93] Borsay, *Leisure*, 14–15.

those in the textile towns of the north), whose rising real incomes released money for recreational pursuits such as association football, the music hall and a seaside holiday. Between 1880 and 1900 average per capita consumer expenditure grew by about 50 per cent, and between 1911 and 1915 and 1939 and 1940 by 25 per cent; overall between 1880/1 and 1939/40 by 231 per cent.[94] By the late-nineteenth century we are seeing the emergence of an economy increasingly defined by its capacity to generate large-scale surplus wealth and structured to meet the demand that this generated. Though the distribution of surplus wealth was heavily socially skewed to the middle and upper class, and widespread poverty remained a serious problem, large elements in the working class were beginning to share in the fruits of economic growth.

The growth in surplus wealth and the demand for leisure that built upon this did not of itself turn the landscape into a recreational good. That said, without such wealth the development of domestic tourism would have been impossible. Time and space were also key factors. During the early phases of the Industrial Revolution working hours may have been extended, reducing the time for leisure, though never eliminating it entirely, even for the working class, but from the middle of the nineteenth century the trend was in the opposite direction. An aspect of this was the development of formal periods of holiday such as the Saturday half holiday, the 'weekend', bank holidays, and the extended summer holiday, all of which provided more opportunity not only for leisure but also for the sort of structured leisure involved in tourism.[95] The middle class in particular, for all its apparent devotion to the cult of hard work, made time for recreation, as can be seen in the emergence of organized domestic and overseas tourism serviced by travel agencies such as those of Thomas Cook, Sir Henry Lunn and John Frame.[96] A major consequence of urbanization was a fundamental change in the relationship of the majority of the population to space. When most people were employed and resided on the land, the countryside was perceived as predominantly working and living space. This imposed limits to how far it could be treated as recreational in character. With large-scale urbanization, this balance was reversed. Rural space took on a quite new dimension. Not only did a declining proportion of the population live in the countryside but its share of the national workforce and economic output began rapidly to diminish. These trends were accelerated from the later nineteenth century by the mechanization of agriculture, which reduced the rural demand for labour, and by growing imports of core foodstuffs such as grain and meat from overseas. As the rural landscape's role as a productive resource declined comparatively, its recreational potential increased. 'England', as W. A. Eden observed in *Britain and the Beast* (1937), 'is no longer a predominantly agricultural country, and her highly industrialized state makes it essential that a large part of our foodstuffs should be imported.' In future, he concluded, the function of the land would consist

[94] John Benson, 'Consumption and the Consumer Revolution', *Refresh*, 23 (1996): 8, https://files.ehs.org.uk/wp-content/uploads/2020/07/29061006/Benson23b.pdf, accessed 30 Jul. 2022.
[95] Reid, 'Playing and Praying', 746–57; F. M. L. Thompson, *The Rise of Respectable Society. A Social History of Victorian Britain* (London: Fontana, 1988), 272–7; Borsay, *Leisure*, 193–4; Hugh Cunningham, *Time, Work and Leisure: Life Changes in England since 1700* (Manchester: Manchester University Press, 2016), 92–123.
[96] Thompson, *Rise of Respectable Society*, 260–4.

of the production of perishable foodstuff and 'the provision of space for the recreation of the urban population'.[97] No longer constrained by the everyday needs of agriculture, for the majority of people, the countryside was opened up, to use A. G. Street's term, as 'a playground'.[98]

Much the same was happening to the rivers that interlaced the rural landscape. They had been a vital part of the communications infrastructure, and there is every reason to believe that role increased during the early Industrial Revolution. But with the introduction of railways and then motorized transport their function as working spaces became more and more marginalized, and their potential as recreational spaces, for fishing and boating, developed. The case for the sea is less clear. From the early 1700s its potential as leisure space was becoming clear, as it began to be valued as a source of natural health cures, and as seaside resorts first emerged. But the sea, and the ports which serviced it, continued to be a fundamental, and in terms of overseas trade, an unavoidable part of the communications system, to which must be added their role in the fishing industry. Over time, however, there was a tendency to concentrate these commercial functions in larger ports, or zones within these ports, freeing up the smaller ports or areas within the bigger ports (Yarmouth, for example, developed both a major fishing/commercial zone and leisure zone), along with the sea more generally, for recreational pursuits.

The same sort of spatial separation was occurring within the urban system itself. The long-term concentration of industrial activity in the towns and cities of the North West, North East and West Midlands was changing the economic rationale of towns outside these zones, such as in East Anglia, the South East and the South West. They continued to play important regional functions, particularly as administrative and agricultural service centres, but many among them experienced a diminishing manufacturing base and, by way of compensation, began to exploit their potential as attractive residential centres and historic locations. A similar process had occurred in the early modern period with towns like York, Salisbury, Worcester and Bath, which saw a loss of their traditional textile industries and a growing concentration on their roles as regional/county capitals and centres of leisure.[99] It was these historic towns that were to benefit particularly with the growth of the heritage industry in the nineteenth century.

It is difficult to assess how much weight to ascribe to what Harry Batsford called the 'instinctive reaching of our souls towards the fields and woods'. Was the yearning for Arcadia part of a primeval urge among those trapped in industrial towns to re-integrate with Nature? Was the fascination with old England an attempt to re-connect with a lost, more human past, prompted by the de-humanizing and disruptive effects of mechanization and modernization? That is certainly how it seemed to many contemporaries. But it might be more realistic by way of explanation to think in terms of the growing *opportunities* for turning landscape into a recreational good provided

---

[97] Clough Williams-Ellis (ed.), *Britain and the Beast* (London: J. M. Dent & Sons, 1937), 59–60, 70.
[98] Ibid., 122.
[99] Paul Slack, 'Great and Good Towns', in *Cambridge Urban History of Britain. Vol. II*, ed. Clark, 347–76.

by changes in patterns of wealth, time and space instigated by industrialization and urbanization. To these must be added the way that these opportunities were capitalized on by interwoven negative discourses surrounding industrialization and urbanization, and positive ones associated with the countryside and heritage. Because these discourses were constructed and delivered at the level of printed and visual texts, it was possible never to leave the confines of the modern suburb and simply engage in virtual tourism. No doubt this sort of armchair tourism was widely practised. But facilitating real access to the 'other' was always going to be a crucial aspect of turning the landscape into leisure, and it is travel and the journey that is the subject of the next chapter.

8

The transport revolution and the journey

'London is becoming miserably hot and dusty; everybody who can get away is rushing off', wrote J. Arthur Gibbs in the opening lines to *A Cotswold Village* (1898), the book that reputedly put the Cotswolds on the tourist map. He continues, as he describes the view from his railway carriage window,

> Who will fly with me westwards to the land of the golden sunshine and silvery trout steams, to the land of breezy uplands and valleys nestling under limestone hills, where the scream of the railway whistle is seldom heard and the smoke of the factory darkens not the long summer days? Away, in the smooth 'Flying Dutchman'; past Windsor's glorious towers and Eton's playing-fields.

It is a journey that takes him along 'the glorious valley of Father Thames', past views of the Chilterns and Wittenham Clump, 'a conspicuous object for miles', into the Valley of the White Horse, the animal 'cut into the velvety turf of the rolling chalk downs', before the 'Cotswold Hills rising out of a dreamy haze' hove into view, and his destination Cirencester is finally reached, 'the ancient capital of the Cotswold country'.[1] From there he ventures out to discover 'a small village [Ablington], nestling amid a wealth of stately trees', and the manor house that was to be his new home, with 'quaint old Elizabethan gables and sombre bell-tower, the old-fashioned entrance gates, the luxuriant growth of ivy, combined together to give that air of peace, that charm which belongs so exclusively to the buildings of the middle ages'.[2] At one level Gibbs's journey is a very practical one. The railway provides him with the technological means to be transported from London to the Cotswolds in a matter of hours, something unthinkable in the age of horse-drawn travel; it also, perhaps more importantly, allows him to undertake the reverse journey and to remain in regular and easy touch with the Metropolis. But it is also clearly a metaphorical journey, from the present to the past, and from the urban to the rural. Moreover, the journey is an experience in its own right with almost filmic qualities:

> From a Great Western express, running at the rate of sixty miles an hour through picturesque country, you may watch the sun setting amidst every variety of scenery. Now some hoary grey tower stands out against the intense brightness of

[1] Gibbs, *Cotswold Village*, 1–10.
[2] Ibid., 12, 14.

the western sky; now a tracery of fine trees shades for a time the dazzling light; then suddenly the fiery furnace is revealed again, reflected perhaps in the waters of some stream or amid the reeds and sedges of a mere, where a punt is moored containing anglers in broad wideawake hats.[3]

Dr Watson's account of his rail journey with Sir Henry Baskerville, as the scene of action in Conan Doyle's *Hound of the Baskervilles* shifts from London to Dartmoor, is much terser; indeed it is difficult to see why it is included in his report to Sherlock Holmes, who we are led to believe has remained in London since it includes nothing of significance to the case. But from the reader's perspective the account fills a critical role. First, it brings an air of familiarity. Many will live in the capital, be used to making train journeys and observe the changing landscape from the window. Some by this point in time will have made the exact journey of Watson and his companion. Since 1849 the London to Plymouth line around the southern skirts of Dartmoor had been operational; the Moretonhampstead branch line from Newton Abbot was opened in 1866, providing access to the eastern side of the moor; and by the turn of the century cheap tickets, the promise of a four-hour journey, and the possibility of a day excursion from the Metropolis were being advertised.[4] In 1935 it was said that 'the peculiar merit of a holiday in Cornwall, [is] that you are separated from London by five thousand years and yet you can get back in five hours'.[5] Second, short as the account of the journey is, Doyle captures the essence of the change in landscape:

> In a very few hours the brown earth had become ruddy, the brick had changed to granite, and red cows grazed in well-hedged fields, where the lush grasses and more luxuriant vegetation spoke of a richer, if a damper, climate. … Over the green squares of the fields and the low curve of a wood there rose in the distance a gray, melancholy hill, with a strange jagged summit, dim and vague in the distance, like some fantastic landscape in a dream.[6]

Here, encapsulated in a few phrases is the shift from the civilization of the city to that of the pastoral but still ordered landscape of the countryside, to the primitive wilderness of the moor.

As with Gibbs, the rail journey facilitates but also symbolizes the transition from the urban to the rural, and the present to the past. But even more than Gibbs, because of its fictional character, the journey opens the door to another sort of consciousness, 'the fantastic landscape in a dream'. The journey has become a trigger for the mind to enter an imaginative landscape, ripe for discovery, and in that sense an essential part of the tourist experience. Watson and Sir Henry's journey does not end at the rail station. Awaiting them is a 'wagonette' to convey them to Baskerville Hall. This brings its own landscape experience – 'The road in front of us grew bleaker and wilder over

---

[3] Ibid., 7–8.
[4] Milton, *Discovery of Dartmoor*, 115, 161–2.
[5] Mais, *See England First*, 71.
[6] Conan Doyle, *Hound of the Baskervilles*, 103–4.

huge russet and olive slopes, sprinkled with giant boulders' – and is a reminder that other means of transport were involved in recreational travel, some of which, such as horse and foot, harked back to more traditional modes of movement and worked hand in hand with newer ones.[7] As Michael Thompson pointed out, 'Far from displacing horses, the railways created new and expanding demands for horse-labour.'[8]

This chapter will begin by looking at the so-called transport revolution and its impact on landscape tourism. The emphasis here will be on facilitating access: the practicalities of getting the consumers to the product (a significant difference form other sorts of consumption, where the focus is upon getting the product to the consumer). Improved modes of transport might be thought to have undermined the traditional way of getting around for the mass of the population, that is by foot, but if anything they enhanced its feasibility and attractiveness for tourists, so the next section will explore the role of walks and walking. Modes of transport impacted on and changed the way that landscape was experienced – the filmic qualities of Gibbs's journey as he whistled through the West Country are a case in point – and this will be explored in the final section, which will also explore the journey as cultural metaphor.

The transport revolution and recreational travel

The establishment and expansion of the railway network from the 1830s played a great part in opening up recreational access to the natural and human landscape, as we shall see. But long before the introduction of steam trains, changes in the modes and means of transport were underway that laid the foundations for the transport revolution and the access that it provided to recreational landscape. The seventeenth- and eighteenth-century growth of continental and domestic travel, and the rise of the spa and seaside resort, rested heavily upon developing more efficient and comfortable means of accessing town and countryside. Leaving aside foot and wind power, it was horse power that underpinned human mobility at this stage and indeed would continue to play a vital part even when the steam and combustion engines were introduced.

It was the development of horse-drawn conveyances for personal transport that represented one of the key changes in recreational travel in the pre-railway age. In his *English Pleasure Carriages* (1837) William Bridge Adams had reminded his readers that 'as a measure of simple locomotion, for the purpose of a long journey, a horse's back is, to the majority of human beings a very imperfect mode of conveyance.'[9] For the purposes of leisure travel carriages of one sort or another were more comfortable and convenient than horseback (and for the infirm and disabled essential), reducing the physical strain, allowing opportunities for sociability, and usually providing some level of protection from the elements. The most prestigious private conveyance was the coach, first introduced in the late-sixteenth century, whose ride was improved by

---

[7] Ibid., 107.
[8] F. M. L. Thompson, 'Nineteenth-Century Horse Sense', *Economic History Review* 2nd ser., 29 (1976): 60–81 at 64.
[9] Wiliam Bridge Adams, *English Pleasure Carriages* (London: Charles Knight, 1837), 8.

the introduction of steel springs in 1754. Though it was originally a means for the elite to travel in luxury and privacy, its greatest impact came in its public form, either the town cab for intra-urban transport or the stage coach for longer distance travel. The latter allowed the middling orders access to a relatively comfortable, inexpensive, increasingly rapid mode of travel – the road journey from London to Bath was reduced from twenty-eight hours in 1750 to little more than nineteen hours by 1800, from London to Brighton from nine hours in 1791 to five to six hours in 1833. By 1830, compared to 1750, travel between the major towns was four to five times quicker, and 'almost everywhere else it was at least twice as fast'.[10] This laid the foundations for all forms of public transport in the future and, in the concept of the enclosed carriage, for a physical model that was replicated by the railway, tram and motorcar. Most personal vehicles, however, were not coaches, and by the early-nineteenth century it is clear that a proliferating variety of private carriages were being manufactured to meet the growing market demand. Immersion in the landscape might not be quite as complete from the carriage as from horseback, but many conveyances were open in character and could be used not only to travel to particular destinations but also for the simple purpose of the ride itself. The large-scale remodelling of estates in the eighteenth century to meet the new fashions in landscape gardening often included carriage drives, such as at Alnwick, where the Duke of Northumberland's chaplain Thomas Percy published 'A Ride through Hulne Park from Alnwick Castle to Hulne Abbey' in 1765.[11]

It is easy to focus on the modes of conveyance and forget the great improvements in the communications infrastructure that were taking place. Poor-quality roads represented a potentially serious hindrance for recreational access to the landscape. The first turnpike trusts were established in the late-seventeenth century; permitted to charge travellers using the highways under their remit, they took over responsibility for road care from parishes, ensuring a more systematic and regular programme of maintenance, with wider roads to facilitate the passage of wheeled vehicles. By 1820 about 22,000 miles of British roads were under the care of some 1,000 trusts.[12] Alongside these developments went a widespread upgrading of victualing facilities, with larger and more comfortable inns to accommodate passengers and service the growing number of vehicles and their horses.[13] On the most widely used longer-distance routes, such as that from London to Bath, where journeys might require overnight accommodation, a string of specialist road towns emerged, their main streets packed with hostelries, some on a grand scale, creating the potential for travel to be a pleasurable experience, or at least mitigating the factors that often made it otherwise.[14]

[10] Sylvia McIntyre, 'Bath: The Rise of a Resort Town, 1600–1800', in *County Towns in Pre-industrial England*, ed. Peter Clark (Leicester: Leicester University Press, 1981), 210; Walton, *English Seaside Resort*, 21; H. J. Dyos and Derek Aldcroft, *British Transport: An Economic Survey from the Seventeenth Century to the Twentieth* (Leicester: Leicester University Press, 1969), 79; J. Crofts, *Packhorse, Waggon and Post. Land Carriage and Communications under the Tudors and Stuarts* (London: Routledge & Kegan Paul, 1967), 109–32.

[11] C. Shrimpton, *A History of Alnwick Parks and Pleasure Grounds* (Derby: Heritage House, 2006), 44.

[12] Hey, *Oxford Companion to Local History*, 454–5.

[13] Peter Clark, *The English Alehouse: A Social History, 1200–1830* (London: Longmans, 1983); Alan Everitt, 'The English Urban Inn, 1560–1760', in idem *Landscape and Community in England* (London: Hambledon Press, 1985), 155–208.

[14] Daniel Maudlin, 'Inns and Elite Mobility in Late Georgian Britain', *Past and Present* 247 (2020): 37–76.

Eighteenth- and nineteenth-century guides to spas and seaside resorts frequently included details of horse, coach and carriage rides in the surrounding environs. John Wood's *Description of Bath* (1749), for example, relating the fashionable daily round at Bath, reported how at midday a 'Part of the Company are taking the Air and Exercise' in the surrounding environs, 'some on Horseback, some in Coaches', while the *Original Bath Guide* of 1840, in a section on 'Rides in the Vicinity of Bath', declared the city 'nearly surrounded by hills of towering height', access to which 'is now rendered as safe and easy for carriages, as for the equestrian'.[15] *The New Bath Guide* of 1809 made explicit a key factor in opening up the countryside to visitors: 'The publick roads about Bath have been much improved within these few years, and the access to the hills Claverton and Lansdown, (which was formerly very difficult) is now rendered safe, easy and pleasant, either on horse-back or in carriages.'[16] During the course of the nineteenth century these descriptions of excursions into the environs to view features in the natural and human landscape became increasingly extensive while listing a much wider range of means of access. When visitors to Bath opened their *Ward Lock Red Guide* in 1909, almost one half of it was taken up with trips to locations outside the spa, with reference not only to 'walks around Bath' but 'excursions by electric trams', 'routes by motor bus', 'railway excursions' and 'cycle and motor routes'.[17]

These changes reflected the transport revolution that was to make accessible for pleasurable contemplation every nook and corner of the English landscape. The revolution was initiated by the arrival of steam-powered conveyances. This was first seen in the form of the steamboat, operating as early as the 1810s. It was passenger traffic rather than cargo that underpinned this early phase, and from a recreational perspective it was seaside resorts that were the great beneficiary.[18] By the early 1840 passenger steamship services were covering over 1,400 route-miles of regular sailings, linking ninety ports and harbours.[19] Thereafter the speed and flexibility of rail access generally undermined the competitiveness of the steamboat for personal travel, but it remained a persistent feature of the scene for coastal resorts such as those in North Devon, where land access proved problematic, for island visiting, for excursion traffic, and for those who simply wanted a trip on a pleasure steamer and the sight of the sea, coastline or riverbank that it provided.

As early as 1846 *Black's Picturesque Guide to the English Lakes* informed its readers that Ambleside (at the north end of Windermere) was the terminus of the Lancaster and Preston Canal and that '[t]wo iron boats, drawn by horses at an average speed of eight miles an hour, depart daily with passengers for Lancaster and Preston' Here was a means by which the rapidly expanding population of Dickens' Coketown (Preston's population grew from 12,000 in 1801 to 50,000 by 1851), and the Lancashire textile towns in general, might piggyback on what was essentially a commercial artery of

---

[15] John Wood, *A Description of Bath*, 2nd edn. ([1765]Bath: Kingsmead Reprints, 1969), 439; *Original Bath Guide*, 135-6.
[16] *The New Bath Guide; or Useful Pocket Companion* (Bath: J. Savage, 1809), 48.
[17] *A Pictorial and Descriptive Guide to Bath* (London: Ward Lock, 1909), 116-210.
[18] Walton, *English Seaside Resort*, 21-2.
[19] Philip Bagwell and Peter Lyth, *Transport in Britain, 1750-2000: From Canal Lock to Gridlock* (London: Hambledon and London, 2002), 25.

communications and gain access to the picturesque Lake District. But at 8 miles an hour it was a long haul. More encouragingly the guide went on to advise that the Lancaster Carlisle railway passed within a short distance of Ambleside, and a short line, when complete, would connect to Windermere. When finished the following year, the *porte-cochère* of Windermere station 'became', in John Marshall's words 'the railway gateway to the Lakes in much the same way as the Doric arch at Euston was the gateway to England'.[20] Though the railways did not create domestic tourism, these 'accelerators of pleasure as well as of business'[21] were part of a revolution in transport that facilitated a gear change in the scope and range of recreational travel in Britain. By the early 1850s, after a frenetic burst of construction activity, and though 'a great deal had still to be done', the basic framework was in place with the major cities and towns connected.[22] But there were many gaps, noticeably in areas that were to prove hotspots for landscape tourists: the upland mountainous regions of Wales, the Scottish Highlands and the North Pennines, and a good deal of the south of England, particularly the West Country and East Anglia.[23]

Subsequent expansion in the system helped fill in the spaces. By 1850 just over 6,000 route miles had been opened; three decades later this had climbed to over 15,000 miles and by 1920 over 20,000 miles. By 1870 the network was carrying 336.5 million passengers; on the eve of the First World War, as the network reached its peak, this number had grown to 1,294.3 million.[24] One important aspect of the later evolution of the system was the development in the larger cities of a suburban service, bolstered in London by the construction of the underground (the first stretch was opened in 1863). Though not originally intended for recreational purposes, suburban services, as they extended their reach further and further, provided growing numbers of city-dwellers with a highly efficient means to enjoy a day in the country, as the rail and underground companies came to realize and promote through beguiling posters and the sponsorship of walking guides (see Figure 8.1).[25]

During the second half of the nineteenth century a host of lesser lines and branch lines were added, criss-crossing the country – the lattice-like effect evident in the specialist railway maps produced by companies like Bartholomew's – and providing access to remoter coastal locations and small inland towns and villages.[26] When William Morris leased his Cotswold retreat at Kelmscott in 1871 – a move to the

---

[20] *Black's Picturesque Guide to the English Lakes*, 3rd edn (Edinburgh: A. and C. Black, 1846), 24; B. R. Mitchell and P. Deane, *Abstract of British Historical Statistics* (Cambridge: Cambridge University Press, 1962), 26; J. D. Marshall, *Old Lakeland: Some Cumbrian Social History* (Newton Abbot: David & Charles, 1971), 173.

[21] *Bradshaw*, section 1, 49.

[22] Dyos and Aldcroft, *British Transport*, 145.

[23] Ibid., 145–54, 168–9; Jack Simmons and Gordon Biddle, *The Oxford Companion to British Railway History from 1603 to the 1990s* (Oxford: Oxford University Press, 1997), 492–7.

[24] Simmons and Biddle, *Oxford Companion*, 492; Dyos and Aldcroft, *British Transport*, 156.

[25] Dyos and Aldcroft, *British Transport*, 230–4; Simmons and Biddle, *Oxford Companion*, 291–9; London Transport posters by Herry Perry, 'Whitsun in the Country. Strolls and Rambles', 1934; C. Leighton, 'Week-end Walks', 1938, https://www.ltmuseum.co.uk/collections/collections-online/posters/page/3?, accessed 6 Jun. 2017.

[26] David Spaven and Julian Holland, *Mapping the Railways* (London: Collins, 2013), 94–7, 184–7.

The Transport Revolution and the Journey   185

Figure 8.1 'Whitsun in the Country' (1935), poster design by Herry Perry for London Transport. © TFL from the London Transport Museum Collection.

country that foreshadowed later trends – it was to Faringdon station that he originally travelled, the terminus of a line opened seven years earlier which connected with the GWR main London line at Uffington (of White Horse fame). This still left a carriage journey of roughly 9.5 miles to remote Kelmscott, a distance reduced to 3.5 miles when the station opened at Lechlade in 1873. It was from this station that Morris's corpse was carried from the Metropolis in 1896 to be conveyed on a specially constructed funeral bier to its resting place in the village churchyard.[27] The picturesque but difficult-to-access coastal resorts of Lynton (North Devon) and Lyme Regis (Dorset) did not

---

[27] Tom Hassall, Peter Sawley and Alan Crossley (eds.), *William Morris's Kelmscott: Landscape and History* (London: Society of Antiquaries, 2007); McCarthy, *William Morris*, 674.

get their stations until 1898 and 1903 respectively, while the East Anglian resort of Cromer acquired its first station (Cromer High) in 1877 (the more central Cromer Beach followed ten years later), providing a gateway into Poppyland, the idyllic region 'discovered' by the London theatre critic Clement Scott in 1883.[28]

The railways revolutionized recreational access to coast and country for the nation's growing numbers of city-dwellers.[29] It was not just the improved comfort, cost and above all speed that they provided, it was also the breadth of their reach, as the tendrils of the system penetrated deeper and deeper into England's landscape. In E. M. Forster's *Howards End* (1910) Margaret Schlegel was said, 'like many others who have lived long in a great capital', to have

> strong feelings about the various railway termini. They are our gates to the glorious and the unknown. Through them we pass out into adventure and sunshine ... In Paddington all Cornwall is latent and the remoter west; down the inclines of Liverpool Street lie fenlands and the illimitable Broads; Scotland is through the pylons of Euston; Wessex behind the poised chaos of Waterloo.[30]

Already by 1863 it could be claimed that the South Eastern Main Line 'has been called the "Pleasure Line" ... its iron roads and branches intersect the beautiful county of Kent ... affording the inhabitants of the great metropolis facilities of visiting the numerous watering places on its coast, and enabling them to become acquainted with its picturesque scenery, cities, and baronial halls, and the astonishing fertility of its soil.'[31] Tourists came to depend upon the railways to facilitate their journeys. The Worcestershire Naturalists Club and Herefordshire Woolhope Club regularly used trains, sometimes commissioning special carriages, to service their excursions.[32] The four UCL undergraduates who undertook a river trip on the Wye in 1892 depended on the train to get themselves, their baggage, provisions, a tent and boat from Paddington to Whitney-on-Wye station (opened in 1864), from where they rowed to Chepstow, before catching the train back 'for town to once more undergo the regularity of everyday-life'.[33] Ideally the 120-mile Pilgrim's Road from Winchester to Canterbury was undertaken continuously on foot, but the fallibilities of the human condition were recognized in a guide to the road of *c.* 1920, which acknowledged that '[t]here may be many who would like to travel the Pilgrims' Road by a series of daily excursions. Fortunately it is so served by railways that it can be completely traversed in this way'.[34] During the 1930s the GWR published a series of guides written by Hugh Page, for

---

[28] John Travis, *Lynton and Lynmouth: Glimpses of the Past* (Derby: Breedon Books, 1997), 134–46; John Fowles, *A Short History of Lyme Regis* (Wimbourne: Dovecote Press, 1982), 44; Peter Stibbons and David Cleveland, *Poppyland; Strands of Norfolk History*, 2nd edn (North Walsham: Poppyland, 1985).

[29] Greg Morse, *Holiday Trains* (Amberley: Stroud Publishing, 2019).

[30] Forster, *Howard's End*, 27.

[31] *Bradshaw*, section 1, 29.

[32] Jones, *Lookers-Out*, 64, 67, 88, 119–21, 145, 159–6.

[33] Baker (ed.), *Camping on the Wye*, 2–4, 53.

[34] Elliston-Erwood, *The Pilgrim's Road*, 192.

'rambles' in tourist areas – such as the *Chiltern Country*, *South Devon*, the *Wye Valley* and *Shakespeare Land and the Cotswolds* – which were closely modelled around the railway network and advertised 'cheap day fares for ramblers', 'week-end walking tour tickets' and 'dog tickets'. That for the *Wye Valley* (1938) outlined twenty walks in the Wye and Usk Valleys, the Black Mountains and the Forest of Dean, all based around stations.[35]

Perhaps the most striking evidence of the way in which the railways were releasing the potential of domestic tourism, and reshaping its pattern, was the impact on the guide literature. From very early on specialist railway guides were being produced, notably George Measom's 'official guides' of the 1850s and 1860s, *Bradshaw's Descriptive Railway Hand-Book of Great Britain and Ireland* (1860, 1863), and the 'official' company guides published by Cassell between the 1880s and early 1900s. To this must be added the growing body of attractive guides published from about the 1890s by the companies themselves, such as Payne Jennings's *Sun Pictures of the Norfolk Broads* (Great Eastern Railways, 1897), and the prolific inter-war output of professional guidebook writers like Maxwell Fraser and S. P. B. Mais for the GWR and other companies.[36] Unsurprisingly these publications were geared to the railway tourist. More significant is the way that the general guides adapted to the new context. There was a tradition of modelling guides around road routes, sometimes including strip maps indicating locations and sites to be seen en route. *Black's Guide to England and Wales* (1864) includes, alongside the road strips, ones based on rail routes and stations. *Black's Guide to Dorsetshire* (1872) similarly mixed road and rail routes (though without the strip maps), whereas the guide to Warwickshire (1881) took the form of a gazetteer based on the main towns but incorporated a radial map showing the 'distances by rail' from the major English cities to Warwick, and detailed maps indicating all the lines and stations in the county.[37] In the late-nineteenth century the London-based publisher Edward Stanford produced a similar series of county guides and again railways were given a prominent position; that to Warwickshire (1882) demonstrated where the force now lay in setting the pattern for tourism, with thirteen 'railway excursions' counter-balanced by a mere six 'road excursions'.[38]

Roads were never going to be wholly replaced by rails. There were always going to be spaces that it was physically impossible or financially unviable for track to penetrate. Even when Kelmscott (and Langford) finally acquired a station in 1907, actually getting to the village still involved a journey of a mile and a half.[39] Nonetheless, there must have been a point in later Victorian England when it appeared that rail would come to be the principal means of accessing the recreational landscape of

---

[35] Hugh Page, *Rambles in the Chiltern Country* (London: Great Western Railway, 1932); idem, *Rambles in Shakespeare Land and the Cotswolds* (London: Great Western Railway,1933); idem, *Rambles and Walking Tours in the Wye Valley* (London: Great Western Railway, 1938); idem, *Rambles and Walking Tours in South Devon* (London: Great Western Railway, 1939).

[36] Peter Thorpe, 'Railway Tourist Guides, Parts One and Two', *National Railway Museum*, 2011, http://blog.nrm.org.uk/railway-tourist-guides-part-1/, http://blog.nrm.org.uk/railway-tourist-guides-part-2/, accessed 17 Jun. 2022; Simmons and Biddle, *Oxford Companion*, 39, 108–9.

[37] *Black's Guide to Warwickshire*.

[38] Bevan, *Tourist's Guide to Warwickshire*.

[39] R. V. J. Butt, *The Directory of Railway Stations* (Sparkford: Patrick Stephens Ltd., 1995), 129.

coast and country. In 1908 John Hissey claimed that 'a few years ago, the despised cyclist excepted, no one appeared to know or care anything about the roads … for everybody travelled by railway then'.[40] But just as it seemed that the humble highway was losing ground, it struck back. By the 1920s H. V. Morton could write that 'the roads of England, eclipsed for a century by the railway, have come to life again'.[41] Two innovations – the 'despised' cycle and the combustion engine – made the difference and created the platform for an even more effective penetration of deepest England. Whatever the advantages of rail, particularly in terms of moving people en masse over long distances, when it came to personal mobility and flexibility there was a clear gap in the system. The crude velocipede was introduced in the 1860s followed by the 'penny farthing' in the 1870s, but it was during the 1880s that the modern 'safety' cycle, with its double-diamond frame, chain drive, and equally sized pneumatic tyres, emerged to take cycling as a pastime to a quite new level.[42] It was estimated in 1894 that there were about 500,000 cyclists.[43] A key aspect of the recreational side of cycling was the formation of clubs designed to facilitate touring. The Cyclists Touring Club was founded in 1878 (as the Bicycle Touring Club) and over a short period of time saw a dramatic rise in its membership from 3,356 in 1880, to 10,627 in 1883, and a peak of 60,449 by 1899; this was to drop to 15,474 in 1913, and a low of 8,546 in 1918 after the First World War, but by 1930 had recovered to 28,005.[44] Many of these clubs were locally based, predominantly – though not exclusively – suburban and middle class and provided some scope for female participation, either in single sex or increasingly mixed clubs.[45] The activity of the clubs naturally took them out of the city and into the tourist-scape of small town, country and coast.

To what extent immersion in the landscape was the principal *raison d'être* of the exercise is difficult to say; sociability, sport, and sexual adventure may all have played a part. One man passionately, almost obsessively committed to using his cycle to explore the landscape of his homes in the Malverns and Hereford was Edward Elgar (see Figure 8.2). He came rather late to the cycling craze; it was not until 1900 and the age of 43 that he purchased the first of his two Sunbeam models. But for the next decade he was a highly active cyclist – his surviving maps tracing in ink the routes he took, showing the remarkable range of his expeditions, and depth to which he penetrated the nooks and crannies of his environs.[46] For Elgar cycling was a sociable

---

[40] Hissey, *An English Holiday*, 158.
[41] Morton, *In Search of England*, vii.
[42] https://thevictoriancyclist.wordpress.com; Brian Griffin '"Bad Roads Will Absolutely Nip in the Bud New Development": Cycling Tourism in Ireland in the Late Nineteenth and Early Twentieth Centuries', in *Leisure and the Irish in the Nineteenth Century*, ed. Leeann Lane and William Murphy (Liverpool: Liverpool University Press), 187–206.
[43] Baedeker, *Great Britain*, xxv.
[44] *Cyclists' Touring Club Handbook* (London: Cyclists' Touring Club, 1931), 36–50, http://www.cyclinguk.org/about/history/ctc-history-timeline, accessed 17 Jun. 2022; Borsay, *Leisure*, 187.
[45] Richard Holt, *Sport and the British: A Modern History* (Oxford: Clarendon Press, 1989), 122–4, 195–8; Will Manners, *Revolution: How the Bicycle Reinvented Modern Britain* (Richmond: Duckworth, 2018).
[46] Kevin Allen, *Elgar the Cyclist in Worcester and Hereford: A Creative Odyssey* (Malvern Wells: K. Allen, 1997).

Figure 8.2 Bronze statue of Edward Elgar with his Sunbeam bicycle, Hereford Cathedral Close. © Getty Images.

activity. He was often accompanied by a small number of friends (particularly women) or relations. A favourite companion was a local schoolmistress Rosa Burley:

> There cannot have been a lane within twenty miles of Malvern that we did not ultimately find. We cycled to Upton, to Tewkesbury, to Hereford, to the Vale of Evesham, to Birtsmorton where Cardinal Wolsey is said to have fallen asleep and come under the fatal shadow of the Ragged Stone … Our favourite rides were in the lovely country that surrounded the southern parts of the [Malvern] hills. We made a point of visiting all the churches, many of which are ancient and of rare architectural interest.[47]

---

[47] R. Burley and F. C. Carruthers, *Edward Elgar: The Record of a Friendship* (London: Barrie & Jenkins, 1972), 145–6.

Burley was convinced that these cycle rides – the combination of countryside and history, and of natural and human landscape – inspired much of Elgar's music.

For A. G. Bradley, writing in 1905, it was the flexibility of the machine that lay at the heart of its success: 'A cycle is of course the ideal method by which to see the countryside… I have tested to the full the abiding nature of its manifold and elastic services, and it is impossible to go much about England without a deep sense of the inestimable boon in a more general way it has been to the country.'[48] In the same year H. A. Evans, in his exploration of the *Highways and Byways in Oxford and the Cotswolds*, declared that 'the bicycle is the conveyance we have chosen, and for the firm smooth main roads of our district no easier mode of travelling can be devised'.[49] The general guidebooks were modified to accommodate the needs of the cyclist, and a series of specialist manuals and guides appeared. Some contained extraordinarily detailed practical information about routes, road conditions and contours. *The Contour Road Book of England* (1906) has details of 997 specified routes, which included gradient diagrams and descriptions of the roads. Number 791, Ilfracombe to Minehead, was not for the faint-hearted:

> The worst main road in the south of England. … The road then descends to Lynmouth by a sheer descent with an awkward twist at the bottom – about the most dangerous hill in the country. … the road then descends to Porlock by another sheer descent, with two twists near the bottom; there is scarcely any surface to this part of the road – it is more like a river bed.[50]

Such details and descriptions gave travellers precise warnings of the risks awaiting them, so they could be avoided or mitigated, but they may also have added to the anticipation, excitement and challenge of the journey. On the positive side, there was also the likelihood that the most difficult roads from a gradient perspective were likely to be located in the most spectacular landscapes. *The Contour Road Book* also contained maps and distances between locations, but only brief references to accommodation. The last features much more prominently in *The Modern Cyclist* (1923) and especially in the CTC's annual *Handbook*, which provided club members with details of the special terms negotiated for them.[51] Cycle repairers are also listed in the *Handbook* alongside a plethora of adverts for equipment; indeed, many general guidebooks came to resemble a sandwich in which the meat of the text was squeezed between two large wedges of advertising, especially for B&Bs and hotels. This is a reminder of the importance of the rapidly developing touring infrastructure that allowed the potential of the new modes of transport to be realized.

As Bradley noted, cycles are wonderfully flexible machines for exploring, and it is no accident that their explosion on the transport scene in the late-nineteenth century coincided with a middle-class desire to escape – albeit largely temporarily – the modern city for coastal and rural England. But cycles required human effort

---

[48] A. G. Bradley, *In the March and Borderland of Wales* (London: Archibald Constable & Co., 1905), 24.
[49] H. A. Evans, *Highways and Byways in Oxford and the Cotswolds* (London: Macmillan, 1908), 34.
[50] *Contour Road Book of England* (London: Gall and Inglis, 1906), 584.
[51] *The Modern Cyclist; A Handbook for Cyclists and Other Roadfarers* ([1923]Oxford: Old House, 2013); *Cyclists Touring Club: Handbook and Guide* (London: Cyclists' Touring Club, 1923).

and able bodies, took time to cover long distances, and exposed their riders to the vagaries of the weather. In retrospect it is clear that the future lay with the combustion engine and motorized transport, either in corporate (trams, buses, and coaches) or personal (motorcar, motorcycle) modes. Automobile numbers grew rapidly in the early-twentieth century, especially after the First World War. In 1905 there were 16,000 vehicles on the road; by 1918 this had grown to 100,000. There were roughly the same number of motor cycles as cars in 1925, about half a million, but whereas in the case of cycles numbers dropped slightly over the next decade, in the case of cars they quadrupled by 1938 to around 2 million, showing clearly the way that the market in personal mobility was trending. Alongside these vehicles there were about 50,000 buses and coaches in use in the 1930s for those unable to purchase a car or who were temperamentally unsuited to driving.[52] S. P. B. Mais, a keen walker, whose itineraries in *See England First* (1935) are largely based around bus journeys, claimed, 'I did not learn what Dorset really has to show until I began to explore the county by charabanc from Bournemouth.'[53]

Spearheading the rise of the motor car was the introduction of the affordable small family automobile, and the aspirational middle-class market, predominantly located in the south-east of England. Middle-class incomes were relatively unaffected by the employment crisis of the 1920s and 1930s; in 1938, 25 per cent of households in the south-east possessed vehicles, compared with only 12 per cent in the north. In a 1930s compilation of light-hearted magazine articles describing car trips, most of which seem to start in London, A. S. Jenkinson celebrated the democratization of the automobile, proclaiming, 'We poorer motorists have been born into an age where we *can* go out and enjoy ourselves as much as, and sometimes better than, the Rolls-Royce owner.' If economics, class and location, underpinned the success of the motor car, it was leisure, the flexibility, privacy and convenience of the mode of transport and its capacity to facilitate the weekend trip into the country that gave it much of its rationale at this stage.[54] The car became *the* instrument to explore the landscape of old and rural England, a point stressed in the famous Shell oil company's lorry posters of the 1930s 'of fine landmarks, historical sights and inspiring landscapes, all firmly located in the countryside', and in their initiation of the Shell county guides under the direction of John Betjeman (see Figure 8.3).[55]

The improved accessibility provided by the motor car was often commented on. Early motorists were acutely aware of the advantages over traditional forms of travel: 'The motor, unlike a horse, never tires', wrote John Hissey in 1908, 'and therein, to me, lies its chief charm, for the motorist can always extend his wanderings at will.'[56] By the

---

[52] O'Connell, *Car in British Society*, 17–19; Dyos and Aldcroft, *British Transport*, 359.
[53] Mais, *See England First*, 103; see also 180.
[54] David Jeremiah, *Representations of British Motoring* (Manchester: Manchester University Press, 2007), 14–22, 73, 79–81; O'Connell, *Car in British Society*, 77–111, 150–78; A. S. Jenkinson, *In Search of Romantic Britain* (London: A. Barron, 1936), 186.
[55] John Hewitt, *The Shell Poster Book* (London: Profile Books, 1998); Heathcote, *A Shell Eye on England*, 4–68.
[56] Hissey, *English Holiday*, 148.

Figure 8.3 'Faringdon Folly' (1936), poster design for Shell by Lord Berners. © Shell Heritage Art Collection.

1930s the impact of the car in opening up the backwaters of the English countryside was well acknowledged. In 1938 J. H. Baker noted that Stoke Row, now a part of the Chilterns AONB,

> was little known or visited when I first knew it some thirty years ago. Its remote and elevated position ... was the chief cause of its isolation and obscurity. ... With the coming of the motor transport and subsequent improvement of the roads, and the rise of popular movements for exploring the countryside, Stoke Row and its environment became known to an increasing number of country-lovers.[57]

Some parts old England – notably coaching towns – had, paradoxically, become more inaccessible with the arrival of the railways; so it could be said in 1935 of Broadway, on the edge of the Cotswolds, 'Its lapse into obscurity was but the interval of railway supremacy, and the motor car and coach have now made the village as busy a centre as ever it was in the past.'[58]

Because of a common concern about the state of the road, the guide literature for the cycle and motor car often overlapped, as in Charles Spencer's *Cyclist and Automobilist Road Book* (c. 1912). But the car soon came to develop a distinctive and voluminous

---

[57] Baker, *Land of 'The Gap'*, 154–5.
[58] Noel Carrington (ed.), *Broadway and the Cotswolds* (Birmingham: Kynoch Press, 1933), 39.

guide literature of its own. The first Michelin guides to Britain appeared just before the First World War and were stuffed with practical information to assist motorists in what were still challenging touring conditions. Most of the information was delivered in an alphabetically arranged gazetteer, with 'the curiosities or places of interest' listed for each location, but fifty-one separate 'excursions', many chosen for their 'picturesque' (indicated in the text by the use of the abbreviation *pict.*) landscape features, were also included, taking in classic tourist regions, such as 'The Lake District', 'The Norfolk Broads', 'Gloucester, Hereford and the Valley of the Wye' and 'The Heart of Wessex'.[59] The advantage of the car was immediately obvious since most of these excursions were around 100 miles, beyond the daily range of a cyclist. It was the overly prosaic guide that Charles Harper had in mind when in 1910 he published *The Autocar Road Book* in four volumes:

> Many road-books, on the basis of mileages and hotel information, have been produced of late years, but these have no mention of those things – scenery and the villages, castles, cathedrals, ancient manor-houses, and rural churches of the country – for a sight of which, it may be presumed, most travellers in these days use the roads. … in these pages will be found not only all the most outstanding places with which it behoves those who love their country to be acquainted, but also a very large proportion of those less-known hamlets and rural districts which, not yet *exploités*, should give the traveller who comes, delighted, to their unspoiled beauties, something of the thrilful experience of an explorer.[60]

Harper in fact included a good deal of practical information, such as contours and distances, in his route descriptions (over 150 alone for the 'South of the Thames' volume) but some authors largely eschewed such mundane information in favour of a more whimsical and aesthetic approach. 'Let us be free to wander where we will', declared John Hissey at the start of his motoring tour, 'taking the fortune of the highway and the lane, just driving from time to time in whatever direction the country looks most inviting or the mood of the moment inclines.'[61] John Prioleau opened his *Car and Country: Week-End Signposts to the Open Road* (1929) in extravagant terms: 'The roadfarer and lover of England will find that, like those of Cleopatra and Lady Hamilton, the charms of his passion change, and are renewed and increased incessantly.' The beauty of England, he continued, 'is a thing apart, greater far than the beauty of any other land, in that you do not see it in a fixed portrait, but in countless series of exquisite miniatures, whose subjects have been painted, and are constantly re-painted, in ten thousand moods'. It seems that we have scarcely shifted from the world of the eighteenth-century picturesque tour, only now it was delivered through the modern medium of the motor car, and as the guide makes clear, the 'motor-cruise', the 'comfortable and pleasant Saturday and Sunday cruise'.[62]

---

[59] *Michelin Guide to the British Isles*, 4th Year (1914), 11–12, 49–96.
[60] *The Autocar Road Book*, 4 vols. (London: Methuen, 1910), vol. 1, 'South of the Thames', v.
[61] Hissey, *The Charm of the Road*, 4.
[62] Prioleau, *Car and Country*, vii, 1, 227.

Walking[63]

'To get in touch with the real Dartmoor you have to walk,' declared S. P. B. Mais in 1928, a point he later reinforced when he revealed that 'I did not become conscious of the loveliness of the English countryside until I began to walk through it'.[64] When in 1894 Baedeker pronounced 'the pedestrian ... unquestionably the most independent of travellers', the comparison was with rail and horse-driven coach. By the early-twentieth century, there was a new challenge. 'You must walk and climb' the Wye Valley to see it properly, argued A. G. Bradley: 'It is idle to fancy that a spin along the road at twenty miles an hour will give you anything of its spirit or leave any worthy impressions.' The *Manchester Guardian* journalist Charles E. Montagu (1867–1928) wrote, 'You certainly see most when you walk ... travel by car is only semi-travel, verging on the demi-semi-travel that you get on trains.' The pedestrian, as Harry Batsford insisted, 'alone is free of the land'.[65]

People have walked throughout human history. It is a defining feature of the human physiology and character. But the rise of walking for pleasure, on a significant scale, is often dated to the romantic era. For much of the eighteenth century, it has been argued, little value was placed on walking for pleasure. Towards the end of the century, however, attitudes changed, particularly among the new middle classes who were most affected by the urban-economic changes of the period, and walking came to acquire new value as a recreational activity.[66] Important as this era was, we may need to track a little further back to establish the origins of recreational walking in England. As we saw in Chapters 2 and 5, formal walks began to be constructed in English towns during the seventeenth century, providing fashionable society with outdoor stages on which to perform the rituals of polite sociability and display. By the mid- to later eighteenth century scarcely any town with social pretensions would have been without such a facility, many of which were situated on the urban edge. The peripheral location of these promenades was no doubt in part a practical response to the availability of cheap undeveloped land. But it also suggests a conscious desire to engage with the rural world, particularly since many of the walks were constructed on elevated sites that gave extensive views of the countryside. Nonetheless, it is likely that for those occupying these promenades the focus of their attention was as much, and in all probability a great deal more, upon each other as upon the natural world. The perambulation that took place was what may be termed 'social' walking. Participants were primarily there to exchange conversation, to display themselves and to observe others flaunting their feathers.

One of the major problems, however, is trying to establish the evidence for 'solitary' walking. Whereas there are plenty of visual and literary accounts of formal

---

[63] Much of the following section is taken from Peter Borsay, 'Promenade en bord de ville: espace périphérique et activité récréative dans la ville anglaise at galloises, de 1700 à 1900', in *Esthétiques de la Ville Britannique (XVIIIe-XIXe siècles)*, ed. Pierre Dubois and A. Tadié (Paris: PUPS, 2012), 83–104.

[64] Mais, *Glorious Devon*, 86; Mais, *Round about England*, 15.

[65] Baedeker, *Great Britain*, xxii; Bradley, *Wye*, 59; Moore quoted in Piehler, *England for Everymen*, 35; Batsford, *How to See the Country*, 56.

[66] Bryant, Burns and Readman, *Walking Histories, 1800–1914*, 2; see also Rebecca Solnit, *Wanderlust: A History of Walking* (London: Granta Books, 2014), 81–117.

promenades, those of the informal rural footpath are far scarcer. Take the case of Bath and its guidebooks. John Wood's *Description of Bath* includes accounts of the main fashionable promenades at the spa, all situated close to the water facilities in the southeast quadrant of the city.[67] Wood also described the fashionable daily round at Bath, in particular referring to a relaxed period about noon, when the company went their different ways, some making for the assembly rooms and card playing, some for the bookshops, some for the formal walks, some taking 'air and exercise' on horseback or in coaches, and – intriguingly – some walking 'in the Meadows round the City, particularly in those by the *Avon Side*, between BATH and *Twiverton*'.[68] Wood's account of the extra-mural excursions of the company suggests, as we have seen, that for most this would have been facilitated through horse-powered transport rather than on foot (he refers to 'thirty different rides'), and this assumption pervades guidebooks of the early nineteenth century.[69] However, by the time that *The Original Bath Guide* of 1876 was published, a section had been included on 'Walks and Rides', with specific reference to paths, and by the Ward Lock guide of 1909 the section on rides has disappeared entirely to be replaced by thirteen pages on 'Walks around Bath'.[70]

We should be cautious about reading too much into these changing accounts. On the one hand, it is likely that inhabitants had long strolled in the countryside surrounding their towns, and much of this activity may simply be hidden from us by the nature of the sources. On the other hand, there were pressures – growing during the eighteenth century – that restricted rather than encouraged the use of the urban environs for recreational walking. The trend towards enclosure and the loss of common land would have restricted public access. For working people shrinking leisure time as industrialization accelerated may also have been a problem. For fashionable society the development of the cultural values of politeness and sociability, and the rise of the promenade, could have drawn the elite away from informal perambulations. Many of those attending watering places would of course have been invalids whose ailments restricted their movement, and for the affluent in general their mode of transport – in a carriage or on horseback – would transmit important messages about their status that walking could not. Finally, the traditional economic and social geography of the town – with the better off occupying the urban centre and the poorer the peripheries, and with many industrial processes also situated on the edge – would hardly have encouraged fashionable society to take to the urban margins. Only with middle-class suburbanization, gathering pace in the provinces from the later eighteenth century, but earlier in London, and maturing in the Victorian period, was this pattern of spatial relationships to be decisively reversed and with it the general character of the urban periphery changed.[71]

---

[67] Wood, *Description of Bath*, 224–5, 243–6, 342–3, 349–51; Borsay, *Urban Renaissance*, 350.
[68] Wood, *Description of Bath*, 439–40.
[69] *Original Bath Guide* (1840), 135–49.
[70] *Original Bath Guide: Historical and Descriptive*, 125–43; *Pictorial and Descriptive Guide to Bath* (London: Ward Lock, 1909–10).
[71] Peter Borsay, 'Early Modern Urban Landscapes, 1540–1800', in *English Urban Landscape*, ed. Waller, 105; Carl B. Estabrook, *Urbane and Rustic England: Cultural Ties and Social Spheres in the Provinces, 1660–1780* (Manchester: Manchester University Press, 1998), 253–75.

Yet the growing length of the environs section in the guide literature, particularly during the nineteenth century, suggests that the area on the edge of towns, and in the surrounding countryside, was acquiring a greater significance for visitors and inhabitants, whether accessed on foot or by other modes of transport. This reflected a much broader cultural trend towards the valorization of the natural world, which intensified, as we have seen, at the end of the eighteenth century with the picturesque movement and romanticism.[72] Tourism and travel for pleasure was fundamental to this trend, and embedded within this was the emerging cult of walking and the walking tour. Pioneered and popularized by figures like the poets Thomas Gray, William Wordsworth, Samuel Taylor Coleridge, and John Keats, and associated with visits to 'remote' areas in Britain such as the Wye Valley, the Lake District, and Snowdonia, walking was more than simply a means of accessing wild landscapes. It was felt to allow an intimacy of contact with nature not easily achieved through other modes of movement, and it encouraged an interiority and intensity of psychological response, the opposite of that experienced on the formal promenade.[73] Well before the arrival of the motorcar there was anxiety that the new transport technologies were alienating the traveller from his environment. John Ruskin complained, in the mid-nineteenth century, that 'going by railroad I do not consider as travelling at all; it is merely "being sent" to a place, and very little different from becoming a parcel'. Instead he recommended unhurried travel on foot, so that

> if, advancing thus slowly, after some days we approach any more interesting scenery, every yard of the changeful ground becomes precious and piquant; and the continual increase of hope, and of surrounding beauty, affords one of the most exquisite enjoyments possible to the healthy mind. ... A man who really loves travelling would as soon consent to pack a day of such happiness into an hour of railroad, as one who loved eating would agree, if it were possible, to concentrate his dinner into a pill.[74]

Walking tours were of course usually undertaken with one or two others, but the emphasis would not be upon sociability (in the sense of the promenade or pleasure garden) but upon companionship, and there would be a shared understanding that the focus of attention was the natural landscape.

The cult of walking did not necessarily translate easily to the immediate outskirts of towns – the area most easily accessed by a growing majority of the population – for some of the reasons mentioned above. The most obvious problem was its association with wild and inaccessible places, far removed from areas of intensive urbanization.

---

[72] Thomas, *Man and the Natural World*; Ousby, *The Englishman's England*; Louis Hawes, *Presences of Nature: British Landscape 1780–1830* (New Haven: Yale Center for British Art, 1982); Andrews, *Search for the Picturesque*; Dixon Hunt, *Picturesque Garden in Europe*.

[73] *Thomas Gray's Journal of His Visit to the Lake District in October 1769*, ed. William Roberts (Liverpool: Liverpool University Press, 2001); Hebron, *Romantics and the British Landscape*, 1–95; James Buzzard, *The Beaten Track: European Tourism, Literature, and the Ways to Culture, 1800–1918* (Oxford: Clarendon Press, 2001), 34–5; Solnit, *Wanderlust*.

[74] John Ruskin, *Modern Painters* (London: George Allen, 1904), vol. 3, 311–12.

But remote locations also incurred considerable costs in terms of travel time, monetary expense and simple lack of comfort. The outcome was that despite the problems involved, the thirst for contact with nature and with it the cult of walking radiated out from the town into the surrounding countryside. The idea that this was an entirely novel activity should be treated – as has been suggested already – with caution. It almost certainly built upon long traditions of recreational walking on the periphery of towns and in all probability utilized already existing networks of informal paths and customary rights of way. What changes is that an unconscious tradition was turning into a self-conscious cult, and the pathways utilized from tracks for facilitating movement, often connected with work,[75] were transformed into arteries of leisure. Guidebooks and maps play an important part in re-conceptualizing the practices and spaces involved in this process. It is when the guidebooks begin to identify informal walks, and describe the scenes to be viewed from them, in the way that they had for formal promenades, that change takes place.

This process was reinforced at both a mental and practical level by changes in mapping practices. The establishment of the Ordnance Survey (1791), and its production of maps that could easily be carried around by the general public – essentially the one inch to a mile series, the first of which was published for Kent in 1801 – was critical in structuring recreational perceptions of the landscape. Much depended upon the lines of communication and features depicted. Until 1883 no attempt, with a few exceptions, was made to identify footpaths as such on OS maps. After that date they begin to appear as a specified feature, 'the object ... being that the public may not mistake them for roads traversable by horses or wheeled traffic'. Included were to be 'all footpaths over which there is a well known and undisputed right of way' and 'private footpaths through fields (but not in gardens) ... if they are of a permanent character'. Hinting strongly at the recreational function of this information, specifically excluded were 'mere convenience footpaths, for the use of a household, cottage or farm, or for the temporary use of workmen ... but paths leading to any well-defined subject of use or interest, such as a well, should be shown'. Only after the mid-1880s did footpaths become a specified feature of the one-inch series, with the stipulation being that 'only footpaths that are habitually used by the public should be shown'.[76] It was the presence of well-marked paths that underpinned the value to ramblers of the OS maps, especially the popular series introduced after the First World War.[77] OS maps also provided the template for specialist walkers' maps like the 'Geographia' *Ramblers' Map to London's Countryside* (1920s to 1930s) on which 'footpaths [were] distinctly printed in red; bus routes in green', and railway stations were clearly indicated, providing all the information necessary to access and navigate the capital's rural belt.

---

[75] Clark and Thompson, *Dorset Landscape*, 76.
[76] Richard Oliver, *Ordnance Survey Maps: A Concise Guide for Historians* (London: The Charles Close Society, 2005), 95–7.
[77] Although OS maps also contained the warning 'N.B. The representation on this map of a Road, Track, or Footpath, is no evidence of the existence of a right of way', and as J. R. A. Hockin noted in 1934, 'The Ordnance Survey is not reliable in the matter of paths.' Hockin, *On Foot in Berkshire*, 3. Only after the passage of the National Parks and Access to the Countryside Act (1949) were local authorities required to produce and keep under review definitive maps showing rights of way.

These changes coincided with, and were related to, initiatives that emerged from the blossoming of associational culture in Victorian towns, and which in some respects modified the solitary nature of out-of-town walking. Societies proliferated aimed at protecting and utilizing peripheral urban spaces and footpaths. The foundation of the Commons Preservation Society in 1866 led the way, followed by the establishment of local footpath associations in the 1880s under the umbrella of the National Footpaths Preservation Society, founded in 1884; in 1899 the CPS and the NFPS merged to form the Commons, Open Spaces and Footpaths Preservation Society.[78] From the 1870s the first organized rambling clubs also emerged, many based on the expanding industrial cities, such as London, Manchester, Liverpool, and Sheffield.[79] The rambling clubs followed in the wake of the natural history, archaeological and field societies; among the first was the Berwickshire Naturalists' Field Club founded in 1831 with many more established in the 1840s and 1850s.[80] They aimed to take their members into the countryside to investigate the natural environment, though it is clear that most of those involved were motivated as much by aesthetic and social considerations, as by the desire to further scientific research. Carefully planned and regular excursions were organized. Some of these trips would be held at a good distance from the club's base town and would involve using various modes of transport, including the railways, but all would usually require a lengthy walk once the destination had been arrived at.

Not that the sites visited were always that far away. One of the Woolhope Naturalists' Field Club's favourite locations – as we have seen – was the Woolhope Dome that lay only 4 miles from its home base, Hereford. Some 15 or so miles from the city were the Malvern Hills, the destination for occasional excursions, and where the Woolhope Naturalists would sometimes meet with those of another field society, the Worcestershire Naturalists' Club (founded in 1847).[81] Sometimes they were joined (as in June 1853 and June 1855) in the Malverns by a third society, the Malvern Naturalists' Club, established in 1853.[82] Only 5 to 6 miles from Worcester and 15 from Hereford, the Malverns hovered above the Severn plain, a steep and striking ridge of hills with a complex and dramatic geological history (see Figure 8.4).

If the Malverns had a home town, then this was the rapidly expanding spa of Great Malvern – its population grew from under 1,000 at the start of the nineteenth century to over 16,000 by the end – nestling directly under the Worcestershire Beacon, the highest of the chain of hills.[83] For Great Malvern the hills were in its immediate backyard, and for the businessmen of the town they represented a crucial recreational

---

[78] Readman, *Storied Ground*, 125.
[79] Dave Hollett, *The Pioneer Ramblers 1850–1940* (London: North Wales Area of the Ramblers' Association, 2002), 61–105, 132–47.
[80] Hudson, *Social History of Archaeology*, 15–20; N. Hewitt, 'Encountering Nature: The Tyneside Naturalists' Field Club and the North East, 1846–1900' (M.Res. dissertation, Northumbria University, 2008).
[81] Jones, *Lookers-Out*.
[82] *Transactions of the Malvern Naturalists' Field Club* (1853–1870): 1, 3–4, 12.
[83] Phyllis Hembry, *British Spas from 1815 to the Present: A Social History*, ed. W. Leonard and Evelyn E. Cowie (London: Athlone Press, 1997), 182–98; *Great Malvern Conservation Area: Appraisal and Management Strategy* (Malvern: Malvern Hill Development Council, 2008), 5–11.

Figure 8.4 'View from the Ivy Rock, Malvern', *c.* 1830–40. © The Trustees of the British Museum.

resource, that appealed to the visitors and residents as much – and probably a good deal more – than the waters. It was for this reason that the townspeople were one of the driving forces behind the establishment of the Malvern Hills Conservators, entrusted by a special Act of Parliament in 1884 to care for the hills.[84] The Conservators were required to address and manage the conflicting interests of a range of groups using the hills. These included not only local landowners and commoners but also the general public. It was clear from the outset that one of the Conservators' primary duties was to preserve and develop the hills as an area of natural beauty for the community at large. This meant not only fashionable residents and visitors to the spa but also less well-off local people and excursionists from the heavily urbanized industrial West Midlands, and even as far afield as Derby and Manchester, whose access to the hills was facilitated by the coming of the railways to Great Malvern in the 1860s. Though there was a good deal of local opposition from some quarters to these elements, and efforts were taken to limit the rail services available for them, over the long term the trippers were to prove a key user group.[85]

[84] Hurle, *The Malvern Hills*, 14–31.
[85] Hembry, *British Spas*, 191–2; BBC Hereford and Worcester website, http://news.bbc.co.uk/local/herefordandworcester/hi/people_and_places/history/newsid_8680000/8680618.stm, accessed 30 Jul. 2022.

The 1884 Act stated specifically that those parts of the Malverns covered by the legislation were to 'remain under the management and control of the Conservators for the use and recreation of *the public* [my italics] subject to any existing rights of common'.[86] This meant that among the Conservators' myriad duties was a requirement to protect the appearance of the hills and address issues of public access, including safety matters, the maintenance of footpaths, and the installation of benches. Rangers were appointed to deal with these problems on a day-to-day basis. The chief ranger was constantly concerned about the safety of public footpaths, particularly in proximity to quarries, and by the early 1900s he and his assistants were spending considerable time inspecting and repairing paths and supplying benches (authority to provide seats had been included in the 1909 Malvern Hills Act).[87] Paths and seats for recreational walkers inscribed the hills as leisure space, and the Conservators' early construction of a kiosk with refreshments and toilets on the top of the Worcestershire Beacon reinforced this.[88] The extent to which the hills had become a major walking and recreational facility for Great Malvern is evident from the guidebooks and maps produced for the spa and surrounding area. Charles Grindrod devoted the vast majority of *Malvern* (1904) to extensive descriptions of the views from the hills to 'short excursions' on the hills or in their immediate vicinity (including Worcestershire Beacon which can be accessed by carriage, pony, donkey chair or on foot), and to longer excursions, to places like the Wye Valley, the Forest of Dean, Warwick, Bristol and Shrewsbury.[89]

In fact, as the case of Bath suggests, spa towns, even if they did not possess any single landscape feature of the significance of the Malverns, were increasingly engaged in the process of physically mapping and culturally encoding their environs to meet the needs of excursionists and in particular walkers. The guidebooks to Leamington, for example, one of the fastest growing spas in the early-nineteenth century,[90] include accounts of walks to surrounding villages and historic sites. Beck's guide of 1840 contains seven chapters on 'The Neighbourhood of Leamington', outlining the objects of historical and natural features in the vicinity, promising that the visitor would 'find himself surveying and admiring these amidst scenery eminently picturesque; to several of them it forms a most agreeable walk: to those more distant, a short ride is preferable'.[91] Precise directions are provided about the paths to be taken by pedestrian explorers. The 1868 edition begins its instructions a short distance from the Pump Room at the Holly Walk, which 'winding beneath luxuriant elms, has long been a favourite resort', helped funnel visitors into the countryside.

> Ascending to the Newbold Hills beyond, a beautiful view bursts upon the beholder, embracing Warwick, its Castle and Church, and a vast expanse of richly-wooded and undulating country, dotted with villages and stately mansions; … Proceeding

---

[86] Malvern Hills Act 1884, clause 13.
[87] MHCA, Ranger's Report Book, 24 Jul. 1885, 20 and 31 Aug. 1888, 4 Nov. 1891, 14 Sept. 1904, 8 Mar. 1905, 14 Mar. and 12 Sept. 1910, 13 Nov. 1911, 8 Jan., 8 Jul. and 11 Nov. 1912; Assistant Ranger's Book, 8 May 1911: Malvern Hills Act 1904, clause 7.
[88] MHCA, Committee Minute Book, 6 and 20 Mar. 11 and 17 Apr. 1885; 15 and 29 Oct., 5 Nov.1886.
[89] Grindrod, *Malvern: What to See*.
[90] Hembry, *British Spas*, 8–32.
[91] *Beck's Leamington Guide: Containing also, a Description of the Neighbourhood, and a Directory*, 6th edn (Leamington: J. Beck, 1840), 108–9.

through a plantation, not inappropriately termed 'The Lover's Grove', the church of Lillington presents itself, enshrouded amidst surrounding trees, beyond a fine tract of meadow land, through which a path conducts to the village ... The visitor may pass through the Church-yard ... and proceed down a shady lane into the high road, by which he may return to Leamington, or by going a short distance in that direction and taking a footpath on the right, he may cross the meadows into the Kenilworth road.[92]

Walking on the urban edge had become an essential element of a visit to any watering place. This of course went not only for spas but also the rapidly developing seaside resorts.[93] Here the urban edge was defined in rather different ways. There was a rural margin, but in addition there was the sea. Both land and water represented natural phenomena and in that respect appealed to the counter-cultural responses of townspeople. The maritime resorts took the formal walk of eighteenth-century inland fashionable towns and developed it into the seaside promenade. In some cases existing harbour facilities, such as a stone pier, might be appropriated and adapted; in other cases there was considerable investment in new structures, including 'parades' that ran parallel with the beach and iron piers that plunged into the sea. All these promenades were highly sociable spaces, for parading and performing, as in the case of the formal walks in the inland towns. But the proximity of the sea meant that walkers would have close contact with nature, even if perambulating en masse. Moreover, when the wind blew and the waves pounded the promenade, and most visitors retreated to their lodgings, there was also an opportunity for the solitary walker to engage in that intensive relationship with raw nature that serviced his or her interior psyche.

However, there was also another remoter edge that the solitary walker could exploit at the seaside, that constituted by adjacent cliffs, beach and marshland. Most resorts developed on their margins a network of informal paths that allowed access to these spaces for individuals or small groups. Cliff-side paths, with their dramatic geological forms, elevation, inherent danger, and high exposure to wind and sea, were particularly conducive to the practice of solitary walking and intimate contact with the full forces of nature. Lucy Lawford left a diary of her stay in Tenby in southwest Wales from August 1873 to January 1874. She was an intrepid and frequent walker, sometimes on her own, sometimes with a companion or companions, around the environs of the resort, despite inclement conditions: 'I've worn out one pair of boots, I can't keep them dry for there surely never was such weather.' Her perambulations could take several hours and involve an element of danger and excitement:

> Jane & I went to the top of the cliffs at Giltar-point ... one of the peculiar features of the cliffs here, is that in the sides, (or tops of some) there are large rents or yawning gulfs, they open at the bottom into caves. When the tide comes in the sound is awful, the first I heard frightened me & I fled. This one [a drawing accompanies the text] in the Giltar cliffs is not safe for any one to look into.

[92] *Beck's Guide to Leamington and the Surrounding District*, 14th edn (Leamington: J. Beck, [1868]), 71–2.
[93] Walton, *English Seaside Resort*; Brodie and Winter, *England's Seaside Resorts*; Peter Borsay, 'Health and Leisure Resorts, 1700–1840', in *Cambridge Urban History of Britain. Vol. II*, ed. Clark, 775–803.

One day she embarked on her own for Monkstone Point (on the opposite side of Tenby to Giltar) but soon discovered that she had seriously miscalculated the tides, was cut off, and was forced – having met a family in the same dilemma – to scramble up a precipitous cliff where they discovered a track 'made by previous unfortunate pedestrians'.[94]

The spas and seaside resorts played an important role in developing the idea and practice of recreational walking, both the social and solitary kind. It was the latter that acquired cult status and involved engagement with the landscape. By the inter-war years the cult was becoming a craze – walking was being transformed into something called rambling and hiking – which attracted a widening social clientele and age demographic, proving increasingly appealing to young people. The establishment of the Youth Hostels Association in 1930 (with a membership of almost 50,000 by 1935) and then the Ramblers Association in 1935 crystallized a series of developments and movements that had been growing for some time.[95] Travel on foot, unaided by machine, was valorized. One guidebook of 1936 that charted a series of quite strenuous walking tours, some of eighteen or more miles a day, based around youth hostels, introduced the volume with a declaration that 'ENGLAND IS FIRST and foremost a country for the walker. … only those who walk can ever hope to understand the real spirit of this England of ours'.[96] As with the cycling craze it is difficult to know how much of the enthusiasm was because of the opportunities rambling provided for companionship and sexual liaison and how much for engaging with the landscape. But city-based leisure, such as the cinema and dance hall, provided plenty of contexts for socializing and courting, so it seems reasonable to assume that a good part of the appeal of walking and rambling lay in its environmental attractions. Moreover, by this point there had emerged a cultural model of the open air, open countryside, wayfaring and roaming, which was closely associated with walking. When John Ashton and Arnold Stocks published their *Open-Air Guide for Wayfarers of All Kinds* (1929), they declared 'wayfaring' to be 'the cultivated art of travel' and warned that '[m]odern easy travel gives him [the average townsman] the power to visit nature more often than before … And yet the crowd miss the real thing. They take their town atmosphere with them'. In their book, they explained, they 'tried to show the better way of simple knowledge of country ways'. This was done by a series of chapters on scenery, trees, birds, wayside architecture, weather lore and such like. The use of the motor car 'as an aid to wayfaring' was not ruled out, a sign of how embedded it had already become in travel culture. But it is significant that the first chapter is on walking and climbing: 'We are not concerned with those who walk on roads as fast as they can from one place to another. They are excellent fellows, no doubt, but not wayfarers. This section is for those who roam.'[97]

---

[94] Lucy Amelia Lawford, *Dear Emma. Her Account of Her Stay in Tenby and the Mumbles between 1873 and 1875*, ed. Alan Douglas (privately printed, 1998), unpaginated.
[95] Hollett, *Pioneer Ramblers*, 148–79; Sydney Moorhouse, *Walking Tours and Hostels in England* (London: Country Life, 1936), xiv.
[96] Moorhouse, *Walking Tours and Hostels in England*, xiii.
[97] Ashton and Stocks, *The Open-Air Guide*, 5, 11, 39–42.

Experiencing the journey

There can be little doubt that the rail, cycle and motorized transport greatly enhanced the possibility of recreational travel, and access to England's coastal and rural landscape, for its burgeoning urban population. But did it change the way that landscape was perceived and experienced? There was a good deal of contemporary criticism about the direct impact of the transport revolution on the landscape itself. Railway lines, cuttings, tunnels and stations were seen by some as a scar on the body of Nature itself, hence Wordsworth's famous protest against the projected Kendal and Windermere railway in 1844: 'Is there no nook of English ground secure/From rash assault?'[98] This negative response was accentuated by the engines themselves, with their noise, fire and steam seen as a diabolic presence. Later technologies were not necessarily received more favourably. In 1905 A. G. Bradley complained that '[t]he cycle alone must have swept thousands of ponies and hacks and trappers out of use; and now the motor has arrived, with its unfathomable possibilities and its lengthening shadow over the equine race, as well as its terrors to the peaceful wayfarer'.[99] Along with the automobile came its appurtenances: tarmacked roads, advertising hoardings, and filling stations. In 1938 Colonel Sir Charles Close advised those trying to trace ancient landscape features to

> take a six-inch sheet and one of Dr Grundy's explanations of the Charters, walk round the boundaries therein described, and you will find yourself back in Saxon times – unless you happen to meet with a petrol station in the course of your walk, and you are brought back with a shock to one of the less harmonious features of our modern countryside.[100]

The service station, despite its necessity to facilitate automobile tourism, was a particular object of opprobrium. Alison Murray fumed about the erection of 'these odious eyesores by the roadside in maddening colours like bilious yellow, staring green and fiery red for the benefit of tourists in search of England's "Beauty"'.[101] It was not just a question of the new technologies directly disfiguring the landscape but also damaging the perception of it. Rapid movement of images, as one feature after another flew past the window of the railway carriage or car, disrupted the studied contemplation of a scene, which it was felt was necessary to induce a picturesque response. Landscape appeared simply as a series of disjointed images, a matter not helped in the case of the railways by the presence of cuttings and tunnels constantly obscuring the view. As Wolfgang Schivelbusch has argued, 'visual perception is diminished by velocity': the 'intensity of travel' provided by the coach came to an end with the railway, with

---

[98] Quoted in Christian Wolmar, *Railways* (London: Apollo, 2019), unpaginated.
[99] Bradley, *March and Borderland of Wales*, 216.
[100] Charles Close, *The Map of England: Or about England with an Ordnance Map* (London: Peter Davies, 1938), 138.
[101] Alison Murray, *The Cotswolds*, 2nd edn (Gloucester: British Publishing Co., 1937), 36.

a resulting 'loss of landscape'.[102] Railway guides, it has been suggested, were used by passengers to locate landscape features during a journey, thus providing textual compensation for the visual disruption.[103] Yet we should be cautious about overstating the problem here. What appeared as new and raw features in the landscape soon began to age. Their presence became normalized and they literally became 'part of the landscape' and even eventually part of the landscape heritage.

Despite the growth in new forms of rapid transport, there were still plenty of opportunities for travellers to adopt the picturesque perspective once they had alighted from the train, bus or car and transferred to walking mode. This potential for capturing the static picture was enhanced with the invention of photography, especially once easily portable cameras and roll film were introduced. Significantly, Ashton and Stocks's *Open-Air Guide* contains a section on photography – 'Daily throughout the year but with tenfold intensity in the summer, people are pointing cameras at each other or at "views"' – which includes not only technical details about cameras but also tips on 'composition'.[104] Moreover, a new sort of picturesque was emerging, which incorporated rather than rejected movement. Here was a different way of perceiving landscape, a more dynamic and free-flowing vision, what Schivelbusch has called 'the panaromalization of the outside landscape',[105] that involved an 'extensive transformation in the landscape tradition', and that was to be reinforced from the 1890s by the introduction of moving pictures and familiarized through the cinema.[106] The GWR *Through the Window* series of rail guides of the 1920s, intended to accompany passengers on their journeys, encouraged this cinematic perspective.[107] 'Seeing the country from a railway train' was, in the words of Edmund Vale, 'rather an art'.[108]

For John Betjeman the appeal of the train lay in its slow calm. 'Trains are ... made for meditation. And I advise slow trains on branch lines, half empty trains that go through meadows in the evening and stop at each once oil-lit halt. Time and war slip away and you are lost in the heart of England.'[109] The unscheduled and momentary halt of the London-Oxford-Worcester-Malvern express at the tiny Cotswold village of Adlestrop on 24 June 1914, shortly before the outbreak of the First World War, prompted Edward Thomas's famous evocation of pre-war England, published in 1917 after he was killed by shell blast in France:

> Yes. I remember Adlestrop –
> The name, because one afternoon

---

[102] Wolfgang Schivelbusch, *The Railway Journey: The Industrialisation of Time and Space in the Nineteenth Century* (Berkeley and Los Angeles: University of California Press, 1986), 53, 55.

[103] For the ideas discussed here I am greatly indebted to Charles-Francois Mathis and a paper that he delivered at Aberystwyth University.

[104] Ashton and Stocks, *Open-Air Guide*, 163–71.

[105] Schivelbusch, *Railway Journey*, 67.

[106] Tom Gunning, 'Landscape and the Fantasy of Moving Pictures: Early Cinema's Phantom Rides', in *Cinema and Landscape*, ed. Graeme Harper and Jonathan Rayner (Bristol: Intellect Books, 2010), 31–70.

[107] See, for example, *Through the Window: Paddington to Penzance* (London: J. Burrow & Co. Ltd., 1927).

[108] Vale, *How to See England*, 276.

[109] John Betjeman, *Coming Home: An Anthology of His Prose, 1920–1977*, selected and introduced by Candia Lycett Green (London: Vintage, 1998), 114.

Of heat the express train drew up there
Unwontedly. It was late June.[110]

By the early-twentieth century railways had become a source of nostalgia rather than modernity, a vehicle for a journey into the English past rather than the present and future. In 1923 the journalist and novelist A. G. Macdonell could write of 'the line that used to be called the Great Central' (merged into the London and North Eastern Railway in 1923),

> [I]t is like no other of the north-bound lines. For it runs through lovely, magical rural England. It goes to places that you have never heard of before … It goes to places that do not need a railway, that never use a railway, that probably do not yet know that they have got a railway … It is a dreamer among railways, a poet, kindly and absurd and lovely.[111]

There was, therefore, little difficulty in incorporating the new modes of transport into the *English* picturesque tradition, at the same time as making it available to a much larger volume and wider range of people. But travel was about more than simply the aestheticization of landscape. It was also about turning the journey through landscape into a metaphor. Too much should not be made of this. It is not being suggested that every time someone took to a train to the seaside or went for an afternoon spin into the country they were engaged in a journey of self-discovery. At the same time it is clear from the accounts that opened this chapter, or indeed Betjeman's paean to the railway, that there was more to the journeys undertaken than merely the mechanical exercise of getting from A to B. The passengers involved observed the landscapes that passed before their eyes closely, and in the process these features induced an enhanced consciousness – the 'Cotswold Hills rising out of a dreamy haze', the 'fantastic landscape in a dream', 'trains were made for meditation' – out of which came an awareness of undertaking a more profound and metaphysical type of journey; from the present into the past, from the civilized into the wild, or simply a journey into 'the heart of England'. Some topographical writers signalled the difference between the mundane and metaphysical journey by drawing a distinction between the tourist and the traveller and by implication between the mere guidebook complier and the true travel author. Albert Osborne warned that

> the tourist … may follow the long white roads of the sea, but he thinks of the ship rather than of the waves that follow and which lure … while the traveller … fares along the country ways, under the open sky, and feels akin to the winds that wander there. And to him comes the joy, as to a boy, of the half-formed sense of some impending adventure.[112]

---

[110] Edward Thomas, 'Adlestrop', in *The Annotated Collected Poems*, ed. Edna Longley (Tarset: Bloodaxe books, 2011), 50, 176–7; Mark Bostridge, *The Fateful Year: England 1914* (London: Viking, 2014), 136–40.
[111] A. G. Macdonell, *England, Their England* ([1933]London: Macmillan, 1967), 184–5.
[112] Albert Osborne, *Old-World England: Impressions of a Stranger* (London: E. Nash & Grayton Ltd., 1924), 276.

The idea of the journey is one of the great narrative devices of literary and cultural history. Perhaps the most influential text in this respect, and one of the most widely read books in the nineteenth century, was John Bunyan's *Pilgrim's Progress* (1678). The text is full of landscape features, laced with symbolic meaning – such as the Slough of Despond, Beelzebub's Castle, Hill Difficulty, the Valley of Humiliation, the Valley of the Shadow of Death, the Plain called Ease and the River of Death – which Christian encounters on his journey from the City of Destruction to the Celestial City. Explicit references to religious peregrinations in the guidebook literature, however, are rare. Delineating routes as arduous and perilous, or the experience of the journey as a perpetual and exhausting battle between good and evil, would have been an unlikely strategy for authors intent on selling their volumes. But the language of pilgrimage did allow them to invest the prospective journey with a certain degree of seriousness, significance and even portentousness. H. V. Morton, as he prepared to leave London at the start of his motor tour of England, declared, 'All good knights, pilgrims, sons in search of fortune, seekers after truth, and plain ordinary fools, turn towards the city they have left and take farewell according to their natures. This is a full moment in all journeying, the time when girths are tightened in preparation for the miles that lie ahead.'[113] Ernest Ryan's 'account of an expedition on foot from Putney to Thames Head' with his eighteen-year-old daughter in a hot summer in the 1930s is composed in a low-key light-hearted style, but the author justified the book's compilation as a help to 'those who may feel inclined to engage in similar pilgrimages', and the journey undertaken was clearly meant to cement, celebrate – perhaps even symbolize – the father-daughter relationship:

> We would steadily move on by easy stages and behold at last, somewhere in Gloucestershire, the *fons et origo* of 'our river', as Nancy called it, or perish in the attempt. This had surely been in our hearts that morning, when, having turned our backs on our home, we faced each other and shook hands. I think it also signified implicit faith in one another.[114]

Occasionally the notion of a trial by journey emerges explicitly, as in the Revd Donald Carr's famous account of his *Night in the Snow or Struggle for Life on the Long Mynd* (1865), recounting how he lost his way and almost his life – at one point slipping headlong down a ravine – as he crossed the hill during a storm: 'I knew that, under Providence, all depended on my own powers of endurance, and that the struggle for life must be a very severe one.'[115] Carr in this instance could hardly be said to be on a recreational journey; he was returning home from officiating in one of his own churches. However the Long Mynd, and more broadly the Shropshire Hills, developed, rather like the Malverns, into a recreational space during the nineteenth century, serviced by the small spa town of Church Stretton. What Carr's account does

---

[113] Morton, *In Search of England*, 4.
[114] E. K.W. Ryan, *The Thames from the Towpath. An Account of an Expedition on Foot from Putney to Thames Head* (London: The Saint Catherine Press, 1938), author's note and p. 6.
[115] E. Donald Carr, *A Night in the Snow, or, a Struggle for Life* (London: James Nisbet & Co., 1865), 28.

is to invest the space with imaginative meaning, so that it becomes a place of danger, drama and wildness. The story became so embedded in the location that, in *March and Borderland* (1905) A. G. Bradley makes reference to '[a] blood-curdling account … of a night spent in a snow storm up here by a former vicar of Ratlinghope while following a call of duty' as 'a sort of classic in the neighbourhood' – worth reading but 'quoted with somewhat wearisome reiteration by every local author'.[116] John Henry Garrett's account (1919) of a ramble 'over the great common' on Cleeve Hill outside Cheltenham, on a wild and wet night, 'when I lose the way in the darkness', and 'fall some feet to the bottom of … [a] pit', if not quite as dramatic as Carr's, has the similar effect of wilding the space and the journey.[117]

Jerome J. Jerome's celebrated description of a boat trip along the Thames from London to Oxford, *Three Men in a Boat* (1889), is primarily enjoyed for its humorous content, but there is a brief passage in the novel, where the whole tone changes momentarily, and the protagonist, during a period of disturbed sleep, reflects on the power of the Night:

> Sometimes, our pain is very deep and real, and we stand before her [Night] very silent, because there is no language for our pain, only a moan. Night's heart is full of pity for us: she cannot ease our aching; she takes our hand in hers, and the little world grows very small and very far beneath us, and, borne on her dark wings, we pass for a moment into a mightier Presence than her own, and in the wondrous light of that great Presence, all human life lies like a book before us, and we know that Pain and Sorrow are but the angels of God.[118]

When William Holden Hutton penned the final chapter of *By Thames and Cotswold* in 1908, 'The adventures of G. B. H and W. H. H', it is hard to think that he did not have Jerome's novel in mind. It is a story of a day jaunt on the Thames, undertaken by Hutton and a schoolboy called George from Burford, where Hutton had a home, from Tadpole Bridge (east of Lechlade) to Abingdon. The narrative is predominantly humorous, albeit with (presumably unintended) homo-erotic overtones, but like many of these journeys there is also a deeper sub-text. The pair are unexpectedly delayed in Oxford by the 'City Bumping Races'. Hampered by a leaking boat, descending darkness and a towpath that comes to an abrupt end, they are forced to huddle together on the stern of an 'untenanted' houseboat to get some overnight rest before continuing on to Abingdon the following day. The theme of a journey that descends into darkness and fear – 'Dark it was, and it grew darker. Strange white shapes lay still upon the water … bats flapped their horrid wings in our faces' – and that proves a test of human resilience, is a familiar Christian one. This is not entirely unexpected given that Hutton, like so

---

[116] Bradley, *March and Borderland*, 242–3; see also Henry Thornhill Timmins, *Nooks and Corners of Shropshire* (London: Elliot Stock, 1899), 45–7; Mais, *Welsh Marches*, 102.
[117] J. J. Garrett, *From a Cotswold Height* (Cheltenham: J. J. Banks & Son, 1919), 57–60.
[118] Jerome, *Three Men in a Boat*, 96–7.

many guidebook writers, was ordained (a fellow of St John's College Oxford, and from 1919 Dean of Winchester),[119] and though it was said tongue-in-cheek, he described the space where the two sheltered as 'the narthex [church porch], apodyterium [entry to the public baths in ancient Rome] or ante-chapel of the houseboat.'[120]

The religious interpretation of recreational travel is something we will return to later, but there may be a hint, and a challenge, in some of the cycle and motor car guides and contour books – detailing as they do gradients and road quality – of a choice between the easy and difficult roads. Certainly in some of the hiking literature of the inter-war years there is a sense of abandoning 'civilized', urban society for an ascetic journey into the rural wilderness, the outcome of which may be a greater sense of self-knowledge. In *Hiking* D. Francis Morgan could write, 'For those who have the necessary strength and skills it [hiking] is a glorious experience. It is the real life of the backwoodsman and explorer. The hiker is dependent on himself, and on himself alone, and he learns to be self-reliant, resourceful and patient.'[121] Nineteenth-century editions of *Pilgrim's Progress* were accompanied by colourful maps illustrating the route taken and the landscapes encountered, and in every walker's backpack there should of course be a map: 'The ability to understand and interpret a map is essential to any self-respecting wayfarer.'[122] All this would seem very sensible advice, and the map would appear to offer an overtly objective way – free of the more flowery phrases that tend to colour the guidebooks – of planning a journey. Yet, as we have seen, maps were stuffed with information about where to go and what to see and were profoundly didactic documents. One of the appeals of the Ordnance Survey maps was that this presented an official national vision, though this emotive appeal was often cloaked in claims about their inherent cartographic superiority. Moreover, maps provided a sort of discipline. Christian's journey in *Pilgrim's Progress* can be mapped because there are correct roads and paths to follow. Maps provided travellers, and invested the journeys that they undertook, with a sense of direction and purpose. This was something which Colonel Sir Charles Close, sometime Director General of the Ordnance Survey, felt that the urban population lacked; 'Town-dwellers, in general, have little sense of direction.'[123] He was of course referring to their spatial sense, but there was also more than a hint here of a weakness in their moral compass. Not that 'following orders' was necessarily the right approach for a free-born Briton. It was 'a good thing', Francis Morgan advised the hiker, 'to plan your route roughly beforehand, but … Don't make yourself a slave to it. One of the great joys of hiking is the wonderful sense of freedom it gives you.'[124] In a similar vein John Hissey, having decided on a motoring holiday, responded to his wife's query as to their route, 'Let us be free to wander where we will, taking the fortune of the

---

[119] H. C. G. Matthew, 'Hutton, William Holden (1860–1930), dean of Winchester and historian', *Oxford Dictionary of National Biography*, 23 Sep. 2004, https://www.oxforddnb.com/view/10.1093/ref:odnb/9780198614128.001.0001/odnb-9780198614128-e-34081, accessed 30 Jul. 2022.
[120] Hutton, *By Thames and Cotswold*, 288–303.
[121] D. Francis Morgan, *Hiking* (Plymouth: Mayflower Press, 1927), 1–2.
[122] Ashton and Stocks, *Open-Air Guide*, 63.
[123] Close, *The Map of England*, 1.
[124] Morgan, *Hiking*, 5–6.

highway and the lane, just driving from time to time in whatever direction the country looks the most inviting, or the mood of the moment inclines.'[125] It was of course all a whimsical conceit. Hissey packed a map, and the travelogue he wrote contained a map of his journey, presumably for others to follow. But the sentiments that he articulated would have proved seductive to his target audience, the businessman keen to be freed from his regulated city life. In a very real sense it was possible to conceptualize the journey in whatever form met the recreational and cultural needs of its consumers.

---

[125] Hissey, *Charm of the Road*, 4.

9

Identities

Formally constituted in 1895, the purpose and powers of the National Trust, as set out in the first Act of Parliament passed in 1907, were to promote the 'permanent preservation for the benefit of the nation of lands and tenements (including buildings) of beauty or historic interest and as regards lands for the preservation (so far as practicable) of their natural aspects features and animal and plant life'.[1] (Further acts followed in 1919, 1937, 1939, 1953 and 1971.) At this point it was primarily concerned with conserving green space; it was only after the Second World War that there were large-scale acquisitions of country houses. At its foundation, it attracted the support of some very big guns: its provisional council included the Prime Minister, the Provost of Eton, the Master of Trinity College, Cambridge, and representatives of the Royal Academy of Arts and the Royal Botanical Society plus several members of the aristocracy. It first met at the London home of its president, the Duke of Westminster.[2] But it also provided opportunities for middle-class activism and leadership: the 'social origins' of its three founders being described by David Cannadine as 'quintessentially middle class'.[3] Two were professional men, Robert Hunter, a lawyer and Solicitor to the General Post Office and Canon Hardwicke Rawnsley, a Lake District clergyman; and the third, Octavia Hill, was the daughter of a Wisbech banker. The Trust was to prove the archetypal space in which middle- and upper-class representatives could meet, negotiate their separate interests, and find common ground.

What was special about the Trust was that it was the *National* Trust. Octavia Hill is usually accredited with introducing the idea of a 'trust', as opposed to a 'company', into the naming of the new organization, when in 1885 she proposed that it be called 'The Commons and Gardens Trust'. But it was Robert Hunter, whose work as a professional civil servant and drafter of legislation brought him into close contact with the centralist state, who inserted the 'national' into the title.[4] It was a critical

---

[1] The National Trust Acts 1907–1971, https://nt.global.ssl.fastly.net/documents/download-national-trust-acts-1907-1971-post-order-2005.pdf, accessed 16 Apr. 2020.

[2] Jennifer Jenkins and Patrick James, *From Acorn to Oak Tree: The Growth of the National Trust, 1895–1984* (London: Macmillan 1994), 24–31.

[3] David Cannadine, 'The First Hundred Years', in *The National Trust: The Next Hundred Years*, ed. Howard Newby (London: The National Trust, 1995), 13.

[4] Graham Murphy, *Founders of the National Trust* (London: Christopher Helm, 1987), 104–6; John Gaze, *Figures in a Landscape: A History of the National Trust* (London: Barrie & Jenkins, 1988), 33–4; Merlin Waterson, *The National Trust: The First Hundred Years* (London: National Trust, 1994), 29–37; Jenkins and James, *From Acorn to Oak Tree*, 20–3; Ben Cowell, *Sir Robert Hunter: Co-founder and 'Inventor' of the National Trust* (Stroud: Pitkin Publishing, 2013).

decision because it allowed the Trust to tap into the swelling tide of mythology and sentiment that surrounded the idea of the nation and the practice of nationalism that flourished in late-nineteenth-century Britain and Europe. This chapter explores the way in which landscape, and its consumption, became a critical tool for asserting an English national identity. But this can only be understood by placing it in its complex and paradoxical British and imperial context. Finally, we will explore the manner in which the recreational engagement with the landscape also serviced other religious, class and gender identities.

Landscape, identities and nation

The origins of nationalism in Europe are conventionally traced back to the late-eighteenth century and the Romantic era – its emergence fuelled by the seismic political upheavals of the French Revolution and given philosophical coherence through the theory of the Germanic *Volk* as propounded by Johann Gottfried Herder. In nineteenth-century Britain there was not the political dynamic of unification generated by the need to form a new state, such as in Germany and Italy; consolidation had already been achieved in the UK in 1801 with the formal incorporation of Ireland into the British state (Scotland had already been merged in 1707 and Wales in 1535). However, nationalist sentiments in Britain were stimulated externally by competition and conflict with the nations of Europe and the country's imperialist ventures, and internally by the potential fragility of the British polity and the nationalist feelings among its non-English elements.[5] As far as the British state was concerned, nationalism was a double-edged sword. On the one hand, internally generated nationalism posed a significant threat to the stability and integrity of the state, as the case of Ireland was to prove. On the other hand, nationalist sentiment (and its adjunct imperialism) offered a powerful tool for the state and those who sought to control it, to harness support, particularly popular support, in a political system increasingly subject to democratic influences. To put it simply, nationalism – and the implied politics of identity – provided a means for elites to counter the potential loss of control consequent upon the widening of the electorate.

Political events and structures, and their perceived histories, were clearly central to the development of nationalism, but culture was also critical.[6] Nations are not just defined by geographical borders and political and legal systems. As Benedict Anderson has argued, they are also – in part because they are usually so large that their members can have little intimate knowledge of each other – symbolic or 'imagined' communities, existing as much in the mind as in an external institutional reality.[7] It was at this level that cultural factors played such an important part. Art, literature,

---

[5] Robert Colls, *Identity of England* (Oxford: Oxford University Press, 2004).
[6] David Boswell and Jessica Evans, *Representing the Nation: A Reader. Histories, Heritage and Museums* (London: Routledge, 1999), 1; Anna Green, *Cultural History* (Basingstoke: Palgrave Macmillan, 2008), 108–11.
[7] Benedict Anderson, *Imagined Communities: Reflections on the Origins and Spread of Nationalism* (London: Verso Books, 1991), 5–7.

music and architecture – despite often having an international appeal – were all increasingly deployed towards the celebration of the nation and the identification of a unique national genius.[8] This was, paradoxically, an international phenomenon; artists, composers and writers throughout Europe and beyond were striving to distil a specifically national spirit. Such, for example, was the case in music with Richard Wagner (1813–83) in Germany, Bedřich Smetana (1824–84) and Antonin Dvořák (1841–1904) in Bohemia (Czechoslovakia), and Edvard Grieg (1843–1907) in Norway.

During the eighteenth and nineteenth centuries England had welcomed and lionized foreign composers, like Handel and Mendelssohn. But such was the pressure to discover a national spirit in the last decades of the century that England – pointedly characterized by the German journalist Oskar Adolf Hermann Schmitz in 1914 as '*das Land ohne Musik*'[9] – was eagerly in search of an 'English musical renaissance'. The man most associated with an English musical revival in the period today is Edward Elgar, a rather unlikely champion of a national music, given that he was an enthusiastic and regular visitor to Germany, and a devotee of the German musical tradition (especially of Wagner), the influence of which is clearly discernible in his compositions. Moreover, in a lecture in 1926 he declared, perhaps revealing his ambivalent relationship with the English musical establishment, 'England is not a musical nation, and never will be. As soon as the country is musical it will cease to be English.'[10] But he did draw upon national mythology (as we have seen in the case of *Caractacus*, set in the Malverns) and, in his search for social acceptance and recognition, composed some openly patriotic pieces. More significantly, his music tapped into and came to embody a stream of nostalgia and ruralism that was closely associated with contemporary notions of Englishness.[11] It was the next generation of composers, such as Ralph Vaughan Williams (1872–1958) – who in the 1920s was 'becoming more and more revered as the "national" composer'[12] – that drew on music of the 'olden time' (especially the Tudor period), and the English folk song revival, to create a self-consciously national style of music. Significantly it was a style that eschewed overtly jingoistic elements, which were difficult to articulate in the post-First World War climate in favour of a more introverted and mystical content.

If music and the arts provided one of the strands in the cultural package that articulated national sentiment and identity, landscape was another critical element. Indeed, the arts and the built and natural environments cannot, as we have seen in the cases of landscape painting, be separated since they fed off each other. However, we should not assume that the relationship between landscape and national identity, fundamental as it seems today – in part because of the remarkable growth of the

---

[8] Peter Rietbergen, *Europe: A Cultural History*, 2nd edn (Abingdon: Routledge, 2006), 366–91.
[9] O. A. H. Schmitz, *Das Land ohne Musick; englische Gesellschaftsprobleme* (Munich: Georg Müller, 1914).
[10] *Musical Mirror* VI/4 (1926): 81; quoted in Jürgen Schaarwächter, 'Chasing a Myth and a Legend: "The British Musical Renaissance"', *Musical Times* 149:1904 (2008): 53–60 at 60.
[11] Hughes and Stradling, *English Musical Renaissance*; Jerrold Northrop Moore, *Spirit of England: Edward Elgar and His World* (London: Heinemann, 1984); Lewis Foreman (ed.), *Oh My Horses! Elgar and the Great War*, 2 vols. (Rickmansworth: Elgar Editions, 2001); Nicholas Kenyon, *Elgar: An Anniversary Portrait* (London: Continuum, 2007).
[12] Hughes and Stradling, *English Musical Renaissance*, 98.

National Trust – has always been a close one. As the work of historians such as Alexandra Walsham, discussed in Chapter 2, has shown, the meanings with which landscape was imbued before the eighteenth century were generally associated with local and confessional identities.[13] In the nineteenth century, however, as Paul Readman has argued, the heritage of landscape came to be understood increasingly in terms of national character.[14] It is difficult, however, to see such connections in the eighteenth century. The cultivated and rolling countryside that forms the extensive backdrop to Thomas Gainsborough's *Mr and Mrs Andrews* (*c*. 1750) might now be seen as quintessentially English (see Figure 9.1). Roy Strong includes it in his *Visions of England*, arguing that 'landscape runs through the centuries as an emblem of England', and describing the 'setting for a family portrait' as 'uniquely English'.[15]

But that reflects notions of an idealized landscape, focused especially on the countryside of southern England that emerged after 1800, and especially from the later nineteenth century. There is no evidence that contemporaries of Gainsborough, or the artist himself, saw anything emblematically English in the scene. As John Berger and others have made clear, landscape is used in the painting to depict gentlemanly landlord power rather than nationhood.[16] Significantly, the painting's rise to the status of a national icon only began in the twentieth century, being 'virtually unknown'

Figure 9.1 Thomas Gainsborough, 'Mr and Mrs Andrews' (*c*. 1750). © Getty Images.

[13] Walsham, *Reformation of the Landscape*.
[14] Readman, *Storied Ground*, 4.
[15] Roy Strong, *Visions of England: Or Why We Still Dream of a Place in the Country* (London: Vintage, 2012), 11, 101.
[16] John Berger, *Ways of Seeing* (London: Penguin, 1972), 106–8; John Barrell, *The Dark Side of the Landscape. The Rural Poor in English Painting, 1730–1840* (Cambridge: Cambridge University Press, 1980).

until lent to an exhibition at Ipswich in 1927, and only entering the National Gallery's collection in 1960.[17]

At what point English landscape painting, and given the interrelationship of the two, English landscape, came to embody a national spirit is difficult to say. It is tempting to turn to the famous figures of the genre, Joseph Turner (1775–1851) and John Constable (1776–1837). There is no doubting their significance in the development of the genre and in establishing its importance in the artistic hierarchy. But did they see the scenes they depicted as peculiarly English? The case is probably most strongly made for Constable, whose paintings such as the *Hay Wain* (1821) with their depiction of an apparently fertile and gentle countryside came to be seen as typically English. The influential art critic Nikolaus Pevsner selected Constable as a key figure when in his Reith lectures of 1955 he sought to identify the specifically English element in English art: 'for Constable his England is the countryside', his art embodying 'the eternal qualities of Englishness'. For Pevsner the key aesthetic qualities to be found in English art were the mixture of 'rationalism' and 'fantasy', which he attributes primarily to the country's 'moderate' and 'misty climate'; he is much more ambivalent about the influence of 'race' and 'nation' – unsurprisingly so in the post-Second World War political world.[18] Whether Constable would have made much sense of this analysis is doubtful; it reflects changing attitudes to art and landscape that post-dated his working life. It is true, however, that in the early 1830s Constable published *Various Subjects of Landscape, Characteristic of English Scenery* in five parts, containing twenty-two mezzotints engraved by David Lucas from the artist's paintings (see Figure 9.2).

The prospectus declared that the aim was to 'promote the study of the rural scenery of England, with all its enduring associations'.[19] Although this suggests that there are rural landscapes that are typically English, it does not imply that these landscapes embody, or are emblematic of, something resembling a national spirit. As well as depicting rural scenes, Constable, like Turner, also painted marine views. Because the coast represented a national border, and because of the close association of the sea and the navy with the defence of Britain, then, as Christiana Payne has argued, depictions of coastal and marine scenes may have been charged with a patriotic spirit. Turner's depictions of naval vessels would certainly have fallen into this category.[20] But these were only a small portion of Turner's output, and how far this was a specifically *English* spirit is difficult to say.

If the process by which landscape was invested with national identity was a long-term one, it accelerated decisively in the later nineteenth century. It was not accidental that this was at the same time as guide literature and topographical writings began to proliferate, with references to Englishness suffusing many of these publications. It is not that the term 'England', or its derivatives, appeared in every description of

---

[17] M. Postle, *Thomas Gainsborough* (London: Tate Publishing, 2002), 62–3.
[18] N. Pevsner, *The Englishness of English Art* (New York: Frederick A. Praeger, 1956), 148, 152, 185–6.
[19] Quoted in William Vaughan, 'The Englishness of British Art', *Oxford Art Journal* 13:2 (1990): 11–23, at 17; see also idem, 'Constable's Englishness', *Oxford Art Journal* 19:2 (1996): 17–27.
[20] Payne, *Where the Sea Meets the Land*, 29–32, 67–85; Christine Riding and Richard Johns, *Turner and the Sea* (London: Thames & Hudson, 2013), 102–29; Borsay, 'Le développement des villes balnéaires dans L' Angleterre géorgienne', 33–4.

Figure 9.2 David Lucas after John Constable, 'Summer Evening', from *English Landscape: Various Subjects of Landscape, Characteristic of Scenery from Pictures Painted by John Constable RA* (1829–31). The Metropolitan Museum of Art, New York, Harris Brisbane Dick Fund, 1940, www.metmuseum.org.

a piece of landscape, though they often did so, but rather that directly or indirectly they underpinned many accounts. One strategy was to attach narratives or stories considered part of a received or authorized national past to landscape features to invest them with national meaning. Warwickshire, for example, could be called 'the heart of England. ... the cradle of heroes. On its fair fields the battles of liberty and freedom have been fought'.[21] Of the view of Warwick Castle it could be said, '[W]e feel that we are looking down the corridor of time through English history' and of the ruins of Kenilworth Castle 'there can be none which call up memories richer or more intimately connected with the great names of English history'.[22] The principal actors in these narratives were often members of a national pantheon of heroes reflecting the great person approach to the construction of the past. Mythical or semi-mythical figures like Caractacus and Arthur were attached to particular locations, and medieval and early modern kings, queens and nobility were frequently drawn into the lists, but some heroes could be of much more modern origin. In Bath from the 1890s plaques were affixed to its classical buildings memorializing the residences of famous Georgian visitors and residents, turning the spa into a sort of national mausoleum.[23]

[21] Burgess, *Historic Warwickshire*, 35.
[22] Mee, *Warwickshire*, 270; Hutton, *Shakespeare's Country*, 379.
[23] Borsay, *Image of Georgian Bath*, 229–31.

Another strategy was to see a piece of landscape, in its own right, as inherently English. What were the qualities that made it English? For many observers, it had to be rural. It was a mantra often repeated by authors: 'every sound-minded Englishman is at heart a countryman'; 'all Englishmen are at heart country lovers, as they are by heredity country livers'; 'nearly all Englishmen love the country; it is the one thing that most of us inherit in common'; 'the Englishman is at heart a countryman; towns do not come naturally to him'.[24] For such writers what England was not, was urban: '[R]ural England is the real England, unspoilt by factories and financiers and tourists and hustle,' claimed A. G. Macdonell – a view that his contemporary George Birmingham confirmed: 'I understood that my companions ... when they craved to live in an English village ... wanted to get back to England itself, to that intimate soul of England which eludes us in the great cities.'[25]

Paul Readman, however, has recently challenged the view that late Victorian and Edwardian opinion saw the rural landscape of the past as more essentially English than the urban present. 'This was a culture that accommodated both in its nationalist topography; it celebrated both – in their right place.'[26] He cites in particular the case of Manchester, on the face of it the archetypal shock city of the Industrial Revolution, demonstrating the extent to which contemporaries cherished its history and celebrated its considerable current achievements. A similar case could probably be made for many Victorian manufacturing towns and ports. Whatever maladies the social investigators discovered about urban life in the period, it is difficult to ignore the economic dynamism, technological achievements, and impressive additions to the built environment in the forms of high-class residential accommodation, warehouses, railway stations, bridges, churches, town halls, galleries, libraries, concert halls and schools. Even in a city such as Bath, Victorians valued their own additions to the built environment at least as much, and probably more, than those of their Georgian predecessors. And they would have had no doubt as to their superiority in respect of morality and public spirit.[27]

Not all the guide literature dismissed the urban contribution to national identity. Hilaire Belloc in 1907 called London 'the fullest example of what is peculiarly English in the development of town life'. But such overt associations of Englishness and town life are rare; more common were the descriptions of 'old' and country towns that subsumed the urban into the idea of historic and rural England. Thus Warwick High Street was described by W. H. Hutton in 1914 as 'a picture of English town homeliness' and H. V. Morton considered Yorkshire market towns 'as characteristic as anything in England', and could write of how on the 'ancient streets' of 'your simple country town', 'the rich stream of English country life flows on unaltered'.[28] Such comments evidently

---

[24] Cornish, *Wild England*, 300; Mais, *Round about England*, 109; James Turle, *Out of Doors in England* (London: Constable & Co. Ltd., 1937), 1; W. S. Shears, *This England. A Book of the Shires and Counties*, 2nd edn (London: Right Book Club, 1938), 8.
[25] Macdonell, *England, Their England*, 84; G. A. Birmingham, 'The Country Church', in *Legacy of England*, 163.
[26] Readman, *Storied Ground*, 242.
[27] Borsay, *Image of Georgian Bath*, 66–77, 147–57.
[28] Belloc, *Historic Thames*, 109; Hutton, *Shakespeare Country*, 102; Morton, *Call of England*, 63; Morton, *In Search of England*, 179.

reflected the social class and, perhaps, political inclinations of those who compiled topographical literature. But the essential issue would seem to have been not whether Victorians were proud of their modern cities, or indeed saw them as part of some broad national success story, but the extent to which they associated those cities with the idea of Englishness. It may be wholly misleading to define Englishness in terms of a rural landscape that was rapidly shrinking in significance demographically and economically, but national myths are not necessarily based on reality. There may also be a chronological element to this. As confidence in what the Victorians had achieved began to wane, especially after the First World War, then the desire to locate the English spirit in an idealized pre-industrial world strengthened.

Within the natural landscape certain features were inscribed with national characteristics. Of the River Thames it could be said as early as the 1850s that 'its history is that of England'; almost a century later the refrain had if anything deepened, the river described as 'above everything else, English' and 'perhaps the most English thing in all England. It reflects upon its waters the complexities of the English character'.[29] Trees were an obvious target. James Turle declared 'ash is English through and through', while Richard Jefferies pronounced 'the hawthorn ... part of natural English life – country life. It stands side by side with the English-man, as the palm tree is pictured side by side with the Arab'. This came in an essay on 'Trees about Town', in which Jefferies bemoaned the presence of 'foreign shrubs and trees' and 'the whole host of invading evergreens', complaining of the plane tree 'there are no fragments of English history clinging to it as there are to the oak'. It is difficult to miss here the perceived threat to the national genetic stock of woodland posed by alien species and of the town's role in accommodating these unwelcome immigrants.[30] In Thomas Hardy's *Tess of the D'Urbervilles* the modern 'crimson brick lodge' of the novel's arriviste villain was 'up to its eaves in dense evergreens', a contrast with the surrounding countryside of The Chase (Cranborne Chase in Dorset), 'a truly venerable tract of forest land, one of the few remaining woodlands in England of undoubted primaeval date, wherein Druidical mistletoe was still found on aged oaks'.[31]

Charles Ford argued that the English 'rather than replace their buildings ... have often preferred to watch them evolve almost organically ... and in the process, through the use of native materials ... the buildings have grown into and become almost part of the soil, a legacy from the England past to the England of the present'.[32] This idea that there were 'native' building materials, and that houses constructed in these materials grew 'organically' out of the land, became increasingly fashionable. In a manner that echoes the concerns about alien trees, H. J. Massingham wrote in *Cotswold Country* (first published in 1937) of an 'invader, a barbarian' that 'sprawls all over the geological formations of England. All rocks come alike to contemporary blue slate, red brick and the cement that parodies in imitating stone'.[33] It was the appeal of Cotswold stone that

[29] Hall, *Book of the Thames*, 1; Smith, *Thames*, 1; Green, *The Cotswolds*, 1.
[30] Turle, *Out of Doors in England*, 143; Jefferies, *Pageant of Summer*, 73, 75–6.
[31] Hardy, *Tess of the D'Urbervilles*, 43–4.
[32] M. Fraser, *Companion into Worcestershire* (London: Methuen, 1939), 221; C. Bradley Ford, 'Foreword', *Legacy of England*, vii–viii.
[33] Massingham, *Cotswold Country*, 3.

led many to believe that houses from the region embodied Englishness; that they were, as John Hissey claimed, 'essentially English, as English as roast beef and plum-pudding. They are all built of local material, so they smack of the soil, and look as though they had grown where they stand'.[34] But it was also a question of style and period. For the Victorians and Edwardians it was the 'olden age' buildings that were felt most to represent the national style. 'The Tudor squire', wrote P. H. Ditchfield in 1910, 'clung with whole-hearted affection to the old English style of building, which he considered best suited to the national character and climate'. With the Jacobean house 'the Tudor style became more and more Italianized', and after Inigo Jones 'the golden age of English house-building had passed, and it was left to the humbler building, the smaller manor-houses, the yeoman's house, and country cottages to maintain in some measure the traditions of English Gothic and Tudor art'.[35] In *The Rise of Architectural History*, David Watkin claimed that 'by 1900 a new religion had been invented – or, at least, a new version of an old religion: the worship of England'.[36] J. Alfred Gotch reflected this approach in his account *The English Home from Charles I to George IV* (1918), arguing that the opening up of the country to international influences, especially from the beginning of the eighteenth century, 'led inevitably to the disappearance of a truly national style'. However, in a nod to the Arts and Crafts movement, he maintained that 'the last twenty years have seen something different. Based upon actual needs, and striving after beautiful expression, domestic architecture is slowly progressing on lines characteristically English'.[37]

It was not uncommon for writers to identify landscapes and locations that they considered to resonate especially with Englishness. Some took the view that there was a 'typically English scene';[38] others were less confident and held a more pluralist perspective. Edmund Blunden (1896–1974) observed

> that the inhabitants of this kingdom are not at all consonant in their ideas of the typical English scene. There are those whose feelings create it in semblance, let us say, of Epping Forest; others who make of it perennial Dovedale; others to whom it has been disclosed, a final truth, by John Crome on Mousehold Heath; their rivals whose selection was a little south of that and authorised by Constable. Many a Londoner still escapes from the office to his essential England among the Chilterns. … At once I seem to hear the protests of my friends now staring in deep moods over the Wuthering Heights expanses.[39]

It is not surprising that Blunden, himself a distinguished poet, should recognize the important role that art and literature played in 'authorizing' a piece of landscape as national. And it is certainly the case that different writers had their chosen locations,

---

[34] Hissey, *Charm of the Road*, 172–3.
[35] P. H. Ditchfield, *The Manor Houses of England* (London: Batsford, 1910), 30, 34–5.
[36] Watkin, *Architectural History*, 95.
[37] J. A. Gotch, *The English Home from Charles I to George IV* (London: Batsford, 1918), 391, 394.
[38] Baker, *Land of the Gap*, 140.
[39] Edmund Blunden, 'The Landscape', in *Legacy of England*, 2–3.

though never doubting that there was something called Englishness that could be distilled into a piece of landscape. One visitor to Malvern, viewing the Severn Plain from the town, enthused that 'the landscape seemed so altogether, so surpassingly English', while another, having surmounted Malvern (Worcestershire) Beacon, declared, 'There is England. This is the scene I have dreamed about when I was fighting in North Africa and Italy.'[40] Shropshire could be described as 'neither North, South, East or West England – but just England'; Devon as 'the perfection of England'; the Weald of Kent as 'incredibly English'; 'the lanes of Northamptonshire ... [as] an unforgettable picture of unspoilt England'; the Lake District as 'a national monument'; and Yorkshire as 'an epitome of England'.[41]

If it is true that views varied as to which landscape represented the essential England, nonetheless certain areas were cited a good deal more than others. Generally speaking, southern England was much more likely to be referenced than the North. We saw in Chapter 7 how parts of the north – and by implication the north as a whole – were stigmatized in many guide accounts because of its perceived industrial degradation. When S. P. B. Mais in the inter-war years was encouraging his fellow countrymen to *See England First*, he observed that 'foreign lands ... must be extraordinarily attractive if they can beat what I have seen in the South of England', proceeding to give an account of Cornwall, Devon, Dorset, Hampshire, Oxfordshire, Sussex and Wiltshire, a seven-page chapter on Derbyshire constituting his only excursion into what might conceivably be called the north.[42] At one point in his 1932 guide to Gloucestershire, Edward Hutton was unable to contain his exasperation, launching an extraordinary tirade,

> Why have the sodden Midlands, with all the filthy and immoral industrialism of their Birmingham, their Cowley, their Stourbridge, thrust down into us – our Eden, our demi-Paradise? Is it envy and egoism only, or mere vulgar, bulging, awkward, parvenuism and new riches: just the old barbarian, the old Adam, the old jackass, wickedness – in one word, the Foreigner?[43]

The implication was that there was an invisible border running through the middle of England and that those north of it were uncivilized foreigners, posing a threat to the English Eden to the south. The area that perhaps attracted most attention as representing the essential England lay on this border. Warwickshire was consistently cited as the core of England: 'the centre and heart of English soil', 'no county of England is richer in truly English scenery', 'considered most typically English of the English shires', 'the core and centre of the English world; midmost England, unmitigated England'.[44] It was not of course just geography, or even the Arcadian landscape,

---

[40] Howells, *London Films, 1905* ..., 472; Frederick Cowles, *Vagabond Pilgrimage. Being the Record of a Journey from East Anglia to the West of England* (London: Travel Book Club, 1950), 291.
[41] Darling, *Seeing Shropshire*, 7; James, *English Hours*, 53; Morton, *I Saw Two Englands*, 92, 173; Thomas, *English Landscape*, 175; Morton, *Call of England*, 78.
[42] Mais, *See England First*, 36.
[43] Hutton, *Highways ... Gloucestershire*, 124.
[44] Bevan, *Warwickshire*, 1; Clive Holland, *Things Seen in Shakespeare's Country* (London: Seeley Service & Co. Ltd., 1927), 12; Mee, *Warwickshire*, 1; James, *English Hours*, 113.

that underpinned these claims, but the presence of Stratford-on-Avon, 'the heart of Warwickshire, even of England', 'the small town which may be described as the heart of England', 'a national shrine ... this fat heart of England is the very setting one would ask for the personality of Shakespeare'.[45] It was the spirit of the national bard, along with the associations as the crucible of English history – reflected in Shakespeare's history plays – of the county, which set the seal on Warwickshire's status as the heart of England. Birmingham and Coventry were originally part of the county, occupying its northern parts; however in 1889 they became separate county boroughs. This helped deliver Warwickshire from the stain of industrialization and urbanization; at the same time the very presence of two major industrial cities, and of the notional border between north and south (reflected in the division in the county itself), only added to the sense of Warwickshire's Englishness.

It is because of their proximity to 'the foreigner' that border landscapes are often heightened points of national consciousness.[46] An obvious site was the south coast of England, and particularly Kent and Sussex, which had historically acted as the bridgehead for invasion fleets, and was only a short distance across the Channel from France. A. G. Bradley's *An Old Gate of England*, published at the end of the First World War, played explicitly to the border theme. The core settlements described were the Cinque Ports – Hastings, Winchelsea, Rye, New Romney, Hythe, Dover and Sandwich – which, as Bradley reminded the reader in his opening paragraph 'in the Middle Ages were responsible for the sea defence of England and were the nucleus out of which has grown the British Navy'. The guidebook reached its apotheosis with the account of the view across the English Channel from Lympne Hill (above Hythe in Kent):

> [H]ere ... looking over Romney Marsh is the old, old England. ... furthermore we have the sea, from Dover to Fairlight, shining beyond, and yet more, that particular little bit of sea, with the coast of France lying low upon its further bounds, which of all the seas that wash the shores of England has been the most pregnant with weal or woe for its people; the unceasing danger point from age to age over which the sword of fate has hung continuously from the victorious Roman, Saxon and Norman, to the baffled Napoleon.[47]

The British paradox

When it came to establishing identity, arguably the most important border for England was not that with continental Europe, but those with the other nations within Britain – Scotland, Wales and Ireland. In terms of internal British borders, the attitude of English topographical writers was paradoxical. In some circumstances they chose to

---

[45] Hutton, *Highways ... Shakespeare Country*, 159; Walter Jerrold, *Shakespeare-land* (London: Blackie, 1910), 5; Bradley, *Avon and Shakespeare's Country*, 234.
[46] Readman, *Storied Ground*, 25–89.
[47] Bradley, *Old Gate of England*, 1, 333.

ignore the borders; in other circumstances, they were highlighted. The first case is exemplified by the innumerable examples of where the terms 'England' and 'Britain', 'English' and 'British', were used interchangeably – often in close proximity. In a 1943 broadcast John Betjeman complained that 'when people talk to me about "the British", as though they were all the same, I give up'. However, far from unravelling the differing characteristics of the Scots, Welsh and Irish, it transpires that what he was referring to is variations among the English. 'If I could explain England', he continued, 'if it really were a planned ants' nest which we could all generalize about, I, like thousands of others, would have no home to which to return'.[48] Three years later the opening page of Ruth Cobb's *Country Town Story* pondered what would be the future of 'the ENGLISH COUNTRY TOWN in the 18th century' in the post-war era: 'that small town which represents so many things essentially British? … The English country town is a thing by itself'.[49]

Some heritage literature simply incorporated the non-English parts of Britain under the English umbrella. *Historic Sites and Scenes of England*, a GWR guide of the 1920s, was open about the inclusion, 'in the name "England" we include for the purpose of this book the Principality of Wales'. *The British Heritage* of 1948 recognized it was a British volume but reminded readers that in a brief survey there was scope for nothing more than a 'passing glance at the visible memorials of Welsh, Scottish, or Irish elements in the general story of Britain'. The 'central pivot of progress', it continued, lay in the lowlands 'in which the English settled'. Other publications, such as Edmund Vale's *How to See England*, simply included 'the Celtic fringe' without any acknowledgement of the appropriation of Wales, while an essay on the country town in *The Legacy of England* asserted that 'we are considering something supremely English in the widest sense of the word, which is larger than the seemingly more comprehensive term British'.[50]

If there was a tendency at times to elide Britain and England, while simultaneously making it clear where the real heart of the nation lay, on other occasions it was convenient to recognize the difference between the core and periphery polities. Since the eighteenth century, the English had visited Wales and Scotland as tourists and sometimes established residences there. The mountainous scenery and apparent primitiveness of both areas appealed to the romantic imaginations of the urbane English. But the attraction of the Celtic peripheries, genuine as it was, was heightened by the opportunity it also provided to assert English cultural superiority. It was very much a case of having one's cake and eating it. On the one hand it was possible to luxuriate in the experience of the wild and sublime; on the other hand visiting such locations demonstrated how much more fertile and civilized England was, and how much she had progressed from the primitive state of social development in which her northern and western borders were still marooned. R. H. Mottram observed that 'there is nothing in the [typical English] country town of Celtic Twilight or Celtic fairyland,

---

[48] Betjeman, *Coming Home*, 141.
[49] Ruth Cobb, *Country Town Story* (London: John Crowther, 1946), 1.
[50] *Historic Sites and Scenes of England*, 3; Vale, *How to See England*, 39–44; *The British Heritage: The People, Their Crafts and Achievements as Recorded in Their Buildings and on the Face of the Countryside* (London: Odhams Press, 1948), 78; *Legacy of England*, 130.

nor of that savage nobility that redeems and makes uncomfortable the small towns of Ireland and the Highlands'.[51] The mysterious and capricious Celtic character, appealing as it may be, only underlined the stability and civility of its English neighbour, who used its Celtic satellites to define its national identity. Many of the accounts of Wales dwelt upon its turbulent past, its castles, the warlike character of its people, and their continuing attachment to magical beliefs and superstition.[52] The contrast with a peaceful and ordered England was summed up in the way their different landscapes were described, especially at the border between the two countries. A. G. Bradley described how looking west towards Wales from the top of Bredon Hill in Worcestershire

> the whole of this trans-Severn country shows a broken heaped up surface. What with the Malverns near by, the Clee and Stretton ranges beyond, the long line of the Brecon mountains and the Radnor moors and Glamorgan highlands, the whole west may be described, in the language of metaphor, as in a state of unrest and agitation, while nearer and more southerly are the upstanding billowy ridges that carry the forest of Dean and follow the Wye to its confluence, with the broad tidal waters of the greater river as it opens out towards the Severn sea.[53]

'The language of metaphor' explained the process by which landscape was invested with national political meaning; Wales was 'a broken heaped up surface … in a state of unrest and agitation', whereas to the south lay the 'billowy upstanding ridges' of England. As in the first decade of the twentieth century, John Hissey left Whittington in Shropshire:

> near the Welsh boundary the landscape became less orderly, though not the less beautiful on that account … The whole character of the landscape gradually changed as we drove on, the mellow, homelike look was giving place to one less paternal. The gentle English country of green meadows, carefully tilled fields, and enclosing hedgerows we were leaving behind for a wilder land.[54]

Hissey was generally appreciative of Welsh landscape but only so long as it remained within Wales. At Tetbury in the Cotswolds, he found himself

> gazing at the roofs simply because of the loveliness of their colourings. A century or less ago, before the ease of railway transport, no English builder dreamt of using anything for his roofs but stone 'slats', or pleasing tiles, or homely thatch; now the hideously hued Welsh slate is almost universally employed to the wholesale disfigurement of the landscape: … nothing could be cheaper, nothing could be uglier, nothing could be more out of harmony with the mellow look of the fair

---

[51] R. H. Mottram, 'The Country Town', in *Legacy of England*, 131.
[52] See, e.g., Bradley, *March and Borderland*, 110–13, 247–52.
[53] Bradley, *Avon and Shakespeare's Country*, 70–1.
[54] Hissey, *Charm of the Road*, 109.

English landscape than the chilly blue of Welsh slate … the revenge that Wales has taken upon her English counterpart is complete!'[55]

In reality pockets of 'English' landscape were to be found in Wales and Scotland, though there it was not an intrusion but a beneficent influence, that only served to highlight the contrast between the two environments; 'only a little of Wales and about a third of Scotland is reminiscent of the traditional English landscape', observed the author of *British Heritage*, 'perhaps it is this transition from the bountiful and fertile lowlands to the inhospitable and unproductive highlands that most amazes the visitor from overseas'.[56] The Scottish border, and in particular Hadrian's Wall, prompted similar observations to those that attended the boundary with Welsh. In 1932 Vaughan Cornish found Whin Sill crags, along which the Wall ran in one of its more dramatic locations

> stood in a posture of defence, thrusting their forbidding form northwards against the land of the Pictish tribes. … As I stood in solitude, the scene that was before me appeared but the infinitesimal part of the ancient frontier of civilization whose course of seven thousand miles was unbroken … The distant view to the south beyond the gorge of the Tyne, with woods and fields in the English manner, stood in striking contrast with the stern, wild country in the north, so Caledonian in character.[57]

Six years later William Beach Thomas similarly saw a juxtaposition of distinctively 'Scotch and English' landscapes at Whin Sill crags: 'The wild rocks and the dark waters are themselves more Scotch than English, but from this point and that you see, if you look south, a progressively humanized landscape. If you look north, the rough moorland looks unending.'[58] There was no doubting which side of the border civilization and humanity lay.

Race and empire

One late afternoon in the 1890s in 'our much-abused English autumn', J. Arthur Gibbs was rambling in the 'undulating downland' of the Cotswolds, an area he did much to 'invent'. The sunset and landscape before him, he wrote, 'take your thoughts away into the great unknown – the infinite, – that mysterious world which is ever around us … although no human habitation is anywhere to be seen, the air is full of the spirits of bygone generations and bygone *races* of men'.[59] In the late nineteenth and early-twentieth-century theories of race, boosted by social Darwinism and colonial ventures,

---

[55] Hissey, *English Holiday*, 241.
[56] *The British Heritage*, 117.
[57] Cornish, *Scenery of England*, 92–3.
[58] Thomas, *English Landscape*, 144.
[59] Gibbs, *Cotswold Village*, 114 [original italics].

abounded and were embedded – usually uncritically – in everyday cultural discourse. The notion of race also became closely intertwined with that of national identity, even though there was no necessary fit between them. It became not uncommon to refer to an 'English race'. In the 1940s, for example, Harry Batsford observed that 'the village architecture is one of the quite considerable achievements of the English race'.[60] In this case the built environment is seen as a product of racial characteristics, although how is not explained, something probably deemed unnecessary; in other cases the natural landscape is seen to shape racial features. These are by no means always of a national type. Distinctive environments were believed to influence the development of certain physical and mental characteristics, in part because those environments isolated their inhabitants. Dwellers on the Isle of Portland were said to 'retain much of their primitive simplicity', on Romney Marsh it was claimed that 'there are primitive people still about', while 'the natives of the Forest of Dean ... were a race unto themselves'.[61] Landscape features, such as the Forest, were barriers between the two races; thus A. G. Bradley called the River Severn 'a great racial boundary', and the Malvern Hills, though some distance from the border, 'that stupendous racial barrier'.[62] Users of *Black's Guide to South Wales* (1896) were warned that '[t]he Englishman in South Wales must remember that he is, if not in a foreign land, at least among an alien race'. Half a century later readers of *British Heritage* were still being reminded that the people of Wales, western Scotland and the south-west of England 'are even now racially different, and the difference is one that can be easily discerned in the characteristic appearance of the mountain folk and the lowland people'.[63]

Behind such ideas lay the more sophisticated thinking of geographers like H. J. Fleure (1877–1969) who even in the 1950s was linking together notions of physiognomy, environment, culture and race.[64] The mountain/lowland split by no means conformed to national boundaries in Britain. Nonetheless, England was more clearly associated with the 'lowland people' than the 'mountain folk'. W. H. Hudson recognized that the English were a mixture of races, especially at its borders (he acknowledged, for example, 'the peculiarly Welsh character of the Somerset peasant'), but he found in the 'downland shepherd' of Sussex a particularly pure English archetype due to what he saw as their Saxon origins: 'his best and sterling qualities are undoubtedly of the race. Probably the villagers of the downs and the weald of Sussex have more Saxon blood in their veins than the people of any other part of England'.[65] Contemporaries were well aware that a 'race' of British inhabitants preceded the Saxons, but a Saxon heritage drew a line between the Irish, Welsh and Scots on the one hand, and the English on the other.

---

[60] Batsford, *How to See the Country*, 20.
[61] *Black's Guide to Dorsetshire*, 27; Bradley, *Old Gate of England*, 313; Bradley, *Wye*, 152; see also Fleure, *Natural History of Man*, 196.
[62] Bradley, *Avon and Shakespeare's Country*, 68, 111.
[63] *Black's Guide to South Wales*, 9th edn (London: A. & C. Black, 1896), 6; *The British Heritage*, 7.
[64] Fleure, *Natural History of Man*, 182–201.
[65] W. H. Hudson, *Nature in Downland* (New York: Longmans, Green, 1901), 105; idem, *Afoot in England* (London: Hutchinson & Co., 1909), 81.

The Saxons were believed to have displaced the ancient inhabitants of Britain, the Celts – an assumption that led Dixon Scott, writing about Stratford-upon-Avon, to marry the heart of England thesis with racial theory, all bolstered by the town's surrounding landscape, to claim it was a repository of ancient genetic purity:

> [I]t is because it is buried so deeply in England that it has become so un-English. Glance at the map for a moment, and consider the effect of this midmost position in the past. Across the moat, and all around, the rest of England stretches like a great redoubt – a vast series of encircling outworks. Thus protected, it was left singularly undisturbed. Pressing always from the coasts, up the river-beds, the successive tides of invasion were diluted and absorbed long before they reached this kernel. Fenced by deep forests and begirt by buffer kingdoms, this patch of ground, indeed, might well become a kind of central coffer: a place where the old blood might be preserved with special purity, the heart of England in a yet deeper and more dramatic sense. *Avon*, as we know, is pure Celtic for 'river'; *Arden*, pure Celtic for 'forest'. Almost as completely as in such carved remote corners of the kingdom as Cumberland and Cornwall, has a racial purity been preserved.

Dixon Scott did not go so far as to call Shakespeare a Celt, but he did claim that 'it might not be difficult, were it needful, to prove that Hamlet was a Celt'.[66]

In 1939 John Wyndham was reviewing, for his 'travel-book', the archaeological finds in his home county of Sussex. At Trundle and Whitehawk camps, he reported:

> [T]hey have discovered something of the squalor in which Britons lived more than four thousand years ago. It must have been a very similar life to that of the most primitive African tribes before the white man made them his burden: a semi-nomadic existence, sheltering in ditches and pits. ... That was the beginning of our civilisation. Of pre-civilised Sussex much less is known, but one of the human species – a gibbering creature – chose to live on the sandy soil of my local golf course at Piltdown, not far from the fifth tee.[67]

We now know that Piltdown man ('discovered' by Charles Dawson in c. 1908), the 'missing link' between ape and man, was an audacious fraud, though one that took almost fifty years to finally expose. It was a product of a combination of personal vanity and national ambition, to find the origins of modern humans on English soil. But Wyndham's account, with its casual comparison to African tribes, and references to the 'white man's ... burden' and 'civilization', reveals an embedded racist imperialism which suffuses the wider genre.

Empire was one of the leitmotifs running through politics and culture in nineteenth- and early-twentieth-century England, with the latter years of Victoria's reign constituting the 'climax of imperialism' and the physical extent of the British

---

[66] Scott, *Stratford on Avon*, 44–5.
[67] Wyndham, *Sussex*, 4.

Empire continuing to grow until 1921.[68] Leaving aside the complexity of to what extent the empire was English or British, it represented an identity around which the English nation (and many Scots, Welsh and Irish also) could rally. Imperial themes found their way into many aspects of culture, including panoramas, music hall, popular theatre, literature, cinema, sport and consumer products.[69] From the late-eighteenth century there was a clear, if limited, architectural impact evident in the Middle East- and Asian derived features at the Gloucestershire country house of Sezincote, the Royal Pavilion in Brighton, the Dunbar Wing at Osborne House on the Isle of Wight and the Arab Room at Cardiff Castle.[70] Much of this was for private eyes only, and a more popularly accessible 'imperial' architecture was to be seen at the seaside: as Fred Gray has written, 'by 1900 Oriental architectural styles, although not universal, became a classic decoration of pleasure piers'.[71] Imported flowers and shrubs, and in particular the construction of arboreta, could also deliver subliminal messages of empire.

Structures within the built environment that had a greater potential to convey an explicit imperial message came in the form of memorialization. The complex iconography on the Albert Memorial, erected after the death of Queen Victoria's consort in 1861, but not completed until 1876, contains representations of the four continents, with Britain portrayed as the conduit for progress and civilization, and an underlying tone of moral superiority.[72] Many statues were erected in English cities and towns – not just London – memorializing the achievements of great men, who, one way or another, contributed to the foundation, expansion and defence of the British Empire.[73] From 1861 Lord Clive, MP for Shrewsbury 1761–74, but better known as 'Clive of India', stood in The Square in central Shrewsbury. Public statues of Clive were also erected in London (Whitehall, 1912), and of Major General Sir Henry Havelock in Sunderland (Mowbray Park, 1861).[74] How much all of this registered on the tourist circuit is difficult to say: the Clive statue in Shrewsbury is mentioned in Baedeker's guide to Great Britain of 1890, but the Sunderland Havelock statue goes unremarked, and there is no commentary to explain the significance of the individuals.[75]

Sunderland scarcely registers as a location in Baedeker, despite a population of 130,000. The same was not the case for Bath with a population of only 50,000. The

---

[68] C. C. Eldridge, *Victorian Imperialism* (London: Hodder & Stoughton, 1978), 215, 240.
[69] Dave Russell, *Popular Music in England, 1840–1914* (Manchester: Manchester University Press, 1987), 117–19; J. M. Mackenzie, 'Empire and Metropolitan Cultures', in *The Oxford History of the British Empire, vol. III: The Nineteenth Century*, ed. Andrew Porter (Oxford: Oxford University Press, 1999), 277–80; Joseph McAleer, *Popular Reading and Publishing in Britain, 1914–1950* (Oxford: Oxford University Press, 1992), 253.
[70] John Sweetman, *The Oriental Obsession. Islamic Inspiration in British and American Art and Architecture, 1500–1920* (Cambridge: Cambridge University Press, 1987).
[71] Gray, *Designing the Seaside,* 207.
[72] Colin Cunningham, 'Iconography and Victorian Values', in *The Albert Memorial: The Prince Consort National Memorial: Its History, Contexts and Conservation*, ed. Christopher Brooks (New Haven and London: Yale University Press, 2000), 244–9.
[73] Joan Coutu, *Persuasion and Propaganda: Monuments and the Eighteenth-Century British Empire* (Montreal: McGill-Queen's University Press, 2006).
[74] N. Pevsner, *The Buildings of England. Shropshire* (London: Penguin, 1958), 283; idem, *The Buildings of England. County Durham*, rev. Elizabeth Williamson (London: Penguin, 1983), 459.
[75] Baedeker, *Great Britain*, 2nd edn (1890), 5, 263.

substantial entry makes no specific mention of memorialization, although we are informed that 'among the innumerable visitors of eminence in the 18th and early 19th cent. may be mentioned Chatham, Pitt, Canning, and Burke, Nelson, Wolfe, and Sir Sidney Smith', together with a clutch of artists and authors.[76] In the late nineteenth and early-twentieth century – under economic pressure to extend its appeal beyond that of a watering place – Bath was rapidly turning itself into a site of imperial pilgrimage. An early sign of this was the excavation of the Roman bathing complex from the 1870s and its development as a location for archaeological tourism. Particularly important was the discovery in 1880–1, and subsequent reconstruction, of the Roman Great Bath, so that it became one of the icons of the city. In fact the Great Bath had been discovered in 1755 during work on the Duke of Kingston's baths but was covered over as the building of the new establishment proceeded. The rediscovery of the Great Bath in the late nineteenth century suggests a desire to associate imperial Rome with an ascendant imperial Britain, to link the two 'civilizing' forces, and to develop Bath as one of the premier sites in Britain where *Pax Romana* could be used to justify and celebrate *Pax Britannica*.[77]

Exploiting its Roman connections was one way, albeit rather indirectly, in which Bath could burnish its imperial credentials. Of more direct relevance was the Georgian legacy. During this period a high proportion of the nation's elite visited and lived in the spa. It was a period when the foundations of Britain's empire were being laid, and many of those passing through Bath were directly or indirectly associated with that project. The potential for exploiting this roll call of imperial heroes was noted by Baedeker, but it was turned into bricks (more accurately Bath stone) and mortar by the late Victorian and Edwardian movement to associate buildings with famous visitors and residents. A key figure in the project was a local luminary and councillor, Thomas Sturge Cotterell. He was responsible for compiling and regularly updating a *Historic Map*, intended for the tourist market, linking the famous to particular buildings; by the 1898, it had already amassed over a hundred names, which by the eve of the Second World War had risen to almost 300 in number. Cotterell was also the driving force behind the project initiated at the turn of the century to erect memorial tablets on the city's houses to their celebrated residents: by 1913 thirty-four plaques had been placed commemorating thirty-seven individuals, and by 1939 the list of those honoured had probably grown to sixty-four. A substantial number of these were political and military figures of the Georgian era associated with the making of empire. Several were accompanied by large-scale unveiling ceremonies, aimed at generating publicity for the spa. In 1899 tablets were erected on the houses occupied by two leading eighteenth-century statesmen and prime ministers who visited Bath, the elder Pitt (1708–78, Earl of Chatham, MP for Bath 1757–66) and the younger Pitt (1759–1806). The unveiling ceremonies were undertaken by the leading Liberal Imperialist, Lord Rosebery, who six years earlier had declared it 'part of our heritage to take care that the world as far as it can be moulded by us, shall receive an English-speaking complexion'. A lavish luncheon was laid on

---

[76] Ibid., 110.
[77] Borsay, *Image of Georgian Bath*, 56, 75–6.

at the Guildhall for Rosebery and 200 or more guests, during which he summarized the achievements of the Elder Pitt's administration: 'He sees [presumably seized] one empire in Canada, he took half an empire in India, our ships still supreme on every sea, our armies were victorious on land. There was never a moment at which the power of Great Britain reached so completely its acme.'[78]

The iconography of empire was to be found in the public spaces of many cities and towns. It was also to be discovered in the churches of town and country, where memorials to members of the ruling order extoled their service to the imperial cause. Gordon Home, the editor of Dent's *Cathedrals, Abbeys and Famous Churches* series, declared in his preface to the *Gloucester, Tewkesbury and District* (1925) volume that 'the aim which I have set before me in these books is the presentation, as far as possible, of the *personal aspects of the great buildings*'. He cites as an example the 'stirring account of General Thackwell's brilliant achievement at Sobraon [1846, the decisive battle of the first Anglo-Sikh War], where he ordered his cavalry to attack a heavily-entrenched position, and actually succeeded in taking it'. Later in the volume, in front of a memorial window in Gloucester Cathedral to the hero, we are treated to a three-page account of 'the complete and very murderous British victory', in which 10,000 Sikhs and 2,500 British were killed, and reminded that 'the fate of our Indian Empire depended upon the decision made under fire by this modest general of cavalry'.[79]

The built environment, particularly memorials, provided an easy medium to convey imperialist sentiment. Less explicit in the guide literature, but evocatively potent, was the potential of the natural landscape to convey the same messages. The Homeland Association, founded in 1896, produced a series of photographic guides aimed at 'presenting in pictorial form the natural beauty and architecture of the cities and countryside of the Homeland. ... Delightful presents to send to friends across the seas, and holiday souvenirs'.[80] By 1929 fourteen volumes had appeared, with titles such as *Dear Old Devon*, *The Beauty of West Sussex*, and *Leafy Warwick*. The reference to 'friends across the seas' suggests citizens of the Empire yearning for memories of the motherland. During his motor tour of the early-twentieth century, John Hissey may have had a similar audience in mind, as he concluded, having described the landscape around Nunney in Somerset: 'It is the remembrance of a land like this that makes the Englishman feel, when far from his island home, that for tranquil beauty there is no country to compare with his own, no scenery so peace-bestowing.'[81]

The Empire, though barely mentioned, is in all likelihood a potent backdrop – the ghost in the machine – to much that is written about the English countryside in this period. Touring holidays could be framed, albeit with humorous overtones, in the form of an exploration into the wild. A diary of a camping tour along the River Wye by

---

[78] Borsay, *Image of Georgian Bath*, 102–3, 136–8, 229–31, 320–2.
[79] Edward Foord, *Gloucester, Tewkesbury and District* (London: J. M. Dent & Sons, 1925), 5–6 [original italics], 65–8.
[80] J. Dixon-Scott, *Hereford and the Wye Valley* (London: the Homeland Association, 1929), advert at rear.
[81] Hissey, *Charm of the Road*, 355.

four students in 1892 adopts some of the narrative of an expedition along an uncharted South American or African river:

> Morning was spent … buying stores … Two porters conveyed our luggage across the city [Hereford] … All the able bodied men in the village came round to assist in conveying us to the river … Early morn proved that G. sleeps with one eye open for seizing his air gun he rushed out and fired several times into a crowd of bovine visitors … Once more we board the lugger, and soon a mighty fall is heard. We drift down cautiously and find a singular bed of sand-stone rocks covering three fourths of the river, which confined on the left rushes through a narrow channel roaring over great boulders on either side.[82]

Jerome K. Jerome's holiday on the River Thames is a comic conceit, but there is still the hint of the expedition about it with some racist overtones. George purchased a particularly loud blazer for the trip. The salesman 'told him that it was an Oriental design'. He asked his companions their opinion of it. 'Harris said that, as an object to hang over a flower-bed to frighten the birds away, he should respect it; but that, considered as an article of dress for a human being, except a Margate n****r, it made him ill.' Later in the trip George was tasked with preparing breakfast; 'we did not know what scrambled eggs were, and we fancied that it must be some Red Indian or Sandwich Islands' sort of dish that required dances and incantations for its proper cooking'.[83]

Real landscapes used in fictional contexts were potentially a subtle but powerful medium for conveying the message about empire. In Arthur Ransome's hugely popular *Swallows and Amazons*, the Lake District landscape was deployed by the children as the setting for their imperial game playing.[84] The sense of identity delivered by embracing and enacting the idea of empire would no doubt have strengthened many a person's feeling of Englishness. But empire also complicated identities. In his account of his wanderings through southern England, *The South Country* (1909), Edward Thomas records the sight of a 'young labourer … his eyes blue and deep set, his lips like those of Antinous … his hair short and brown and crisp upon his fair round head … a noble animal', entering 'a cottage that stands worn and old and without a right angle in its timbers or its thatch any more than in its apple trees and solitary quince which all but hide the lilac and massed honesty of the little garden'. Here – in the Anglo-Saxon traits of the labourer and description of the cottage and garden, not to mention the iconic landscape of the 'south country' – are the symbols of a thoroughly English presence. And yet Thomas goes on,

> [F]or a moment or less as he [the labourer] goes under the porch I seem to see that England, that swan's nest, that island which a man's heart was not too big to love

---

[82] Baker (ed.), *Camping on the Wye*, 4–5, 9, 17.
[83] Jerome, *Three Men in a Boat*, 60, 104.
[84] M. Daphne Kutzer, *Empire's Children: Empire and Children in Classic British Children's Books* (New York: Garland Pub., 2000); Julian Lovelock, *Swallows, Amazons and Coots: A Reading of Arthur Ransome* (Cambridge: Lutterworth Press, 2016); Hazel Sheeky Bird, *Class, Leisure and National Identity in British Children's Literature, 1918–1950* (Basingstoke: Palgrave Macmillan, 2014).

utterly. But now, what with Great Britain, the British Empire, Britons, Britishers, and the English-speaking world, the choice offered to whomsoever would be patriotic is embarrassing, and he is fortunate who can find an ideal England of the past, the present, and the future to worship, and embody it in his native fields and waters or his garden, as in a graven image.[85]

Religion, class and gender

Englishness, and the way that landscape mediated this, have been the central themes explored in this chapter. But people identify themselves and are identified by others in many different ways. Religion is one such identity. Chapter 6 examined the way in which landscape was invested with religious meaning, primarily by the sheer prominence given to churches, cathedrals and abbeys in the guidebooks. Although this reflected the clerical backgrounds of many of the authors, it would not have sold books unless the wider public shared these interests. Writers were able to draw on a long tradition of antiquarianism that had received a huge boost with the gothic revival – classically designed churches and furnishing received much less attention – which helped incorporate pre-Reformation Roman Catholic architecture into the national heritage. Indeed, it could be argued that it was the association of the Anglican Church and its estate with the idea of Englishness that underpinned the tourist appeal of churches. In the 1870s Henry James, describing a visit to an unnamed but idealized English village, recorded 'the small weather-worn, rust-coloured church [which] had an appearance of high antiquity', the churchyard and 'medieval-looking cross': 'this was the heart of England, unmistakably; it might have been the very pivot of the wheel on which her fortune revolves. One need not be a rabid Anglican to be extremely sensible of the charm of an English country church'.[86]

Twenty years earlier the Halls had observed that 'poetry and prose have laboured from age to age to describe the pictorial beauty and the moral power of what may be termed the "church-landscape" of England', and suggested that it was different to that in 'foreign countries'. The singular nature of the English church landscape was a theme rehearsed by George Birmingham in an essay on the 'Country Church' in the 1930s: '[T]he English village church, with the nestling cottages and the manor-house, is unique. France, Germany, and Italy have nothing like it.'[87] H. V. Morton finishes his tour *In Search of England* recalling his attendance at a service in a medieval village church, at the end of harvest:

> [T]he little church was full of corn sheaves ... I went out into the churchyard where the green stones nodded together, and I took up a handful of earth and felt it

---

[85] Thomas, *South Country*, 55.
[86] James, *English Hours*, 116.
[87] Hall and Hall, *The Book of the Thames*, 11; G. A. Birmingham, 'The Country Church', in *Legacy of England*, 163.

crumble and run through my fingers, thinking that as long as one English field lies against another there is something left in the world for a man to love. 'Well,' smiled the vicar, as he walked towards me between the yew trees, 'that, I am afraid, is all we have.' 'You have England,' I said.[88]

It is a sentiment John Betjeman would probably have shared. In 1938 he declared that 'of all the old houses of England, the oldest and the most interesting are the Houses of God – the Churches … the old churches of England are the story of England'.[89]

Leaving aside the relationship between Anglicanism and Englishness, it is also likely that visitors explored and rehearsed their specific confessional identity as they progressed their way from church to church. The guide literature embodied the religious sentiments of its authors, so we must be cautious about assuming these reflected the attitudes of readers. That said, it is probably also true that writers of guidebooks, especially those in series that aimed to attract a large market, would avoid too overt expressions of religious position. Generally, a broad Anglicanism prevailed. Notably absent, however, are accounts of nonconformist chapels, even where these were historic or possessed significant architectural features. For example, the impressive Presbyterian Octagon Chapel in Norwich built by Thomas Ivory (1754–6) and the Countess of Huntingdon's Chapel in Worcester (1804, enlarged 1815) were omitted from *The Little Guides*.[90] Geoffrey Clark and W. Harding Thompson's study of *The Dorset Landscape* (1935) contains a list of seventy of the 'best examples of churches of architectural interest' in the county; no nonconformist chapels are included, even though fine early examples of Congregational Chapels survived at Lyme Regis (1750–5) and Poole (1777).[91] This in part reflected the fact that early chapels were largely classical in design, and in the early-twentieth century Georgian classicism was only slowly being incorporated into the architectural heritage canon, especially in the case of religious buildings. But there was also a clear resistance to what was seen as the meanness and poverty of the nonconformist aesthetic: what Henry James termed its 'dusky brick chapels in provincial by-streets'.[92] Methodist chapels, complained George Birmingham, unlike churches, 'are strangely devoid of any kind of beauty. … They are irremediably [sic] ugly'.[93] Birmingham was writing in the 1930s, and attitudes were changing. John Betjeman was a notable revisionist voice, though his comment in 1943 on English towns hints at a continuing ambivalence; 'the nonconformist chapels,

---

[88] Morton, *In Search of England* 279–80.
[89] Betjeman, *Coming Home*, 76.
[90] W. A. Dutt, *Norfolk (The Little Guides)*, Rev. E. T. Long ([1902] London: Methuen/Batsford, 1949), 118–28; F. T. S. Houghton, *Worcestershire* (London: Methuen, 1922), 225–39; N. Pevsner, *The Buildings of England: North East Norfolk and Norwich* (London: Penguin, 1976), 255; A. Brooks and N. Pevsner, *The Buildings of England. Worcestershire*, 2nd edn (London: Yale University Press, 2007), 718–19; see also 'Nonconformist Places of Worship', Christopher Wakeling and Paul Stamper, Historic England, 2016, https://historicengland.org.uk/images-books/publications/iha-nonconformist-places-of-worship/heag139-nonconformist-places-of-worshipi-iha/, accessed 30 Jul. 2022.
[91] Clark and Thompson, *Dorset Landscape*, 105–12; J. Newman and N. Pevsner, *The Buildings of England: Dorset* (London: Penguin, 1972), 260–319.
[92] James, *English Hours*, 42.
[93] *Legacy of England*, 188–9.

especially those belonging to Unitarians, Moravians, Quakers and Congregationalists, Baptists and Methodists are worth seeing, outside at any rate'.[94]

If, on the face of it, there was little to encourage the Protestant nonconformist tourist in the guide literature, Roman Catholic nonconformists were another matter. They could legitimately claim the whole of the pre-Reformation English church fabric to be their heritage. It is unclear what drove Edward Elgar to be such an avid church crawler (and bicycler) in his native Worcestershire and Herefordshire, but it could have been the chance it provided to explore the roots of his faith. For the prominent Catholic Hilaire Belloc (1870–1953), a guidebook was an opportunity to set the record straight. His guide to the Thames valley (1907) identified the location of the medieval monasteries and abbeys, emphasized 'the monastic system's' huge and positive economic influence on the area, and decried the manner in which the Reformation led to the 'rapid enfeeblement of the crown', 'the disappearance of the small men' and the rise of the 'the Oligarchy: the landed class which had been threatening for so long to assume the Government of England [and had] stepped into the shoes of the great (monastic] houses'.[95] Frederick Cowles (1900–49), author of supernatural fiction (such as *The Horror of Abbot's Grange*, 1936) and travel writer, left little doubt where his religious affiliations lay. In a chapter on the 'Faith of England' in *This Is England* (1946), Cowles observed that despite the Reformation, 'when the shrines of the saints were desecrated, and the altars broken down ... The pilgrim shrines of England still represent the spiritual heritage of our nation', before introducing us to 'the ruins of the great monasteries of England ... still eloquent of the days when men did their best work for the glory of God'.[96] Edward Hutton looked through the same 'eyes of faith' when in his guide to Somerset, in the Highways and Byways series, he proclaimed Wells 'the best example of all that we have been compelled to sacrifice to that Moloch of Industrialism which has risen to enslave us upon the ruins of the Protestant heresy'.[97] Other authors are less explicit about their attachment to the 'old faith' but the signs are often there. George Phillips Bevan's *Tourist Guide to Warwickshire* (1882), a county with a history of recusancy, highlighted the presence of medieval rood screens, piscinas, reredos, stained glass and shrines; attacked the iconoclasts of the Reformation; praised local Catholic landowners; and among 'modern' gothic churches picked out for particular plaudits the work of A.W. N. Pugin.[98]

Pugin was a Roman Catholic convert, but he received numerous Anglican commissions, and there were many in the Church of England – reflected in the Tractarian and Oxford Movements – who bought into the need and project to revitalize the national church, by restoring, reproducing and celebrating its medieval

---

[94] John Betjeman, *English Cities and Small Towns* (London: Collins, 1943), 12; K. J. Garner, 'Strange Deliberations: John Betjeman and Protestant Nonconformity', *Christianity and Literature* 63:2 (2014): 225–56. Betjeman published 'Nonconformist Architecture' in *Architectural Review* (Dec. 1940): 160–74, and it seems likely that it was this which was reprinted in *First and Last Loves* ([1952] London: J. Murray, 1969), 90–119.

[95] Hilaire Belloc, *The Historic Thames* ([1907] London: Michael Joseph, 1988), 81, 92–3.

[96] Frederick Cowles, *This Is England* (London: F. Muller, 1946), 40–1, 49.

[97] Hutton, *Highways and Byways in Somerset*, 122.

[98] Bevan, *Warwickshire*, 68; Foster, *Birmingham*, 47–52.

aesthetic and heritage. The majority of guides took a broadly Anglican approach with many focusing on detail and adopting a descriptive technical language. John Betjeman complained that church architecture had been made 'incredibly boring' by the antiquarians. 'In their anxiety to find a Norman window, or to open up an Early English piscina ... they've omitted to see the church as a whole,'[99] but it made commercial sense to avoid too obvious a religious stance, or at least to leave readers to decode the signals in a way that suited their predilections, whether it be High or Low Church. The antiquarian vicar of Barkham, P. H. Ditchfield, is one of those whose guidebooks would very likely have bored Betjeman, but among the detailed accounts of windows, piscinas, aumbrys, rood screens and stairs, brasses and stained glass, it is not difficult to discern High Church Anglicanism; there was the ritual criticism of the 'iconoclastic zeal that has destroyed so much', but the praise for the 'pious and industrious' monks of Beaulieu, the endorsement of the Decorated style 'when English architecture attained to its greatest beauty' – for ecclesiologists the high point of medieval design[100] – and the attention given to the minutiae of medieval church furnishings, pointed in one direction.[101]

If the church constituted an obvious feature of the built landscape through which to play out religious identities, the same was not so easily the case with the natural landscape. Leaving aside the fact that there was nothing inherently religious about a mountain, forest or waterfall, as there was a church, there were two further problems to negotiate. The first was the long-standing issue that extolling the natural world risked slipping from the worship of a single Christian God, into pantheism and paganism, and ultimately the veneration of Nature alone. The second grew out of the Scientific Revolution, and especially the emergence of geology as a science, aspects of which, as we have seen, represented a potentially serious challenge to Christian origin narratives. These were tricky areas, and compilers of travel literature were understandably cautious about confronting them too directly. Occasionally legends associating locations with religious events are recalled, such as the curse of Raggedstone Hill near Little Malvern Priory, the Devil's Churchyard on Checkendon Common in the Chilterns, Skirrid Fawr or 'Holy Mountain' (whose summit was supposed to have split apart at the Crucifixion) in the Black Mountains, and the many legends associated with Glastonbury and the adjacent Tor. Much of this drew on a rich pre- and post-Reformation mythology coupling religion and natural landscape.[102] But this was a dying mode of thinking and such examples were probably introduced to add a little folkloric colour rather than with the intention of stimulating any strong religious sentiment. More in touch with contemporary concerns was the relationship between geology and religion. In 1834 it was still possible for George Roberts, in his guide to Lyme Regis, to claim plausibly that 'inferences' drawn from the pioneering fossil discoveries in the area 'exactly coincide

---

[99] Betjeman, *Coming Home*, 77.
[100] Roy Strong, *A Little History of the English Church* (London: Vintage, 2007), 210.
[101] Ditchfield, *Byways in Berkshire*, 67, 180, 239.
[102] C. F. Severn Burrow, *A Little City Set on a Hill: The Story of Malvern* (Malvern: Priory Press, 1948), 59–61; Baker, *Land of the Gap*, 152; Bradley, *March and Borderland*, 76; *A Pictorial and Descriptive Guide to Bath* (London: Ward Lock, 1926–7), 153–8; Walsham, *Reformation of the Landscape*.

with the narrative of Genesis'. But for C. F. Severn Burrow, in a guide to Malvern written over a century later, still to be suggesting a reading of the hills' geology based on 'a profound imaginative expansion of the Bible story in Genesis', pushed the boundaries of credulity.[103]

Others took a more nuanced approach. *Black's Picturesque Guide to the English Lakes* (1846) prefaces a long section on geology with the observation that 'the landscape may, and indeed must, charm alike the Geologist and Tourist; but the former … beyond this long vista of geological time and physical change, beholds, with higher admiration, exempt from change, and independent of time, the power of the INFINITE and WISE'.[104] There can be little doubt who this refers to, but the failure to actually name God, and the claim that there was a period beyond geological time, bespeaks the problems in dealing with this controversial subject, where new information and interpretations were regularly emerging.

Lyme Regis, the Malverns and the Lake District were areas where it was difficult for a guide not to engage with geology. Generally, however, travel literature was catering more and more for the tourist and less and less for the geologist, and with this came a mode of discourse that was more aesthetic than scientific. This helped to avoid contentious aspects of the landscape. Picturesque beauty was something around which a broad consensus could be constructed. If needs be, it was possible to see in the natural world a justification and celebration of God's existence. For H. V. Morton the Somerset hills appeared to provoke such a response; 'When the sun is over them, the cloud shadows moving like smoke, the scent of warm hay in the air, and larks holding up the blue sky with their little wings, the hills of North Somerset bring a man very near to prayer and make him thank God for life … ' (the ellipsis is Morton's).[105]

However, it is unclear whether this was intended to stimulate in the reader admiration for God's works, in the manner of natural theology, or was simply a conventional way of signalling the intensity of the experience. By this point in time most guides were avoiding any serious association between institutional religious belief and the natural landscape. This is not to argue that religious-type experiences were not being invoked, but increasingly the subject was not God but Nation and Nature. Nature had become an agent in its own right, an object to contemplate, celebrate and even worship. Both John Hissey and Vaughan Cornish refer at remote locations in the Cotswolds and Devon, to being 'alone with Nature'.[106] At 'the rolling brown and purple hills of the great heath' to the rear of Poole Harbour (Hardy's Egdon Heath), claimed Clark and Thompson, 'Nature has retained her mastery'.[107]

Some observers leave little doubt that in their eyes engagement with Nature was a sacred experience and were happy to appropriate the language and structures of formal religion to make their case. It had been while walking the Wye above Tintern

---

[103] Roberts, *History and Antiquities of Lyme Regis and Charmouth*, 331; Burrow, *Little City Set on a Hill*, 13.
[104] *Black's Picturesque Guide to the English Lakes*, 203.
[105] Morton, *In Search of England*, 126.
[106] Hissey, *An English Holiday*, 343; Cornish, *Scenery of England*, 64.
[107] Clark and Thompson, *Dorset Landscape*, 2.

Abbey that Wordsworth, as we have seen, implicitly invoked the power of Nature as a sacred force. Richard Jefferies and William Hudson were among the most prominent nature writers in the period and freely mixed the discourses of Nature and religion. Jefferies, who wrote an essay on 'Nature and Eternity' and sprinkled his autobiography with references to 'soul' and 'soul-life', recalled how 'the subtle influence of Nature penetrates every limb and vein, [and] fills the soul with a perfect contentment'.[108] During one of his 'Rural Rides' in southern England in the early-twentieth century Hudson recorded how the 'beeches grew among the firs, and the low sun on my left hand shining through the wood gave the coloured translucent leaves an unimaginable splendor. This was the very effect which men, inspired by a sacred passion, had sought to reproduce in their noblest work – the Gothic cathedral and church, its dim interior lit by many-coloured glass'.[109]

Stonehenge was a particularly iconic feature when it came to the relationship between Nature and religion, not just because of its historical prominence but because it was seen to be associated with worship of the sun and therefore of the natural world.[110] It was the monument where Thomas Hardy chose to place Tess in her final moments of liberation, before capture by the authorities, and represented his damning indictment of conventional Anglicanism; "'Did they sacrifice to God here?" asked she [Tess]. "No," said he [Angel]. "Who to?" "I believe to the sun."'[111] For Vaughan Cornish the builders of Stonehenge were also sun-worshippers, prompting him to indulge in a fantastical day dream in which his soul joined the original worshipers in adoration of nature:

> I have dreamed that there were men of vision in those ancient days and that by transmigration of the soul backward in the stream of time I stood with them at worship in the Courts of Stonehenge. The rays of the rising sun, the blue vault above, the far horizon and the spreading plain, the fragrant breeze from the dewy Downs, with the song of the lark and the peewit's cry, united in such fellowship of beauty that the earthly scene vanished and the soul was in heaven.[112]

The idea of sun- or Nature-worship as a religion would, on the face of it, have been a minority belief. However, sunbathing, heliotherapy, naturism and 'the cult of the sun' were emerging as powerful forces at the European seaside in the early-twentieth century.[113] Moreover, the man in his motor car who undertook the weekend 'pilgrimage' into the countryside along with the hikers and ramblers who swarmed out of the cities at the same time using cycles, trams and charabancs were driven by something akin to the worship of Nature, though they would never have described it as a religion. This is not to argue that conventional religion no longer had a hold on tourists. The heavy

---

[108] Jefferies, *Hills and the Vale*, 31–3, 284–305; Jefferies, *Story of My Heart*.
[109] Hudson, *Afoot in England*, 91.
[110] Edgar Barclay, *The Ruined Temple Stonehenge* (London: St Catherine Press, 1911), 50.
[111] Hardy, *Tess of the D'Urbervilles*, 417.
[112] Cornish, *Scenery of England*, 45–6.
[113] Gray, *Designing the Seaside*, 31–5.

church content of many of the guidebooks would suggest otherwise. It would seem that a distinction was drawn between religion in a formal sense (as represented for the majority by Christian worship) and something else that might broadly be called 'the sacred'. Both included a form of spiritual experience and the two were not mutually contradictory but could be participated in together.

There was also another factor at work here, closely related to issues of identity. The Anglican Church, which possessed the bulk of the built religious heritage that attracted the 'tourist gaze', was tied closely to the state and the traditional structures of authority. It continued to cater for the religious needs of the working class (especially in relation to rites of passage) and made considerable efforts to counter the threat from popular dissent and indifference. But it was becoming increasingly the church of the higher social classes. Adherence to it was a badge of middle- and upper-class identity.[114] This was signalled not only by regular attendance at services but also in the use of leisure time, such as visiting Anglican churches in a tourist capacity. Indeed, more generally it is clear that much of the travel and topographical literature was directed at the better off. Chapter 4 showed how such literature was subtly framed to instruct those using it in how to perform in a manner which conveyed a proper sense of their social class. Detailed knowledge about church architecture, for example, would enable a tourist to convey an educated and respectable persona. Choice of destination and accommodation also help define social image. Certain areas of the countryside were more accessible to the discerning traveller than others. As late as the 1930s Alison Murray found it 'a matter of satisfaction', in the case of the Cotswolds 'that the railway has not marred this least spoilt of all England's touring areas to any appreciable extent. There are no "cheap trips" and "day excursions" … Motor coaches run to the principal towns on the high roads and to other accessible places, but even these ubiquitous vehicles cannot penetrate into those delectable corners where Cotswold hides its greatest charms'.[115]

In the same period one of the leading hotels in the Cotswolds, the Lygon Arms in Broadway, was advertising its gourmet delights, and old world comfort and charm, in a handsomely illustrated booklet; 'I cannot imagine the man or woman who will not succumb to the atmosphere of well-being that pervades the Lygon … It must be a positive rest-cure to captains of industry.' Given the purported difficulties of accessing the area the booklet also noted, '[L]astly, if master is well served, so is his chauffeur and his car. Two or three expert mechanics are always at hand in the Lygon's own garage.'[116] Guides were often geared towards middle- and upper class country recreations. *Burrows Guide to the Wye* has information on fox and otter hunting, racing, shooting, fishing and golf. The same guide to Wessex has an advert quoting a review from *Antiquity*, which claimed that unlike most guide books, the Burrows series were written in 'a gentlemanly style: as if the many items of interest were recalled over a glass of port by a genial friend after a leisurely tour in a chaise and four'.[117] 'If ever I become

[114] Edward Royle, *Modern Britain: A Social History, 1750–1997*, 2nd edn (London: Arnold, 1997), 291–348, esp. 330–47.
[115] Murray, *Cotswolds*, 17.
[116] Carrington (ed.), *Broadway and the Cotswolds*, 57.
[117] *Burrows Guide to the Wye*, 13–14, 44–5, 60–1, 70; *Burrows Guide to Wessex*, 78.

a rich man', mused S. P. B. Mais, 'I shall not buy a car or a large country house. I shall hunt the fox for six days a week from November to March and get through the summer as well as I can chasing the otter and the stag, with a little cricket on the village green thrown in.' There is more than an element of fantasy about this, and not just because of the dream of becoming a rich man. For many, perhaps most readers, this gentrified vision of the countryside was largely an imaginary one, but the very endorsement of its values and effort to access it was an assertion of class identity.[118]

All this is not to argue that there were not also many working- and lower-middle-class people who turned to recreations such as cycling and hiking as a way of escaping the city and consuming the rural landscape. Moreover, as leisure options for the better off among these groups began to grow, a trip to or holiday at the seaside became a feature of their annual routine. But a visit to the seaside was as class-riven as one to the countryside. This had been clear from the very origins of resorts and was to continue to be the case.[119] In 1933 H. A. Piehler's *England for Everyman* gave potted accounts of the nation's resorts, which carefully delineated their social stratigraphy: at Sheerness 'part of the north shore … is set aside for lower-class pleasurable activities'; Minster-on-Sea 'is a lower-middle-class bungalow colony'; Herne Bay 'is a large middle-class resort'; Deal a 'distinctly bourgeois resort'; Folkestone 'a large, fashionable, and well laid-out resort'; Eastbourne 'is a large, well-planned, and select resort'; Peacehaven 'is the most notorious example of the vandalism that is defiling so much of the south coast'; Worthing and Bognor Regis were both 'large, middle-class resort[s]'; Sidmouth 'is a small but fashionable summer and winter resort'; Ilfracombe 'is the most popular seaside resort in Devon, and no place for the aesthete'; Sheringham 'is a pleasant, high-class, and expensive resort'; Clacton 'a modern, uninspiring, "trippery" resort'; Coney Island 'is a bungalow colony of the lower middle classes'; and Yarmouth 'a great seaside resort of the popular variety'.[120] Albert Osborne was less complimentary about the last of these:

> It is a far cry from beautiful Lynmouth [North Devon] to Yarmouth [Norfolk], the 'People's Play-ground by the Sea', as the posters call it. … Rather fortunately, it seems to me, there is no other resort in England just like Yarmouth. … And such a free and easy, rollicking crowd, without an 'h' in it. It jams the walks that line the interminable line of hotels and bazars, moving-picture shows, bar-rooms, lunch counters, concert halls and penny theatres that face the sea. … The immense crowd is very familiar and decidedly bad mannered. Young women call out to young men they never saw before. Young men crudely, and rather more than impudently, discuss the passers-by. Hand in hand men and women fight through the crowd singing shrilly. Clasped in each other's arms, half-grown boys and girls sprawl on the sand. In pairs, and sometimes a dozen couples at a time, men and women, yes, and boys and girls in their teens, openly enter the saloons, and emerge rather the worse for wear. … It is all huge, crude and barbaric.[121]

[118] Mais, *See England First*, 37.
[119] Walton, *English Seaside Resort*; Walton, *The British Seaside*, 51–72.
[120] Piehler, *England for Everyman*, 231–61.
[121] Osborne, *Old-World England*, 223–4.

It would be tempting in the face of such a verbal assault, to write off the appeal of the seaside to working people as merely 'social', satisfying at best their gregarious instincts and having little to do with environment. But there is a built and natural landscape at work here, of beach, promenade, and entertainment facilities. Moreover, we should not write off the aesthetic attraction of sea and coastline to 'the people'. In 1913 the suffrage campaigner Ada Nield Chew asserted that ordinary Lancashire folk possessed 'a keen sense of beauty, [which] was gratified to the full by the ever-changing panorama of sea, sky, rocks and tree-clad hills', and Andy Croll's recent study of Barry supports the notion that a key attraction of the resort for the miners of South Wales was its picturesque qualities.[122]

In his foreword to the Dunlop-sponsored *Picturesque Towns and Villages of England and Wales* [c. 1928], Harold Eley comments, 'I like to imagine this book in the hands of a busy man – set free for a spell from the toils of commerce'.[123] This apparently innocuous observation conceals a number of assumptions about identity. One, given that the volume is targeted at car owners, is that the busy man is a businessman and a member of the middle class, and that a holiday is justified as a relief from 'the toils of commerce'. Another, though it is implied rather than stated, is that it is men, and not women, who are 'busy' and need recuperation. If women were to have a holiday, it must be as companions to their hardworking husbands. It has to be said that it was not always quite as simple as this. One of John Hissey's summer car tours was prompted by the realization 'that we both needed a change … for of late I had felt, and had even dared to complain, that the children had become noisier and more rampageous than ever; on the other hand, my wife declared that housekeeping was a burden, and the management of tradespeople and servants simply a drudgery'.[124]

However, though middle-class women clearly did travel and holiday, sometimes independently, they are largely invisible as agents in the commercial guide and landscape literature of the period. A key reason was the fact that the vast majority of this material was written by men, reinforcing the notion that recreational consumption of the landscape was a male activity, and a way of expressing male identity. There was a 'hard' reality to this in that there were many barriers to women accessing leisure on equal terms with men.[125] For example, the scientific and natural history societies were reluctant to accommodate women members, reflecting a trend in club culture as a whole. Women were not admitted as ordinary members to the Worcestershire Natural History Society (1833–80) or the Worcestershire Naturalists' Club (f. 1847) until 1895. Although they formed a third of the club's membership between 1909 and 1914, 'it was many years before they took any active part in running it', and it was not until 1931 that the first lady president was appointed.[126] Similarly, women were excluded from membership of the prestigious mountaineering Alpine Club founded in 1857. The 'soft' reality was that men were much more effective in commandeering the literature

---

[122] Quoted in Walton, *British Seaside Resort*, 51; Croll, *Barry Island*.
[123] Stevens, *Picturesque Towns and Villages*, viii.
[124] Hissey, *English Holiday*, 5.
[125] Borsay, *History of Leisure*, 111–21.
[126] Jones, *Lookers-Out*, 36–7, 136–7, 191.

of landscape exploration. A significant number of women were active in the Alpine mountaineering scene in the late nineteenth and early-twentieth century and went on to form the Ladies Alpine Club in 1907 (which did not merge with the Alpine Club until 1975), but as Clare Roche has shown, men were far more prolific and effective in publicizing their achievements and framing these in terms of male characteristics.[127]

There were a number of strategies open to male authors, drawing on gender stereotyping, to emphasize men's close relationship with the landscape and its exploration, and to diminish that of women. One was to note the physical limitations of women as walking companions. *The Tourist's Guide to Bridgnorth* (1875) advised that 'for the benefit of lady tourists and those who may not be disposed to rough it by going up the ravine, we may mention the that the same bone-bed occurs above the farm house, on both sides of the valley', while William Hudson recorded that his companion was slow – 'slower than the poor proverbial snail or tortoise – and I would leave her half a mile or so behind to force my way through unkempt hedges, climb hills, and explore woods and thickets', though admitting that as a consequence of this burst of activity he was so exhausted that she had to slow down when they eventually met up again.[128] For C. E. M. Joad, in an essay 'In Praise of Walking', the problem went deeper than physical inadequacies. Women were simply distracting companions for those seeking true communion with Nature:

> [Y]ou must not … expect to enjoy or even notice Nature, if you make one of a chattering party; or to absorb something of Nature's spirit, if you are in the woods with the girl you love; or in deep conversation along the roads with a friend … it is better that he [the male rambler] should be alone … he can more easily go across country when alone without being under the necessity of explaining to others why he chose this particular gap in the hedge, or why it is necessary for the women to expose their silk stockings to the embraces of brambles.

Joad uses a potent sexualized image to describe the male walker's relationship with Nature; 'a man walks that he may be impregnated by Nature … if Nature is to fertilize she must be given her chance to do her work. Hence, it is good that man should sometimes be alone with Nature'. Though in this case Nature is described as female, she in fact possesses male characteristics – she impregnates rather than being impregnated – creating an ambivalent sexual presence that ultimately subverts, as does the whole account, the agency of real women.[129] Joad does not rule out walking with a companion, but he specifically refers to that being a man, and it is notable that where real and fictional tours are undertaken, such as Jerome's *Three Men in a Boat* (1889), it is often men who are considered the ideal soul mates.[130]

---

[127] Clare Roche, 'Women Climbers 1850–1900: A Challenge to Male Hegemony?', *Sport in History* (2013): 1–24, at 17.

[128] *Tourist's Guide to Bridgnorth*, 128; Hudson, *Afoot in England*, 18.

[129] C. E. M. Joad, *The Untutored Townsman's Invasion of the Country* (London: Faber & Faber, 1946), 52–4.

[130] See also Hutton, *By Thames and Cotswold*, 288–303; Baker (ed.), *Camping on the Wye*.

In reality young women did cycle and hike their way around the countryside, sometimes in the company of young men – for both parties that was probably a good part of the appeal of the activity. At Chester S. P. B. Mais observed a 'boy cyclist' leaning over the parapet of the city walls as he 'ogled five schoolgirl cyclists in shorts who were standing below, each of them with a different-coloured ribbon in her glossy hair'. By and large, Mais approved of women cyclists, formerly a subject of controversy: 'those bare-legged girl cyclists are only asserting their freedom by wearing shorts. They stand for a fine principle'. Of course, he would have not written the same thing about men and their apparel, and he rather gives the game away when he adds, '[I]t is only for the sake of beauty that I found myself wishing that those shorts were kilts'.[131]

The notion of female beauty, so instrumental in reconciling Mais to female cyclists, finds its way into a number of travel accounts both as an index of regional differences and as a source of aesthetic and sexual pleasure. Mais thought it 'jolly to pretend that the girls of Devon owe their exquisite pink and white complexions … to the incessant beating of the rain on their cheeks' and later went on to observe that 'the West Country, like a bashful maiden, has a habit of refusing to reveal her beauty to those who are peremptory or high-handed'.[132] While on tour, H. V. Morton discovered near Kirkdale 'apple-faced girls, whose hair is straight and yellow, stand[ing] knee-deep in the grass, their pinafores full of buttercups', and at Whitby he found 'here and there … a slim sturdy blonde beauty, whose hair has never known scissors, and who I am willing to bet, has never smoked a cigarette in her life'. Sheffield, he learned, 'glorifies its women. Against the blue-blackness of the smoke bath a pretty girl wearing a scarlet hat is more marvellous than in any city on earth'. In the chocolate factory at York he was invited on a guided tour by 'a pretty girl wearing a brown overall', and his 'first impression of Gloucester was that of a city full of small, comely maidens between the fortunate ages of fifteen and twenty-five'.[133] Unsurprisingly, no equivalent remarks are made about men's sexual appearance. Women are treated as ornamental features of a landscape seen through and defined by a male gaze. The gendering of landscape along male lines extended to the perception of physical geography itself. Geoffrey Clark and W. Harding Thompson, writing of the 'steep chalk hills' that rise to the rear of Chesil Bank on the Dorset coast, observed 'a masculine vigour about the lines of these hills which demands respect both from the motorist and the walker'. Comparing the Isle of Purbeck in Dorset with the 'hilly limestone districts of Derbyshire' they argued that whereas the 'hard northern climate' of the latter lent a harshness to the landscape, the southern climate of Dorset had 'allowed a gentler, kinder character to soften the masculine vigour of the material and given it a silver harmony unexcelled elsewhere'.[134]

Applying gender characteristics to non-living forms gave observers a good deal of scope for interpretation. William Beach Thomas, for example, found the 'suave uplands' of 'the limestone country of the Peak' in Derbyshire, 'pale, arid, flecked with spots of

---

[131] Mais, *Highways and Byways in the Welsh Marches*, 33–4; see also Mais, *Round about England*, 98–9.
[132] Mais, *Glorious Devon*, 2, 7.
[133] Morton, *Call of England*, 49, 71, 82, 173; Morton, *In Search of England*, 161.
[134] Clark and Thompson, *Dorset Landscape*, 8, 44.

white rock which gives them an air not so much feminine as effeminate'.[135] Whether it is 'masculine vigour' or 'effeminacy', it is a case of men measuring their identity as men against the landscape. On some occasions this could go so far as turning landscape forms into erotic objects of the male gaze: William Henry Hudson described the down land of southern England as

> the succession of shapely outlines; the vast protuberances and deep divisions between, suggestive of the most prominent and beautiful curves of the human figure, and of the 'solemn slope of mighty limbs asleep.' That modern poet's [Algernon Charles Swinburne, 'In Memory of Charles Baudelaire', 1867] vision of a Titanic woman reclined in everlasting slumber on the earth, her loose sweet-smelling hair lying like an old-world forest over leagues of ground … has seemed a mere outcome of a morbid imagination. Here, among the downs, the picture returns to the mind with a new light, a strange grandeur … a startling vivid reminder that we ourselves are anthropomorphic and mythopoeic, even as our earliest progenitors were, who were earth-worshippers in an immeasurably remote past, before the heavenly powers existed.[136]

In acknowledging the tendency in humans to anthropomorphize the world around them, Hudson was also recognizing the way the built and natural landscape was invested with meaning. Human beings tended to shape the material world in their own image.

The aim of this chapter has been to examine the process by which landscape forms were modelled culturally to reflect various identities. Primarily the focus has been on the way in which in an age that increasingly celebrated the idea of the nation, landscape became a vehicle, in many respects the principal cultural vehicle, for expressing Englishness. Though there was no universal agreement as to precisely which landscape type or location did this above all others, the dominant (but not necessarily the majority) view would have placed this somewhere in the south rather than the north of England, and in the countryside rather than the city. The issue was complicated by the fact that England was embedded in a British state that was both unitary and multinational, leading to a paradoxical position. Where it was to the benefit of England in defining itself, Englishness and Britishness were elided together; where it was not, England was treated as a separate entity. On the one hand, it was helpful to picture the Welsh, Scottish and Irish landscape as relatively wild, disordered and uncultivated because this highlighted the ordered and civilized character of England's natural landscape. On the other hand, eliding together England with Britain enabled England to fully exploit its prestige as the leader of the hugely powerful British Empire. Imperial Britain was reflected most in the built environment, but it also could be seen in the treatment of the natural landscape. In both scenarios – integration and separation – race was seen to play an important part in the perception of landscapes and in defining Englishness. National sentiment was not the only form of identity being invested in

---

[135] Thomas, *English Landscape*, 154.
[136] Hudson, *Nature in Downland*, 19.

landscape. Religion was also important. With its extensive built heritage the Anglican Church was a natural focus of attention, allowing recreational visitors to explore their own positioning on the confessional spectrum. In the long term – though this should not be overplayed in the period – a new form of religious experience and a new notion of the sacred were developing, expressed especially through the natural landscape, in which Nature rather than God became the focus of attention. The fact that the Anglican Church was the Church of England meant that much of its architectural appeal arose from its embodiment of Englishness. It has also to be said that this appeal owed a good deal to the Church of England becoming an increasingly middle-class organization. Visiting old churches was a way of asserting class identity, and it is clear that much of the touring literature was geared to servicing a middle- and upper-class market. It is also clear that this literature was framed in a way that invested landscape features with gender identities that privileged the male gaze.

10

Conclusion:
The Second World War and beyond

By the Second World War it is possible to talk not only of the making of the English landscape but also its invention. The former process was spread over thousands of years, but the latter was very largely concentrated in the previous two and a half centuries c. 1700–1939. This chapter will speculate on how the process of invention unfolded after 1939 in a series of phases; firstly during the Second World War, then in the post-war decades up until the 1970s, and finally in the period up until the beginning of the new millennium. But first, it is important to establish what had been achieved by 1939.

In 1700 it is difficult to conceive of the English landscape as an object of touristic, even consciously pleasurable consumption. Many people would have used it as a space for recreational activities (such as hunting or football), but consuming the landscape itself, taking an interest and pleasure in its material forms and adopting the 'tourist's gaze' would have been the pastime of a few. Except for a small number of antiquarians there was little interest in old buildings and ancient monuments. Inquisitiveness was growing, as part of the Scientific Revolution and Enlightenment, in the natural world, but this was still a minority interest. The countryside was, for the vast majority of people, still a place of work, and there was little incentive to conceive of it as something to be enjoyed in its own right. Substantial landowners built grand houses and landscaped portions of their estates and in some cases encouraged their fellow members of the gentry and aristocracy to visit their properties. But all this activity was confined to a narrow elite.

By 1939 all this had changed. The landscape had become a recreational commodity, and consuming it an established and substantial feature of the leisured life of the middle and lower middle classes, and even the working class, especially if we include the seaside experience. Underpinning this transformation were major shifts in the economic and geographical environment. Rapid and heavy industrialization and urbanization played a critical role in generating both the growth in per capita income, and transformation in cultural perspective, that made it possible to turn the landscape into a marketable recreational commodity. There was simply more money around to spend on leisure in general, so that what was once a comparatively esoteric pastime – the aesthetic appreciation of landscape – became available to a far wider range of social classes. In brief, the picturesque was democratized. Industrialization shifted the profile of the economy, so that agriculture, once the key sector, occupied a declining proportion of the workforce, a process accelerated by rising imports of foodstuffs from abroad. This opened up the countryside as a recreational resource, for a population that was increasingly concentrated in towns, cities and urban conurbations. Access to country and coast was hugely facilitated by a revolution in the means of public and private transport. Economic and cultural change moved in step, though often in a dialectical fashion. Rapid change stimulated an interest in past, present and future, so that visiting landscapes became a way of exploring time; predominantly this was old time, though modernity also had an appeal. It also engendered a reconfiguration of space along more overtly touristic lines, with working grey (urban), green (rural) and blue (water) environments reconstructed as recreational imaginative spaces with, for example, the rise of the seaside or the emergence of imagined regions like the Cotswolds.

The link between economic and cultural change was never a simple one. Quite apart from the dialectical element, culture had a certain life of its own. Intellectual movements like the Enlightenment, Romanticism, and the eclectic mélange of ideas we call Victorianism played a crucial if complicated part in shaping events. It is argued here, for example, that science was less influential than aesthetics in determining the popular appeal of landscape. Poets, novelists, painters and polemicists were more important than boffins. Though substantial figures such as Hardy and Ruskin were able to reach large audiences, the more elevated aspects of culture were refracted and popularized through newspapers, magazines and guidebooks. It was the compilers of these mediums – along with popular illustrators and painters – that did the heavy lifting when it came to modelling and remodelling public attitudes to landscape. It was they who invested landscape with new meanings, where such meanings had scarcely existed before. It was they, rather than any 'reality', that created representations that, for example, demonized the city and its suburbs and elegized the countryside. It was they who also convinced a receptive public that selective parts of the landscape that they occupied were authentically 'English'.

Economic change wrought political change. But again, it was a complicated process. Property – and therefore landscape – and power were inextricably linked. A process by which the ownership and control of land was concentrated in fewer hands during the early modern period and eighteenth century was checked and to a degree reversed. It was more a matter of control rather than ownership since even today a tiny number of aristocrats, organizations (including the public sector, the church and the crown) and companies own a large proportion of Britain's landscape. According to the Country Land and Business Association, half the rural land of England and Wales is owned by 36,000 landowners (under 0.1 per cent of the population), and Guy Shrubsole has calculated that companies own 18 per cent of these countries' acreages.[1] The growing wealth and numbers of the middle class, and collective activism of an increasingly assertive working class, forced the traditional landowning elite to concede a measure of control over access to the landscape. It was, however, more a matter of negotiation than confrontation. The middle class in particular used their economic and political muscle to strike a new contract with the traditional ruling class in which the latter were able to retain much of the trappings and realities of power, in return for more widespread

---

[1] Guy Shrubsole, *Who Owns England?* (London: Collins, 2019), 21, 297–307.

recreational access to the landscape. It was done partly through a reconfiguration of the state's objectives, in which a broadly defined public interest could trump the once sacred imperatives of private property. To a degree there was a democratization of the landscape. But this was accompanied by a reconfiguration of the structure of the state so that it became larger, and more multi-faceted, interventionist and powerful. There was a growth of the central and local state, and critical from our perspective of the informal state, since it was through the last of these, through organizations such as the National Trust, that control was negotiated between upper and middle class, and access to the built and green heritage protected.

In the new world of 'democratic' politics that emerged during the course of the nineteenth and early twentieth centuries, the state had to be seen to be acting in the 'national interest', even if in reality that interest might be quite narrowly defined. In this era the idea of the nation was energized by the rise of nationalism. Landscape, which previously had been relatively free of national associations, became heavily invested with national sentiment. In a society riven by social divisions, and facing increasing democratic accountability, appealing to such sentiment became a valuable way for the nation state to counter the fissiparous forces of class and legitimize its existence. What was meant by the nation state when it came to a specific national identity was problematic. Was it England, Britain, or the British Empire? Contemporary accounts of the landscape played with and between all three of these identities, but the ultimate aim was to facilitate the invention of the *English* landscape.

The Second World War

At the outbreak of the Second World War, all the elements that made for incorporating the landscape, really or virtually, into the leisured routine and ideological profile of the English nation had been established. The First World War had done little to interrupt this process. Whatever the trauma and conflicting emotions induced by the war, guidebook writers appear reluctant to draw directly on them. A. G. Bradley, in his 1918 account of Sussex, described 'the Battle of Hastings as the opening scene in one stage of our national existence, another of which has so recently closed, is altogether too big a business for passing notice'.[2] That said, the contrast between the scarred landscape of the battlefields in France and the tranquillity of old England must have intensified the appeal of the latter for those involved in the war. In an account of a tour published by the Council for the Preservation of Rural England in 1932, Vaughan Cornish recalls how

> it was during the Great War that I became well acquainted with the lawn of King's [College, Cambridge] between the stately Tudor chapel and the slow waters of the Cam, where weeping willows droop their slender branches to the stream. Here the convalescent wounded whiled away the summer hours sculling and punting

[2] Bradley, *Old Gate*, 165.

leisurely along, and the bells of the college chapels marked the peaceful progress of the day. The devastated fields of France were my mental background for the green lawns and grey walls of the hospitable precincts of piety and learning, for I had come from the battle of the Somme.[3]

For some it was not so much the war itself as the changes that followed it that heightened sensitivity to the value of old England and to the threat of its loss. In the late 1920s Clough Williams-Ellis bemoaned rapid changes that England had undergone in recent decades: 'Since the War, indeed, it has been changing with an acceleration that is catastrophic, thoroughly frightening the thoughtful among us, and making them sadly wonder whether anything recognizable of our lovely England will be left for our children's children.'[4] The proliferation of preservation organizations and flood of guidebooks and nature publications that appeared in the inter-war years suggest that the First World War accelerated trends already in place.

The impact of the Second World War was more complicated. The powerful link between national identity and landscape that had been forged over the previous century or so proved an irresistible cultural asset to draw upon to sustain national morale during the 1940s. The domestic film industry and government film units exploited it brilliantly with deeply evocative films such as Michael Powell and Emeric Pressburger's *A Canterbury Tale* (1944). Filmed in the Kent countryside and Canterbury itself, it drew heavily upon elements discussed in previous chapters – such as the idea of the village and historic town, nature mysticisms, medievalism, the notion of the journey and pilgrimage, and southern Englishness – at the same time as developing a sophisticated and nuanced case for why the war was being fought.[5] In 1939–40 a project was initiated, called the 'Scheme for Recording the Changing Face of Britain', funded by the Pilgrim Trust, which ran until 1943, and led to the production – by a variety of artists – of 1,549 'topographical watercolour drawings of places and buildings of characteristic national interest'. Though industry was present it was 'pushed to the margins', and the four categories of subject matter envisaged by Sir Kenneth Clark, the Director of the National Gallery and a key promoter of the scheme, give a good idea of what was conceived to constitute 'places and buildings of characteristic national interest'; 'A. Fine tracts of landscape which are likely to be spoiled by building developments or factories … B. Towns or villages where old buildings are about to be pulled down … C. Parish Churches … D. Country Houses and their Parks'.[6] Direct references to the war were 'strangely absent',[7] but there is little

---

[3] Cornish, *Scenery of England*, 77.
[4] Williams-Ellis, *England and the Octopus*, 15.
[5] Tilson Pugh, 'Perverse Pastoralism and Medieval Melancholia in Powell and Pressburger's "A Canterbury Tale"', *Arthuriana* 11:3 (2009): 97–113; David Lowenthal, 'British History and the English Landscape', *Rural History* 2:2 (1991): 208–30; Stella Hockenhull, 'Romantic Landscapes: Visual Imagery in Three Films of Powell and Pressburger', *Journal of British Cinema and Television* 2:1 (2005): 152–66; Maroula Joannou, 'Powell, Pressburger and Englishness', *European Journal of English Studies* 8:2 (2004): 189–203.
[6] Gill Saunders, 'Introduction', in *Recording Britain*, ed. Saunders, 8–51.
[7] Ibid., 24.

doubt that it was anxieties about the destruction of the historic English landscape (Scotland spawned a separate scheme, and Wales was represented by only seventy-six pictures) both before and as a consequence of war, that underpinned the project.

Five historic English cities were bombed by the Lufwaffe – Exeter, Bath, Norwich, York and Canterbury – and though this was in reprisal for Bomber Command's attack on the medieval Hanseatic port of Lübeck, it was reported in the British press as evidence of German contempt for civilized culture.[8] A local newspaper in Bath described how 'fire lit by the barbarism of the Nazi "New Order", gutted the interior of the stately Assembly Rooms, the restored Georgian monument that belonged to all civilisation' and characterized the ruins as 'a monument to German savagery'.[9] There is no evidence that the Luftwaffe High Command used the Baedeker guides specifically to decide on their targets (though a German official did refer to the guides), but it is clear that the cities were chosen because of their cultural significance, and that this significance owed much to the role of guidebooks in defining cultural value before the war. In 1943 John Betjeman saw – paradoxically – the destruction and revulsion wrought by the German bombardment as a way of protecting Britain's heritage in the future: 'while Ludlow stands, while Burford High Street rises from the Windrush … we have an England to protect … Nazi bombing has built up an affection for the old

Figure 10.1 Frank Newbould, 'Your Britain – Fight for It Now' (1942). © The Imperial War Museum.

---

[8] Niall Rothnie, *The Baedeker Blitz: Hitler's Attack on Britain's Historic Cities* (Shepperton: Ian Allan, 1992), 3–11, 130–4.
[9] Borsay, *Image of Georgian Bath*, 82.

towns of England among those many who formerly thought little about them.'[10] The same could be said of the countryside.

Frank Newbould's deeply evocative 1942 poster (produced for the Army Bureau of Current Affairs) of the South Downs, complete with farmstead, shepherd, shepherd dog and sheep, scarcely needed the textual addition 'your BRITAIN fight for it now' (see Figure 10.1).[11] It was the same message from Vera Lynn, though in this case the nation to be saved was explicitly England, 'There'll always be an England / While there's a country lane / Wherever there's a cottage small / Beside a field of grain'.

For some observers a key way in which war enhanced the appeal of rural England was the migration from city to country, especially through evacuation. The publisher Harry Batsford, who transferred much of his business from London to the Malverns just before the war, observed that thousands of town-dwellers were led or compelled to a first-hand acquaintance with the country for the first time: 'Bank clerks have spread themselves in the historic mansions of the chairman of directors, civil servants have been deported *en masse* to country billets, and teachers and children have experienced the strange conditions of village life.'[12] John Betjeman was confident that '[no] child who has migrated from the towns to the country, will ever again despise country life ... Evacuation may have brought about what is badly needed, the return to the land'.[13] But evacuation could provoke negative attitudes to the countryside. Edith Olivier observed that 'townspeople love the thought of the country'. But nearly half the evacuees returned home after two months or less. 'They would rather be bombed than bored.'[14]

The ambivalent impact of evacuation underpins much of the complex reaction that war induced in public attitudes to the landscape. The militarization of town and country – with large tracts of land taken over for urban defences, airfields, camps, and training and testing facilities, and hotels and country houses/estates requisitioned for purposes such as war administration, officers' messes and hospitals – would have been seen by many as a necessary but irritating blot on the landscape, that was to take many years after the end of the conflict to eradicate.[15] H.V. Morton, who sought to compare pre-war and war-time England, by undertaking journeys in 1939 and 1942, thought that 'only in and around cities and towns was the war atmosphere noticeable'. He was rather taken by the 'exquisite beauty of Salisbury Cathedral in the black-out' but felt that the 'industrial Midlands, a region always hideous and deformed', was made even worse by the means taken to protect it 'in the form of municipally erected shelters, sand-bags, home-made dug-outs and trenches'.[16] This reinforced the pre-war city/country, historic/modern narrative. Others were less sure about the countryside's escape from the effects of war: Bernard Newman described how the 'little hedge-lined lanes' of

---

[10] Betjeman, *English Cities*, 41.
[11] Saunders, *Recording Britain*, 18, 25.
[12] Bolitho, *Batsford Century*, 90–3; Batsford, *How to See the Country*, 1, 5.
[13] Betjeman, *Coming Home*, 106.
[14] Newman, *British Journey*, 143; Edith Olivier, *Country Moods and Tenses* (London: Batsford, 1942), 19.
[15] Trevor Rowley, *The English Landscape in the Twentieth Century* (London: Hambledon Continuum, 2006), 307–47.
[16] Morton, *I Saw Two Englands*, 216, 238, 281.

Devon 'now shuddered under the impact of tanks and guns'; how in villages outside Cambridge 'the housing problem is acute' being 'grossly accentuated by the influx of evacuees and industrial personnel' and how East Anglia generally had become a 'region of vast airfields'.[17]

There is no doubt that the bombing of British cities during the war, and the damage done to their historic features, provoked a wave of revulsion that drew a good deal of its strength from growing sensitivity to this heritage prior to the war. However, the reaction to these attacks – and more broadly to the impact of the war in general – was not as straightforward as it might seem. The focus on the injury to the historic fabric, and the understandable disgust that this prompted, ran the risk of underplaying the attendant human suffering and loss. In the case of Bath, the worst hit of the Baedeker cities, the damage to the Georgian fabric was significant but largely superficial; the brunt of the bombings of the evenings of 25 and 26 April 1942 was borne by the predominantly working-class areas of the city, and it is estimated that about 400 people were killed (a figure comparable to the terrible death toll of 550 during the Coventry air raid of November 1940). For most people it is likely that it would have been the human cost of the attacks that would have registered most deeply in their psyche. One major piece of Bath's eighteenth-century fabric that was severely damaged, though by no means wholly destroyed, was the eighteenth-century upper assembly rooms. These had been meticulously restored in the late 1930s, the centre-piece of Bath's Georgian revival in the inter-war years. In the post-war climate there was considerable local opposition to rebuilding the rooms, so much so that the local council opposed their reconstruction. This reflected a widespread feeling that the city ought to look to the future rather than the past and invest in modern housing and facilities that met the needs of the indigenous population, rather than servicing the aesthetic pretensions of well-off residents and outsiders. It was only pressure from external bodies like the National Trust (to whom the ownership of the rooms had been transferred in the 1930s, and who leased the rooms to the council) that forced its rebuilding and reopening, not to occur until 1962, seventeen years after the end of the war. It would seem that for the majority of Bath's citizens, war-time devastation, far from prompting an intensified concern to preserve and protect the city's exclusively defined heritage, had generated a reaction against the past and in favour of a more socially inclusive modernity.[18]

The response seen in Bath to the war was to a lesser or greater degree replicated elsewhere. Without rejecting the past wholesale, the need for a new vision of the future was recognized, especially as embodied in the notion of planning. Edith Olivier argued that 'there must first … be regional planning on a large scale. One lesson has been cruelly bombed into us: our cities are too big'.[19] Her vision for the future did draw on historic examples of town planning, such as early modern Bath, Blandford Forum and London, but it also recognized the need to build new and intervene on a large scale. Bernard Newman, emphasizing the 'necessity for modernity', noted that at Plymouth 'they are planning boldly for the [city's] reconstruction … taking advantage

---

[17] Newman, *British Journey*, 33, 264.
[18] Borsay, *Image of Georgian Bath*, 82–4, 172–4, 311–12, 314–15.
[19] Olivier, *Country Moods*, 113–14.

of the opportunity the German bombers helped to create', and at Birmingham and Hull where 'war wounds' were 'as severe as those of any city in England' progressive housing schemes were underway.[20] Gilbert McAllister summed up the mood in the country, arguing 'the more the cities of Britain were bombed and blasted by the Luftwaffe, the more the people of this country were inspired by a vision of the new cities which they were to build after the war'.[21] In 1937 John Betjeman might have opined, 'Come, friendly bombs and fall on Slough/It isn't fit for humans now', but when the bombs really did fall, the destruction they wrought was to inspire a vision closer to Slough than Chipping Campden.[22]

Modernity and the post-war decades

War had provoked an ambivalent response to the touristic landscape. On the one hand it and its connection with national identity were exploited to justify war ends and boost morale. On the other hand, that landscape, and the values underpinning its meaning, became seen as part of a past that needed to be jettisoned in favour of a more modern, efficient and socially inclusive vision. For the two to three decades after 1945 it was this vision that was to hold sway. At the heart of it was the notion of town and country planning. This was not a new phenomenon: its intellectual and theoretical basis was established during the early-twentieth century and had gained considerable purchase among influential figures within a state (national, local and informal) increasingly willing to intervene in matters of property and landownership. At this stage planning was not seen as a threat to preservation. Quite the opposite. The creation of National Parks under the National Parks and Access to the Countryside Act of 1949 (between 1950 and 1955, seven were established in England: Dartmoor, Exmoor, Peak District, Yorkshire Dales, North York Moors, Northumberland and the Lake District) was in one way a triumph of the marriage of preservation and planning and of the whole movement towards the creation of an accessible touristic landscape – a fulfilment of Wordsworth's dream in 1835 that 'the Lake District should be deemed a sort of National property in which every man has a right and interest who has an eye to perceive and a heart to enjoy'. The same could be argued for Areas of Outstanding Natural Beauty (AONB), authorized under the same legislation of 1949 as the National Parks; by 1969 these included the Quantocks, the Sussex Downs, the Kent Downs, the Surrey Hills, the Cotswolds, the Chilterns, the Malverns and the Shropshire Hills.[23] Effectively the post-war legislation formalized, and at least in theory protected and made easily accessible, many of the imagined landscapes that had been established before the war. Green belt legislation, pre- (London and the Home Counties) and post-war, could be said

---

[20] Newman, *British Journey*, 20, 242–6, 278, 327.

[21] McAllister, *Homes, Towns and Countryside*. xiii.

[22] John Betjeman, *Collected Poems*, ed. Earl of Birkenhead ([1958] London: John Murray, 1980), 22–4; Tony Pilmer, 'Slough Booms: Slough between the Wars', *Berkshire Old and New: Journal of the Berkshire Local History Association* 33 (2016): 26–40.

[23] Alan J. Patmore, *Land and Leisure in England and Wales* (Newton Abbot: David & Charles, 1970), 39, 193–9, 208–10.

to have achieved the same thing. Indeed, respect for, and the protection of, what were deemed historic features (effectively established through the antiquarian and guide literature of previous generations) was a key part of the extensive plans proposed for cities and towns in the post-war period. Those produced by the leading town planners of the post-war era, such as Thomas Sharp, Patrick Abercrombie and Colin Buchanan, recognized the importance of a town's history in shaping the vision for its future and generally sought to protect and incorporate in their proposals landscape features that were considered of historical significance.

However, the concept of planning, as it pertained in this period, contained two elements that posed a potential threat to landscape tourism. First, the priority was to facilitate the creation of a working urban and rural landscape that met the needs of a modern economy and population. That could mean, for example, the introduction of more efficient modes of farming, the construction of an effective urban road network, and the building of large-scale public housing projects, and with this the inevitable corollary, the destruction of small fields, hedgerows, and historic but what was considered low-grade urban fabric – particularly where it got in the way of what was considered essential modernization. The second problem was that all the post-war legislative measures put into place to protect the historic landscape – such as National Parks, AONB's, Green Belts, the listing system (established under the Town and Country Planning Act of 1947, grading, and to a degree protecting, buildings according to their perceived aesthetic and historical significance)[24] – had the effect of downgrading landscape features not included in their designations and left them doubly exposed. When it came to the new projects proposed by the planners, these spaces were considered expendable. Countryside not included in the designatory framework, and unlisted urban buildings, could be easily appropriated and bulldozed to accommodate the planners' visions. The outcome was the loss of urban and rural landscape features that later generations were to bitterly regret.

That said, in the immediate post-war decades many of the features that had propelled the growth of the landscape as a leisure resource continued to flourish. The rail network reached its peak in 1930 with 20,243 miles opened. By 1960 it had decreased to 18,369 miles, but it was only with the cuts that followed the so-called Beeching reports in 1963 and 1965 that the real reduction in the system set in; by 1970 the number of miles had been reduced to 11,799.[25] Access to the landscape consequent on rail cuts was more than compensated for by the growth in motorized transport: buses, coaches and especially motor cars. The number of licensed vehicles in Britain grew from about 4 million in 1950 to 15 million by the early 1970s, with private and light goods vehicles accounting for the vast majority of the increase.[26] The road network was greatly upgraded, and the introduction of the first full-length motorway (M1) in 1959 marked, it has been

---

[24] Andrew Saint, 'How Listing Happened', in *Preserving the Past: The Rise of Heritage in Modern Britain*, ed. Michael Hunter (Stroud: Alan Sutton, 1996), 114–53.

[25] Simmons and Biddle, *Oxford Companion to British Railway History*, 29, 492.

[26] Department for Transport, Transport Statistics Great Britain, 2011, https://assets.publishing.service.gov.uk/government/uploads/system/uploads/attachment_data/file/8995/vehicles-summary.pdf; for figures see also Bagwell and Lyth, *Transport in Britain,*130 and Rowley, *English Landscape*, 39, which places the number of motor cars in 1970 at 12.2 million and in 2001 at just over 25 million.

said, 'the beginning of the full motorization of British society', facilitating – at least until gridlock set in – more rapid access to recreational landscapes.[27] The guidebook, adapting to the arrival of the motor car since the early-twentieth century, focused more and more on the form of transport that epitomized, par excellence, modernity. The *Ward Lock Red Guides* could advertise a 'SPECIAL SECTION FOR MOTORISTS', the popular *Shell Guides* inevitably assumed a motoring public, while even the scholarly Nikolaus Pevsner was forced – in the foreword to his 1951 *Middlesex Buildings of England* volume – to acknowledge that 'the work of compilation could not have been done if my wife and Miss Marjorie Stearn, who was then my secretary, had not, day-in day-out, driven an obstreperous vintage 1932 car through the country'.[28] Churches still figure heavily in these volumes, a sign that the powerful antiquarian/religious tradition still exerted a considerable influence over how tourists were expected to read the built landscape. But tastes were changing or, more accurately, broadening. The dominance of the medieval and early modern periods of what was considered to be of historical and architectural interest was challenged first in the inter-war years by the appeal of the Georgian era and then after the Second World War by an emerging appreciation of Victorian eclecticism. In this way the character of the tourist value of the landscape was constantly being reappraised.

Access was not only a function of transport but also of free remunerated time. The inter-war years had made considerable advances here. The number of manual workers with holiday pay agreements rose from 1 million in the early 1920s to 4 million by late 1938, and 10 million by 1945. By the early 1950s many manual workers had acquired two weeks paid holiday plus public holidays; by 1973 three quarters had three or more weeks, and non-manual workers had longer holiday breaks. Perhaps as significant in respect of later trends was the introduction of pension schemes and the development of the idea of retirement. Important here was not so much the state pension (introduced in 1908), given its very limited provisions, but the growth of occupational pensions (especially for those in salaried as opposed to waged employment), where the proportion of the workforces covered rose from 13 per cent in 1936 to 33 per cent by 1956, inaugurating what has been called 'mass retirement'.[29] The demand released by these developments fuelled the continued growth through the inter-war years, and the continued buoyancy during the post-war years, of one of the great landscape inventions of the eighteenth century, the seaside resort. Adaptation was seen – the growing importance of holiday bungalows, the static caravan and of the retirement market – but the widely trumpeted demise of the British seaside was still some time away, if indeed it has ever arrived.[30] Political developments after the war, especially with the arrival of Labour governments, favoured a continued extension of the central and local state. This was apparent not only in the planning legislation, with its protection of and greater access to green space, but also in the support given to the 'informal' state

---

[27] Bagwell and Lyth, *Transport in Britain*, 202.
[28] *Red Guide Bath. Cheddar. Wells. Glastonbury*, 13th edn (London: Ward Lock, c. 1960), title page; N. Pevsner, *The Buildings of England: Middlesex* (Harmondsworth: Penguin, 1951), foreword.
[29] Cunningham, *Time, Work and Leisure*, 111–12, 117–18.
[30] Walton, *British Seaside*, 27–50.

in the guise of the National Trust. This was the most high profile of the organizations established since the later nineteenth century which together created an infrastructure to support the recreational/touristic landscape. It was after the Second World War that the Trust started to acquire country houses on a large scale, facilitated by the newly elected Labour government, especially by the establishment of the National Land Fund and the provision to take property, which was then transferred to the Trust, in lieu of tax, notably death duties.[31] Though the growing inclusion of country houses in the Trust's portfolio may have reflected the 'narrower, more exclusive' vision of its post-war leadership,[32] arguably more houses enhanced its appeal to urban dwellers seeking a historic rural destination – and one that offered both protection from inclement weather and catering facilities – and may have accounted for the rise in membership, from 7,850 in 1945, to 157,581 by 1965, and 226,000 by 1970.[33]

Towards the millennium and beyond

The growth in the National Trust in the immediate decades after the war was impressive enough. But it hardly compared with what was to come. By 1981 membership had crossed the 1 million mark, by 1990 2 million, at which point David Cannadine observed that it was 'the most important and successful voluntary society in modern Britain. ... Its present membership ... is more than the Conservative, Labour and Liberal Democratic parties combined'.[34] Three decades later (2020) its membership had almost trebled to 5.6 million. This is just under one-in-ten of the entire population of England (68 million), and – if it is assumed that there is a connection between social class and membership, which it cannot be easily proven – perhaps a fifth to a quarter of the entire middle class.[35] A quiet revolution was and is underway, at the heart of which was and is an organization founded in the late Victorian era and dedicated to presenting the landscape as a recreational good. A series of factors were at work both in stimulating the explosive growth of the National Trust, but also more generally in reshaping consumption of the landscape.

The post-war decades, building on pre-war foundations and the rising opportunities for leisure, had seen a growing recreational interaction with the landscape. However, the full impact of this trend was moderated by the post-war enthusiasm for modernity. From the late 1960s and early 1970s the appeal of the modern began to wane in critical areas of life. There was a resurgence of the influence of the past, something

---

[31] Gaze, *Figures in a Landscape*, 145–7.
[32] Cannadine 'The First Hundred Years', 21–2.
[33] Gaze, *Figures in a Landscape*, 113, 216; National Trust, Our History: 1945–2000, https://www.nationaltrust.org.uk/lists/our-history-1945-2000.
[34] Cannadine, 'The First Hundred Years', 11.
[35] Using the National Statistics socio-economic classification, and based on the July–September 2014 quarterly Labour Force Survey, 32 per cent of those surveyed were placed in occupational categories 1 (Higher managerial, administrative and professional occupations) and 2 (Lower managerial, administrative and professional occupations). Mike Savage, *Social Class in the 21st Century* (London: Penguin Books, 2015), 41.

widely noted by a variety of observers – sociologists, historians, geographers and archaeologists. In 1987 Robert Hewison ominously warned that 'the past begins to loom above the present and darkens the path to the future', while five years later Peter Fowler speculated, 'I doubt if anyone before this moment can have been subject to quite so much "pastness" as there is around now *and be so aware of it*.'[36] The length and consequence of this reaction, which permeated deep into the cultural fabric of society, is still difficult to determine. Even more problematic are the causes. It is arguable that a series of major economic crises, especially the oil crisis of the 1970s and the financial crash of 2008, and more drawn-out processes such as de-industrialization and globalization, have proved critical, with the damaging impact on living standards, such as through unemployment or long-term declines in real income. This led to a loss of faith in the prevailing economic system and a retreat into an imagined past of prosperity and stability. The destabilizing effects of economic change would also reinforce anxieties among the English, prompted by globalization, entry into the European Union and Devolution, about a loss of local and national identity, and a quest for an equally fictive past in which Englishness seemed an unchanging, unproblematic and virtuous brand. This blast from the past did not necessarily enhance engagement with the landscape. As previous chapters have argued, modernity could have a touristic appeal. But these had not been the principal themes propelling the interest in landscape in England before the Second World War, when the past and nationalism held sway. Modernism had been an important feature of the seaside, but by the later 1960s several of the principal English resorts were facing increasing competition from overseas destinations, as domestic tourists sought their holidays abroad in guaranteed sunshine. It is true that England itself drew rising numbers of international tourists, but their sights were firmly set on its historic attractions, and a version that owed much to the picture created in the late Victorian and Edwardian eras. It has also to be said that the products of much of post-war English modernism – council housing, high-rise flats, schools, hospitals, office blocks and road systems – were not by their nature obvious tourist sites. Cultural buildings were far more likely to be in the tourist sight lines. The ten most visited attractions in the UK in 2019 were all in London.[37] One, the Southbank Centre, could claim to be a modernist structure, and part of the legacy of the 1951 Festival of Britain, perhaps the moment when there was a genuine national enthusiasm for the new. The internal contents of Tate Modern (opened 2000) undoubtedly meet the modernist criteria. But it is housed in a converted piece of redundant industrial heritage, the Bankside Power Station originally designed by Sir Giles Gilbert Scott in the late 1940s, and decommissioned in 1981. The rest are accommodated in gothic or classical buildings predating the First World War and redolent of Britain's imperial past.

These iconic national cultural buildings have been modified over time, though when the National Gallery (originally designed by William Wilkins 1832–8) attempted

---

[36] Borsay, *Image of Georgian Bath*, 3.
[37] Statista, Number of visits to leading visitor attractions in the United Kingdom in 2019, https://www.statista.com/statistics/559616/leading-visitor-attractions-in-the-united-kingdom-uk/, accessed 14 Jul. 2020.

to add a new wing in a thoroughly modernist design in the early 1980s this was widely criticized, with the then Prince of Wales describing it as 'a monstrous carbuncle on the face of a much-loved and elegant friend'. It was replaced by a tamer post-modernist structure. This reflected the major shift in public sentiment from about the 1970s already discussed. The political and cultural leaders and organizations stimulating and directing this sentiment adopted an increasingly assertive and confrontational approach, challenging – as they saw it – the modernist hegemony of the post-war establishment, notably the architectural and planning professions. The critics had plenty of ammunition to fire: the apparent failure – structurally and socially – of large-scale public housing projects, especially those based on high-rise accommodation; the deterioration of the nation's country house heritage (which prompted the Destruction of the Country House exhibition at the Victoria and Albert Museum in 1974); the damage to the centres of many old towns and cities to accommodate the rapacious needs of the motor car and shopper. The inherent 'flaws' in the post-war planning regime now became exposed – the need to subordinate everything to efficiency and the failure to protect 'minor' elements of heritage. The latter was forcibly demonstrated in the case of Bath, where unlisted Georgian terraces were demolished to make way for modern buildings and the motorcar, highlighted by the highly effective 'Sack of Bath' campaign of the early 1970s.[38] The sea change in attitudes did not overthrow the concept of planning as such. In many respects the state became even more involved in the building process than before. But it was a process that now paid greater respect to the past, with the emphasis on conservation (reflected in the development of the notion of the conservation area, which protected whole zones of historic towns)[39] and the higher social-class residential and tourist markets.

Much of the inter-war and immediate post-war literature on Bath had highlighted the role of its celebrated eighteenth-century architects (John Wood father and son) as pioneers of urban planning. But the emphasis in this commentary subtly changed over time, from what might be called hard formal to soft informal types of planning. The former emphasized the macro-scale and the urban quality of the architecture. The latter focused on minor buildings and smaller-scale features, such as door cases and windows, in some instances projecting Bath as a type of almost accidental planning. Writing during the 'Sack of Bath' campaign in 1971, Peter Smithson claimed that the city 'has no town-plan in the sense of Karlsruhe or Baroque Berlin with their avenues, formal parks and civic palaces ... Bath demonstrates above all that it is perfectly possible to build a memorable, beautiful, and cohesive community of *fragments*'.[40] All this was a reaction to the perceived failure of large-scale post-war town planning. Above all the Woods were praised for their sensitivity to the natural world, creating forms of urban design (such as the crescent) that acknowledged the importance of the surrounding countryside and merged town and country.

---

[38] Adam Fergusson and Tim Mowl, *The Sack of Bath – and After: A Record and an Indictment* (Salisbury: Bath Preservation Trust, 1989).
[39] Borsay, *Image of Georgian Bath*, fn 60, 184.
[40] Peter Smithson, *Bath: Walks within the Walls – A Study of Bath as a Built-Form Taken over by Other Uses* (Bath: Adams & Dart, 1971), 2, 17.

This new green attitude to planning reflected a growing sensitivity to the importance of Nature in the later twentieth century.[41] The 'recovery' of the English countryside after the problems faced by agriculture in the late Victorian, Edwardian and inter-war years was facilitated by the full commercialization and modernization of the rural economy, through mechanization and the use of agro-chemicals, and the single-minded pursuit of efficiency and profitability. But this had led to what many saw as the destruction of the traditional countryside and the natural life that it supported.[42] A new ecological agenda emerged, aspects of which were already present in the inter-war years,[43] and that dovetailed closely with the wider conservation campaign for the built landscape. A plethora of books were published which not only charted the decline of the English countryside but also extolled elements of Nature from hedgerows to hares, and forests to foxes. There was a call for re-wilding and more broadly for a re-engagement with Nature. One writer, Tistan Gooley, produced a book on *How to Connect with Nature* (2014), full of practical tips and exercises on how this might be done: 'Spend ten minutes sketching a tree. Now write a short story about the experience of looking at the tree in this way', or 'Notice how the sun is due south in the middle of the day', but with no definition of what Nature is.[44] Richard Mabey, one of the most influential and prolific authors and broadcasters on the natural world, does not take us any nearer a definition, but in *Nature Cure* (2005) he is unequivocal in his belief about the centrality of Nature to our lives: 'we constantly refer back to the natural world to try and discover who we are. Nature is the most potent source of metaphors to describe and explain our behavior and feelings. It is the root and branch of much of our language'.[45] Such books rarely possess a formal religious content, but they do imbue their subjects with a tone sometimes bordering on the sacred, reflecting the pre-war trend by which God was being displaced for many by Nature as the source of belief and legitimacy.

It would be seriously misleading to represent the post-1970s as the death of modernism. The regular erection of ever-taller skyscrapers in city centres, and the extraordinary developments in communications, data storage and analysis systems are indicative of a society that welcomes and celebrates technological innovation and the new. At the same time there is also a parallel cultural stream that seeks to slake the thirst for the past and mitigate the deep anxiety at its destruction. So powerful is this that even relatively recent pasts – especially those that conform with a notion of an English national heritage – can be swept into its path, including industrial and military survivals, and the products of modernity and post-modernity themselves.[46] In 2018 '17 bold, playful, brightly coloured Post-Modern buildings of the late 1970s to 1990s' were listed by Historic England (the latest manifestation of the Royal Commission on the

---

[41] Borsay, *Image of Georgian Bath*, 168–206.
[42] Tom Williamson and Liz Bellamy, *Property and Landscape: A Social History of Land Ownership and the English Countryside* (London: George Philip, 1987), 208–28; Rackham, *History of the Countryside*, 25–30; Rowley, *English Landscape*, 245–68.
[43] Matless, *Landscape and Englishness*.
[44] Gooley, *How to Connect with Nature*, 43, 45.
[45] Richard Mabey, *Nature Cure* (London: Vintage, 2008), 19–20.
[46] Nigel Whiteley, 'Modern Architecture, Heritage and Englishness', *Architectural History* 38 (1995): 20–37.

Historical Monuments of England founded in 1908), adding to a developing list of post-war buildings recognized as part of the national heritage.[47] These more recent examples of heritage were not part of the pre-Second World War vision of what constituted the nation's past, but much of what now attracts the tourist's gaze in the landscape was in place by the 1930s. Take, for example, the reissuing for a contemporary audience of some of the guide and ruralist literature of the late-nineteenth and early-twentieth century, such as that of Richard Jefferies, W. H. Hudson, Edward Thomas, H. V. Morton and Richard Wyndham. A further sign is that the culture and infrastructure of recreational walking, such a feature of earlier developments, has resulted in recent decades in an efflorescence of waymarked trails and guide literature in town and country, and growing pressure for effective Right to Roam legislation in England.[48] The invention of the English landscape between 1700 and 1939 has left a legacy that continues to exert a huge influence on the way that the modern town-dweller and tourist shape their leisure lives.

---

[47] Historic England, 1980s Buildings Officially Become Heritage, 10 May 2018, https://historicengland.org.uk/whats-new/news/post-modern-buildings-listed/, accessed 16 Sep. 2020.

[48] The Right to Roam campaign estimates that the 2000 Countryside and Rights of Way Act gives a partial right to roam over about 8 per cent of England, https://www.righttoroam.org.uk, accessed 18 Sep. 2020.

Select bibliography

A Handbook for Travellers in Gloucestershire. 4th edn. London: John Murray, 1895.
A New Pictorial Guide to Oxford and District. 4th edn. London: Ward Lock, 1949.
Abelson, E. (ed.). *A Mirror of England: An Anthology of the Writings of H. J. Massingham (1888–1952)*. Bideford: Green Books, 1988.
Alfrey, Nicholas and Stephen Daniels (eds.). *Mapping and Landscape: Essays on Art and Cartography*. Nottingham: University Art Gallery and Castle Museum, 1990.
Andrews, Malcolm. *Landscape and Western Art*. Oxford: Oxford University Press, 1999.
Andrews, Malcolm. *The Search for the Picturesque: Landscape Aesthetics and Tourism in Britain, 1760–1800*. Aldershot: Scolar Press, 1989.
Andrews, William and Elsie M. Lang. *Old English Towns*. London: T.W. Laurie, 1923.
Ashton, J. R. and F. A. Stocks. *The Open Air Guide*. Manchester and London: John Heywood Ltd., 1928.
Austen, Jane. *Northanger Abbey*. 1817. Edited by R. W. Chapman. 3rd edn. Oxford: Oxford University Press, 1969.
Austin, Linda M. *Nostalgia in Transition, 1780–1917*. Charlottesville and London: University of Virginia Press, 2007.
Baddeley, M. J. B. *The Peak District of Derbyshire and Surrounding Counties*. 3rd edn. London: Dulau, 1884.
Baedeker, K. *Great Britain: A Handbook for Travellers*. 3rd edn. Leipzig: Baedeker, 1884.
Bailey, Peter. 'Ally Sloper's Half Day Holiday'. *History Workshop Journal* 16:1 (1983): 4–31.
Baker, J. H. *Land of 'The Gap'*. Oxford: Basil Blackwell, 1937.
Baker, S. K. (ed.). *Camping on the Wye: The Tale of a Trip along the Wye from Whitney in Herefordshire to Chepstow in 1892*. Almeley: Logaston Press, 2003.
Barclay, Edgar. *The Ruined Temple Stonehenge*. London: St Catherine Press, [1911].
Baring-Gould, Sabine. *Devon*. London: Methuen, 1907.
Barrell, John. *The Dark Side of the Landscape. The Rural Poor in English Painting, 1730–1840*. Cambridge: Cambridge University Press, 1980.
Barrett, J. *A Description of Malvern and Its Environs*. Worcester: T. Holl, 1796.
Bath: Guides, Newspapers, Directories. 3rd edn. Bath: Bath Municipal Libraries, 1988.
Batsford, Harry. *How to See the Country*. London: Batsford, 1940.
Beck's Guide to Leamington and the Surrounding District. 14th edn. Leamington, J. Beck, 1868.
Beck's Leamington Guide; Containing also, a Description of the Neighbourhood, and a Directory. 6th edn. Leamington: J. Beck, 1840.
Beckett, John. *Writing Local History*. Manchester: Manchester University Press, 2007.
Belloc, Hilaire. *The Historic Thames*. 1907. London: Michael Joseph, 1988.
Betjeman, John. *English Cities and Small Towns*. London: Collins, 1943.
Betjeman, John. *Coming Home: An Anthology of His Prose, 1920–1977*. Selected and introduced by Candida Lycett Green. London: Vintage, 1998.
Bevan, G. P. *Tourist's Guide to Warwickshire*. London: Stanford, 1882.
Bingham, Jane. *The Cotswolds: A Cultural History*. Oxford: Signal Books, 2009.

Black's Guide to Dorsetshire. 6th edn. Edinburgh: A. & C. Black, 1872.
Black's Guide to Warwickshire. 6th edn. Edinburgh: A. & C. Black, 1881.
Black's Picturesque Guide to the English Lakes. 3rd edn. Edinburgh: A. & C. Black, 1846.
Blunden, Edmund. *English Villages.* London: Collins, 1941.
Bolitho, Hector (ed.). *A Batsford Century. The Record of a Hundred Years of Publishing and Bookselling, 1843–1943.* London: Batsford, 1943.
Borsay, Peter. 'The Rise of the Promenade: The Social and Cultural Use of Space in the English Provincial Town'. *British Journal for Eighteenth-Century Studies* 9 (1986): 125–40.
Borsay, Peter. 'Urban Development in the Age of Defoe'. In *Britain in the First Age of Party, 1680–1750. Essays Presented to Geoffrey Holmes,* edited by Clyve Jones. 195–219. London: Hambledon, 1987.
Borsay, Peter. *The English Urban Renaissance: Culture and Society in the Provincial Town, 1660–1770.* Oxford: Oxford University Press, 1989.
Borsay, Peter. 'Fat Sources and Big Ideas: Society, Enlightenment, and the Town', *Journal of Urban History* 24:5 (1998): 647–52.
Borsay, Peter. 'Early Modern Urban Landscapes, 1540–1800'. In *The English Urban Landscape,* edited by Philip J. Waller. 99–124. Oxford: Oxford University Press, 2000.
Borsay, Peter. 'Health and Leisure Resorts, 1700–1840'. In *The Cambridge Urban History of Britain. Volume III. 1540–1840,* edited by Peter Clark. 775–804. Cambridge: Cambridge University Press, 2000.
Borsay, Peter. *The Image of Georgian Bath, 1700–2000. Towns, Heritage and History.* Oxford: Oxford University Press, 2000.
Borsay, Peter. 'The Culture of Improvement'. In *The Eighteenth Century, 1688–1815,* edited by Paul Langford. 183–212. Oxford: Oxford University Press, 2002.
Borsay, Peter. 'Urban Life and Culture'. In *A Companion to Eighteenth-Century Britain,* edited by H. T. Dickinson. 196–208. Oxford: Blackwell Publishers, 2002.
Borsay, Peter. *A History of Leisure.* Palgrave: Houndmills, 2006.
Borsay, Peter. 'New Approaches to Social History. Myth, Memory and Place: Monmouth and Bath, 1700–1900'. *Journal of Social History* 39:3 (2006): 867–89.
Borsay, Peter, 'Le développement des villes balnéaires dans l'Angleterre géorgienne'. In *Les villes Balnéaires d'Europe occidentale du XVIIIe siècle à nos jours,* edited by Yves Pettert-Gentil, Alain Lottin and Jean-Pierre Poussin. 13–34. Paris: PUPS, 2008.
Borsay, Peter. 'The Georgian House: The Making of a Heritage Icon'. In *Valuing Historic Environments,* edited by Lisanne Gibson and John Pendlebury. 157–78. Farnham: Ashgate, 2009.
Borsay, Peter and John Walton (eds.). *Resorts and Ports: European Seaside Towns since 1700.* Bristol: Channel View, 2011.
Borsay, Peter. 'Promenade en bord de ville: espace périphérique et activité récréative dans la ville anglaise at galloises, de 1700 à 1900'. In *Esthétiques de la Ville Britannique (XVIIIe-XIXe siècles),* edited by Pierre Dubois and Alexis Tadié. 83–104. Paris: PUPS, 2012.
Borsay, Peter. 'Town or Country? British Spas and the Urban-Rural Interface'. *Journal of Tourism History* 4:2 (2012): 155–69.
Borsay, Peter. 'A Room with a View: Visualizing the Seaside, c. 1750–1914'. *Transactions of the Royal Historical Society* 6th ser., 23 (2013): 175–201.
Borsay, Peter. 'Nature, the Past and the English Town: A Counter-Cultural History'. *Urban History* 44:1 (2017): 27–43.
Bourne, Henry. *Antiquitates Vulgares: Or, the Antiquities of the Common People.* Newcastle: J. White, 1725.

Bowden, Mark. *The Malvern Hills: An Ancient Landscape*. London: English Heritage, 2009.
Brabant, F. G. *Sussex*. 3rd edn. London: Methuen, 1910.
Brabant, F. G. *Oxfordshire*. 3rd edn. London: Methuen, 1919.
Bradley, A. G. *In the March and Borderland of Wales*. London: Constable, 1905.
Bradley, A. G. *Avon and Shakespeare's Country*. London: Methuen, 1910.
Bradley, A. G. *The Wye*. London: A. & C. Black, 1910.
Bradley, A. G. *An Old Gate of England. Rye, Romney Marsh, and the Western Cinque Ports*. London: Robert Scott, 1918.
Bradshaw's Descriptive Railway Handbook. 1863. Oxford: Old House, 2012.
Brodie, Allan and Gary Winter. *England's Seaside Resorts*. Swindon: English Heritage, 2007.
Brodie, Allan and Matthew Whitfield. *Blackpool's Seaside Heritage*. Swindon: English Heritage, 2014.
Browne, J. P. *Map Cover Art: A Pictorial History of Ordnance Survey Cover Illustrations*. Southampton: Ordnance Survey, 1991.
Bryant, Chad, Arthur Burns and Paul Readman. *Walking Histories, 1800–1914*. Basingstoke: Palgrave, 2016.
Buckland, William and William Daniel Conybeare. *Ten Plates Comprising a Plan, Sections, and Views, Representing the Changes Produced on the Coast of East Devon, between Axmouth and Lyme Regis by the Subsidence of the Land and Elevation of the Bottom of the Sea, on the 26th December, 1839, and 3rd of February, 1840*. London: John Murray, 1840.
Budden, Charles W. *English Gothic Churches*. London: Batsford, 1927.
Burgess, J. Tom. *Historic Warwickshire: Its Legendary Lore, Traditionary Stories, and Romantic Episodes*. London: Simpkin, Marshall & Co., 1873.
Burke, Thomas. *The English Townsman: As He Was and as He Is*. London: Batstford, 1946.
Burrow, C. F. Severn. *A Little City Set on a Hill: The Story of Malvern*. Malvern: Priory Press, 1948.
Cannadine, David. 'The First Hundred Years'. In *The National Trust: The Next Hundred Years*, edited by Howard Newby. 11–31. London: The National Trust, 1995.
Carr, E. Donald. *A Night in the Snow, or, a Struggle for Life*. London: James Nisbet & Co., 1865.
Carrington, Noel (ed.). *Broadway and the Cotswolds*. Birmingham: Kynoch Press, 1933.
Castree, Noel. *Making Sense of Nature: Representations, Politics and Democracy*. Abingdon: Routledge, 2014.
Clark, Geoffrey and W. Harding Thompson. *The Dorset Landscape*. London: A. & C. Black, 1935.
Clark, Geoffrey and W. Harding Thompson. *The Sussex Landscape*. London: A. & C. Black, 1935.
Clarke, David. *The Broads in Print*. Norwich: Joy and David Clarke, 2010.
Close, Charles. *The Map of England: Or about England with an Ordnance Map*. London: Peter Davies, 1938.
Cobb, Ruth, *Country Town Story*. London: John Crowther, 1946.
Cobbett, William. *Rural Rides in Surrey, Kent and Sussex …* London: A. Cobbett, 1853.
Cole, Beverley and Richard Durack. *Happy as a Sand-Boy: Early Railway Posters*. London: HMSO, 1990.
Cole, Beverley and Richard Durack. *Railway Posters, 1923–47*. York: Laurence King, 1992.
Conlin, Jonathan. *Evolution and the Victorians: Science, Culture and Politics in Darwin's Britain*. Bloomsbury: London, 2014.

Contour Road Book of England. London: Gall and Inglis, 1906.
Conway, Hazel. *People's Parks: The Development and Design of Victorian Parks in Britain*. Cambridge: Cambridge University Press, 1991.
Corbin, Alain. *The Lure of the Sea: The Discovery of the Seaside in the Western World*. Cambridge: Cambridge University Press, 1994.
Corfield, Penelope. *The Impact of English Towns, 1700–1800*. Oxford: Oxford University Press, 1982.
Cornish, C. J. *Wild England of Today and the Wild Life in It*. London: Seeley and Co., 1895.
Cornish, Vaughan. *The Scenery of England: A Study of Harmonious Grouping of Town and Country*. London: Alexander Maclehose & Co., 1932.
Cowles, Frederick. *This Is England*. London: F. Muller, 1946.
Cowles, Frederick. *Vagabond Pilgrimage. Being the Record of a Journey from East Anglia to the West of England*. London: Travel Book Club, 1950.
Croll, Andy. *Barry Island: The Making of a Seaside Playground, c. 1795–c. 1960*. Cardiff: University of Wales Press, 2020.
Crossing, William. *Amid Devonia's Alps: Or, Wanderings & Adventures on Dartmoor*. London: Simpkin, Marshall & Co., 1888.
Cunningham, Hugh. *Time. Work and Leisure: Life Changes in England since 1700*. Manchester: Manchester University Press, 2016.
Cyclists Touring Club: Handbook and Guide. London: Cyclists' Touring Club, 1923.
Cyclists' Touring Club Handbook. London: Cyclists' Touring Club, 1931.
Darling, E. Moore. *Seeing Shropshire*. Shrewsbury: Adnitt & Naunton Ltd., 1937.
Darwin, Charles. *The Origin of Species*. 1859. London: Penguin, 1978.
Daunton, Martin (ed.). *The Cambridge Urban History of Britain Volume III. 1840–1950*. Cambridge: Cambridge University Press, 2000.
Davies, G. Christopher. *The Handbook to the Rivers and Broads of Norfolk and Suffolk*. 11th edn. London: Jarrold & Sons, 1888.
Defoe, Daniel. *A Tour thro' the Whole Island of Great Britain*. 3 vols. London: G. Strahan, 1724–6.
Delicata, Aldo and Beverley Cole. *Speed to the West. Great Western Publicity and Posters, 1923–1947*. Harrow Weald: Capital Transport, 2000.
Ditchfield, P. H. *Our English Villages: Their Stories and Antiquities*. London: Methuen, 1889.
Ditchfield, P. H. *The Story of Our English Towns*. London: Methuen, 1897.
Ditchfield, P. H. *Picturesque English Cottages and Their Doorway Gardens*. Philadelphia: John C. Winston, 1905.
Ditchfield, P. H. *The Charm of the English Village*. London: Batsford, 1908.
Ditchfield, P. H. *The Manor Houses of England*. London: Batsford, 1910.
Ditchfield, P. H. (ed.). *Memorials of Old Gloucestershire*. London: George Allen, 1911.
Ditchfield, P. H. *The Village Church*. London: Methuen, 1914.
Ditchfield, P. H. *Byways in Berkshire and the Cotswolds*. London: R. Scott, 1920.
Ditchfield, P. H. *Old Village Life; or, Glimpses of Village Life through all the Ages*. London: Methuen, 1920.
Dixon-Scott, J. *Stratford on Avon with Leamington and Warwick*. London: A. & C. Black, 1923.
Dixon-Scott, J. *Hereford and the Wye Valley*. London: The Homeland Association, 1929.
Doyle, Arthur Conan. *The Hound of the Baskervilles*. 1902. Edited by Francis O'Gorman. Peterborough, OT: Broadview Press, 2006.

Drake, Francis. *Eboracum: Or, the History and Antiquities of the City of York*. London: William Bowyer, 1736.
Dyos, H. J. and Derek Aldcroft. *British Transport: An Economic Survey from the Seventeenth Century to the Twentieth*. Leicester: Leicester University Press, 1969.
Eastwood, David. *Government and Community in the English Provinces, 1700–1870*. London: Macmillan, 1997.
Engels, Friedrich. *The Condition of the Working Class in England in 1844*. 1892. Edited by V. G. Kiernan. London: Penguin, 1987.
Erwood, Frank C. Elliston. *The Pilgrim's Road*. London: Frederick Warne & Co., 1910.
Evans, E. J. and J. Richards. *A Social History of Britain in Postcards 1870–1930*. London: Longman, 1980.
Evans, H. A. *Highways and Byways in Oxford and the Cotswolds*. London: Macmillan, 1908.
Feigel, Lara and Alexandra Harris (eds.). *Modernism on Sea: Art and Culture at the British Seaside*. Oxford: Peter Lang, 2009.
Fenton, E. (ed.). *A Brief Jolly Change: The Diaries of Henry Peerless, 1891–1920*. Charlbury: Day Books, 2003.
Finnemore, John. *Peeps at Many Lands: England*. 2nd edn. London: A. & C. Black, 1912.
Fleure, H. J. *A Natural History of Man in Britain*. London: Collins, 1951.
Foord, Edward. *Gloucester, Tewkesbury and District*. London: J. M. Dent & Sons., 1925.
Forster, E. M. *Howard's End*. 1910. Harmondsworth: Penguin, 1975.
Fox, Cyril. *The Personality of Britain: Its Influence on Inhabitant and Invader in Prehistoric and Early Historic Times*. Cardiff: National Museum Wales, 1932.
Fraser, Maxwell. *Companion into Worcestershire*. London: Methuen, 1939.
Fretton, William. *Geography of Warwickshire*. London: Collins, 1872–4.
Gard, Robin (ed.). *The Observant Traveller: Diaries of Travel in England, Wales and Scotland in the County Record Offices of England and Wales*. London: H.M.S.O., 1989.
Garrett, J. J. *From a Cotswold Height*. Cheltenham: J. J. Banks & Son, 1919.
Gernsheim, Helmut. *The History of Photography from the Earliest Use of the Camera Obscura in the Eleventh Century Up to 1914*. London: Oxford University Press, 1955.
Gibbs, J. A. *A Cotswold Village, or, Country Life and Pursuits in Gloucestershire*. London: Murray, 1898.
Gibbs, J. A. *Cotswold Country: A Survey of Limestone England from the Dorset Coast to Lincolnshire*. London: Batsford, 1937.
Gill, Stephen. *The Prelude*. Cambridge: Cambridge University Press, 1991.
Gilpin, William. *Observations on the River Wye*. London: R. Blamire, 1782.
Gilpin, William. *Observations on the River Wye*. 1782. Introduction by Richard Humphreys. London: Pallas Athene, 2005.
Gilpin, William. *Remarks on Forest Scenery and Other Woodland Views*. 2 vols. London: R. Blamire, 1791.
Girouard, Mark. *The English Town*. New Haven and London: Yale University Press, 1990.
Godfrey, Walter H. *Our Building Inheritance*. London: Faber & Faber, 1944.
Gooley, Tristan. *How to Connect with Nature*. London: Macmillan, 2014.
Gotch, J. A. *The English Home from Charles I to George IV*. London: Batsford, 1918.
Goulden, R. J. *Kent Town Guides, 1763–1900*. London: British Library, 1995.
Gray, Fred. *Designing the Seaside*. London: Reaktion, 2006.
Green, Kenneth H. *The Cotswolds: An Introduction*. Bristol: Garland Press, 1947.
Greenslade, M. W. 'Introduction: County History'. In *English County Histories: A Guide*, edited by C. R. J. Currie and C. P. Lewis. 9–25. Stroud: Alan Sutton, 1994.

Grindrod, C. F. *Malvern: What to See and Where to Go*. Malvern: Thompson: 1904.
Guide to the Cotswolds. 2nd edn. London: Ward Lock, 1948.
Hall, S. C. and A. M. *The Book of the Thames from Its Rise to Its Fall*. London: James S. Virtue, 1859.
Hannett, John. *The Forest of Arden, Its Towns, Villages and Hamlets*. London: Simpkin, Marshall and Co., 1863.
Hardy, Thomas. *The Return of the Native*. 1878. Penguin: Harmondsworth, 1985.
Hardy, Thomas. *The Life and Death of the Mayor of Casterbridge: A Story of a Man of Character*. 1886. London: Macmillan, 1966.
Hardy, Thomas. *Tess of the D'Urbervilles*. Edited by Simon Gatrell and Juliet Grindle. 1891. Oxford: Oxford University Press, 2005.
Harley, Brian. *Ordnance Survey Maps: A Descriptive Manual*. Southampton: Ordnance Survey, 1975.
Harman, Peter M. *The Culture of Nature in Britain, 1680–1860*. New Haven and London: Yale University Press, 2009.
Harper, Charles G. *Summer Days in Shakespeare Land*. London: Chapman & Hall, 1912.
Harris, Alexandra. *Romantic Moderns: English Writers, Artists and the Imagination from Virginia Woolf to John Piper*. London: Thames & Hudson, 2010.
Harrison, W. Jerome. *Shakespeare-Land*. Edited by A. Crosby. Warwick: Warwickshire Books, 1995.
Harvey, L. A. and D. St Leger-Gordon. *Dartmoor*. London: Collins, 1953.
Hawes, Louis. *Presences of Nature: British Landscape 1780–1830*. New Haven: Yale Center for British Art, 1982.
Heath, Charles. *The Excursion down the Wye*. Monmouth: Charles Heath, 1808.
Heath, Charles. *Descriptive Accounts of the Kymin Pavilion and Beaulieu Grove*. 1809. repr. Monmouth, 2002.
Heathcote, David. *A Shell Eye on England: The Shell County Guides 1934–1984*. Faringdon: Libri Publishing, 2011.
Hebron, Stephen. *The Romantics and the British Landscape*. London: The British Library, 2006.
Hembry, Phyllis. *The English Spa, 1560–1815: A Social History*. London: Athlone, 1990.
Hewitt, John. *The Shell Poster Book*. London: Profile Books, 1998.
Hewitt, N. 'Encountering Nature: The Tyneside Naturalists' Field Club and the North East, 1846–1900'. M.Res thesis, Northumbria University, 2008.
Hewitt, Rachel. *Map of a Nation: A Biography of the Ordnance Survey*. London: Granta Books, 2010.
Hey, David (ed.). *The Oxford Companion to Family and Local History*. 2nd edn. Oxford: Oxford University Press, 2008.
Hill, C. W. *Picture Postcards*. Princes Risborough: Shire, 1987.
Hissey, J. John. *An English Holiday with Car and Camera*. London: Macmillan & Co., 1908.
Hissey, J. John. *The Charm of the Road. England and Wales*. London: Macmillan & Co., 1910.
Hockin, J. R. *A. On Foot in Berkshire*. London: A. Maclehouse & Co., 1934.
Holland, Clive. *Things Seen in Shakespeare's Country*. London: Seeley Service & Co. Ltd., 1927.
Hollett, David. *The Pioneer Ramblers 1850–1940*. North Wales Area of the Ramblers' Association, 2002.
Holmes, Edric. *London's Countryside*. London: R. Scott, 1927.
Home, G. *Through the Chilterns to the Fens*. London: J. M. Dent & Sons, 1925.

Hoskins, W. G. *Midland England: A Survey of the Country between the Chilterns and the Trent*. London: Batsford, 1949.
Hoskins, W. G. *The Making of the English Landscape*. London: Hodder & Stoughton, 1970.
Houghton, F. T. S. *Worcestershire*. London: Methuen & Co. Ltd., 1922.
Howells, W. D. *London Films and Certain Delightful English Towns*. London: Harper & Brothers, 1905.
Hudson, Kenneth. *A Social History of Archaeology*. London: Macmillan, 1981.
Hudson, W. H. *Nature in Downland*. New York: Longmans, Green, 1901.
Hudson, W. H. *Afoot in England*. London: Hutchinson & Co., 1909.
Hunt, Peter (ed.). *Devon's Age of Elegance: Described by the Diaries of the Reverend John Swete, Lady Paterson, and Miss Mary Cornish*. Exeter: Devon Books, 1984.
Hurle, Pamela. *The Malvern Hills. A Hundred Years of Conservation*. Chichester: Phillimore, 1984.
Hutton, Edward. *Highways and Byways in Somerset*. London: Macmillan, 1912.
Hutton, Edward. *Highways and Byways in Gloucestershire*. London: Macmillan, 1932.
Hutton, W. H. *By Thames and Cotswold: Sketches of the Country*. 2nd edn. Westminster: A. Constable, 1908.
Hutton, W. H. *Highways and Byways in Shakespeare's Country*. London: Macmillan, 1914.
Ingram, John. *The Haunted Homes and Family Traditions of Great Britain*. 3rd edn. London: W. H. Allen & Co., 1886.
James, Henry. *English Hours*. 1905. Oxford: Oxford University Press, 1981.
Jefferies, Richard. *The Story of My Heart: My Autobiography*. 2nd edn. London: Longmans, Green, 1891.
Jefferies, Richard. *The Hills and the Vale*. London: Duckworth, 1909.
Jenkins, Jennifer and Patrick James. *From Acorn to Oak Tree: The Growth of the National Trust, 1895–1984*. London: Macmillan 1994.
Jenkinson, A. S. *In Search of Romantic Britain*. London: A. Barron, 1936.
Jerome, Jerome K. *Three Men in a Boat*. 1889. Harmondsworth: Penguin 1957.
Joad, C. E. M. *The Untutored Townsman's Invasion of the Country*. London: Faber & Faber, 1946.
Johnson, Walter (ed.). *Journals of Gilbert White*. Newton Abbot: David & Charles, 1970.
Jones, F. *The Holy Wells of Wales*. Cardiff: University of Wales, 1954.
Jones, M. M. *The Lookers-Out of Worcestershire*. Trowbridge: The Worcestershire Naturalists' Club, 1980.
Kearsey, E. Maslin, *Malvern and District*. London: Homeland Association, 1932.
Keating, P. J. (ed.). *Into Unknown England, 1866–1913. Selections from the Social Explorers*. Glasgow: Fontana, 1976.
Lambourne, Lionel. *Victorian Painting*. London: Phaidon Press, 1999.
Lawford, Lucy Amelia. *Dear Emma. Her Account of Her Stay in Tenby and the Mumbles between 1873 and 1875*. Edited by Alan Douglas. Privately printed, 1998.
Lees, E. *Picture of Nature in the Silurian Region around the Malvern Hills and Vale of Severn*. Malvern: H.W. Lamb, 1856.
Lees, E. *The Botany of Worcestershire*. Worcester: H.W. Lamb, 1867.
Lord, Peter. *The Visual Culture of Wales: Industrial Society*. Cardiff: University of Wales Press, 2003.
Lowenthal, David. 'British History and the English Landscape'. *Rural History* 2:2 (1991): 208–30.
Lyell, Charles. *Principles of Geology, or, The Modern Changes of the Earth and Its Inhabitants Considered as Illustrative of Geology*. 12th edn. London: John Murray, 1875.

Mabey, Richard. *Gilbert White: A Biography of the Naturalist and Author of the Natural History of Selborne*. London: Pimlico, 1999.
Macdonell, A. G. *England, Their England*. 1933. London: Macmillan, 1967.
Mackinder, H. J. *Britain and the British Seas*. London: William Heinemann, 1902.
Mais, S. P. B. *Glorious Devon*. London: Great Western Railway Co., 1928.
Mais, S. P. B. *See England First*. London: Richards, 1933.
Mais, S. P. B. *Round about England*. London: Richards, 1935.
Mais, S. P. B. *Highways and Byways in the Welsh Marches*. London: Macmillan & Co., 1939.
Mais, S. P. B. *Hills of the South*. London: Southern Railway Company, 1939.
Making History: Antiquaries in Britain. London: Royal Academy, 2006.
Mandler, Peter. *The Fall and Rise of the Stately Home*. New Haven and London: Yale University Press, 1997.
Manners, William. *Revolution: How the Bicycle Reinvented Modern Britain*. Richmond: Duckworth, 2018.
Massingham, H. J. *Heritage of Man*. London: Jonathan Cape, 1929.
Massingham, H. J. *Wold without End*. London: Cobden-Sanderson, 1932.
Massingham, H. J. *Chiltern Country*. 2nd edn. London: Batsford, 1943.
Matless, David. *Landscape and Englishness*. London: Reaktion, 1998.
McAllister, Gilbert and Elizabeth Glen (eds.). *Homes, Towns and Countryside: A Practical Plan for Britain*. London: Batsford, 1945.
McCarthy, Fiona, *William Morris: A Life for Our Time*. London: Faber & Faber, 1994.
McKendrick, Neil, John Brewer and J. H. Plumb (eds.). *The Birth of a Consumer Society: The Commercialization of Eighteenth-Century England*. London: Hutchinson, 1983.
Mee, Arthur. *Buckinghamshire: Country of the Chilterns*. London: Hodder & Hodder, 1947.
Mee, Arthur. *Warwickshire: Shakespeare's County*. London: Hodder & Stoughton, 1949.
Milton, Patricia. *The Discovery of Dartmoor: A Wild and Wondrous Region*. Chichester: Phillimore, 2006.
Moir, Esther. *The Discovery of Britain. The English Tourists, 1540–1840*. London: Routledge & Kegan Paul, 1964.
Moorhouse, Sydney. *Walking Tours and Hostels in England*. London: Country Life, 1936.
Morgan, F. C. 'An Outline of the History of the Woolhope Club, 1851 to 1951'. In *Herefordshire: Its Natural History, Archaeology and History*. 1954. repr. East Ardsley: S. R. Publishing, 1971.
Morgan, D. Francis. *Hiking*. Plymouth: Mayflower Press, 1927.
Morris, John E. and Humfrey Jordan. *An Introduction to the Study of Local History and Antiquities*. London: George Routledge and Sons, 1910.
Morris, William. *News from Nowhere*. 1890. Oxford: Oxford University Press, 2009.
Morton, H. V. *In Search of England*. London: Methuen, 1927.
Morton, H. V. *The Call of England*. 9th edn. London: Methuen, 1932.
Morton, H. V. *I Saw Two Englands*. London: Methuen, 1942.
Muirhead, Findlay. *England*. 3rd edn. London: Macmillan & Co., 1930.
Murchison, Roderick. *The Silurian System ... in Two Parts. Part I*. London: John Murray, 1839.
Murphy, Graham. *Founders of the National Trust*. London: Christopher Helm, 1987.
Murray, A. D. *Burrows Guide to Wessex: The Hardy Country*. Cheltenham: E. J. Burrow, n.d.
Murray, Alison. *The Cotswolds*. 2nd edn. Gloucester: British Publishing Co., 1937.
Newman, Bernard. *British Journey*. London: R. Hale, 1945.
Newth, J. D. *Gloucestershire*. London: A. & C. Black, 1927.

O'Connell, Sean. *The Car in British Society: Class, Gender and Motoring, 1896–1939*. Manchester: Manchester University Press, 1998.
Oliver, Richard. *Ordnance Survey Maps: A Concise Guide for Historians*. London: Charles Close Society, 1993.
Olivier, Edith. *Country Moods and Tenses*. London: Batsford, 1942.
Osborne, A. B. *Old-World England: Impressions of a Stranger*. London: Nash and Grayson, 1924.
Ousby, Ian. *The Englishman's England*. Cambridge: Cambridge University Press, 1990.
Owen, Sue. et al. (eds.). *Rivers and the British Landscape*. Lancaster: Carnegie Publishing, 2005.
Page, Hugh. *Rambles in the Chiltern Country*. London: Great Western Railway, 1932.
Page, Hugh. *Rambles in Shakespeare Land and the Cotswolds*. London: Great Western Railway, 1933.
Page, Hugh. *Rambles and Walking Tours in the Wye Valley*. London: Great Western Railway, 1938.
Page, Hugh. *Rambles and Walking Tours in South Devon*. London: Great Western Railway, 1939.
Parry, Graham. *The Trophies of Time: English Antiquarians of the Seventeenth Century*. Oxford: Oxford University Press, 1995.
Payne, Christiana. *Where the Sea Meets the Land: Artists on the Coast in Nineteenth-Century Britain*. Bristol: Sanson & Co., 2007.
Pevsner, Nikolaus. *The Englishness of English Art*. New York: Frederick A. Praeger, 1956.
Pictorial and Descriptive Guide to Bath. London: Ward Lock, 1909–10.
Pictorial and Descriptive Guide to Cromer. 10th edn. London: Ward Lock, 1939.
Picture of Lyme-Regis and Environs. Lyme Regis: Tucker and Toms, 1817.
Piehler, H. A. *England for Everyman*. London: J. M. Dent & Sons, 1933.
Piggott, Stuart. 'The Origins of the English County Archaeological Societies'. *Transactions of the Birmingham and Warwickshire Archaeological Society* 86 (1974): 1–15.
Piggott, Stuart. *Ancient Britons and the Antiquarian Imagination: Ideas from the Renaissance to the Regency*. London: Thames & Hudson, 1989.
Pimlott, J. A. R. *The Englishman's Holiday: A Social History*. London: Faber & Faber, 1947.
Porter, Roy. *The Making of Geology: Earth Science in Britain, 1660–1815*. Cambridge: Cambridge University Press, 1977.
Power, Charles. *English Medieval Architecture in Two Parts*. London: Talbot & Co., 1912.
Priestley, J. B. *English Journey*. London: William Heinemann Ltd., 1934.
Prioleau, John. *Car and Country: Week-End Signpost to the Open Road*. London: J. M. Dent & Sons, 1929.
Prioleau, John. *Enchanted Ways*. London: J. M. Dent & Sons, 1933.
Pryor, Francis. *The Making of the British Landscape: How We Have Transformed the Land, from Prehistory to Today*. London: Allen Lane, 2010.
Quennell, Marjorie and H. B. Charles. *The Good New Days*. London: Batsford, 1935.
Rackham, Oliver. *The History of the Countryside*. London: Dent, 1986.
Randall, J. *The Tourist's Guide to Bridgnorth*. Bridgnorth, Evan: Edkins & McMichael, 1875.
Raymond, Walter. *A Short History of Somerset*. 3rd edn. London: Methuen, 1923.
Readman, Paul. *Storied Ground: Landscape and the Shaping of English National Identity*. Cambridge: Cambridge University Press, 2018.
Roberts, George. *The History and Antiquities of the Borough of Lyme Regis and Charmouth*. London: Samuel Bagster, 1834.

Roberts, George. *An Account of the Mighty Landslip of Downlands and Bindon*. Lyme: Daniel Dunster, 1840.
Robinson, W. *The English Flower Garden*. 13th edn. New York: Charles Scribner, 1921.
Robinson's Popular Brighton Directory. Brighton: A.M. Robinson and Son, 1886.
Ross, J. H. 'Founders of the Woolhope Club'. In *A Herefordshire Miscellany: Commemorating 150 Years of the Woolhope Club*, edited by David Whitehead and John Eisel. Hereford: Lapidge Publications, 2000.
Rouse, Clive. *The Old Towns of England*. London: Batsford, 1936.
Rowley, Trevor. *The English Landscape in the Twentieth Century*. London: Hambledon Continuum, 2006.
Rudder, Samuel. *A New History of Gloucestershire*. Cirencester: Samuel Rudder, 1779.
Rudge, Thomas. *The History of the County of Gloucester*. 2 vols. Gloucester, 1803.
Ryan, Ernest K. W. *The Thames from the Towpath. An Account of an Expedition on Foot from Putney to Thames Head*. London: The Saint Catherine Press, 1938.
Saunders, Gill (ed.). *Recording Britain*. London: V&A Publishing, 2011.
Scarfe, Norman (ed. and transl.). *Innocent Espionage: The La Rochefoucauld Brothers' Tour of England in 1785*. Woodbridge: Boydell Press, 1995.
Schama, Simon. *Landscape and Memory*. London: Fontana Press, 1996.
Scharf, Aaron. *Pioneers of Photography: An Album of Pictures and Words*. London: BBC, 1975.
Scott, Clement. *Poppy-Land: Papers Descriptive of Scenery on the East Coast*. London: Carson and Comeford, 1886.
Seaside Watering Places. Being a Guide to Strangers in Search of a Suitable Place in Which to Spend Their Holidays. London: L. Upcott Gill, 1900–1.
Sharp, Thomas. *English Panorama*. London: Architectural Press, 1950.
Shears, W. S. *This England: A Book of the Shires and Counties*. 2nd edn. London: Right Book Club, 1938.
Shoesmith, R. *Alfred Watkins: A Herefordshire Man*. Little Logaston: Logaston Press, 1990.
Shoesmith, R. *Hereford: History and Guide*. Stroud: Alan Sutton, 1992.
Simmons, Jack. 'The Writing of English County History'. In *English County Historians*, edited by Jack Simmons. Wakefield: EP Publishing, 1978.
Simmons, Jack and Gordon Biddle. *The Oxford Companion to British Railway History from 1603 to the 1990s*. Oxford: Oxford University Press, 1997.
Smith, C. Fox. *The Thames*. London: Methuen, 1931.
Snell, F. J. *A Book of Exmoor*.1923. Tiverton: Halsgrove, 2002.
Solnit, Rebecca. *Wanderlust: A History of Walking*. London: Granta Books, 2014.
Stamp, Laurence Dudley. *Britain's Structure and Scenery*. London: Collins, 1946.
Stevens, H. Beresford. *Picturesque Towns and Villages of England and Wales*. London: J Burrow, 1928.
Stibbons, Peter and David Cleveland. *Poppyland; Strands of Norfolk History*. 2nd edn. North Walsham: Poppyland, 1985.
Suffling, Ernest R. *The Land of the Broads*. Stratford: B. Perry, 1895.
Sweet, Rosemary. *Antiquaries: The Discovery of the Past in Eighteenth-Century Britain*. London: Hambledon and London, 2004.
Symonds, W. S. *Old Stones: A Series of Geological Notes on the Plutonic, Volcanic, Laurentian, Cambrian, Silurian, and Devonian Rocks in the Neighbourhood of Malvern*. London: Simpkin, Marshall & Co., 1880.
Taylor, John. *A Dream of England: Landscape, Photography and the Tourist's Imagination*. Manchester: Manchester University Press, 1994.

Thacker, Fred S. *The Thames Highway*. 2 vols. London: Fred S. Thacker, 1914 and 1920.
The Autocar Road Book. 4 vols. London: Methuen, 1910.
The British Heritage: The People, Their Crafts and Achievements as Recorded in Their Buildings and on the Face of the Countryside. London: Odhams Press, 1948.
The Improved Bath Guide; Or Picture of Bath and Its Environs. Bath: Wood, 1812.
The Legacy of England. London: Batsford, 1935.
The Modern Cyclist; a Handbook for Cyclists and Other Roadfarers. 1923. Oxford: Old House, 2013.
The New Bath Guide; or Useful Pocket Companion. Bath: J. Savage, 1809.
The Original Bath Guide, Historical and Descriptive. Bath: William Lewis, 1876.
The Original Bath Guide. Bath: Meyler & Son, 1840.
The Visitor's Guide to Malvern. Malvern: H.W. Lamb, 1862.
Thomas, Edward. *Richard Jefferies; His Life and Work*. Boston: Little, Brown and Co., 1909.
Thomas, Edward. *The South Country*. London: J. M. Dent & Co., 1909.
Thomas, K. V. *Religion and the Decline of Magic*. Harmondsworth: Penguin, 1978.
Thomas, K. V. *Man and the Natural World*. London: Penguin, 1984.
Thomas, William Beach. *The English Landscape*. London: Country Life, 1938.
Thompson, M. W. *General Pitt-Rivers: Evolution and Archaeology in the Nineteenth Century*. Bradford-on-Avon: Moonraker Press, 1977.
Thompson, M. W. (ed.). *The Journeys of Sir Richard Colt Hoare: Through Wales and England, 1793–1810*. Gloucester: Alan Sutton, 1983.
Through the Window: Paddington to Penzance. London: J. Burrow & Co. Ltd., 1927.
Timmins, Henry Thornhill. *Nooks and Corners of Shropshire*. London: Elliot Stock, 1899.
Timmins, Henry Thornill. *Nooks and Corners of Herefordshire*. 1892. Hereford: Lapridge Publications, 1992.
Timperley, H. W. *Ridge Way Country*. London: J. M. Dent & Sons, 1935.
Tompkins, Herbert W. *Stratford-on-Avon*. London: J.M. Dent & Co., 1904.
Travis, John. *An Illustrated History of Lynton and Lynmouth*. Derby: Breedon Books, 1995.
Travis, John. *Lynton and Lynmouth: Glimpses of the Past*. Derby: Breedon Books, 1997.
Treuherz, Julian. *Victorian Painting*. London: Thames & Hudson, 1993.
Trezise, Simon. *The West Country as a Literary Invention: Putting Fiction in Its Place*. Exeter: University of Exeter Press, 2000.
Turle, James. *Out of Doors in England*. London: Constable & Co. Ltd., 1937.
Urry, John. *The Tourist Gaze: Leisure and Travel in Contemporary Societies*. 2nd edn. London: Sage Publications, 2002.
Vale, H. E. T. *How to See England*. London: Methuen, 1937.
Vaughan, John. *The English Guidebook*. Newton Abbot: David & Charles, 1974.
Wade, G. W. and J. H. Wade. *Herefordshire*. London: Methuen, 1917.
Wade, G. W. and J. H. Wade. *Somerset*. 7th edn. London: Methuen, 1926.
Wade, J. H. *Rambles in Shakespeare's Country*. London: Methuen, 1932.
Walling, R. A. J. *The West Country*. London: Blackie & Son, 1935.
Walsham, Alexandra. *The Reformation of the Landscape: Religion, Identity and Memory in Early Modern Britain and Ireland*. Oxford: Oxford University Press, 2012.
Walton, John. *The English Seaside Resort: A Social History, 1750–1914*. Leicester: Leicester University Press, 1983.
Watkins, A. *The Old Straight Track: Its Mounds, Beacons, Moats, Sites, and Markstones*. 3rd edn. London: Methuen, 1945.
Walton, John and Jason Wood. *The Making of a Cultural Landscape: The English Lake District as Tourist Destination, 1750–2010*. Farnham: Ashgate, 2013.

Watts, W. W. *Shropshire: The Geography of the County*. 2nd edn. Shrewsbury: Wilding & Son, 1939.
Wenham, Simon M. 'Oxford, the Thames and Leisure: A History of Salter Bros, 1858–2010'. DPhil thesis, University of Oxford, 2013.
West, G. H. *Gothic Architecture in England and France*. London: G. Bell & Sons, 1911.
Weston, W. H. *Gloucestershire*. Oxford: Clarendon Press, 1912.
Whately, Thomas. *Observations on Modern Gardening, Illustrated by Descriptions*. London: Thomas Payne, 1770.
White, Gilbert. *The Natural History of Selborne*. Edited by Paul Foster. Oxford: Oxford University Press, 1993.
White, Walter. *All Round the Wrekin*. London: Chapman and Hall, 1860.
Whitehead, F. and C. Holland. *Warwickshire*. 2nd edn. London: A. & C. Black, 1922.
Willett, Mark. *An Excursion from the Source of the Wye*. Bristol: John Evans & Co., 1810.
Williams-Ellis, Clough. *England and the Octopus*. London: Geoffrey Bles, 1928.
Williams-Ellis, Clough (ed.). *Britain and the Beast*. London: J. M. Dent & Sons, 1937.
Williamson, Tom. *Polite Landscapes: Gardens and Society in Eighteenth-Century England*. Stroud: Alan Sutton, 1995.
Williamson, Tom. *The Norfolk Broads: A Landscape History*. Manchester: Manchester University Press, 1997.
Winbolt, S. E. *The Chilterns and the Thames Valley*. London: G. Bell & Sons, 1932.
Winbolt, S. E. *Kent, Surrey and Sussex*. Harmondsworth: Penguin Books, 1939.
Wood, Christopher. *Paradise Lost: Paintings of English Country Life and Landscape, 1850–1914*. London: Barrie & Jenkins, 1988.
Wood, John. *A Description of Bath*. 2nd edn. 1765. Bath: Kingsmead Reprints, 1969.
Woodbridge, Kenneth. *Landscape and Antiquity. Aspects of English Culture at Stourhead 1718–1838*. Oxford: Clarendon Press, 1970.
Woodbridge, Kenneth. *The Stourhead Landscape*. London: National Trust, 1974.
Wylie, John. *Landscape*. London: Routledge, 2007.
Wyndham, Richard. *Sussex, Kent and Surrey*. London: Batsford, 1939.

Index

Note: Locators in italics represent figures in the text.

Abercrombie, Patrick 170, 253
Ablington, near Bilbury 115, 179
Adams, William Bridge, *English Pleasure Carriages* 181
Adlestrop, Cotswolds 204–5
agriculture 95–6, 110
   hop-pickers 166
Aldbury, Hertfordshire 145
Alfriston, Sussex 145
All Saints, Kent 135
Allingham, Helen 145
   'At the Cottage Gate' *68*
   The Cottage Homes of England 68–9
   Happy England 68–9
Ally Sloper's Half Holiday 85
Alnwick, Northumberland 182
Alpine Club 239–40
Ambleside 183–4
Ancient Monuments Protection Act (1882) 124, 126, 129
Anderson, Benedict 212
Andrews, Malcolm 45
Andrews, William, *Old English Towns* 139–40
Anglesey, Parys Mountain 157
Anglicanism 29, 231–2, 234, 237
Anning, Mary 120
antiquarianism 26, 29, 78
archaeology
   barrow digging 25
   field studies 23
   maps 78
   sites 124–6, 129
   study of 22–4
   tourism 228
architecture
   classical 134–5
   classicism 148
   domestic 129–30
   Georgian 141–3, 228
   gothic revival buildings 50, 91, 134–5, 149, 231

   historic buildings 91–2
   history of 23
   'imperial' 227
   inspired by the past 50–1
   'medieval' 140–1
   medieval gothic architecture 25–6
   Roman 129
   seaside resorts 150–2
Areas of Outstanding Natural Beauty (AONB) 113, 252
Arkwright, Richard 157
Arnold, Matthew 95
Arts and Crafts Movement 114–15, 149, 219
Arun, Sussex 107
Ashbee, Charles 115, 173
Ashton, John R., *The Open-Air Guide for Wayfarers of All Kings* 101, 173, 202, 204
Auden, W. H., 'Letter to Lord Byron' 164
Austen, Jane, *Northanger Abbey* 39, 44
Avebury 22
Avon 173

Bacon, Francis 33
Baconian empiricism 23, 33
Baddeley, M. J. B., *Thorough Guide Series* 54, 57
Baedeker, K., *Great Britain: A Handbook for Travellers* 90, 126, 160, 194, 227–8, 249, 251
Bagshot Heath, Surrey 20
Baker, J. H. 172–3, 192
Baldwin, Oliver 172–3
Baring-Gould, Sabine 127
Barnsley, Sidney 114
Barrington, Daines, *Naturalist's Journal* 19
Barry Island, South Wales 148, 239
Bartlett, Revd J., *Description of Malvern* 17–18
Bath
   archaeological tourism 228
   architectural development of 89

Assembly Rooms 251
bombing of 249, 251
Georgian architecture 143
guidebooks 56
horse, coach and carriage rides 183
imperial pilgrimage 227–8
Improved Bath Guide, 1812 41–2
leisure activities 146–7
modernization 217
The New Bath Guide 41–42, 183
The Original Bath Guide 56, 183, 195
pagan mythology and archaeology 31
plaques 216, 228–9
post-baroque classicism 135
posters 75
Roman baths 129, 228
Roman past 24–5, 228
Royal Victoria Park 93
'Sack of Bath' campaign 257
as tourist centre 24–5
town planning 251, 257
views from 94
walking 195, 200
Batsford, Harry 59–60, 176, 194, 225, 250
  English Gothic Churches 133
  Face of England series 118
  How to See the Country 163–4, 173
  The Old Towns of England 139
Beckett, John 1
Beck's Leamington Guide 200–1
Beeching reports 1963 & 1965 253
Belloc, Hilaire 217, 233
Bell's Pocket Guides 57, 132, 134
  Chiltern district 97
Benson, E. F., *Mapp and Lucia* novels 141
Berger, John 214
Berkshire 101, 103
Bernard Shaw, George 161
Berners, Lord, 'Faringdon Folly' (1936) 192
Berwickshire Naturalists' Field Club 123, 198
Betjeman, John 191, 204–5, 222, 232–4, 249–50, 252
  English Cities and Small Towns 143
Bevan, G. P. 101, 130
  Tourist Guide to Warwickshire 233
Bidford 173

Birmingham 90, 91, 130, 173, 221, 252
  Aston Hall 132
  Town Hall 148
Birmingham, George 217, 232
  'Country Church' 231
Black, Adam and Charles 57
  Black's Guide to Dorsetshire 98, 130, 187
  Black's Guide to England and Wales 187
  Black's Guide to South Wales 225
  Black's Guide to the Lake District 235
  Black's Guide to Warwickshire 92, 130, 137, 148, 187
  Black's Picturesque Guide to the English Lakes 183–4
Blackdown Hills, Somerset 31, 68
Blackmore, R. D., *Lorna Doone: A Romance of Exmoor* 65, 104
Blackpool 150–2, *151*
Blandford Forum 251
Blenheim Palace 135
Blewbury 170–1
Blockley, near Chipping Campden 116
Blue Guides 57, 160
Blunden, Edmund 219
  English Villages 143–4
Boars Hill, Berkshire 95
boating holidays 108
Bognor Regis 238
bombing 249–51
Booth, Charles, *Life and Labour of the People in London* 168
Booth, William, *In Darkest England and the Way Out* 168–9
Boscobel House, Shropshire, Royal Oak 101
Boughton, Rutland, *The Immortal Hour* 67
Bourne, Henry 32
Bournemouth 126, 150, 171, 191
Bournville 149
Bow Bells 138
Bowshot Wood, near Wellesbourne, Warwickshire 101
Bradley, A. G.
  Avon and Shakespeare's Country 73
  Beauchamp Chapel in St Mary's, Warwick 137
  cycling 190–1, 203
  Dome, Woolhope valley 123
  English race 225

First World War 247
forests 101
Georgian architecture 141
In the March and Borderland of Wales 82, 207
An Old Gate of England. Rye, Romney Marsh, and the Western Cinque Ports 142, 221
townspeople visiting the countryside 173
Wales 223
walking 194
Bradshaw's Descriptive Railway Handbook of Great Britain and Ireland 90, 187
Brayley, E. W. *17*
Bredon Hill, Worcestershire 223
Breidden Hills 103
Brice, Andrew, *Grand Gazetteer* 34–5
Brighton 69, 113
   Royal Pavilion 227
British Association for the Advancement of Science 60
British borders 221–4
British Empire 224–31
   'imperial' architecture 227
The British Heritage series 59–60, 222, 224, 225
British nations 221–3
Britton, John *17*
   Beauties of England and Wales 43, 80
Broadway 114, 115, 192, 237
Buck, Nathaniel 43
Buck, Samuel 43
Buckinghamshire 163–4
Buckland, William 121, *122*
Buck's Antiquities 43
Budden, Charles W., *English Gothic Churches* 133
Bullock, William 120
Bunyan, John, *Pilgrim's Progress* 206, 208
Burford, Oxfordshire 133, 141
Burley, Rosa 189–90
Burlington, 3rd Earl of 148
Burrow, C. F. Severn 235
Burrows Guide to Devon and Cornwall 83
Burrows Guide to the Wye 237–8
Burrows Guide to Wessex: The Hardy Country 65
Burrows Guides 57
buses 191

Cabot, John 10
Cambridge 247–8, 251
Cambridge University Press, *County Geographies* 111, 130
Camden, William 34
   Britannia 23
Camden Town Group 68
camera/mirror technology 44–5
cameras 204
campaigning and pressure groups 113–14
camping tours 229–30
Canaletto, Antonio 42
Cannadine, David 211, 255
Canterbury 56, 248, 249
A Canterbury Tale (1944) 248
Cardiff Castle 227
Carlyle, Thomas 167
Carr, E. Donald, *A Night in the Snow, or, a Struggle for Life on the Long Mynd* 206–7
carriages 126, 181–3
cars 191–3, 203
   tours 239
cartography 10, 76–8
Cassell, 'official guides' 187
Castle Combe, Wiltshire 147
Celts 97, 222–3, 226
charabanc 191
Charlecote House 136
Cheltenham 143
Chepstow 186
Cheshire-Lancashire border 163
Chesil Bank, Dorset 241
Chester 138, 241
Chew, Ada Nield 239
Chilterns 97, 172–3, 252
Chipping Campden 73, 115, 141, 173
cholera pandemic (1831–2) 166
Church Stretton, Shropshire 206–7
churches 231–2
   architecture 133, 254
   and human stories 137
   interior decoration 28–29
   manuals to visiting 132–4
   medieval ecclesiastical heritage 29
Cinderford 164
Cinque Ports 221
Civil Wars 130
Clacton 238

Clark, Geoffrey 98, 172, 235, 241
  The Dorset Landscape 232
Clark, Sir Kenneth 248–9
class, social 231–43
Claverton 183
Clayhidon, Applehayes Estate 68
Cleeve 173
Cleeve Hill, Cheltenham 207
cliffs 14, 119–21, 201–2
Clifton 143
Clive, Robert, statues 227
Close, Charles 203, 208
Clovelly, Devon 71, *72*, 147
coaches (horse-drawn) 181–3
coaches (motor) 191
Coalbrookdale, Shropshire 22, 157, *157*
coastal views 69
Cobb, Ruth 171
  Country Town Story 222
Cobbett, William 114
Coleford 164
Collins' Britain in Pictures series, *English Cities and Small Towns* 143
Collins' County Geographies 60, 111
Collins' County Geographies. Warwickshire 92
Colt Hoare, Sir Richard 25, 39, 78
  History of Ancient Wiltshire 25
Commons, Open Spaces and Footpaths Preservation Society 198
Commons Preservation Society (CPS) 198
Condition of England question 162, 167
Coney Island 238
Conlin, Jonathan 53
Constable, John *216*
  Hay Wain 215
  Various Subjects of Landscape, Characteristic of English Scenery 215
The Contour Motoring Map of the British Isles 163
The Contour Road Book of England 163, 190
Conybeare, Williams 121, *122*
Cooke, Captain James 10
Cook's 'Holiday Tours' 84
Cornbury Park, near Charlbury, Oxfordshire 137

Cornish, C. J., *Wild England of Today and the Wild Life in It* 58–9, 171
Cornish, Vaughan 171–2, 224, 235, 236, 247–8
Cornwall 57, 112, 160, 180
Cotswolds
  Areas of Outstanding Natural Beauty (ANOB) designation 252
  Civil War period 117
  detached from modern life 141
  distinctive landscape characteristics 113–16
  forests 101
  Gibbs, J. A. 224
  Guild of Handicraft 173
  middle- and upper-class country recreations 237
  motorized transport 192
  natural features 21
  'Nature' 235
  publicists 115–16
  railways 179–80, 184–5
  stone 218–19
  urban tourism 92
  Vaughan Williams, Ralph 66
Cotswolds Conservation Board 113
'cottage idyll' 68–9, 145–6
Cotterell, Thomas Sturge
  Historic Map 228
  plaques 228–9
Coughton, Warwickshire 99
Council for the Preservation of Rural England 247–8
counties 110–12
country house visiting 26, 131–2
Country Land and Business Association 246
country recreations, middle and upper class 237–8
countryside
  as green space 95–106
  as a playground 174–8
county histories 12, 111–12
Coventry 92, 221, 251
Coventry, George William, 6th Earl of Coventry 48
Cowles, Frederick, *This Is England* 233
Cox, Thomas 34
Cranborne Chase, Dorset 124–6

Crane, Nicholas, *The Making of the British Landscape* 2–3
Croll, Andy 148, 239
Cromer 186
Cromford, Derbyshire 157
Croome Park, Worcestershire 48
Crossing, William, *Amid Devonia's Alps* 160
Cross's Illustrated Hand-Book to Malvern 62
cultural consumption, landscape as object of 27–48
cultural media 54–78
cultural nationalism 148
Cumnor House 136
Cunnington, William 25
Cusop, Hay on Wye 95
cycling clubs 188
cyclists 188–91, *189*, 192, 238
　specialist manuals for 190
　women 241
Cyclists Touring Club 188
　Handbook 190

Darling, E. Moore, *Seeing Shropshire* 164
Dartington Hall, Devon 152
Dartmoor, Devon
　exploration 127
　industrialization 160
　National Parks 252
　railways 180–1
　wild, lonely and primitive 31, 34–5, 97–8, 106, 169
Dartmoor Exploration Committee 127
Darwin, Charles 52–3
　The Descent of Man 52
　On the Origin of Species 52, 60
Davies, G. Christopher 108
　The Handbook to the Rivers and Broads of Norfolk and Suffolk 81, 82
De la Beche, H. T. L. 120
Deal, Kent 238
deep history 119–22
Deerhurst, Gloucestershire 133
Defoe, Daniel 28, 156
　A Tour thro' the Whole Island of Great Britain 12, 20, 22, 56, 91
Dent's 'Cathedrals, Abbeys and Famous Churches series' 132
　Gloucester, Tewkesbury and District 229

Derbyshire 57, 241
Derwent Gorge, Derbyshire 157
Devon 57, 98, 127, 183, 220, 235, 241, 251
diaries 12–13, 40–2, 83–5, 130–1, 229–30
Dickens, Charles 162
　Hard Times 159, 183–4
Ditchfield, P. H. 61, 101, 145–6, 219, 234
　Byways in Berkshire and the Cotswolds 61, 64
　Memorials of Old Gloucestershire 112
　The Story of Our English Towns 138–9
　Vanishing England 139
Dixon Hunt, John 46
Dorchester 94, 104
Doré, Gustave, 'Dudley Street in the Seven Dials' *168*
Dorset 65, 98–9, 164, 191
Dorset County Museum 124
Dorset Natural History and Antiquarian Field Club 124
Dorset Natural History and Archaeological Society 124
Dorstone, Arthur's Stone 124, *125*, 127
Dover 135–6
downlands 102–4, 170–1, 242
Doyle, Arthur Conan, *The Hound of the Baskervilles* 104, 169, 180–1
Drake, Francis, *Eboracum* 43, 80
Drake, Nathan *14*
drawings, in guide literature 73–5
Dugdale, William
　Antiquities of Warwickshire 23
　Monasticon Anglicanum 25, 29, 43
Durham Cathedral 163
Dutch landscape painters 42

East Anglia 32, 58, 251
Eastbourne 238
ecological agenda 258
economic and social change 155–77
economic crises 256
economics, distribution of wealth 174–5
Eden, W. A., *Britain and the Beast* 175–6
Edinburgh New Philosophical Journal 121
Eley, Harold, *Picturesque Towns and Villages of England and Wales* 239
Elgar, Edward 66, 188–90, *189*, 213, 233

Elmhirst, Leonard 152
Engels, Friedrich, *The Condition of the Working Class in England in 1844* 167
English Heritage, *English Landscape* 2
English race 224–6
Englishness 211–21, 230, 231, 248
engravings 43
Enlightenment 33–5, 49–50, 76
etiquette manuals 82
eugenicist movement 169
European Grand Tour 11
evacuation 250
Evans, H. A., *Highways and Byways in Oxford and the Cotswolds* 190
Evans, Sir Arthur 95
evolution, theory of 52–3
Ewen, Cirencester 114
Exeter 138, 249
Exmoor 98, 252
exploration
   as national and local patriotism 10
   and tourism 9–14

Faussett, Revd Bryan 25
Feigel, Lara, *Modernism on Sea: Art and Culture at the British Seaside* 150
Festival of Britain, 1951 256
films 248
First World War 247–8
Fleure, H. J. A. 225
flora and fauna 18–19
Folkestone 238
footpath associations, local 198
footpaths 197, 200
Ford, Charles 218
Ford, James Bradley 143
Forest of Arden, Warwickshire 99–101, *100*
Forest of Dean, Gloucestershire 21, 88, 114, 164, 225
forests 99–102
Forster, E. M., *Howard's End* 146, 171, 186
fossils 120–1, 234–5
Foster, Myles Birket 147
Fox Talbot, Henry, *Pencil of Nature* 45
French landscape painters 42
Fry, Charles 59

Gainsborough, Thomas 42
   Mr and Mrs Andrews 214, *214*
Gard, Robin 41
Garden City Movement 149–50, 170
gardens 35, 38, 45–8, 106, 145–6, 182
Garrett, John Henry 207
Gaskell, Peter 167
Gateshead 163
gazetteers 112
gender 231–43; *see also* women
'Geographia' *Ramblers' Map to London's Countryside* 197
geography 16, 87–116
Geological and Linnean Society 124
Geological Society 63
Geological Survey Act (1845) 51
Geological Survey of Great Britain 51, 160
geology 16–18, 24, 34, 51–3, 62, 119–28, 235
Georgian architecture 141–3, 228
Georgian Group 135
Gibbs, J. A. 224
   A Cotswold Village 115, 179–80
Gilpin, William 41, 114, 156
   Observations on the River Wye, and Several Parts of South Wales etc 36, *36*, 44, 48
Gimson, Ernest 114
Glastonbury Abbey and Tor 22
Glastonbury Festival 67
Gloucester 66, 241
Gloucester Cathedral 229
Gloucestershire 110, 112, 130, 220
Godfrey, Walter H. 162–3
Goodrich Castle 131
Gooley, Tristan, *How to Connect with Nature* 258
Gotch, J. A., *The English Home from Charles I to George IV* 219
gothic revival buildings 50, 91, 134–5, 149, 231
Goulden, R. J. 56
Grand Tour 10–11
Gray, Fred 227
Great Bindon and Downlands Landslip, Christmas 1839 121–2, *122*
Great Eastern Railways, *Sun Pictures of the Norfolk Broads* 187

Great Western Railway (GWR) 185
  guidebooks 187
  guides for rambles 186–7
  Historic Sites and Scenes of England 222
  posters 75
  Through the Window series 204
Great Yarmouth 176, 238
green belt legislation 252–3
Gregory, Edward John, *Boulter's Lock, Sunday Afternoon* 107
Griggs, Frederick 73
Grignion, Charles, 'A Noble Terras Walk' 14
Grindrod, C. F. 62–4
  Malvern: What to See and Where to Go 200
guide literature
  drawings in 73–5
  landscape painting in 73–5
  'popular' texts 55–63
  pre-history 126
  and railways 187
  and religion 232
  specialist writers of 79–81
  and stories 118–19
  towns and Englishness 217–18
guidebooks
  anti-urbanism 172–3
  country house visiting 131
  for cyclists 190
  forests 101
  motorcars 254
  religious buildings 231, 233–4
  series-based 56–57, 80
  visual representations of landscape 44
  volume of 55–8
  walking 197, 202
  water landscapes 107–8
Guild of Craftsmen 115
Guild of Handicraft 173
Gurney, Ivor 66
Gutch, John Wheely Gough, 'View of Tenby from the Croft' 71
Guy's Cliff, Warwickshire 136

Hadrian's Wall 224
Hall, S. C. and A. M. 231
  The Book of the Thames from Its Rise to Its Fall 119

Hampshire 57
Hampstead 95
Hampton Court 131
Hannett, John, *The Forest of Arden, Its Towns, Villages and Hamlets* 100–1
Hansom, Joseph 148
Hardy, Thomas 140–1
  The Return of the Native 104, 155
  Tess of the d'Urbervilles 159, 218, 236
  Wessex 65
Harper, Charles G. 99, 101, 134–5
  The Autocar Road Book 193
  The Great North Road 83
  Summer Days 73–5
Harper's Magazine 83
Harper's New Monthly Magazine 115
Harris, Alexandra, *Modernism on Sea* 150
Harrison, W. Jerome 71
Haslehurst, Ernest William 73
  'Anne Hathaway's Cottage' *74*
Heath, Charles, *Descriptive Account of the Kymin Pavilion and Beaulieu Grove* 44–5
Henshaw, Frederick Henry
  'A Forest Glade, Arden' 100, *100*
  'An Old Oak, Forest of Arden' 100
Hereford 66, 123–4, 138, 188, *189*
Herefordshire 78, 127, 233
Herne Bay 238
Hewison, Robert 256
Hewitt, Rachel 77
hiking 202, 208–9, 238
Hill, Christopher 29–30
Hill, Octavia 211
Hissey, J. John
  Cotswolds 115–16
  empire 229
  An English Holiday with Car and Camera 58
  Englishness 219
  motorcars 191, 193, 208–9
  'Nature' 235
  railways 188
  village archetype 145
  Wales 223–4
  women 239
Historic England 258–9

Historic Warwickshire: Its Legendary Lore, Traditionary Stories, and Romantic Episodes 136
Hoare, Henry, II 46–8
Hockin, J. R. A. 87, 104, 170–1
   On Foot in Berkshire 132
Hog's Back, North Downs 171
holiday
   development of formal periods of 175
   pay 254
   seaside resorts 43
   souvenirs 229
Holland, Clive 100
   Warwickshire: the Land of Shakespeare 73, 92
Hollar, Wenceslaus 43
Holmes, Edric 171
Holst, Gustav, *Cotswold Symphony* 66
holy springs and wells 30–2, 108–9
Home, G. 229
Homeland Association 57, 229
   Malvern and District 62
horse-drawn conveyances 181–3
Horspath, Oxford 143–4
Hoskins, W. G.
   The Making of the English Landscape 1–3
   Midland England: A Survey of the Country between the Chilterns and the Trent 118
Housman, A. E., *Shropshire Lad* poems 65–6
Howard, Peter 104
Howells, Herbert, *Missa Sabrensis* or *Mass of the Severn* 66
Howells, W. D., *London Films and Certain Delightful English Towns* 83
Hudson, W. D. 103–4
Hudson, W. H. 55, 225, 236, 240, 242
Hull 252
Hunter, Robert 211
hunting 237–8
Huntsham, Queen Stone 128, *128*
Hutton, Edward 103–5, 148, 220
   Highways and Byways in Oxford and the Cotswolds 115
   Highways and Byways series 58, 73, 132, 233
Hutton, James, *Theory of the Earth* 16

Hutton, W. H. 92, 99, 217
   By Thames and Cotswold: Sketches of the Country 116, 207–8

identities 211–43
Igtham Motte 132
Ilfracombe, Devon 190, 238
Ilkley Moor, Cow and Calf 84–5
Industrial Revolution 80, 155–63, 217
industrialization 89–91, 148, 155–64
inner cities 167–9
Ironbridge, Shropshire 164
Isle of Portland 225
Isle of Purbeck, Dorset 241
Isle of Wight, Osborne House 227
Italian landscape painters 42
Ivington Camp, Herefordshire 129

James, Henry 115, 141, 231, 232
   English Hours 138
Jarrold's, Norwich 57–8, 71, 75
Jefferies, Richard 88, 101–3, 218, 236
   'On the Downs' 102–3
   The Graphic 101
   'Trees about Town' 218
Jekyll, Gertrude 146
Jenkinson, A. S. 191
Jennings, Payne, *Sun Pictures of the Norfolk Broads* 187
Jerome, Jerome K., *Three Men in a Boat* 108, 207, 230
Jerrold, William, *Shakespeare-Land* 73, 74
Joad, C. E. M.
   'In Praise of Walking' 240
   The Untutored Townsman's Invasion of the Country 172
Jordan, Humfrey, *Introduction to the Study of Local History and Antiquities* 117
journalists 59
journey
   experiencing the 203–9
Jurassic Coast 124

Kay, James 167
Kelmscott, Oxfordshire 114, 144–5, 184–5, 187
Kendal 203
Kenilworth Castle 130, 136, 216

Kent 132, 166, 186, 197, 221, 248
   Downs 252
   guidebooks 56
   Weald of 220
Kent, William 46
Kingsley, Charles, *Westward Ho!* 65
'Kingsley country' 64
Kirkdale 241
Knole 132
Kymin 44–5

La Rochefoucauld brothers 22
Lacock, Wiltshire 145, 147
Ladies Alpine Club 240
Lake District
   campaigning and pressure groups 113
   empire 230
   Englishness 220
   geology 235
   guidebooks 57
   historicization 117
   mountains 103
   National Parks 252
   'Nature' 4
   transport 183–4
   wild, lonely and primitive 20, 105–6
Lake District Defence Society 113
Lamb House, Rye 141, *142*
Lambarde, William, *A Perambulation of Kent* 12, 111
Lancashire 163
Lancaster 183–4
Lancaster and Preston Canal 183–4
Lancaster Carlisle railway 184
land ownership 246–7
landed gentry 79
Land's End, Cornwall 106
landscape
   discourse 39
   'dreary' 104–6
   early modern 9–26
   gardening 182
   human 21–6
   ideas and representations of 27–48, 49–54
   man-made 43
   of memory and myth 118–19
   as modernism 148–53
   as object of cultural consumption 27–48
   poetical images of 39–40
   political messages in landscape design 48
   possession by 31
   production and performance 78–82
   reception 83–5
   reconfiguring the 49–86
   representations of 38–48
   stories 118
   visual representations of 41–2, 67–78
   wild nature 100–1, 104–6, 196–7
landscape artists 81
landscape painters
   Dutch 42
   French 42
   Idyllist group 68–9, 73
   Italian 42
landscape painting 42–3, 50–1, 67–9
   fictional or semi-fictional representations of 64
   in guide literature 73–5
   human inhabitants included in 69, 70
   and national spirit 213–15
   watercolours 43
Lang, Elsie, *Old English Towns* 139–40
Lansdown 183
Lawford, Lucy Amelia 201–2
Lea, Herman, *A Handbook to the Wessex Country of Thomas Hardy's Novels and Poems* 65
Leamington, Warwickshire 143, 200–1
Leatherhead, Surrey 171
Lechlade 185
Leckford estate, Hampshire 152
Leeds Castle, Kent 132
Lees, E., *Pictures of Nature in the Silurian Region around the Malvern Hills and Vale of Severn* 63, 102
The Legacy of England 222
leisure 174–7
Leith Hill, Surrey 173
Leland, John 12, 34
   Itinerary 23
Letchworth, Hertfordshire 149–50
letter writing 41
ley lines 127–8
Lhwyd, Edward 12
Liddington Hill, near Ridgeway 102–3
Lincoln 28

Linnaean system 18–19, 52
Linnean Society 63
literary associations 64
Little Doward 131
Little Guides 57, 111, 112, 126–7, 132, 133, 135, 137, 232
    Devon 98
Liverpool 90–1, 139
living conditions, urban 167–9
local footpath associations 198
local knowledge 110–11
local natural history association networks 63
local societies 60–1, 123
'localization of space' 48
London
    Albert Memorial 227
    architectural development of 89
    Bullock's London Museum of Natural History 120
    'civilized' countryside 96–7
    Docks 90
    Englishness 217
    'Great Stink' 166
    leaving 173
    living conditions 168
    modernity 90
    Paddington 186
    paintings of 42
    railways 185
    Southbank Centre 256
    suburbia 94
    Tate Modern 256
    tourist attractions 256
    town planning 251
    underground 184
    urbanization 93, 138, 165–6
    West End 56, 90
    Woolwich Arsenal 90
London, Midland and Scottish Railway (LMS) 75
London Transport, posters *185*
Long Mynd, Shropshire 103, 206–7
Lord, Peter 158
Loutherbourg, P. J. de, *Coalbrookdale by Night* 22, 157, *157*
lowland-highland divide 96–9
lowlands 225
Lucas, David, 'Summer Evening' 215, *216*

Luckin, Bill 166
Lyell, Charles, *Principles of Geology* 52
Lyme Regis, Dorset 120–1, 185–6, 234–5
Lymington, Hampshire 156
Lynmouth, Devon 84
Lynton, Devon 13–14, 84, 122–3, 185–6
    Glen Lyn 84
    Valley of the Rocks 14, 17, *17*, 122–3, 129

Mabey, Richard, *Nature Cure* 258
Macdonell, A. G. 205, 217
magazines 80
Magnis, Kenchester 129
Maiden Castle, Dorset 129
Maidenhead 106–7
Maidstone 56
Mais, S. P. B.
    architectural aesthetics 135–6
    Brighton 113
    'civilized' countryside 96–7
    cyclists 241
    'discovery' 9
    escape from the city to the country 173
    fictional or semi-fictional representations of landscapes 65
    Hills of the South 103
    middle- and upper-class country recreations 238
    Ordnance Survey (OS) 78
    photography 71
    See England First 191, 220
    villages 143
    walking 194
    wild, lonely and primitive 106
male gaze 241–2
Malvern Naturalists' Club 198
Malvern 17–18, 62–3, 84, 88, 133, 220, 235
    'View from the Ivy Rock, Malvern,' c. 1830–40 *199*
Malvern Hills 161–2, 198–200, 225
Malvern Hills Act (1884) 113
Malvern Hills Conservators 113, 161–2, 199–200
Malvern Naturalists' Club 62–3
Malverns 66, 188, 252
    British Camp 127
    Great Malvern 122–3, 198–200
    Little Malvern 63–4

Manchester 90, 91, 139, 167, 217
Manchester Guardian 194
Mandler, Peter 131–2
Mansell-Pleydell, J. C. 124
maps 76–8, 87–8, 98, 126, 190, 197, 208–9
    mental 87–8
    'period' 126
Marshall, John 184
Martin, Ellis 77
Masefield, John 95
Massingham, H. J. 170
    Cotswold Country 116, 218
    Wold without End 116
Matless, David 3, 78, 107, 152
Matlock, Derbyshire 22
May Day celebrations 32
Mayhew, Henry, *London Labour and the London Poor* 167
McAllister, Gilbert 252
Mearns, Andrew, *The Bitter Cry of Outcast London* 168
Measom, George, 'official guides' 187
mechanization, anti-mechanization 158–9
media
    cultural 54–78
    image of the city 167–9
    revolution 55
Mee, Arthur 140
    county guides 132
    King's England series 58, 111, 149
memorialization 227–9
Mendips 104–5
Methodists 29–30, 232–3
Michelin guides 193
migrant workers 87
militarization 250
mining 159–61
Minster-on-Sea 238
'Miss Mitford's country' 64
The Modern Cyclist 190
modernism 50–1, 148–54, 256–9
Modernist Movement 150–2
modernity 22, 152, 251–6
Monmouth 44–5
Montagu, Charles E. 194
Morgan, D. Francis, *Hiking* 208
Morris, John E., *An Introduction to the Study of Local History and Antiquities* 117

Morris, William 114, 162, 184–5
    News from Nowhere 144–5
Morton, H. V.
    country house visiting 132
    Dartmoor, Devon 97
    'discovery' 9
    Englishness 217
    industrialization 163
    journey 206
    'olden time', cult of 140
    In Search of England 231–2
    Second World War 250
    Somerset 235
    transport 188
    urban tourism 93
    villages 145
    water landscapes 107
    women 241
Moss, Brian 107
motorcars 191–3, 203
motorcycles 191
motorized transport 253–4
motorways 253–4
Mottram, R. H. 140, 222–3
mountains 103–4
Mousehole, Penzance *152*
Murchison, Roderick 16, 62, 123
Murray, Alison 203, 237
Murray, John 57
    Handbook for Travellers in Gloucestershire 114
music 66–7, 127, 188–90, 212–13, 233
mythical timescapes 117–54

Nash, Paul, 'The Wood on the Hill' 104, *105*
National Footpaths Preservation Society (NFPS) 198
National Gallery, London 256–7
'national interest' 247
National Land Fund 255
National Observer 138
National Parks and Access to the Countryside Act (1949) 252
National Parks Commission 97
National Photographic Record Association 70
National Trust 113, 132, 211–12, 251, 255
nationalism 211–21
    cultural 148

'native' building materials 218–19
natural history 12, 62, 119–21, 124
    local association networks 63
natural philosophy 33–4
naturalist and scientific societies 101–2
'Nature' 33–8, 54, 234–6, 258
    human improvement of 35–7
    and religion 235–7
    sea as unbridled 109–10
    women and 240
Nature magazine 107
Nene Valley 164
New Forest 88, 126
    Knightwood Oak 101
Newbould, Frank, 'Your Britain – Fight for It Now' (1942) *249*, 250
Newcastle 163
Newman, Bernard 151–2, 160, 163, 250–2
newspapers 80
Newth, J. D. 111–12
Newton, Isaac 33
Nicholson, Francis, 'The Waterfall or Cascade falling into the Paddock Pond opposite Garden Lake' *47*
nonconformists 29–30, 232–3
Norfolk Broads 71, 75, 81, 107–8, 132
North East 163
north south divide 220–1
North York Moors 252
Northamptonshire 220
Northern Hay, Exeter 94
Northumberland 252
Norwich 249
Nunney, Somerset 229

The Observer 59
Ode to the Genius of the Lakes in the North of England 11
Ogilby, John, *Britannia* 76, 77
'olden time'
    architecture 134
    buildings 219
    country house visiting 131–2
    cult of the 26
    music 213
Olivier Edith 250
Ordnance Survey (OS) 77–78, 79, 126, 129, 197, 208
    Map of Roman Britain 126

Neolithic Wessex, Roman Britain 78
    Popular Series 77, 126
    XVII Century England 78
Osborne, A. B. 105–6, 140, 205, 238
Owlpen, Gloucestershire 148
Oxford 107
Oxford Movement 50, 233–4
Oxford Preservation Trust 95
Oxford University Press, *County History* series 111, 130
Oxfordshire 127

paganism 29, 31, 234
Page, Hugh, guides for GWR 186–7
pageant movement 135–6
painting *see* landscape painting
Palmer, Arthur 77
panoramic views 94
pantheism 47–8, 234
parks, public 93
Patterson, Arthur Henry 107
Payne, Christiana 69, 215
Peacehaven 238
Peak District, Derbyshire 20, 22, 54, 147, 241–2, 252
Peerless, Henry 83–5, 90–1
Pendle Hill, Lancashire 93
Penguin Guides 57
    Kent, Surrey and Sussex 132–3, 174
Pennant, Thomas, *British Zoology* 19–20
Pennines 96–7
Penshurst Place 132
pensions 254
Percy, Thomas, 'A Ride through Hulne Park from Alnwick Castle to Hulne Abbey' 182
Perry, Herry, 'Whitsun in the Country' *185*
Pevsner, Nikolaus 215
    Buildings of England series 111, 133
    Middlesex Buildings of England 254
photographic survey 70–1
photography 45, 67, 69–73, 81, 204
picturesque
    agriculture 114
    buildings 50
    coastal views 69
    movement 196
    old towns 138

and religion 235
  tourism 44–5
  and transport 204–5
Picturesque Towns and Villages of England and Wales 163, 239
Piehler, H. A., *England for Everyman* 163, 238
Pilgrim Trust, 'Scheme for Recording the Changing Face of Britain' 248–9
pilgrimage 10, 30
Pilgrim's Road, Winchester to Canterbury 186
Piltdown man 226
Pitt, the elder 228–9
Pitt, the younger 228–9
Pitt-Rivers, Augustus 124–6
plaques 47, 216, 228–9
Playden, Rye 95
pleasure boats 106–7
Plymouth 251–2
poetry 39–40
Poole Harbour 235
Pope, Alexander 35, 40, 47
Pope, Cornelius, *The New Bath Guide* c. 1762 56
Poppy Land 64, 186
Porter, Roy 15, 33
postcards 73, *151*
posters 75–6, *152*, *185*, *192*, 250
Power, Charles, *English Medieval Architecture* 133–4
prehistoric monuments 29, 31
preservation movement 26
Preston, Lancashire 159, 183–4
Priestley, J. B. 116, 117, 149
  English Journey 150–2
printing 43, 79–80
  colour lithography 75–6
Prioleau, John
  Car and Country: Week-End Signpost to the Open Road 164, 193
  Enchanted Ways 59
promenades 14, 94, 194, 201
property 246–7
Protestantism 28–32
Pryor, Francis, *The Making of the British Landscape* 2–3
publishers 79–80
Pugin, A. W. N. 233–4
Puritanism 29–30

Quantock Hills, Somerset 103, 252
quarrying 119–20, 159–61
Quennell, Marjorie and H. B. Charles
  The Good New Days 149–50
  History of Everyday Things in England 149–50
Quinton, Alfred 73

race 224–31
Rackham, Oliver 99
railways
  guides 204
  journeys 179–81, 204–5
  maps 184–5
  network 253
  posters 75–6
  scarring the landscape 203–4
  to see pre-history 126
  transport revolution 183–8
rambling 202
rambling clubs 198
Randall, J., *The Tourist's Guide to Bridgnorth* 130, 240
Ransome, Arthur, *Swallows and Amazons* 230
Rawnsley, Hardwicke 113
Raymond, Walter, *A Short History of Somerset* 130
Readman, Paul 4, 88, 90, 106, 148, 214, 217
Reformation 23, 28–33
regional
  composers 65–7
  guides 112–13
  novels 64–6
religion 231–43
  buildings 28–32, 132–3
  disenchantment of the non-sacred world 32
  domestic space and religious meaning 29–30
  and geology 234–5
  and natural landscape 234–7
  open air worship 30
  sites of special spiritual significance 31
  travel and religious interpretation 208–9
Renaissance 23
retirement 254

Rider Haggard, H. 166, 170
rights of public access 129
rivers
    guides 107–8
    as leisure 176
roads
    network 253–4
    quality 182, 192
    service stations 203
Roberts, George 120–2, 234–5
Robinson, W. 146
Robsart, Amy 136–7
Roche, Clare 240
Rodger, Richard 167
Rollright Stones, Oxfordshire 127
Roman Britain 23, 24, 129, 228
Roman Catholicism 28–9, 233–4
Romanticism 35–8, 40, 48, 50, 113, 196
    and industrialization 157–158
romantic thriller stories 136–7
Romney Marsh 225
Rooker, Michael Angelo 42
Rosebery, 5th Earl of 228–9
Ross on Wye 84
    Wilton Bridge 84
Rouse, Clive, *The Old Towns of England* 139
Rowntree, Benjamin Seebohm, *Poverty: A Study of Town Life* 168
Royal Commission on Historical Monuments 111, 135
Royal Forests 99–100
Royal Geographical Society 16
Rudder, Samuel, *A New History of Gloucestershire* 21, 113
Rudge, William 114
rural space 175–6
Ruskin, John 49–50, 113, 162, 196
    The Two Paths 159
Ryan, Ernest K. W. 206
Rye, Sussex 141

Salisbury Cathedral 22, 250
Salters Brothers 107
Sandby, Paul Munn, *Ironbridge*, 22
Sandys, Sampson 11
Sandys, William 11
Sanford, William 13–14
Savernake (or Marlborough) Forest 101

Saxon heritage 225–6
Schama, Simon 28, 99, 118
    Landscape and Memory 3
Schivelbusch, Wolfgang 203–4
'scholarly' texts 55, 60–1
science
    geology and natural history 119
    institutionalization of 53–4
    professionalization of 53–4
    'scientists' 12
    specialization in 53
Scientific Revolution 23, 33, 51, 120, 234–5
Scotland 221–5
Scott, Clement 64, 186
Scott, J. Dixon 226
    Stratford-on-Avon with Leamington and Warwick 80–1
Scott, Samuel 42
Scott, Walter 137
    Kenilworth 136
sea, as unbridled Nature 109–10
seaside resorts
    architecture 150–2
    class, social 238
    establishment of 13
    guidebooks 56
    health cure 30–1, 176
    holidays 43
    landscape painting 69
    modernism 150–2
    'Nature' 109–10
    overseas competition 256
    promenades and cliff-top walks 14
    towns 89
    transport 183
    walking 201–2
Second World War 247–52
    and beyond 245–59
Sezincote, Gloucestershire 227
Selborne 18–20
Select Committee on Public Walks 93
Seven Dials, Dudley Street *168*
Severn, River 48, 225
Severn Gorge 164
Severn Plain 220
Seymour, Aubrey, *A Square Mile of Old England* 110
Shaftesbury, Park Walk 14, 94

Shakespeare 221, 226
'Shakespeare-Land' 71
Sharp, Thomas 170
Shears, W. S. 156
Sheerness 238
Sheffield 156, 241
Shell
   county guides 58, 111, 132, 191, 254
   posters *152*, 191, *192*
Sheringham 238
shires 110–12
Shrewsbury, Shropshire 227
Shropshire 103, 130, 220, 252
   and the Border Country 65–6
Shrubsole, Guy 246
Sidmouth 238
Simmons, Jack 112
Simms, George, *How the Poor Live and Horrible London* 168, 170
Sinodun Hills 104
Slough 252
'Slowdon-in-the-Soke' 140
Smith, C. Fox 104
   The Thames 107
Smith, William (Strata) 16
Smithson, Peter 257
Snell, Keith 64
sociability 34, 39, 181, 188, 194–6, 201
social Darwinism 224–5
social exclusion 48
societies
   local 60–1, 111, 123
   naturalist and scientific 101–2
   science 16
Society for the Protection of Ancient Buildings 149
Society of Antiquaries, London 23, 24
Solihull 95
Somerset 84, 127, 225, 233, 235
South Downs 250
South Eastern Main Line 186
south of England 220–1
South Wales 39, 41, 164, 225
Southern Railway Company 103
spas
   churches 133
   development of 13
   guidebooks 56

   health and leisure tourism 30–1, 89, 109
   in Roman times 24
   transport 183
   and walking 198–201
The Spectator 59
Spencer, Charles, *Cyclist and Automobilist Road Book* 192
St Austell, Cornwall 160
Stamp, Laurence Dudley 97–8
Stanford's 'Tourist Guides' 57, 187
Stanton Drew, Somerset 127
statues *189*, 227
steam power 157–9
steamboats 183–4
steam railways 183–5
Stocks, F. Arnold, *The Open-Air Guide for Wayfarers of All Kinds* 101, 173, 202, 204
Stoke Row, Chilterns 192
Stonehenge 22, 126, 236
stories
   human 136–7
   and landscape 118
Stourhead, Wiltshire 25, 46–8, *47*
Stowe landscape gardens 48
Stratford-on-Avon 83, 130, 221, 226
Street, A. G. 176
strip maps *76*, 77, 187
Strong, Roy, *Visions of England* 214
Stroudwater Valley, Gloucestershire 156
Stuart history 129–31
Stuart-Hill, Alexander, 'Mousehole, Penzance' *152*
Stukeley, William 22–4
sublime 42, 69, 104–5, 156–8
suburbia 94–5, 166–8, 170–172
Suffling, Ernest R. 132
Suffolk Broads 71
Sumner, Heywood 124–6
Sunderland 227
Surrey 171, 252
Sussex 98–9, 103, 221, 225, 226, 247, 252
Swete, Revd John 17
Symonds, W. S., *Old Stones* 63

Taylor, John 71
Tenby, Wales 69, 201–2

Tetbury, Cotswolds 223–4
Tewkesbury, Gloucestershire 164, 173
Thackwell, General 229
Thames, River
  empire 230
  Englishness 218
  guidebooks 107–8, 119, 233
  industrialization 90
  journey 206
  recreational use 106–7
  Sinodun Hills 104
  trial by journey 207
Thames Conservancy 106
Thames Preservation Act (1885) 106, 113
Thanet, Kent 56
Thomas, Edward 103, 204–5
  The South Country 103, 170, 230–1
Thomas, K. V., *Man and the Natural World* 15
Thomas, William Beach 50, 54, 117, 163, 224, 241–2
Thompson, W. Harding 98, 172, 235, 241
  The Dorset Landscape 232
Thomson, James, *The Seasons* 39–40
The Times 83, 161
timescapes 117–53
Timmins, Henry Thornhill 78, 123
  Nooks and Corners of Herefordshire 73, 80
Timperley, H. W., *Ridge Way Country* 103
Tintern Abbey 36–7, *36*, 235–6
Tissington, Derbyshire 147
Tompkins, Herbert W. 83
topographical drawings 43
topographical literature, subscription to 79–80
topography 10, 87–116
Torquay 84
tourism
  archaeological 228
  domestic industry 13
  Grand Tour 10–11
  health and leisure 30–1, 89, 109
  industrial 148
  literature 58–9
  organized 175
  representations of landscape 38–9
  as theatre 81–2

'tourist gaze' 49, 53, 73, 78–9, 81, 237
tourists
  armchair 58
  publications 41
  societies 131–2
  using guides 83–5
tours
  camping 229–30
  car 239
  domestic 42–3
  holidays 229–30
  walking 196–7, 202
town halls 91
town planning 149–53, 251–3, 257
  green attitude to 257–8
towns 89–95, 140
  guidebooks 56–8, 112–13
  and historic style 91
  and modernity 89–92
  'new towns' 138
  'old towns and villages' 138–47
Tractarian Movement 233–4
transport 75–6, 131–2
  network 126
transport revolution
  and the journey 179–209
  and recreational travel 181–93
travel journals 108
trees 101–102, 218
Trezise, Simon 65
Trundle camp, Sussex 226
Tunbridge Wells 56
Turle, James 218
Turner, J. M. W. 67, 158, 215
turnpike trusts 182
Twyford, Kent 144

UCL undergraduates 186, 229–30
Uffington 185
underground railway 184
unemployment 160
urban
  development 139
  improvement 169
  modernity 89–92
  'renaissance' 89
  sprawl 170–2

urbanization 164–76
  anti-urbanism 92–3
  'deep' 170–2
  see also suburbia
Ure, Andrew 167
Urry, John 49

Vale, H. E. T. 21, 78, 204
  How to Look at Old Buildings 149
  How to See England 64, 135, 222
Vaughan Williams, Ralph 213
  A Cotswold Romance 66
  Hugh the Drover 66
The Victoria County History of England 111
Victorianism 49–51
viewing platforms 81
villages 143–7, 231–2
Virgil
  influence on descriptions of countryside 40
  influence on garden design 46–7
The Visitors' Guide to Malvern 62

Wade, J. H. 137
Wales 42, 221–4
walking 14, 186–7, 194–202
  solitary 194–202
  tours 196–7, 202
  women 240, 241
walks, formal 94
Wall, George 138
Walling, R. A. J., *The West Country* 160
Walmer Castle 132
Walpole, Horace 109
Walsham, Alexandra 3–4, 29
Walton, John 109
Ward Lock guides 73, 113, 147, 195
  Malvern 133
  Oxford 82
  Red Guides 57, 112, 132, 183, 254
Warwick 134–5, 137, 140, 148, 187, 217
Warwick Castle 22, 130, 132, 216
Warwickshire 70–1, 110, 130, 136, 216, 220–1
water 106–10
water features 106
Waterhouse, Alfred 91
Watkin, David, *The Rise of Architectural History* 219

Watkins, A. 70, *128*
  The Old Straight Track 127–8
Webb, Mary 65
Wegener, Arnold 52
Wells, Somerset 233
wells and springs, holy 30–2, 108–9
Welwyn Garden City 149
Wessex 65, 237–8
West, G. H., *Gothic Architecture in England and France* 133–4
West Country 65, 160, 163
West Midlands 66, 173, 250
Westerham, Quebec House 132
Weston-super-Mare 84
Westward Ho, Devon 65
Weymouth 172
Whately, Thomas 38–9
Wheatley, Oxford 143–4
White, Gilbert 110
  The Natural History of Selborne 18–21, 41
White, Walter 103
Whitehawk camp, Sussex 226
Whitehead, F. 73
Whitlingham Vale from Postwick 72
Whitney-on-Wye 186
Whittington, Shropshire 223
wild nature 100–1, 104–6, 196–7
Willett, Mark, *An Excursion from the Source of the Wye* 44
William of Worcester 12
Williams-Ellis, Clough 248
  England and the Octopus 172
Williamson, Tom 46, 107
Wilson, Richard 42
Wiltshire 78, 103
Winbolt, S. E. 143–4, 145
Winchester 138
Windermere 84, 184, 203
Windle, B. C. A., *The Wessex of Thomas Hardy* 65
Windsor Castle 22, 131
Windsor Forest 101
witchcraft 31, 32
Wittenham Clumps 104
Wixford, Warwickshire 101
women 239–40
  cyclists 241

and 'Nature' 240
    walking 240, 241
Wood, Christopher 145
Wood, John, *A Description of Bath* 31,
    183, 195
Woodcraft Folk 128, *128*
woodlands 99–102
Woolhope Naturalists' Field Club 70, 102,
    123, 124, *125*, 127–8, 186, 198
Woolhope valley, Dome 123–4, 198
Worcester 66, 84
Worcestershire 110, 233
Worcestershire Natural History Society 239
Worcestershire Naturalists' Club 63,
    101–2, 186, 239
Wordsworth, William 37–8, 40, 203, 236,
    252
    Prelude 37–8
Working-class trippers 148, 151–2
Worthing 69, 238

Wrekin, Shropshire 103
Wright, Joseph 157–8
Wye, River 123, 130–1, 156, 186, 229–30,
    235–6
Wye gorge 37, 101, 114
Wye Valley 41, 44–5, 113, 164, 194
Wyndham, John 226
Wyndham, Richard 135, 171
Wyre Forest, Sorb Tree or Whitty Pear of
    102

Yalding, Kent 144
York 43, 80, 168, 241, 249
    Assembly Rooms 148
    New Walk 14
    'A Noble Terras Walk' *14*
Yorkshire 220
    market towns 217
Yorkshire Dales 252
Youth Hostels Association 202

www.ingramcontent.com/pod-product-compliance
Lightning Source LLC
Chambersburg PA
CBHW071807300426
44116CB00009B/1226